Rudyard Kipling's Fiction

Edinburgh Critical Studies in Victorian Culture

Series Editor: Julian Wolfreys

Volumes available in the series:

In Lady Audley's Shadow: Mary Elizabeth Braddon and Victorian Literary Genres
Saverio Tomaiuolo

Blasted Literature: Victorian Political Fiction and the Shock of Modernism
Deaglán Ó Donghaile

William Morris and the Idea of Community: Romance, History and Propaganda, 1880–1914
Anna Vaninskaya

1895: Drama, Disaster and Disgrace in Late Victorian Britain
Nicholas Freeman

Determined Spirits: Eugenics, Heredity and Racial Regeneration in Anglo-American Spiritualist Writing, 1848–1930
Christine Ferguson

Dickens's London: Perception, Subjectivity and Phenomenal Urban Multiplicity
Julian Wolfreys

Re-Imagining the 'Dark Continent' in fin de siècle *Literature*
Robbie McLaughlan

Roomscape: Women Readers in the British Museum from George Eliot to Virginia Woolf
Susan David Bernstein

Women and the Railway, 1850–1915
Anna Despotopoulou

Walter Pater: Individualism and Aesthetic Philosophy
Kate Hext

London's Underground Spaces: Representing the Victorian City, 1840–1915
Haewon Hwang

Moving Images: Nineteenth-Century Reading and Screen Practices
Helen Groth

Jane Morris: The Burden of History
Wendy Parkins

Thomas Hardy's Legal Fictions
Trish Ferguson

Exploring Victorian Travel Literature: Disease, Race and Climate
Jessica Howell

Spirit Becomes Matter: The Brontës, George Eliot, Nietzsche
Henry Staten

Rudyard Kipling's Fiction: Mapping Psychic Spaces
Lizzy Welby

The Decadent Image: The Poetry of Wilde, Symons, and Dowson
Kostas Boyiopoulos

Forthcoming volumes:

Her Father's Name: Gender, Theatricality and Spiritualism in Florence Marryat's Fiction
Tatiana Kontou

British India and Victorian Culture
Máire ni Fhlathúin

The Sculptural Body in Victorian Literature: Encrypted Sexualities
Patricia Pulham

Visit the Edinburgh Critical Studies in Victorian Culture web page at www.euppublishing.com/series/ecve

Also available:
Victoriographies – A Journal of Nineteenth-Century Writing, 1790–1914, edited by Julian Wolfreys
ISSN: 2044-2416
www.eupjournals.com/vic

Rudyard Kipling's Fiction

Mapping Psychic Spaces

Lizzy Welby

EDINBURGH
University Press

For Bruno and our children

Edinburgh University Press Ltd
The Tun – Holyrood Road
12(2f) Jackson's Entry
Edinburgh EH8 8PJ
www.euppublishing.com

Typeset in 10.5/13 Sabon by
Servis Filmsetting Ltd, Stockport, Cheshire,
and printed and bound in the United States
of America

A CIP record for this book is available from the
British Library

ISBN 978 0 7486 9855 4 (hardback)
ISBN 978 0 7486 9856 1 (webready PDF)
ISBN 978 1 4744 0444 0 (epub)

Contents

Series Editor's Preface

'Victorian' is a term, at once indicative of a strongly determined concept and an often notoriously vague notion, emptied of all meaningful content by the many journalistic misconceptions that persist about the inhabitants and cultures of the British Isles and Victoria's Empire in the nineteenth century. As such, it has become a by-word for the assumption of various, often contradictory habits of thought, belief, behaviour and perceptions. Victorian studies and studies in nineteenth-century literature and culture have, from their institutional inception, questioned narrowness of presumption, pushed at the limits of the nominal definition, and have sought to question the very grounds on which the unreflective perception of the so-called Victorian has been built; and so they continue to do. Victorian and nineteenth-century studies of literature and culture maintain a breadth and diversity of interest, of focus and inquiry, in an interrogative and intellectually open-minded and challenging manner, which are equal to the exploration and inquisitiveness of its subjects. Many of the questions asked by scholars and researchers of the innumerable productions of nineteenth-century society actively put into suspension the clichés and stereotypes of 'Victorianism', whether the approach has been sustained by historical, scientific, philosophical, empirical, ideological or theoretical concerns; indeed, it would be incorrect to assume that each of these approaches to the idea of the Victorian has been, or has remained, in the main exclusive, sealed off from the interests and engagements of other approaches. A vital interdisciplinarity has been pursued and embraced, for the most part, even as there has been contest and debate amongst Victorianists, pursued with as much fervour as the affirmative exploration between different disciplines and differing epistemologies put to work in the service of reading the nineteenth century.

Edinburgh Critical Studies in Victorian Culture aims to take up both the debates and the inventive approaches and departures from convention that studies in the nineteenth century have witnessed for the last half century at least. Aiming to maintain a 'Victorian' (in the most positive sense of that motif) spirit of inquiry, the series' purpose is to continue and augment the cross-fertilisation of interdisciplinary approaches, and to offer, in addition, a number of timely and untimely revisions of Victorian literature, culture, history and identity. At the same time, the series will ask questions concerning what has been missed or improperly received, misread, or not read at all, in order to present a multi-faceted and heterogeneous kaleidoscope of representations. Drawing on the most provocative, thoughtful and original research, the series will seek to prod at the notion of the 'Victorian', and in so doing, principally through theoretically and epistemologically sophisticated close readings of the historicity of literature and culture in the nineteenth century, to offer the reader provocative insights into a world that is at once overly familiar, and irreducibly different, other and strange. Working from original sources, primary documents and recent interdisciplinary theoretical models, Edinburgh Critical Studies in Victorian Culture seeks not simply to push at the boundaries of research in the nineteenth century, but also to inaugurate the persistent erasure and provisional, strategic redrawing of those borders.

Julian Wolfreys

Acknowledgements

I would like to thank Professor John Thieme, whose dedication to my project coupled with his unfailing energy and tireless perseverance would have, I am certain, surprised even Kipling. I am grateful to Professor Jan Montefiore for her generosity in sharing her scholarly expertise with me on Kipling's art. I wish to thank Julian Wolfreys at Edinburgh University Press for being an insightful and always-available editor. I would also like to acknowledge The Kipling Society, both for its electronic research tool, 'The Reader's Guide' and its warm human contact. Many thanks are due to, in particular, John Walker, David Page, John Radcliffe and John Lambert, who replied to my frequent questions, large and small, about Kipling's life and art with grace, good humour and speedy efficiency. Their encyclopaedic knowledge of the man and his fiction is both enviable and astounding. I would like to acknowledge the critical works of Kelly Oliver that helped me find an uncluttered path through the complexities of Julia Kristeva's arguments on the formation of identity.

Most of all, I would like to thank five people whose love and support has been a constant source of strength during the course of my writing. To my children, Tom, Izzy, Caitlin and Harriet, and my partner, Bruno, I owe profound debts of gratitude.

Part of Chapter 2 has been previously published in *The Kipling Journal* as 'The Lords of Misrule and the Pleasant Isle of Aves', June 2010.

A version of part of Chapter 4 has been previously published as 'Solar Midnight: Traversing the Abject Borderline State in Rudyard Kipling's "The City of Dreadful Night"', in *The Domination of Fear*, ed. by Mikko Canini (Amsterdam: Rodopi Press, 2010), pp. 147–77.

Abbreviations

A&R	*Actions and Reactions*
BOW	*A Book of Words*
DW	*The Day's Work*
JB	*The Jungle Book*
LH	*Life's Handicap*
L&S	*Land and Sea Tales for Scouts and Guides*
PPH	*Puck of Pook's Hill* and *Rewards and Fairies*
PT	*Plain Tales from the Hills*
S&C	*Stalky & Co.*
SJB	*The Second Jungle Book*
SOM	*Something of Myself*
WWW	*Wee Willie Winkie*

Note on the Text

Rudyard Kipling's Fiction: Mapping Psychic Spaces examines Kipling's artistic journey of separation from his biological mother, the surrogate mother figure of his *ayah*, and his 'best beloved' Indian homeland. Born in Bombay but spending his formative years lodged in a boarding house with strangers on the south coast of England, Kipling experienced a traumatic 'exile'. Kipling's exile mirrors the more universal exilic position of the child as it begins the process of socialisation and moves away from the covetous space of the semiotic and into the paternal authority of the symbolic, as put forward by Julia Kristeva and Hélène Cixous. In this study, Kipling's writing is not presented chronologically but arranged to follow the trajectory of infancy into adulthood.

Introduction: Two Separate Sides to His Head – Kipling's Ambivalent India

> The two of them, laying [Kim] east and west, that the mysterious earth-currents which thrill the clay of our bodies might help and not hinder, took him to pieces all one long afternoon – bone by bone, muscle by muscle, ligament by ligament, and lastly, nerve by nerve. [. . .] Kim slid ten thousand miles into slumber [. . .] sleep that soaked like rain after drought. [. . .] And Mother Earth was as faithful as the Sahiba. She breathed through him to restore the poise he had lost lying so long on a cot cut off from her good currents. His head lay powerless upon her breast, and his opened hands surrendered to her strength. The many-rooted tree above him, and even the dead-manhandled wood beside, knew what he sought, as he himself did not know. Hour upon hour he lay deeper than sleep.[1]

> Water was trickling from a score of places in the cut face of the hill, oozing between the edges of the steps and welling up between the stone slabs of the terrace. Trees sprouted in the sides of the tank and hid its surroundings. It seemed as though the descent had led the Englishman, *firstly*, two thousand years away from his own century, and *secondly*, into a trap, and that he would fall off the polished stones into the stinking tank, or that the Gau-Mukh [cow's mouth] would continue to pour water placidly until the tank rose up and swamped him, or that some of the stone slabs would fall and crush him flat.[2]

Rudyard Kipling's descriptions of India, particularly in his verse and fiction, frequently contain images of a 'feminine' landscape, and his urban and rural environments are painted with brushstrokes that can be both hazily impressionistic and finely detailed. As the above epigraph from *Kim* shows, Kipling can seamlessly move from the healing Sahiba to the tender and protective Mother Earth who repairs Kim's fragmented soul at her breast. Yet Mother India can also be a terrifying entity for England's colonial sons, as these lines from his 'A Vision of India' demonstrate:

> Mother India, wan and thin,
> Here is forage come your way;

> Take the young civilian in,
> Kill him swiftly as you may.[3]

His 'feminised' settings cast India in the conflicting roles of a nurturing, life-affirming mother figure and an uncontrollable, fecund she-devil. The stories of India can be read as a succession of conflicts between restorative and abjected feminised spaces, populated with a host of colonial characters that are as desirous of India as they are repulsed. Menaced by the heart of an Indian darkness, they must rely on survival techniques learned as schoolboys on the playing fields of England if they are to survive imperial service.[4]

The multiplicity of Kipling's fiction – frame-tale narrative technique, diverse narrators, ambivalent subject positions as well as conflicting attitudes toward British imperialism – serve to underscore his already complex and difficult relationship to India. Kipling's England, in contrast, is usually rendered as an asexual space devoid of menace, a place to which the white man returns when his punishing stint in the colonies is done, notwithstanding the alarming descriptions of London in 'In Partibus' (1889), the horror of the theatre in the story 'For One Night Only' (1890), or the brutalised Cockneys in 'The Record of Badalia Herodsfoot' (1890). England is, for the most part, a country where 'the night-air cools on trout-ringed pools', where father and son can share a smoke and confidences in 'the shadow of the old house [that] lay long across the wonderful English foliage, which is the only living green in the world'.[5] A pastoral vision of England such as this encourages what Homi Bhabha argues are 'memories of the "deep" nation crafted in chalk and limestone; the quilted downs [. . .] the quiet cathedral towns'.[6] The profound sense of one being an important but fleeting part of the ceaseless continuum of England's settler past marks Kipling's post-India fiction. Identity is tied to a sense of 'belonging' to the soil, as Kipling makes clear in 'An Habitation Enforced'. 'It's not our land', says George, the wealthy American who buys an estate in East Sussex and comes to call this corner of a foreign field 'Home', '[w]e've only paid for it. We belong to it, and it belongs to the people.'[7] Kipling's 1902 poem 'Sussex', which contain the lines 'our close-bit thyme that smells/ Like dawn in Paradise',[8] not only captures Kipling's attraction to England's verdant countryside, but also his deep desire to feel his genealogical way down through the layers of its ancient past. Kingsley Amis argues that 'Sussex' is the 'work of a man pushing down his roots by will-power'.[9] For Kipling, allegiance to England's green and pleasant land means alienating himself from the country of his birth and necessitates imaging India, to borrow from Homi Bhabha, as England's 'daemonic double'.[10]

A clue as to why Kipling's fictional characters demonise India and beatify England as they move into adulthood can be found in the India of Kipling's childhood.

'I have always felt the menacing darkness of tropical eventides, as I have loved the voices of night-winds through palm or banana leaves, and the song of the tree-frogs,' says Kipling of his childhood India.[11] It is a space that contains both menacing darkness and cherished voices and songs, and these are among Kipling's earliest memories of his birthplace, Bombay. Those memories, like his representation of India and its peoples, are marked by ambivalence. Kipling's feminised Mother India has two faces. One is vampiric, endlessly draining the coloniser's life force, and the other is benevolent, providing a safe and familial environment for the writer's child characters to explore. Kipling's India can be seen in terms of Barbara Creed's notion of the 'monstrous feminine', which is, she argues, powerfully connected to the reproductive female body. The 'monstrous feminine' is a source of horror for a society that is structured according to a phallogocentric law[12] as well as the Kristevan ubiquitous pre-symbolic mother. According to Julia Kristeva, before a child enters the linguistic realm of the symbolic, s/he exists in a preoedipal psychic space, what she terms the 'semiotic chora', which is a 'nonexpressive totality formed by the drives and their stases in a motility that is as full as it is regulated'.[13] Maternal authority exists before a paternal law for the mother begins the process of socialisation by regulating her child's oral and anal drives. The semiotic, Kristeva argues, is a prototype of the symbolic in so far as the child begins to recognise a maternal authority before submitting to the law of the father.[14] With a terrain that is represented as dangerous and fecund, sacred and nourishing, Kipling's fictional India can potentially maim or heal the young English men who come to colonise its wild spaces.

Hidden within its rural and urban spaces are unspeakable horrors. Kipling's English men find snickering wells ('Bubbling Well Road', in *Life's Handicap*) and erupting cemeteries ('The City of Dreadful Night', in *Life's Handicap*), dismembered limbs (the eerie 'Towers of Silence' as described in *Something of Myself)* and whispering ghosts ('The Lost Legion', in *Many Inventions*). But viewed through the child and adolescent eyes of characters like Mowgli and Kim, the fertile jungle spaces and ancient mountains, broad vistas and lush fields are sources of meditation and rejuvenation, places of learning and unrestricted playgrounds. We see Kipling's ambivalent relationship to India played out in his artistic representation of a gendered geographical terrain where India as a maternal space is represented as either polluted and corrupt (a source of psychic and physical contamination) or a vital earth-mother that, like Hélène Cixous' '*materrenelle*', 'sings from a time before the law [. . .] before the symbolic took [her] breath away'.[15] The mother, in Cixousian topography, is fused to the sea. Using the homophony between *mer/mère*, as well as inserting the French *terre* (earth/terrain), Cixous proclaims 'it's my mother! The sea floats her, ripples her, flows together with her daughter, in all our ways. Then unseparated they sweep along their changing waters, without fear of their bodies, without bony stiffness, without a shell [. . .] and sea for mother (*mer pour mère*) gives herself up to pleasure in her bath of writing.'[16] Kipling's restorative, 'feminine' landscapes can be interpreted as reinstating Freud's 'dark continent' of female sexuality as a site of 'feminine' discourse, even if it must remain within the phallotext where binary oppositions are still rigidly and solidly set in place.[17] Julia Kristeva, after Freud, maintains that men were once within their mothers' bodies and must learn to include the feminine in their psychic maps. In this respect the feminine and the pre-symbolic maternal realm (what Kristeva terms the semiotic) are inextricably bound together. The fluidity with which Kipling renders his cathartic Indian landscapes characterises a 'feminine' elsewhere that lies outside the borders of the phallocentric economy. The aqueous mother, according to Cixous, is a potent marker of alterity. In Kipling's texts, the ancient windswept Himalayas with their icy covering that thaws and drips from the roofs of remote village houses, the watermill that bubbles through Dan and Una's Sussex glade in *Puck of Pook's Hill*, the rhythmic waves that break upon the cliff where Stalky constructs his dens in the gorse in *Stalky & Co.*, the dew-drenched fecund jungle spaces, can be read in terms of a feminine fluidity that both Cixous and Kristeva regard as powerfully expressive. However, the poetic maternal voice seems to be confined to Kipling's stories concerning children. His colonial foot soldiers and administrators in *Life's Handicap*, *The Day's Work* and, to an extent, *Plain Tales from the Hills* invariably demonise a feminised terrain. In these collections, Kipling toes the imperial line, generally associating masculinity with rationality and the feminine with horror.

Central to Kipling's positioning of India as a maternal space is a psychic ambivalence associated with this notion of a rebellious fecund female body and a pre-symbolic nurturing mother who satiates the child's desires. Post-Freudian psychoanalytic theory maintains that the infant's relationship to its caregiver plays an instrumental part in the development of subjectivity. Frustrated desires, which become narrativised in stories of 'loss', are an integral part of the child's first objects of love. Gaining entry into the symbolic, the child understands that its union with its primary carer must be compartmentalised into self and Other. Desire for the fantasy of coalescence, the impossibility of reclaiming the mother in the pre-linguistic space, establishes the child as a desirous being marked by longing, nostalgia and alienation. In the case of Kipling, I aim to demonstrate that the specifics of his childhood condition of migration and exile (of literally being separated from his early childhood landscape and caregivers) can be seen as a heightened example of what Kristeva would posit as a human universal, and his Indian stories become emblematic of that difficult dual exile.

'I met a hundred men on the road to Delhi and they were all my brothers,'[18] says Kipling in the epigraph to *Life's Handicap*. And a connection with his 'native brothers' seems to be borne out in other stories. In 'Lispeth' (in *Plain Tales from the Hills)*, for example, he castigates the English chaplain and his wife for their easy lies to the eponymous Hill girl waiting in vain for her beloved Englishman. 'It takes a great deal of Christianity', says the narrator of 'Lispeth' with savage irony, 'to wipe out uncivilised Eastern instincts.'[19] But the supposed affinities with 'native' India that the author cultivated belie the tone of 'knowing' white narrator who speaks for the 'native' in many of the stories in these collections. In 'The Incantation of Krishna Mulvaney' (in *Life's Handicap*) Kipling makes a mockery of Hindu religion, and in 'The Mark of the Beast' (in *Life's Handicap*), he allows his Hindu 'brothers' to be brutally tortured at the hands of hysterical Englishmen. In this respect, Kipling was tiresomely conforming to the prejudices of the Anglo-Indian community toward the Hindu religion (much respect was accorded to the Muslim faith, as well as their supposed 'masculine' traits, which the British saw as ennobling).[20] He infantilises his native 'brothers' in 'The House of Suddhoo' (in *Plain Tales*) and castigates them for their gullibility and belief in superstition. An elderly Suddhoo in Lahore is concerned for the health of his son in Peshawar. One of his tenants, known only as the seal-cutter, sees Suddhoo's concern as a way to extort money from the old man. Relying on daily telegraph reports, the seal-cutter pretends to perform a magic that enables him to ascertain the state of the son's illness. Only the narrator can see through the seal-cutter 'magic', but can do nothing. 'The Incantation of Krishna Mulvaney' sees Kipling's favourite Irish soldier, Private Mulvaney, carrying out one of his many boorish schemes (usually involving alcohol). Having been duped by a fellow soldier, Mulvaney finds himself in the midst of temple celebrations where he is mistaken for the god Krishna. After a farce-like escape, he manages to procure money for beer for himself and his comrades. J. M. S. Tompkins is not the first critic to point out that had this incident taken place in a Christian church, the story's reception would assuredly have been different.[21] 'The Mark of the Beast' is a darker take on a similar theme. The Englishman, Fleete, at the end of a drunken evening desecrates the temple of Hanuman, the Monkey God. For this disrespectful act, he is bitten and cursed by a leper priest. Fleete begins to transform into a wolfish creature that howls and devours raw meat. Fleete's friend Strickland, together with the narrator, gruesomely torture the leper priest who, in excruciating pain, agrees to reverse the curse, and Fleete is returned to his old self.

Kipling's attitude toward those perceived as a threat to the British imperial project is similarly ambivalent. In 'On Greenhow Hill' (in *Life's Handicap*), a sepoy deserter has been taking pot-shots at the British cantonment. So that his grievances do not infect the rest of the company, Privates Learoyd, Mulvaney and Ortheris have been charged to kill the deserter. The narrator appraises the artistry of Private Learoyd's unemotional execution and the assumption, despite such a cold-blooded murder, is that the threat to army morale has been averted. The 'Mutiny' of 1857 (now known as the First Indian Rebellion) was a continued source of great fear and distrust amongst the Anglo-Indian community and whilst not mentioned directly in the story, the changed attitude – both Indian and British – toward British rule of the Indian subcontinent is certainly a subtext.[22] However, this attitude is in sharp contrast with the perceived failing of a British rule that allows the eponymous orphan in 'Little Tobrah' (in *Life's Handicap*) to murder his blind sister by pushing her into a well. Frightened by her desperate calls, he leaves her to perish, saying 'it is better to die than to starve'[23] (*LH*, p. 270).

Kipling acknowledges an internal ambivalence in *Kim*, venerating the 'two/Separate sides to [his] head' (*Kim*, p. 179). And in this respect, his conflicting attitudes toward the colonial project and its effect upon his best beloved India mirror a psychic splitting. Hybrid characters like Kim and Mowgli must construct an identity that is contained within the profoundly phallogocentric and ethnocentric matrix of British imperialism, yet Kipling's texts exalt 'foreignness' and dissent at the same time as they struggle to contain and gag those prohibited voices of criticism that the nineteenth-century Anglo-Indian community finds so intolerable. To understand how Kipling came to cultivate such antithetical views of England and the English, and India and its peoples, it is necessary to go back to what is noted by many commentators of Kipling's art as a defining moment in the author's childhood, that of his expatriation to England. Along with his three-year-old sister Trix, Kipling was taken to a boarding house on the south coast of England and left in the care of Mrs Sarah Holloway, a woman deemed capable, on the strength of a newspaper advertisement, of bringing up a desperately young boy and his toddler sister. It was not unusual at that time for Anglo-Indian parents to send their children 'Home' for a spell to counteract what they saw as the corrupting influence of the native servants and *ayahs* and to eradicate the frowned-upon sing-song '*chi-chi*' accent British children developed, but this in no way lessened the trauma that a young brother and sister undoubtedly felt at the loss of their parents. 'Orphaned' by his biological mother as well as his devoted *ayah* and 'exiled' from his Bombay home, Kipling was left to map the psychic terrain of his identity according to the Christian edicts of his evangelical foster mother, which took the place of the maternal authority of his biological mother and beloved *ayah*.

Kristeva argues that the maternal authority is 'the trustee of that mapping of the self's clean and proper body; it is distinguished from paternal laws within which, with the phallic phase and acquisition of language, the destiny of man will take shape'. The maternal authority, which maps the territory of the child's body, is an 'authority without guilt at a time when there is a harmonious 'fusion between mother and nature'. This is in stark contrast to the authority that is linked to the phallus and exists in a 'universe of socially signifying performances where embarrassment, shame, guilt and desire come into play'.[24] Kipling's physical exile from his mother and his homeland makes the process of psychic separation from the maternal body more complex. Five and a half years would elapse before either of the children was to see their mother again, and Kipling would not set foot in India for a further five years. British psychiatrist John Bowlby in his pioneering work on attachment theory argues that '[w]henever a young child who has had the opportunity to develop an attachment to a mother figure is separated from her unwillingly he shows distress; and should he also be placed in a strange environment and cared for by a succession of strange people such distress is likely to be intense'.[25] At Southsea, Kipling experienced a dual 'exile'. He was not only cut off from his first home, its cultural shape and language, but also separated from his biological parents. By exploring his troubling exilic moment within a psychoanalytic framework, I hope to uncover the particular factors operating in the exchange and interchange with a maternal authority and its threat to the stability of the symbolic that informed Kipling's early socialisation.

The ideas on the necessary but problematic rupture of the mother/child dyad in the work of Julia Kristeva, and the Kleinian ideas of psychic splitting, form an important substratum of my Kristevan analysis. In her biography of Melanie Klein, Julia Kristeva celebrates the innovative Kleinian notion of the mother/child bond as a vital relationship in the child's psychic development. Kristeva also discusses the act of matricide that the child must perform as part of his/her psychic development.

Kristeva acknowledges the impact of Klein's conceptual framework of the mother/child dyad on her own notions of the evolution of identity.[26] Together with Kristeva and Klein, Hélène Cixous' work on writing from the margins of phallogocentric discourse will form the methodological scaffolding on which my analysis of Kipling's fiction is constructed.

Kristeva's writings on the 'semiotic' are an exploration of the fluidity which exists between verbal and non-verbal meaning and her work on the pre-verbal codes, which permeate language to produce signification and lie in the gap between words and their meaning, resonates in Kipling's writings. Like Kipling, she has travelled the 'exile's' line, born in Bulgaria but moving to Paris in 1965 at the age of twenty-four. Her own personal situation as a 'foreigner' on the borders of French culture, as well as her own marginalised position as a woman on the Parisian intellectual scene in the 1960s, has been integral to her notion of exile and her understanding of what it means to be 'foreign'. She says it was necessary for her to 'attempt to take up that exorbitant wager of carrying the rational project to the outer borders of the signifying venture of men'.[27] Hélène Cixous has, since the 1960s, advocated a 'feminine' style of writing that is both conceptually complex and playfully creative. She was born in 1937 in Algeria to a mother with Austro-German roots and a Jewish French-colonial father whose early death saw her expatriated to France. Her experience of 'exclusion' and 'exile' in Algeria, as well as her notion of using the experience of death, loss and lack to create a celebratory, life-affirming art, will inform my analysis of the maternal realm associated with landscape in Kipling's fiction of both the Punjab and Sussex.

On 30 December 1865, after his mother, Alice Kipling, experienced a difficult and drawn-out labour, Kipling was born on the Indian subcontinent. At that time in England's colonial history, India was considered to be the 'jewel in the crown' of the Empire and, ruled over by a queen, elevated to almost mythic status as 'The Centre of the World's Desire'.[28] Raised almost extensively by his beloved *ayah*, a Portuguese Roman Catholic, Kipling was reminded to 'Speak English now to Papa and Mamma' in the evenings (*SOM*, p. 4). Looking back across the decades in his autobiography, Kipling's first impressions were of early morning walks in the sunshine to the Bombay fruit market, of 'golden and purple fruits at the level of [his] shoulder'. He would remember naps in the afternoon heat where his *ayah* would sings Indian nursery rhymes and tell stories 'all unforgotten', a mother who 'sang wonderful songs at the black piano' and a father who worked in a 'marvellous place filled with the smells of paints and oils, and lumps of clay with which [he] played'. He would wander into Hindu temples to peer at 'dimly-seen, friendly gods' or sit beside his *ayah* as she prayed at a wayside cross. He remembered watching Arab dhows on the sparkling water embarking on faraway voyages, and brightly dressed Parsees splashing out into the waves to meet the glowing sunset (*SOM*, pp. 4–5). This vibrant, noisy country, backlit with sharp sunshine and soft sunset hues, was, in Kipling's imaginative geography, an edenic space filled with loving, patient caregivers. In these 'green spaces' of his Elysium, childhood fears could be easily assuaged. Meeta, his Hindu bearer, could diminish the totemic significance of a stuffed leopard's head on his nursery wall (*SOM*, p. 4). His father, Lockwood Kipling, would devise limericks to ward off his son's fear of a 'winged monster' on a foot-deep 'ravine', which was only a hen. His *ayah* could explain the reason behind the sudden appearance of a dismembered child's hand in the garden. It had come from the ominous Towers of Silence, where vultures waited on turrets for the dead to be brought in. Alice Kipling had forbidden the boy's insistent questioning on the subject, but his *ayah* satisfied his curiosity (*SOM*, p. 4). His lost Eden would be a source of comfort through the grey and wretched years he would spend in a boarding house in Southsea. Thus Bombay took on talismanic significance to a boy and his sister ejected from their very own paradise.

Kipling's formative years were spent in an India where little was prohibited, curiosity for the kaleidoscopic nature of his environment was encouraged and stable, loving relationships in the Anglo-Indian and Indian communities abounded. His English parents and Indian carers, his filiative relationships and affiliative identifications, provided the opportunity to express his desire to be loved as a person and have his love accepted in return. In his discussion of filiation and affiliation, Edward Said argues that new affiliative political and cultural ideas, orders, religions or belief systems can compensate for a breakdown in filiative concepts or roles, providing us with different forms of relationships and allegiances. Kipling's 'lost' mother in his real and psychic world, and his filiative relationship with her, is mourned throughout his earlier fiction. However, I will argue that Kipling's fascination with the mythic ideal of Empire, embodied in its goddess of Albion, 'Britannia', acted as an antidote to his 'orphanhood', and bestowed upon him an affiliative identification that, in one ideological puff, blew away his alienated childhood self.[29] These are potent feelings that would characterise his later stories for children. The *Just So Stories*, written in cathartic remembrance of his daughter Josephine, who died of pneumonia in New York at the age of eight, have at their heart the welcoming, secure intimacy that characterised his notion of 'home'. In the phantasmagorical *Kim*, the orphan Anglo-Indian finds his 'home' not in any one particular urban or rural space but in the whole of the Indian subcontinent, and all of its peoples are his family. One side of Kipling's imagination firmly fixed the India of his childhood as a sunny, inclusive space. When those 'days of strong light and colour passed' to be replaced with a 'dark land', the children were left to eke out their lonely existence in a boarding house 'smelling of aridity and emptiness' (*SOM*, pp. 3, 5). A paradisiacal polychromatic landscape given a multicultural shape and weight by a babble of harmonious English and Indian voices was, as Kipling's autobiography emphasises, exchanged for a drab and wretched abyss presided over by a desiccated matriarch whose brutality was matched only by her self-righteous evangelical rhetoric. An experience of moving between cultures, languages and power hierarchies gives rise to what Caren Kaplan argues is 'the ability to read and write culture on multiple levels'.[30] Commentators of Kipling's art have traced the influence of what Sandra Kemp calls his '"other self" of childhood'[31] as well as the effects of his early 'abandonment' on his stories, but few have addressed the desire for and fear of the 'lost' mother figure, which, operating as a Kristevan maternal metaphor, runs through Kipling's fiction.

The complexity that is evident in Kipling's ambivalent attitude toward India, as well as the narrative techniques he employs in his prose, has been much commented upon by critics of his art. In the following section of this chapter, I will offer a brief survey of the commentary that forms the basis of my own analysis of Kipling's fiction. Concentrating on his love for the India of his childhood, with what he sees (through the tinted lens of nostalgia) as its variegated landscape peopled by a multiplicity of ethnic groups, allows critics to conveniently diminish his deeply entrenched sense of imperial ideology. Bonamy Dobrée tried to reappraise Kipling's imperial ideology in a more objective manner, arguing that his ideal of Empire was founded on a sense of moral purpose, and called attention to what he saw as the humanist dimension of Kipling's fiction.[32] However, to study Kipling solely in terms of his wholehearted belief in the British imperial project and the 'superior clay' of the white man is to consign him to history as a racist.[33] In this duality Salman Rushdie locates the paradoxical 'Ruddy Baba as well as Kipling Sahib' and his writing, Rushdie asserts, has 'the power simultaneously to infuriate and to entrance'.[34] Thomas Metcalf succinctly summarises Kipling as an artist continually 'coping with contradiction', arguing that he 'made visible the psychic tensions that lay hidden beneath the seemingly placid surface of the late Victorian Raj'.[35] Kipling's contemporary critics, however, were uneasy with what they (justifiably) saw as his loathsome political polemic. Robert Buchanan famously vilified the author's undisguised enjoyment of brutality and cruelty in 'The Voice of the Hooligan' (1899), establishing a strand of criticism that became *de rigueur* well into the twentieth century. Orwell, though recognising Kipling's artistic talents, cited his 'definite strain of sadism' that cannot easily be 'accepted or even forgiven by any civilised person'.[36] Kipling's celebration of masculinity, which characterises particularly the *Soldiers Three* collection, does much to disguise what I will argue are the maternal spaces in his fiction. In this sense, the feminised spaces underlie the superstructure of male activity. His Punjab and wider Indian landscapes can be read as terrains that have to be negotiated through a paternal discourse as well as poetic spaces that are liberated from the domain of masculinity. Hence Mowgli's wild jungle spaces, Stalky's out-of-bounds dens, Kim's resting places on the Grand Trunk Road, the Sahiba's compound or the Hill people's houses under the eaves of the Himalayas, whether in a subversive or reactionary way, image the feminine in its 'difference' to a monolithic masculine conservatism and western ethnocentrism.

From Edmund Wilson (1941) to Andrew Rutherford (1964),[37] much has been done to wrest Kipling from his hard-line imperial propagandist image, delivering tired aphorisms and revelling in revenge. However, cruelty and revenge are recurring themes in Kipling's fiction. Stories that centre on characters possessed by a thirst for vengeance can be found throughout his long writing career. In 'Dray Wara Yow Dee' (in *Soldiers Three*), an elderly Pathan horse dealer has discovered his wife's infidelity and after a grisly mutilation (cutting off her head and breasts) throws her corpse into the river. 'The Limitations of Pambé Serang' (in *Life's Handicap*) sees the Malay sailor, Pambé Serang, dishonoured by a drunken African stoker. Serang, exacting his revenge, eventually kills the stoker but remains unperturbed by the death sentence imposed upon him. 'Mary Postgate' and 'Swept and Garnished' (in *A Diversity of Creatures*) deal with the psychological effects of repressing situations too horrific to confront consciously. Wilson was especially important in initiating what Martin Seymour-Smith calls a 'sensible criticism of Kipling'.[38] Biographers Charles Carrington and Lord Birkenhead provide much material that has since been lost due to Kipling's daughter Elsie Bambridge destroying many of her father's papers, with Andrew Lycett's lengthy and in-depth historical study of the man and his art filling in many of the biographical gaps. Modern biographer David Gilmour's study of Kipling's imperial and political life is a thoughtful examination of Kipling's many identities,[39] particularly when read in conjunction with Harry Ricketts' biography where he aims to 'bring out the full range of these diverse Kiplings'.[40] Angus Wilson's *The Strange Ride of Rudyard Kipling* is an important biography for my analysis, particularly his notion that Kipling's India represented a 'Garden of Eden before the Fall [. . .] making the Indian peasantry – what most people thought of as "the Indian people" – his first love, his beloved children for the rest of his life'.[41] His study was, said Wilson, 'intended to suggest that Kipling's art is suffused with a personal and mysterious despair and apprehension' that caused the author to create 'a rigid social rule (The Law) to shield the individual (and himself) from a constant nagging anxiety about his ultimate fate'. Wilson notes that Kipling's insistence on his notion of the 'Law' is not based on any Puritanical joylessness and contempt for those who do find life pleasurable. It is more, Wilson argues, an essential psychological buttress that, through a sense of selfless duty, shores up the crippling realisation of the meaninglessness of existence.[42] Shamsul Islam's *Kipling's Law* attempts to disentangle Kipling's ideology from British imperialism and sees a more profound personal philosophy contained within a universal 'Law' to which all his (male) characters are bound regardless of race or class. Like Wilson, Islam sees Kipling's 'Law' as an antidote to the horror of meaninglessness, nameless 'Powers of Darkness, Disorder and Chaos'.[43] This study will build upon this notion of Kipling's ubiquitous 'Law', deploying the Kristevan notion of the interplay between the semiotic and the symbolic to read the horror of the abyss as that which we most dread, the (feminine) object of primal repression. Kipling's 'abyss' represents a border beyond which lies the abjected maternal space, the feared, hidden parts of colonial identity and community, that which 'disturbs identity, system and order',[44] against which, I will argue, the white man defines and validates his masculinity.

Philip Mason, having been a member of the ICS (Indian Civil Service) during the last twenty years of British rule, and engaged in his pioneering work into advancing the study of minority and race problems during his time as director of the Institute of Race Relations, is well positioned to understand the nature of the Anglo-Indian community to which Kipling belonged. In *The Glass, the Shadow and the Fire* he argues that the structure of society was responsible for 'binding [Kipling] within a surface that reflected back his immediate surroundings but beneath which something far more important was astir'.[45] What is astir in Kipling's fiction is the construction of an abjected maternal figure, and I will relate this to Kristeva's notion of the mapping of the child's clean and proper self. Kristeva argues that individual subjectivity and group identity are founded upon the abjection of that which lies beyond the borders of society. The main threat to individual autonomy is the child's unitary relationship with the mother and his/her dependence on the maternal body (for psychological as well as physical nourishment). Kristeva's notion of *abjection* is therefore closely related to the maternal function. She argues that in order for a child to free his/herself from the mother figure and enter into the symbolic, s/he must perform a necessary 'matricide'. In order to exist in a patriarchal society the child must abject the maternal body. Images of horror and abjection point to the division between the maternal authority and the law of the father. For example, lethal crevices and polluted vaginal spaces, such as those in 'The Strange Ride of Morrowbie Jukes' (in *Wee Willie Winkie*); pockmarked, scarred and missing faces, such as the terrifying leper in 'The Mark of the Beast' or the Boer farmer's son of 'A Sahib's War' (in *Traffics and Discoveries*) whose nostrils have been eaten away by disease; bloodied, decomposing corpses, such as those in 'Thrown Away' and 'The Return of Imray' (in *Plain Tales* and *Life's Handicap*) as well as the sleepers that are mistaken for corpses in 'The City of Dreadful Night'. On one hand these images of corruption threaten a 'clean and proper' subjectivity and thus fill Kipling's white men with disgust and horror. On the other hand they look back across time to the unifying mother/child relationship in the semiotic where prohibitions on 'waste' were not yet in place and corporeal expulsions and leaking breasts were merely part of the undifferentiated fabric of the infant's relation to his/her mother. The eponymous Little Tobrah pushes his starving blind sister down a well, turning her body into living waste matter. Part of the sympathy we feel for this desperately pitiful act is evoked by the absence of loving parents who have died of smallpox, leaving their children to fend for themselves in an unrelentingly harsh economic and climatic environment.

The critical voices sympathetic to Kipling's art, such as J. M. S. Tompkins and T. S. Eliot, amongst others, argue that the discrepancy that exists between Kipling the artist and Kipling the imperial apologist point to a corresponding ambivalence in his writing. Tompkins argues that Kipling should be approached in a historical context but the centre of his work concerns 'permanent human nature, reactions and relationships of men within a defined territory'. His stories, she argues, are 'stuffed with human beings under various stresses of duty, command, anguish, error, hatred and love'.[46] T. S. Eliot concedes that Kipling was, unfairly in his opinion, considered a Tory, but crucially, 'knew some of the things that are underneath, and of the things which are beyond the frontier'.[47] Eliot's observation corresponds to Kipling's notion that imagination was a 'form of imperfect memory'.[48] The 'deeper and darker caverns' of 'experience or [. . .] imagination',[49] which blur the demarcation between the 'I' and its object of desire, find their narrative expression in tales of madness and terror such as 'At the End of the Passage' (in *Life's Handicap*), of worlds beset with neuroses such as 'As Easy as ABC' (in *A Diversity of Creatures*), of realities transformed into unrealities in stories like 'The Dream of Duncan Parrenness' (in *Life's Handicap*) and dream worlds overshadowing and encroaching upon waking worlds like those found in 'The Brushwood Boy' (in *The Day's Work*). Yet, as Angus Wilson notes, India as an edenic place of bliss informs much of the narrative of stories such as *Kim* amongst others, and 'made childhood the sacred age from which all growth was more or less a painful lesson of cunning endurance'.[50] Kipling's art is engaged in the psychic mapping of his Anglo-Indian child and adult characters in their responses to colonial edicts, as well as their ambivalent relationships to India and its peoples existing in a psychic 'elsewhere', a dangerous post-Freudian 'dark continent' on the symbolic map, as it were.

In spite of Eliot's sympathetic appraisal of Kipling's art in 1941, it seemed likely (especially after the horror of the First World War) that Kipling would be consigned to history as, to borrow from John Osborne, 'just one of those sturdy old plants left over from the Edwardian Wilderness who can't understand why the sun isn't shining anymore'.[51] George Orwell's 1942 essay, 'Rudyard Kipling', coherently summarised widespread critical opinion that Kipling presented himself through his narrative voice as a 'jingo imperialist [. . .] morally insensitive and aesthetically disgusting'.[52] Similarly, Lionel Trilling's 'Kipling' (1943) and Edmund Wilson's 'The Kipling that Nobody Read' (1952) are typical of the body of harsh criticism of the post-war period. Like Orwell, Trilling takes issue with Kipling's narrative voice, which he identifies as nothing less than 'swagger and swank' filled with tones of 'bullying, ruthlessness, and self-righteousness'.[53] Wilson categorises Kipling's fiction as 'crude in writing [and] trashy in feeling'.[54] However, Tompkins argues that 'no one should pass judgement on the "tone" of a writer more than one generation away from him',[55] and in the decades that followed Kipling began to be appraised more sympathetically[56] by critics who were responding to his art through the distancing effects of time, as captured in Auden's 'In Memory of W. B. Yeats': 'Time with this strange excuse / Pardoned Kipling and his views, / And will pardon Paul Claudel, / Pardons him for writing well.'[57] Sandra Kemp in *Kipling's Hidden Narratives* focuses on the irony used by Kipling's narrators in stories such as 'One View of the Question' (in *Many Inventions*). Kemp argues that this story, told from the point of view of a Muslim visiting London writing a letter to his brother, reverses the 'usual "play" of discourse' by positing the English, and not the 'native' as Other.[58] Philip Mason argues that Kipling seemed to align himself with the ruling British with his patronising treatment of native Indians in stories like 'In the House of Suddhoo', but adds a codicil: 'then again he has a second thought and adds an ironic hint which implies: "This isn't really what I think".'[59]

Elliot Gilbert also notes Kipling's use of irony to acerbically criticise the British Establishment. In 'The Gardener' (in *Debits and Credits*), Gilbert argues that the conventional way of life of the village is emblematic of pre-war respectability and has the means of 'imposing upon its members, at whatever cost, its own way of life'.[60] Kipling's structuring of Helen Turrell's forlorn story (she is silently grieving for the loss in the First World War of a son who has been brought up as her 'nephew') relies on a second-hand account that is littered with sharply ironic sentences. The effect of these, Gilbert argues, is to portray a woman 'who has been defeated by a repressive, parochial society'.[61]

Kipling's use of irony, which amplifies the plight of his most wretched Anglo-Indian and Indian characters, can, Kemp argues, 'define India as an unknown Other in the terms established by a European racism which ignores process and history'. However, she goes on to stress that 'ambivalent or multiple perspectives undermine their assertion of a colonialist will to power and knowledge'.[62] Edward Said argues that, following in the tradition of other western writers of the eighteenth or nineteenth century with little university endorsement and even less academic discipline, Kipling constructs colonial narratives that evaluate the 'Orient' according to a western ethnocentricity.[63] 'At Howli Thana' and 'Gemini' (in *Soldiers Three*), which highlight the supposed thievery and dishonesty of the 'Oriental', do much to support Said's argument, but this complex author can also be viewed in terms of Homi Bhabha's notion that colonial subjectivity is constructed on the foundations of mimicry, the white man's need to 'see' his colonised peoples as sort of European-in-negative, 'as a subject of a difference that is almost the same, but not quite'.[64] Kipling undermines the authority of the educated Bengali, Hurree Chunder Mookerjee, in *Kim* with his pastiche of the Babu's speech, in particular the mispronunciation of English words and idioms which are misplaced in the mouth of an Indian national, '*all*so', 'tommy-rott' (*Kim*, p. 271). But even in his pastiche Kipling is ambivalent as just a little further on he writes (with sincerity, it seems) of Kim's 'envy' of the babu: 'The Hurree Babu of his [western] knowledge – oily, effusive, and nervous – was gone; gone, too was the brazen drug-vendor of overnight. There remained – polished, polite, attentive – a sober, learned son of experience and adversity, gathering wisdom from the lama's lips' (*Kim*, p. 275). In short, this is *everything* that Kim, in part, aspires to be but is not. Hurree Chunder may be a resourceful, well-respected and courageous player in the Great Game, but he is no match for the illiterate Anglo-Indian street boy. A western-style education and knowledge of anthropology and medicine will not be sufficient to gain him entry into the exclusive Royal Society. Kipling's treatment of the Bengali babu is by no means exclusive to him. *Kim* was written at a time of growing change in the political landscape in India, as British rule was gradually being brought under scrutiny. The National Congress, founded in 1885, included many educated Bengalis who, amongst many members of the Anglo-Indian community, were regarded with suspicion.[65]

Lewis Wurgaft[66] touches upon this in his analysis of the political effect of Indian resistance and the change in perception of the Anglo-Indian psyche that now looked upon India as a less stable, more frightening continent to rule. Wurgaft argues that the British increasingly imaged India as an alluring 'female', libidinous, corrupting and languid. This 'Orientalised' vision provided a handy contrast to what Anglo-Indians considered 'manly' virtues: order, cleanliness, vigorous activity and discipline. These were qualities that the British believed justified what they saw as their innate right to rule. After the watershed of the Indian 'Mutiny', the British (politically with the likes of Lord Curzon, and creatively in the fiction of Kipling) developed a heroic mythology as a means to counteract their faltering imperial confidence. A new breed of imperial hero emerges in collections like *The Day's Work*. The long-suffering Findlayson in 'The Bridge Builders' and the exhausted Scott in 'William the Conqueror' are assigned the role of self-sacrificing martyrs to the cause of Empire. George Cottar in 'The Brushwood Boy' is the dedicated, duty-bound hero who safeguards the Empire's northwest frontiers. Noel Annan, in a seminal article in the early 1960s, recognises this 'problem set by the concept of roles'.[67] Underlining Kipling's proficiency in examining the conflict existing between cultures in a sociological context, he suggests that Kipling was nevertheless unable to adequately address his own internal conflict.[68] Kemp, too, recognises the duality inherent in an author who can authoritatively write of India in a dispassionate journalistic style, commenting on coloniser and colonised alike from a knowing and objective observer, but is undermined by the shadowy 'fluidity of the self which interprets and commands'.[69] In my analysis, the fluid voice that Kemp identifies belongs to the substructure of Kipling's Anglo-Indian self. It is a voice that speaks from the unconscious, and is connected to a nostalgic notion of childhood. Kipling even had a name for the unconscious force that articulated his artistic inspiration into verse and prose. Long before Freud formalised his classification of the unconscious, the ego and the id, first mentioned in his 1920 essay 'Beyond the Pleasure Principle', Kipling used the word 'Daemon' to describe the unconscious creative process that he argued was responsible for much of what he considered his best writing. 'When your Daemon is in charge,' he wrote, 'do not try to think consciously. Drift, wait, obey' (*SOM*, p. 123). It is very tempting to replace the word Daemon with *id*.

In *Something of Myself*, Kipling describes the false starts he encountered writing the *Puck* stories but, as with *Kim*, he was certain that the writing process was completed without his conscious control, 'Evidently my Daemon would not function in the brickyards and school rooms. Therefore, like Alice in Wonderland, I turned my back on the whole thing and walked the other way. Therefore, the whole thing set and linked itself [. . .] and I knew it must be very good or very bad because the whole series turned itself off just as *Kim* had done' (*SOM*, pp. 110–11).

As early as 1965 critics were interested in a psychoanalytic reading of Kipling's fiction. T. N. Cross explored the effects of Kipling's parental abandonment in Southsea on the subsequent formation of his identity.[70] In 1975, Leonard Shengold produced a more comprehensive study of Kipling's childhood experiences, incorporating his years at the United Services College (USC) in Westward Ho! as part of that study.[71] Shengold argues that Kipling was the victim of 'soul murder', initiated by his parents leaving him and his sister Trix at the 'House of Desolation' in Southsea without preparation or explanation. He goes on to argue that Kipling was, in effect, orphaned, and this resulted in a psychic 'splitting [of] the victim's identity into contradictory fragments that function without effective synthesis'. According to Shengold, the evidence for Kipling's psychic fragmentation can be found in his portrayals (especially in *Stalky & Co.*) of authority figures as simultaneously good and bad. According to Shengold, the personal hatred, directed firstly toward his parents but then transposed onto Sarah Holloway, which Kipling insisted he was drained of at Lorne Lodge (*SOM*, p. 12), emerges continually in his narratives. His chief motivation for beginning writing at USC, Shengold argues, was revenge. The range of reading material available to a young boy who saw literature as a 'means to everything that would make him happy' was vast and eclectic (*SOM*, p. 6). From Horace to James Thomson, Swinburne to Longfellow, Kipling was soon producing pastiche and parodies. He discovered that words had not only the power to wound, but also the potential to settle scores, a potential the heavily bespectacled aesthetic Kipling much valued in the masculine, athletic environment of UCS. The 'personal and well-appointed limericks' which 'worked well' on his companions were exchanged for a Dantesque tale that pre-emptively meted out punishments for teachers and pupils alike: 'I bought a fat, American cloth-bound note-book, and set to work on an *Inferno*, into which I put, under appropriate torture, all my friends and most of the masters. This was really remunerative because one could chant his future doom to a victim walking below the windows of the study' (*SOM*, p. 22).

Diane Simmons argues that children who have been raised in environments where their self-esteem has been continuously undermined develop personalities that need to exercise control (physical or psychological) over others to counteract their inner vulnerability. These fears, she argues, 'can translate into a deep-seated and compulsive desire for revenge'.[72] Following the work of Heinz Kohut, W. R. D. Fairburn and D. W. Winnicott, Simmons maintains that Kipling's fiction is the tortured creation of a 'full-fledged [sic] narcissist'[73] and the undercurrent of revenge fantasy that runs through the stories can be located in the boy's experience of loss in Southsea. Simmons' notion of narcissism follows Winnicott's idea of narcissism as a 'false self', which is initiated by a 'not good enough mother'. He argues that: 'in the cases on which my work is based there has been what I call a true self hidden, protected by a false self. This false self is no doubt an aspect of the true self. It hides and protects it, and it reacts to the adaptation failures.' Simmons points to the lack of care that Kipling experienced in Southsea as crucial to the formation of his narcissism.[74]

Retribution, particularly cruel and sadistic retribution, has long been noted as a dominant feature of Kipling's stories. Tompkins devotes a chapter to the twin themes of hatred and revenge in her important book on Kipling's art, *The Art of Rudyard Kipling*. John Kucich cites the many instances of sadomasochism in Kipling's fiction. The bullyings, beatings, torture and cruelty both in the military and out of it that pervade his fiction actually, Kucich argues, determine his characters' moral judgements and sanctify their colonial injustices.[75] Michael Berkeley's opera *Baa Baa Black Sheep* points to the deprivation the young Rudyard endured at the 'House of Desolation' as the source for much of the dark tones of his adult writings. Berkeley merges Kipling's thinly disguised autobiographical account of his time in Southsea, 'Baa Baa, Black Sheep' (in *Wee Willie Winkie*) with the Mowgli tales, and sees much in the original tale that is evident in Kipling's later writings, 'all the elements of revenge and cruelty'.[76] In Berkeley's opera, the fiction becomes a means through which the abused child Kipling can cope with his childhood isolation and bullying, as well as a means to face and master his daily miseries.[77]

The narrative retranslating of childhood separation, together with the seemingly magical abilities to address those complex and difficult issues, are among the psychoanalytic explorations of this study. The anger that Punch in 'Baa Baa, Black Sheep' feels, in a sinister twist, links the bullying 'foster mother' Aunty Rosa with his parents. Ulrich Knoepflmacher argues that the story 'bitterly yokes a boy's rosy memories of a benign father and mother to their parental surrogate, the decidedly unrosy

Aunty Rosa, Punch's relentless tormentor'.[78] The link between Punch's feelings toward Aunty Rosa and his repressed anger toward his parents, in particular his mother, will be more fully developed in Chapter 1 of this study. The implication in the text is that both parents are complicit in the beatings that Punch receives from Aunty Rosa. Connecting Aunty Rosa to his perceived abandoning parents enables Punch to safely split his mother(s) into their good and bad elements as a way of working through the grief of his separation without endangering the goodwill of his loving but absent biological mother. This division is mirrored in the fiction, where Kipling's colonial adults will subsequently split Mother India into her coveted and abjected geographical and climatic component parts. India becomes the location where the 'good' mother resides but it is, crucially, a place that threatens psychic disintegration and potential orphanhood.

Kipling's ambivalent attitude toward the Eden of his childhood is played out with a new Eve that is both mythic and monstrous, and provides a trope for his split mother figures. The Eve of the Genesis story is subject to a doubling identity. She is the first woman and sacred of her sex, but is also responsible for Adam's ejection from paradise by her defiance of the word of God. Hélène Cixous points to Eve's story as an illustration of questioning the law of the father, in which her transgressions become a threat to the phallogocentric order.[79] Kipling's colonial adults in collections such as *Plain Tales* and *Life's Handicap* demonstrate a desire and fear of an India that has the potential to place them in psychic as well as physical exile. Julia Kristeva examines the cult of the Virgin Mary as a way in which women can be identified with the word of the father. The Virgin is the sacred, ideal mother but is also defined by the word of the father.[80] Kipling's adulation of what I will argue is his goddess of Empire, 'Britannia', in collections such as *The Day's Work* and *Puck of Pook's Hill* has parallels with Kristeva's notion of the Virgin's duality and will be developed in more detail in Chapter 5 of this study. Kipling never, to my knowledge, named 'Britannia', but in 'Song of the English', he has England address her colonial sons as 'your old grey mother who bore you on her knees'. The closest he comes to it is in 'Centurion of the Thirtieth' (in *Puck of Pook's Hill*), where the Roman soldier Parnesius invokes 'Roma Dea!' when talking about his childhood memories of his mother (*PPH*, p. 87). For the purposes of this study, the personification of Britannia belongs to the trope of maternal figures.

Jane Hotchkiss touches upon the issue of what she argues is the 'radically orphaned' child and how that child is seen outside of cultural markers in 'The Jungle of Eden: Kipling, Wolf Boys and the Colonial Imagination'.[81] She discusses the implications of existing outside of both language and human society. The Victorians, she argues, were fascinated with feral children, for they represented 'an impossible connection and irremediable alienation'.[82] Denied access to human contact, the feral child establishes familial bonds with the non-human world and is thus able to establish, Hotchkiss argues, 'an oceanic dyadic connectedness'[83] with animals. The idea of the wilderness is thus intimately connected to the idea of the child. Hotchkiss's article is concerned with Mowgli as willing subaltern. His colonial self is caught between two worlds. The preoedipal relationship with his biological and adoptive mothers (Messua and the she-wolf Raksha) is crucial to Hotchkiss's analysis, for it ends, she argues, in an implied incestuous union with the native mother. In one narrative stroke, Kipling dissolves India and its cultural heritage by hailing a new colonial Adam whose actions are bound by a mixture of Jungle law and Forestry code, which in turn lessens the threat of the Mutiny that was still fresh in the minds of the Anglo-Indian community. My study follows on from Hotchkiss's in that the wolf mother is representative of primal desire that must be abjected if Mowgli is to move forward into society (she is continually associated with blood, violence and infant suckling). I depart from Hotchkiss in suggesting that *The Jungle Book* is not only a fictive piece to assuage Mutiny fears, but also highlights the importance of the natural terrain and the sustenance that Kipling's orphans find therein. Mother India can compensate for the grief of separation and becomes the translation for the desirous semiotic mother. In *The Jungle Book* and *Kim*, the natural environment of India becomes the stage on which the struggle of separating from the maternal realm is played out. As I will make clear, however, the 'wild' side of India is always 'off limits' or beyond the boundaries in a Kristevan sense for Kipling's post-adolescent characters. The 'wilderness' represents an internal battleground where these boys struggle to become 'good' colonial citizens. John Kucich argues that Kipling's notion of society is organised around a 'sadomasochistic psychology and cultural logic' and that his 'sadomasochistic groups underwrote a remarkably unilateral class politics, which accommodated contrary attitudes toward imperialism'. Kucich makes a case for the school environment in the *Stalky* stories becoming a training ground for the 'intersubjective dynamic' of 'good' and 'bad' bullying. How the boys respond to and manage such a brutalising regime has a bearing on the future success (or failure) of Kipling's empire builders, whether that is in bloody border wars, isolated outposts or the claustrophobic atmosphere of the Anglo-Indian hill stations.[84]

In a similar critical vein to Hotchkiss, Ulrich Knoepflmacher analyses Kipling's preoccupation with female power, which he argues is inseparable from a mother figure, in 'Female Power and Male Self-Assertion: Kipling's Preoccupation with the Maternal'. Kipling highlights the importance of powerful male camaraderie in story collections such as *Soldiers Three*. The bond of friendship that is created in a beery, raucous male environment 'conceals a boy's ambivalent perception of a matriarch's power'.[85] Knoepflmacher argues that the stories Kipling began to write for children after the publication of 'Baa Baa, Black Sheep' cathartically reconciled the betrayal that he felt as a result of his mother's abandonment.[86] Focusing on 'Baa Baa, Black Sheep', 'The Potted Princess', *The Light that Failed* and the *Just So Stories*, Knoepflmacher argues that Kipling 'depended on maternal goodwill to sanction the exile he came to accept'[87] and his stories become a way of working through the grief of his childhood loss.

Using Knoepflmacher's perceptive analysis as a springboard, Chapter 1 of this study will extend his ideas by tracing Kipling's exilic moment and the ensuing anxiety it caused back to the suffering of an earlier separation from the maternal body in the pre-linguistic realm. On one level, the exilic experience is a universal one. In a Kleinian/Kristevan configuration, pre-symbolic identity is locked into an undifferentiated mother/child dyad. However, when the child begins the process of socialisation it must begin to address the linguistic boundaries and barriers that draw a distinction between it and its mother. The child, until the moment of entry into the symbolic, has been able to identify with a life-giving and nourishing mother, an ideal object, in effect. From a Kleinian perspective, the ideal object is the mother's breast and as such is, for the child, both life-giving and protective. The successful integration of the child into the symbolic is dependent upon the successful negotiation of its anxiety toward the newly abjected mother figure. Klein was to have an important influence on Kristeva's ideas about the mother/child dyad. In her early work, Kristeva deals in depth with the infant's relationship to the surface of the mother's body and the ways in which internal identification and a 'lack' (*manque*) are already operating within this relationship, due to the mother's role as regulator of the child's drives and desire.[88] Although separating from the maternal body is a prerequisite for entrance into the symbolic realm, it is invariably a painful process. The child often experiences trauma due to its psychic exile from the seamless fabric of the maternal realm.

Of course, for Kipling, psychic exile was made more complex by his physical removal from his first home in Bombay. Like his ink-and-paper twin Punch, who is transformed from the 'unquestioned despot of the house at Bombay' (*WWW*, p. 268) into a forlorn outcast black sheep, the psychic mapping that Kipling underwent in Southsea aggrandises his 'Englishness' by diminishing (but not eradicating) his Anglo-Indian self. Kipling's return to India after a hiatus of twelve years brought his repressed 'forgotten' Anglo-Indian self back from the dead, as it were, and made him 'deliver in the vernacular sentences whose meanings [he] knew not' (*SOM*, p. 39). Harish Trivedi's comprehensively researched essay in Jan Montefiore's *In Time's Eye* deals with Kipling's use (or misuse) of Hindustani.[89] He neglects to mention, however, the malignant influence of the evangelical Sarah Holloway charged with bringing up two infants expatriated 'Home' to *Belait*. Under her cruel eye, Indian 'vernacular' and all its associated cultural markers were reimaged as shameful; to align oneself with it was to be in a state of 'sin', outcast from the Christian *mores* of the metropolis. Kipling and his sister, 'exiled' from their homeland, had only their shared childish conversations, in which Hindustani was fast diminishing, to try and recapture what was in danger of being irretrievably eradicated, to voice their memories and give shape and meaning to their ambivalent identities. In Kipling's 'Indian' writings, it is certain that the 'vernacular' does not always come out in the right way; there may be errors in grammar, structure or usage; it may appear misshapen and irregular; nevertheless, it represented a best-beloved India from which two small children were wrenched and to which there was no returning save through half-remembered snatches of words from 'home'.

There are echoes of Kipling's struggle with identity in *The Jungle Book*. Confused by his dual status of 'man-cub', Mowgli remains, quite literally, the product of two communities, the human and animal, the savage and civilised. In contrast to Kim, who can comfortably move between communities and languages – Anglo-Indian and Indian, Christian, Sikh, Hindu and Muslim – Mowgli is unable to be posited in either the jungle or the man-village, and his dilemma remains somewhat open-ended. The epilogue to *The Jungle Book* (written twelve months prior to the Mowgli stories), 'In the Rukh' (in *Many Inventions*), is a resolution of sorts, as we see Mowgli married and in the employ of the Forestry Department. But Mowgli's rebirth as dutiful native of the British Empire ignores the vengeful, devil-may-care streak that Kipling had vigorously written into the character of his anarchic wolf-boy in 'Letting in the Jungle' (in *The Second Jungle Book*). Elliot Gilbert notes that 'Kipling considered pain, violence and even brutality to be necessary elements in the creative process.'[90] Certainly, Mowgli's curiously acquiescent end in the service of the Forestry Commission lends a pageant, almost mythic air to the collection that transcends the mercilessly violent scenes in 'Tiger! Tiger!', 'The Red Dog' and 'Letting in the Jungle' that have preceded 'In the Rukh'. Critics such as Mark Paffard argue that elements of the Mowgli tales can be read as allegories of Empire. 'Mowgli', he argues, 'is undoubtedly the young "sahib" of the jungle, and he has to contend with the native ingratitude that his superiority arouses'.[91] John McClure sees *The Jungle Book* collections as a composite 'fable of imperial education and rule'.[92]

Similarly, Zohreh Sullivan, in her Lacanian reading of Kipling's fiction, *Narratives of Empire*, finds much in the fiction that can be read as complex colonial metaphor and allegory rather than simple imperial propaganda. Taking the trope of family as the starting point for her study, Sullivan argues that 'Kipling constructs a pathology of selves which illuminates the pathology of empire. Understanding Kipling's stories requires us to reread their representations of self in terms of the culture of empire, and then again of representations in terms of the self.'[93] The primary 'site of psychic splitting and division'[94] is, Sullivan argues, located in Kipling's Empire/child configuration. This split site is full of contradictions. The stories that revolve around the relentless struggle of 'Britannia's overburdened imperial sons' demonstrate the 'obsession with the private and the unconscious as a source of terror and fascination [that] lies at the heart of the Kipling myth and informs all his tales'.[95] In her postcolonial and historical study, Sullivan concentrates on Kipling's early Indian tales and an extensive investigation of *Kim*. Her analysis of the fiction is reinforced with autobiographical details from *Something of Myself*. She argues that Kipling's use of the family trope taps into a very nineteenth-century social construct. Queen Victoria was seen as the all-powerful matriarch and the natives her unruly children that had to be kept in order by her colonial sons. The imperial space is like an English 'drawing room' where exacting (British) standards of behaviour expected of Anglo-Indians and natives were judged by them. Sullivan argues that Kipling occupies an ambivalent position in this totalitarian view of Empire. As 'the quintessentially divided imperial subject',[96] he is both the master and the child, part Englishman, part native.

Her innovative ideas as to the 'constitution of the colonial subject'[97] will form the substratum of my examination of Kipling's ambivalent attitude toward imperial ideology. In particular, my analysis of *The Day's Work* collection owes a debt to Sullivan's groundbreaking study, especially her excellent interpretation of 'The Bridge Builders' and 'The Brushwood Boy', which features substantially in Chapter 5 of this study. Aiming to position Kipling within the timeframe of colonial history, she sees the purpose of the stories, particularly those of the 1890s, as the author's response to the 'turbulent times of imperial self-examination and expansion'.[98] However, I depart from her historical reading of

Kipling's texts by suggesting that his ambivalent desire for and fear of a feminised India and his gradual acceptance of imperial edicts mirror the Kristevan notion of abjecting the mother in the semiotic in order for the child to become a socialised subject in the symbolic. The word of the father transforms the abject mother into a desexualised 'symbolic' mother, which in Kipling's stories is achieved by adopting an imperial mythology that worships the mother of Empire, Britannia. My study will follow Sullivan's postcolonial concept of subjectivity built upon the binary opposition in the colonised/coloniser relationship, but I diverge from her Lacanian analytical route by concentrating upon the importance of a Kristevan maternal realm, which does not feature in her study, together with the influence of Kipling's bicultural upbringing in structuring his ambivalent attitude toward his homeland and Britain.

Like Kemp's Modernist interpretation of Kipling's prose, Sullivan highlights his use of irony as a defence mechanism to ward off the greater terror of a 'breakdown into an India of the mind'.[99] She concentrates her reading on the adult Kipling as all-knowing narrator commenting upon his childhood self in *Something of Myself*. She omits, however, a detailed analysis of 'Baa Baa, Black Sheep'. Kipling was still a relatively young man when this story was written – the more abstruse tales, where his narrator manipulates our reading of the narrative, would come later in his writing career. For example, 'The Ship that Found Herself' (in *The Day's Work*), a tale ostensibly about (anthropomorphised) component parts of a ship having to be 'run-in' to be more efficient, contains the following comment on life, made all the more striking for its understated irony:

> Their [the machine parts'] conversation, of course, is not half as wise as our human talk, because they are all, though they do not know it, bound one to the other in blackness, where they cannot tell what is happening near them, nor what will overtake them next. (*DW*, p. 87)

Similarly, 'They' (in *Traffics and Discoveries*) is Kipling's moving tale of the ghosts of dead children finding a haven on earth in the house of a blind woman who loves them all. Only those who have lost a child are able to see the children flitting through the house and its grounds. When we know that Kipling's eldest daughter, Josephine, died of pneumonia in New York just five years before this story was written, the tightly controlled emotion that pervades the narrative reaches a haunting climax, especially at the moment the narrator recognises his own dead child among the children at the house by a kiss that is planted on his palm, a gesture of tenderness that they shared when she was alive. While the narrator of 'Baa Baa, Black Sheep' is more explicit on the consequences of Punch's move to England than the imperfectly informed narrator of 'They', both stories plumb the depths of grief. Sullivan's investigation of Kipling's fiction ends with *Kim*. My analysis will extend beyond India to what I will argue is Kipling's 'feminised' Sussex landscape in *Puck of Pook's Hill* and *Rewards and Fairies*.

While acknowledging the influence of Sullivan's work on my own, I intend to approach Kipling's texts using a Kristevan methodology to focus on the psychoanalytic trajectory of the child's development as it moves from the undifferentiated realm of the semiotic to the symbolic. In order to move into the socialised space of the symbolic, the child must, firstly, abject the maternal body and, secondly, perform a necessary symbolic matricide that then guarantees its subjectivity. However, desire for the pre-linguistic semiotic realm is never completely eliminated and the whispers of the 'lost' semiotic continually irrupt into the symbolic. According to Kristeva, imprints of the semiotic can be 'read' in literature and I aim to uncover these imprints of a feminine space in Kipling's art. Coupled with Kristeva's notions of the semiotic and the feminine, I will use Cixous' ideas of a feminine writing (as outlined earlier) that can be read as a site of positive transgression from the autocratic paternal law. The American writer Joyce Carol Oates has argued that for most novelists, the act of writing serves as a way to engage with 'the instinct to memorialize'[100] one's past and the 'complex bittersweet' feelings of homesickness such instincts engender. With regards to Kipling's own history, the exilic moment in childhood serves to magnify the impulse to 'memorialize'. Kipling's fiction is informed by what I will argue is a tenderness for, and fear of, a 'lost' maternal realm that exists in his fiction in a sort of suspended 'present'. From the early tales concerning Kipling's orphaned children through to the adult stories set in India, and finally swinging back to the time of the child in the eternal sunshine of the Sussex downs, the maternal realm is omnipresent.

Chapter 1, 'Paradise Lost: Kipling's Southsea Years', will deal with Kipling's fictionalised exile from India as a small boy in the 1888 story 'Baa Baa, Black Sheep' and his transformation from the Anglo-Indian demi-god Punch to the devil Black Sheep. The splitting of Punch's mother and foster mother into a longed-for and abjected mother mirrors the Kristevan notion of a desirous and frightening maternal realm that must be brought under the jurisdiction of the law of the father. This chapter will aim to explore the primitive relationship with the archaic maternal figure that in its evolution not only widens to reveal an intimate space, but also paradoxically turns the child toward a horizon of estrangement. 'Baa Baa, Black Sheep' mourns that most intimate of connections, the unity with the maternal figure in the realm of the undifferentiated semiotic, before the constraints and demands of the symbolic draw demarcations of difference and break apart that eternal continuity.

Chapter 2, 'Mastering the Law-of-the-Father in *The Jungle Book* and *Stalky & Co.*', looks at the notion of orphanhood, though in Mowgli's case, he experiences a host of would-be caregivers vying to offer protection as he learns the law of the jungle. The chapter will deal with the idea that 'jungle' spaces, wild terrains and hideaways in the Devon countryside provide vital relief from having to learn and adopt the stern edicts of the paternal law. My analysis, dealing primarily with *The Jungle Book*, will concentrate on a close textual reading of the Mowgli stories together with 'Rikki-Tikki-Tavi' and 'Little Toomai'. In this analysis, I will endeavour to uncover three mother figures: the protective Mother Wolf; the phallic mother, in the guise of the terrifying Shere Khan; and finally the abjected mother, imaged in natural landscape that is trampled under the mighty feet of the gargantuan emblems of the servants of Empire, the worker elephants. The chapter will also look at the construction of Kipling's ubiquitous 'Law' as an organising social code to which, Noel Annan argues, 'all races and creeds held [. . .] good'.[101] To uncover maternal figures and spaces, I would argue that *Stalky & Co.* is not only a more pertinent critical companion to *The Jungle Book*, but also an important collection with regards to the psychic development of Kipling's adolescents, hence an analysis of *The Second Jungle Book* will remain peripheral in this study. In the absence of a protective female presence in *Stalky & Co.*, the natural landscape is a nurturing maternal space and provides welcome relief from the rigours of a masculine school regime. Again, Kipling's boys are cut off from their parents at this English boarding school but their age, their experience and their friendships leave the reader in no doubt that their 'orphan' status doesn't bother them in the slightest. Read as a precursor to *Kim*, *Stalky and Co.* sees Kipling's sleeker, more successful colonial adolescents emerge from the complex issues surrounding Kipling's child orphans.

Chapter 3, 'Empire of Contradictions: Desire for the Impossible Mother India in *Kim*', is constructed according to Kristeva's notion of the Imaginary Father who provides Kim with a proto-symbolic relationship. Kim navigates his way through a sustaining Indian landscape with ease and gusto. Knowing the intricacies of all castes, ethnic and religious groups, he has the unlikely ability to blend into any background, and is loved by all who meet him. Becoming a subject mastered by love, Kim is never stationary. He moves through the novel as a restless voyager, in transit between one state of love and another. Kipling's last word on India, *Kim* remains Kipling's fantasy of an India where a maternal authority and a paternal law can co-exist and harmoniously articulate Kim's hybrid Anglo-Indian identity.

Chapter 4, 'The "Sorrowful State of Manhood": Kipling's Adults in India', will address Kipling's darker vision of India and the threat of annihilation it holds for his colonial administrators and foot soldiers in his fiction of the late 1880s and early 1890s. The protagonists of these more frightening tales are engaged in conflict with an India that in narrative terms is represented as an abjected maternal space. Climatic conditions, coupled with relentless hardships and imperial ennui, conspire to undermine the health and morale of his colonial workers, driving them to ghastly suicides, madness, despair, disease and loneliness. Each homesick soldier, fevered engineer, insomniac wanderer or overworked administrator deprived of an inner coalescence and a nurturing maternal presence represents the nihilism that characterises Kipling's view of the colonial enterprise in his fiction at this point.

Chapter 5, 'The Ascent from the Abyss: Dedication to Duty in *The Day's Work*' charts the stalwart dedication to imperial duty of Kipling's colonial engineers and exhausted famine relief workers and the flawless progress of the subaltern groomed for imperial life as a means with which to divert the horror of the abyss. This collection sees a shift in Kipling's writings from raging against the autocratic authority of the imperial law to a broader vision of the cause and not the rhetoric of Empire. It is a collection that sees Britannia, which I will argue is Kipling's 'sanitised' goddess of his vision of Empire, replace the fecund, seeping, uncontrollable Mother India as the site of colonial desire, which, in turn, anticipates his polished ideal of Empire in *Puck of Pook's Hill* and *Rewards and Fairies*.

These collections, with which I will conclude my study, detail the restoration of fragmented identities by utilising the echoic reverberations of a 'lost' time in childhood, harking back to an age of unity, continuity and wholeness in the enveloping space of the Sussex downs. By restructuring England's pluralist past and giving it a Norman, Roman, Elizabethan or Stone Age gloss, Kipling not only created an exemplar of a hybridised society that could embrace his own biculturalism, but also found a profoundly welcoming space for his hybrid orphaned children to be woven within its pluralist cultural fabric. In a sense Kipling had to leave the problematic pastoral space of India to find restoration in the Sussex Downs. This tiny corner of a reimagined England, which is based on the polyvalent experiences of long-since-vanished Empires, finally embraces a profoundly all-inclusive maternal space that is reconstructed and articulated through the cult of Britannia. 'What else could I have done?' implores character after character in the *Puck* stories, faced with the arduousness of duty over individuality and responsibility over self-interest. Kipling's allegiance to his goddess of Empire enables him not only to give meaning to the deeds of his wretched colonial adults, but also to avert the horror of the abject mother and rediscover a symbolised feminised landscape as a restorative space, thus completing the process of psychic mapping. My analysis will ask a similar question, given the complexities of the exilic moment in Kipling's childhood and his subsequent struggle to balance two disparate subject positions. To borrow from Kipling in another context: 'What else could [he] have done?' (*SOM*, p. 111).

Notes

1. Rudyard Kipling, *Kim*, pp. 324, 332. Further references are given after quotations in the text.
2. Rudyard Kipling, *Letters of Marque*, p. 126.
3. Rudyard Kipling, 'A Vision of India', in *The Works of Rudyard Kipling, XVII: Early Verse*, p. 63.
4. British poet Sir Henry Newbolt saw virtues learned on the school cricket pitch as transferable skills in the horror of battle. It was a common nineteenth-century notion that achieved classic expression in his (much satirised) poem 'Vitaï Lampada' penned in 1892. The following lines typify the tone of the poem:

   The sand of the desert is sodden red,
   Red with the wreck of a square that broke [. . .]
   And England's far, and Honour a name,
   But the voice of a schoolboy rallies the ranks:
   'Play up! Play up! And play the game!'

   Quoted in Lawrence James, *The Rise and Fall of the British Empire*, p. 277.
5. Rudyard Kipling, 'The Way Through the Woods', in *Puck of Pook's Hill and Rewards and Fairies*, p. 241; 'The Brushwood Boy', in *The Day's Work*, p. 302. Further references to this text are given after quotations in the text.
6. Homi Bhabha, *The Location of Culture*, p. 243.
7. Rudyard Kipling, 'An Habitation Enforced', in *Actions and Reactions*, p. 36.
8. Rudyard Kipling, *The Definitive Edition of Rudyard Kipling's Verse*, p. 215. Further references to this text are given after quotations in the text.
9. Kingsley Amis, *Rudyard Kipling and his World*, p. 97.
10. Bhabha, *The Location of Culture*, p. 243.
11. Rudyard Kipling, *Something of Myself and Other Autobiographical Writings*, p. 3. Further references are given after quotations in the text.

12. Barbara Creed, *The Monstrous Feminine: Film, Feminism, Psychoanalysis.*
13. Quoted in Kelly Oliver, *Reading Kristeva: Unravelling the Double-bind*, p. 46.
14. Julia Kristeva, *Desire in Language: A Semiotic Approach to Literature and Art*, pp. 6–7.
15. Hélène Cixous, 'Sorties: Out and Out: Attacks/Ways Out/Forays', in *The Newly Born Woman*, p. 93.
16. Quoted in Hélène Cixous, *The Poetics of Gender*, p. 169.
17. In this study, the 'feminine' is seen from a French rather than an Anglo-Saxon perspective. That is to say, that feminine (*féminine*) in French relates more to a woman's corporeality as opposed to the Anglo-Saxon term which, Anne-Marie Smith argues, connotes a 'culturally-imposed gender difference [that] stands in opposition to feminist'. Anne-Marie Smith, *Julia Kristeva: Speaking the Unspeakable*, p. 10.
18. Rudyard Kipling, *Life's Handicap* (Oxford University Press), p. 1.
19. Rudyard Kipling, *Plain Tales from the Hills*, p. 7. Further references are given after quotations in the text.
20. Pamphleteer and philosopher James Mill, writing in 1818, argued that the Hindu religion consisted chiefly of 'despotism and priestcraft' which taken together ensured that 'the Hindus, in mind and body, were the most enslaved portion of the human race'. Eric Stokes, *The English Utilitarians and India*, p. 54.
21. J. M. S. Tompkins, *The Art of Rudyard Kipling*, p. 225.
22. David Saul, *The Indian Mutiny*.
23. Rudyard Kipling, *Life's Handicap* (Penguin), p. 270. Further references are given after quotations in the text.
24. Julia Kristeva, *Powers of Horror: An Essay on Abjection*, pp. 72, 74.
25. John Bowlby, *Attachment and Loss, Volume 2: Separation, Anxiety and Anger*, p. 46.
26. Julia Kristeva, *Melanie Klein*.
27. Julia Kristeva, *Desire in Language*, p. x.
28. Elizabeth Longford, *Victoria R.I.*, p. 549.
29. Edward Said, *The World, the Text and the Critic*, pp. 18–19.
30. Caren Kaplan, 'Deterritorializations: The Rewriting of Home and Exile in Western Discourse', *Cultural Critique*, p. 187.
31. Sandra Kemp, *Kipling's Hidden Narratives*, p. 1.
32. Bonamy Dobrée, *Rudyard Kipling: Realist and Fabulist*.
33. Peter Levi, in his Introduction to the *Just So Stories*, rightly points out that 'Kipling uses the word 'nigger' [. . .] but so does Conrad.' The word was in everyday use in the nineteenth century. However, it is important to remember that Kipling no doubt had, as Levi argues, 'deeply offensive thoughts at the back of his head' (Peter Levi, Introduction to *Just So Stories*, p. 15). Stories such as 'His Chance in Life' (in *Plain Tales*), where the heroic actions of Michele D'Cruz in averting imperial disaster are attributed to his 'drop' of European blood, amply demonstrate Levi's argument.
34. Salman Rushdie, *Imaginary Homelands: Essays and Criticism 1981–1991*, p. 74.
35. Thomas Metcalf, *Ideologies of the Raj*, p. 161.

36. George Orwell, 'Rudyard Kipling', in *Dickens, Dali and Others: Studies in Popular Culture*, pp. 140–1.
37. Edmund Wilson, 'The Kipling that Nobody Read'; Andrew Rutherford, 'Officers and Gentlemen'.
38. Martin Seymour-Smith, *Rudyard Kipling*, p. 6.
39. David Gilmour, *The Long Recessional: The Imperial Life of Rudyard Kipling*.
40. Harry Ricketts, *The Unforgiving Minute: A Life of Rudyard Kipling*, p. xi.
41. Angus Wilson, *The Strange Ride of Rudyard Kipling: His Life and Works*, p. 4.
42. Ibid., pp. 124–5.
43. Shamsul Islam, *Kipling's 'Law': A Study of his Philosophy of Life*, p. 5.
44. Kristeva, *Powers of Horror*, p. 4.
45. Philip Mason, *Kipling: The Glass, the Shadow and the Fire*, p. 9.
46. Tompkins, *Art of Rudyard Kipling*, p. xi.
47. T. S. Eliot, *A Choice of Kipling's Verse*, p. 20.
48. Quoted in Wilson, *The Strange Ride of Rudyard Kipling*, p. 3.
49. Eliot, *A Choice of Kipling's Verse*, p. 20.
50. Wilson, *The Strange Ride of Rudyard Kipling*, p.4.
51. John Osborne, *Look Back in Anger*, p. 66.
52. George Orwell, 'Rudyard Kipling', p. 70.
53. Lionel Trilling, 'Kipling', p. 92.
54. Wilson, 'The Kipling that Nobody Read', p. 23.
55. Tompkins, *Art of Rudyard Kipling*, p. xi.
56. For example, C. S. Lewis, *Selected Literary Essays* and Eliot, *A Choice of Kipling's Verse*, with Eliot's caveat that Kipling's artistic dexterity was largely accidental, and Amis, *Rudyard Kipling and His World*.
57. *W. H. Auden: Selected Poems*, p. 35.
58. Kemp, *Kipling's Hidden Narratives*, p. 21.
59. Mason, *The Glass, The Shadow and The Fire*, p. 69.
60. Elliot L. Gilbert, *The Good Kipling*, p. 83.
61. Ibid., p. 84.
62. Ibid., p. 6.
63. Edward Said, *Orientalism*, p. 224.
64. Bhabha, *The Location of Culture*, p. 122.
65. See, for example, David Reynolds, *Britannia Overruled: British Policy and World Power in the 20th Century*, pp. 24–7.
66. Lewis Wurgaft, *The Imperial Imagination: Magic and Myth in Kipling's India*.
67. Noel Annan, 'Kipling's Place in the History of Ideas', p. 124.
68. Ibid, p. 124.
69. Kemp, *Kipling's Hidden Narratives*, p. 11.
70. T. N. Cross, 'Rudyard Kipling's Sense of Identity', pp. 245–52.
71. Leonard Shengold, 'An Attempt at Soul Murder: Rudyard Kipling's Early Life and Work', *The Psychoanalytic Study of the Child*, pp. 683–724.
72. Diane Simmons, *The Narcissism of Empire: Loss, Rage and Revenge in Thomas De Quincey, Robert Louis Stevenson, Arthur Conan Doyle, Rudyard Kipling and Isak Dinesen*, p. 6.

73. Ibid., p. 81.
74. Steven T. Levy and Andrew C. Furman, *Influential Papers from the 1950s*, p. 197.
75. John Kucich, 'Sadomasochism and the Magical Group: Kipling's Middle-Class Imperialism', *Victorian Studies*, 33–68.
76. Quoted in Robert Hanks, 'A sheep that bites: the revival of Rudyard Kipling's fortunes has now spawned an opera'.
77. Michael Berkeley, *Baa Baa Black Sheep: An Opera in Three Acts*.
78. Ulrich Knoepflmacher, 'The Hansel and Gretel Syndrome: Survivorship Fantasies and Parental Desertion', *Children's Literature*, p. 180.
79. Hélène Cixous, 'Extreme Fidelity'.
80. Julia Kristeva, 'Stabat Mater', in *The Kristeva Reader*, pp. 160–86.
81. Jane Hotchkiss, 'The Jungle of Eden: Kipling, Wolf Boys, and the Colonial Imagination'.
82. Ibid., p. 435.
83. Ibid., p. 435.
84. Kucich, 'Sadomasochism and the Magical Group', pp. 33, 36.
85. Ulrich Knoepflmacher, 'Female Power and Male Self-Assertion: Kipling and the Maternal', *Children's Literature*, p. 15.
86. Ibid., p. 15.
87. Ibid., p. 33.
88. Melanie Klein, 'Some Theoretical Conclusions regarding the Emotional Life of the Infant', in *Envy and Gratitude and Other Works – 1946–1963*, pp. 61–93.
89. Harish Trivedi, 'Kipling's "vernacular": what he knew of it – and what he made of it', in Janet Montefiore, *In Time's Eye*, pp. 177–206.
90. Elliot L. Gilbert, 'The Aesthetics of Violence', p. 208.
91. Mark Paffard, *Kipling's Indian Fiction*, p. 92.
92. John A. McClure, *Kipling and Conrad: The Colonial Fiction*, p. 59.
93. Zohreh Sullivan, *Narratives of Empire: The Fictions of Rudyard Kipling*, p. 180.
94. Ibid., p. 138.
95. Ibid., p. 136.
96. Ibid., p. 6.
97. Ibid., p. 6.
98. Ibid., p. 115.
99. Ibid., p. 13.
100. Joyce Carol Oates (ed.), *Telling Stories: An Anthology for Writers*, p. xiii.
101. Annan, 'Kipling's Place', p. 109.

Chapter 1

Paradise Lost: Kipling's Southsea Years

> Neither the harps nor the crowns amused, nor the cherubs' dove-winged races –
> Holding hands forlornly the Children wandered beneath the Dome,
> Plucking the splendid robes of the passers-by, and with pitiful faces
> Begging what Princes and Powers refused: – "Ah, please will you let us go home?"[1]

> Punch and Judy, through no fault of their own, had lost all their world [. . .] They wanted Papa and Mamma gone to Bombay beyond the seas, and their grief while it lasted was without remedy.[2]

Just short of his sixth birthday, Kipling and his three-year old sister Trix boarded a boat in Bombay bound for England with their parents Alice and Lockwood Kipling. After a short stay with various relatives, the children were taken to a boarding house in Southsea and left in the care of Sarah Holloway. Six years would pass before either of them saw their mother again. To our twentieth-century eyes such an act is shocking, but it was usual at that time for Anglo-Indian parents to send their children 'Home' for a spell to counteract the supposedly negative influence of their Indian servants. A contemporary of Kipling's, Maud Diver, now largely forgotten but hugely popular during her writing life (she was a favourite of the Royal Family), writes of the well-established practice of Anglo-Indian expatriates sending children back to England:

> She will be zealous in guarding her children from the promiscuous intimacy with the native servants, whose propensity to worship at the shrine of the *Baba-log* is unhappily apt to demoralize the small gods and goddesses they serve [. . .] the sooner after the fifth year a child can leave India, the better for its future welfare. One after one the babies grow into companionable children. One after one England claims them, till the mother's heart and house are left unto her desolate.[3]

In this respect Lockwood and Alice Kipling were no different from their contemporaries. But for the children, the consequences of such an accepted social practice were devastating. Kipling's sister Trix underscores Kipling's fictionalised children's fears in her account of their Southsea experience.[4] Trix, throughout her life, supported her brother's version of events, the validity of which has been questioned by critics; the pain and trauma of abandonment is terrifyingly present in both her and her brother's fictional accounts.

Diane Simmons argues that to understand the trauma of separation that Kipling and his sister experienced, it is necessary to examine the harshness of the children's forlorn existence in England in conjunction with their happy, carefree life in Bombay.[5] Kipling's first memories of his Indian homeland are of 'daybreak, light and colour' (*SOM*, p. 3). He was surrounded by a succession of servants all willing to recount 'stories and Indian nursery songs' that in the autobiography he was to write six decades later remained 'all unforgotten'. His bearer, Meeta, was remembered as protectively holding a young Rudyard's hand while he visited 'little Hindu temples' and peered through the gloom at 'dimly-seen, friendly Gods,' and providing a rational explanation for a stuffed leopard's head on the nursery wall, thus averting 'night terrors or dread of the dark'. His *ayah* took him in the dazzling early morning sunshine to the Bombay fruit market (*SOM*, pp. 3–4). Enclosed in this solicitous, intimate space were Kipling's parents. 'Far across the green spaces round the house', writes Kipling, 'was a marvellous place filled with smells of paints and oils, and lumps of clay with which I played' (*SOM*, p. 4). This was his father's atelier, which was a playground in the children's eyes, and a place where they could come to no harm. A hen, 'a winged monster as big as myself', once frightened Kipling, and his father (just as Meeta had done with the leopard's head) shrank a young boy's terror with a drawing and a limerick, which, he stresses, not only 'consoled' him at the time but also ensured he was not frightened of hens in the future (*SOM*, pp. 4–5).

In sharp contrast to Kipling's memories from early childhood are his recollections of England, which he describes as a 'dark land and a darker room full of cold' where 'a white woman made naked fire' and made the author cry 'aloud with dread'. Later came Sarah Holloway's boarding house, Lorne Lodge, what Kipling was to call the 'House of Desolation', 'smelling of aridity and emptiness', where Alice Kipling, without preparing the children in any way for what was to happen to them, stole away to join her husband in London before sailing back to Bombay without them (*SOM*, p. 5). Charles Carrington underscores the desolation both children must have undoubtedly felt at their 'abandonment':

> In December the parents deposited their children in lodgings at Southsea before returning to India. Perhaps unwisely, they made no effort to forewarn

> little Rudyard of this calamity, but slipped away without stirring the children's emotion by any passionate display of affection. Rudyard, just before his sixth birthday, was left to discover for himself the meaning of separation from his father and mother; Trix was still too young to know what was the nature of her misfortune.[6]

Their parents had no idea of the dreary life to which they were consigning their children. After their idyllic existence in India, Southsea became a place akin to a prison for young Rudyard and his infant sister.

Kipling's poem 'The Return of the Children' was written as the epigraph to 'They' (in *Traffics and Discoveries*). It tells the story of dead children wandering through heaven, longing to go 'home', and the theme of the poem resonates with what we know of Kipling's Southsea experience. The children of the poem, like Rudyard and Trix, are held captive 'against their will' in an environment that to outsiders seems idyllic. Kipling's heaven is an odd place: ostensibly a paradise where celestial choirs accompany cherubs racing over jewelled floors and past sumptuously dressed onlookers, it is actually rather sinister, an enclosure that is gated by a locked door, guarded by armed soldiers and ruled over by the disembodied voice of the Father, whose word represents the paternal law. There is a discrepancy between a traditional mythologised heaven and Kipling's vision of heaven, which is an imposing man-made edifice populated by a host of acutely unemotional and undemonstrative strangers. The passionate entreaties of the 'weeping' Mother Mary, who intervenes on the children's behalf, eventually move her son to allow them to cross the Void and go home:

> Over the jewelled floor, nigh weeping, ran to them Mary the Mother,
> Kneeled and caressed and made promise with kisses and drew them along to the gateway –
> Yea, the all-iron unbribeable Door which Peter must guard and none other.
> Straightway She took the Keys from his keeping, and opened and freed them straightway.
> Then, to Her Son, Who had seen and smiled, She said: 'On the night that I bore Thee,
> What didst Thou care for a love beyond mine or a heaven that was not my arm?
> Didst Thou push from the nipple, O Child, to hear the angels adore Thee
> When we two lay in the breath of the kine?' And He said: – 'Thou hast done no harm.'[7]

Kipling's Mary is not the untouchable, Virgin goddess of Christian theology, but the fleshy earth mother who reminds her son that on the night he was born heaven extended as far as her embrace and of the intimacy of her 'nipple' as they were warmed by moist breath of living cattle. From a Kristevan point of view, his Mary represents the mother before the law that is joined to her child in the undifferentiated space of coalescence, the semiotic. 'The Return of the Children' could be read as an antidote for Kipling's children of Empire who must relinquish their protected Anglo-Indian environments, which sees them swathed at the centre of a solicitous maternal space, in order to assimilate an English language and patriarchal law. Similarly, in Kipling's heavily autobiographical 'Baa Baa, Black Sheep', Punch and Judy, the Anglo-Indian siblings at the centre of the narrative, are separated from their Bombay home by a vast ocean that cannot be traversed without adult help. However, no one comes to the children's aid, their mother remains in Bombay and the sea represents an impassable 'abyss' (as the 'Void' is to the children in heaven), a psychological as well as physical barrier that lies between India and England.

For a young Kipling, the emotional cost of his 'exile' to England was a separation from his cherished *ayah*, his mother and his motherland. An unknown, chilly foreign country, the terrifying figure of Sarah Holloway and her bullying son, Harry, replaced these stabilising reference points. The children were off their known psychological map, as it were. Kipling's suffering resulted in a psychic collapse. He writes of himself at this time as experiencing a 'sort of nervous breakdown', accompanied by hallucinations of 'shadows and things that were not there' (*SOM*, p. 17). Kipling was to be plagued by intermittent breakdowns early in his adult life, usually set off by overwork, although after his marriage to Carrie (sister of his friend and collaborator on *The Naulakha*, Wolcott Balestier) in 1891, there is no biographical evidence that the author suffered from a breakdown.[8] The despair, depression and anxiety that accompanied his bouts of nervous disorder became potent themes that would resonate in his later fiction. For example, the hallucinations he experienced as a young boy anticipate the terrifying visions that his overworked and isolated colonial engineer, Hummil, experiences as he descends into madness in 'At the End of the Passage'. Despair rings through the narrative in 'The House Surgeon' (in *Actions and Reactions*) as the narrator is engulfed in a 'Horror of great darkness' (*A&R*, p. 270) that emanates from the 'spirit' of the house. Deep anxiety characterises his poem 'La Nuit Blanche', with its ghastly, sightless creature that cries and cannot wipe its eyes. Melanie Klein argues that instances of depression can be traced to a specific loss in the depressive's life, and the resulting breakdown shares important characteristics with mourning.[9] It is certain that the Kipling children experienced a profound sense of bereavement at 'losing' their parents. Kipling's sister wrote of the 'grief' that their parents' abandonment provoked in her autobiographical rejoinder to 'Baa Baa, Black Sheep', 'Through Judy's Eyes':

> Their trouble was that everything had gone at once. Papa and Mama had left them 'deserted almost as much as on a doorstep', Punch said, not because they were dead [. . .] No: they had gone back to Punch and Judy's lovely home and had not taken the children with them. As Punch said 'There was no getting out of that' [. . .] Yes – everything had gone at once, Papa, Mama, home, garden, sunshine.[10]

Klein argues that if the separation is traumatic, the depressive becomes trapped, neither able to confront nor banish, forgive nor accept the object of his/her love. In place of the 'fullness' of maternal love there is a void of loss. For Kipling, losing his parents in the real world created a vacuum that was filled with the edifying strictures of a new social order in England.

In Kipling's early fiction, this vacuum or 'abyss' can be read as a site of separation between the paternal law of the symbolic represented by the cultural codes of England and the maternal authority of the semiotic which is incorporated in the author's childhood memories of India. The competing discourses of England and India are present in the anxieties toward loss that resonate through his art: the horror of psychic fragmentation, the conflict between desire and dread, the terror of colonial breakdown, the panic that prolonged isolation induces, and the difficulties of working in an unrelentingly harsh climate. In certain stories Kipling details his characters' attempts to fend off bouts of loneliness, fatigue and depression that can lead to breakdown. For example, the crushing heat and exhaustion that plague the regiment in 'With the Main Guard' (in *Soldiers Three*), is staved off by Private Mulvaney recounting the tale of a brutal fight between the 'Ould Regiment' and a band of Pathan warriors. His storytelling enables the men to make it through the suffocating June night. In other stories we see Kipling's characters fear separation from their familiar cultural environments, and the imprints of this fear can be identified in his Indian stories. Physical isolation invariably provides the catalyst for a terrifying psychic collapse, as in 'At the End of the Passage', which takes place in a remote outpost. The protagonist, Chief Engineer Hummil, exhausted by overwork, is literally haunted to death by an eerie spectre of himself.

Angus Wilson argues that the desolate states of his characters have their beginnings in Kipling's childhood experiences of suffering and isolation in England, and refers to it as the 'horror of experience'.[11] Zohreh Sullivan identifies an undercurrent of 'loss and horror' running through Kipling's later writing. She argues that it is 'easy to explain these wounds in terms of English education, of repressed sexuality and denied homoeroticism, of Kipling's childhood, or of a system that victimized its children in schools that concealed ruthlessness with rigidity and discipline'. But she goes on to stress that the 'texts refuse to allow such single explanations for events that signify multiple possibilities of competing political, social and psychological meanings'.[12] Sullivan, in her Lacanian reading of Kipling's writings, argues that the repeated motif of breakdown is the author's way of 'internalizing the unacceptable, the terror of annihilation or boundary slippage in the troubling structures of gender, race and identity'.[13] Sullivan concentrates her insightful argument on an adolescent Kipling and his adolescent and adult characters to explain the author's troubling sense of identity and his ambivalent commitment to the imperial project. She deals only very briefly with Kipling's problematic childhood and its place in the formation of his identity (colonial or otherwise). And while she argues that his childhood suffering is not 'the only explanation' for the suffering and fear in his stories, it will be the focus of this chapter. I will attempt to further Sullivan's analysis by retracing Kipling's 'troubling structures' of identity beyond his stories concerning adolescents and back to the time of the child. This chapter will explore what I would argue is the trauma of Kipling's dual separation, which can be read as a Kristevan account of the universal interpellation of the subject when the child leaves the maternal realm to take its place in the symbolic that, for Kipling, was made more problematic by his childhood repatriation to England.

Simmons argues that the author's early Indian experience, which resulted in an 'unhealthily prolonged primary narcissism',[14] together with his suffering in Southsea, permanently damaged Kipling's fragile psyche. The revenge fantasies that occur repeatedly in his fiction have their origins, she argues, in his early narcissistic disturbance. I would argue that the sense of completeness and fulfilment with which he shapes his Indian memories across the decades contrasts sharply with his account of the desolate Southsea experience. England is a cold and forbidding country where rules must be obeyed and pedagogical lessons must be learned and exists, at the beginning of his 'exile', on the margins of a warm and desirable India. This image of a dreary English-style schooling contrasted with the stimulating environment of India can be seen clearly in *Kim*. The eponymous hero of the novel agrees to stay at St Xavier's school for boys and attend his English lessons on the condition that he is allowed to roam free in India's vast and revitalising countryside. He tells his friend Mahbub Ali, 'I will learn their teaching upon a condition – that my time is given to me without question when the *madrissah* is shut. Ask that for me of the Colonel' (*Kim*, p. 183). The India of Kipling's Anglo-Indian childhood, where the fulfilment of his desires was paramount and his servants were complicit in ensuring his continued pleasure, is akin to the Kristevan notion of the undifferentiated realm of the semiotic where consciousness is inseparable from the maternal body and all desires are satisfied. Kipling's repatriation to England is representative of the move toward the symbolic. The iron-cast rigorousness of the symbolic is concretised in his descriptions of the Portsmouth docks and the outlying areas of Southsea that were his roaming grounds during that time:

> The House itself stood in the extreme suburbs of Southsea, next to a Portsmouth unchanged in most particulars since Trafalgar [. . .] The timber for a Navy that was only experimenting with iron-clads such as the *Inflexible* lay in great booms in the harbour. The training-brigs kept their walks opposite Southsea Castle, and Portsmouth Hard was as it had always been. Outside these things lay the desolation of Hayling Island, Lumps Fort, and the isolated hamlet of Milton. (*SOM*, p. 5)

The description is dominated by images of perpetual, desolate rigidity, of ships complying to harbour regulations, of isolated outposts, of the rapidly expanding city of Portsmouth, of the naval machine of war and trade. Compared with his descriptions of the 'green spaces' and 'light and colour' of Bombay, Southsea was a desolate place indeed for five-year-old Kipling.

His formative years were spent in this grey landscape, absorbing a way of life that was alien to him. In a Kristevan sense, following the loss of symbiotic unity with the maternal body, the child's identity is mapped out by his/her desire for the irretrievable mother (a sort of paradise lost), and in Kipling's fiction this is forever deferred by the mirror-like reflections of the phallic domain of England that he experienced on walks around Portsmouth with Captain Pryse Holloway. 'The Burning of the "Sarah Sands"' (in *Land and Sea Tales*) is a tale that has gone largely unnoticed by critics and biographers. The story details the power of naval vessels in the service of Empire along with the emotional cost of soldiering. It concerns the heroic actions of a detachment of the 54th Dorchester Regiment en route to India when their ship catches fire. The epigraph that accompanies this story is telling with regard to 'the behaviour of bodies of untried men under trying circumstances'.[15] Kipling details the men's courage and bravery 'in the face of danger, difficulty and death' (*L&S*, p. 161). The new life in England to which a very young Kipling had to adjust has echoes in the trying situation of the soldiers in this tale. To leave behind the idyllic existence of his childhood home and weather the psychological storm he encountered in Southsea required an immense inner strength. 'The Burning of the "Sarah Sands"', collected in a didactic anthology primarily for children, tackles important issues of actions performed under duress and highlights Kipling's lifelong conviction that discipline, hard work and an obligation to see the situation through to its end was the cornerstone of moral integrity. And it was in the barren soil of his difficult life experiences in England, rather than in India, that the seeds of this philosophy were sown.

Physically (but not psychically) disconnected from their Indian surroundings, the Kipling children had nobody with whom they could articulate what had gone missing culturally, linguistically and socially in journeying from their Bombay home to what was essentially a foreign English 'home'. Not only were the children culturally disadvantaged, they were also linguistically handicapped. In India, Kipling and his sister were cautioned by their *ayah* to '[s]peak English now to Papa and Mama' when presented to them in the evenings. So, he writes, 'one spoke "English," haltingly translated out of the vernacular idiom that one thought and dreamed in' (*SOM*, p. 4). This memory is particularly revealing in his use of the inverted commas that surround the word 'English'. Clearly, at this point in his childhood, Kipling believed that, like Kim, the 'vernacular idiom' was the language with which his identity was expressed, a notion that is reinforced in the epigraph to Chapter One in *Something of Myself*. The chapter covers the period between 1865 and 1878, some thirteen years, yet the epigraph, which echoes the Jesuit maxim, reads 'Give me the first six years of a child's life and you can have the rest' (*SOM*, p. 3). This is an indication, perhaps, that at the age of seventy Kipling considered himself first and foremost an Anglo-Indian despite living the greater part of his life elsewhere. In *Something of Myself*, he talks of his parents' house in Lahore as 'the only real home I had yet known' (*SOM*, p. 62). And on a fleeting visit to Bombay he was reunited with his *ayah*, whom he found 'so old but so *unaltered*' (emphasis mine) (*SOM*, p. 63). A poem much derided for its pompous advocation of British imperial expansion, 'The English Flag', contains the much-quoted line, 'And what should they know of England who only England know?'[16] While the declarative tone of the poem jars on a post-imperial ear, its viewpoint of seeing England from the position of 'outsider' is not easily missed. For a young Kipling, an impaired proficiency in English coupled with a lack of knowledge about the country is in contrast to his fluency in 'Hindustani'[17] and an intimate experience of some of the customs and religious practices of 'native' India. This in turn anticipates the cultural division that a young Kipling would experience in Southsea.

Sarah Holloway's boarding house, he tells us, was 'run with the full vigour of the Evangelical as revealed to the Woman'. The 'friendly Gods' of Indian temples are replaced with 'Hell [. . .] in all its terrors' (*SOM*, p. 6). Fruit-laden perambulators in Bombay give way to 'beastly' tomatoes stewed in sugar and 'string-boiled mutton' that was 'hard to get down' (*SOM*, p. 11). Where he had been afforded unconditional love by parents and servants, Kipling now suffered regular beatings and 'calculated torture' at the hands of the 'Woman' and her bullying son (*SOM*, p. 6).[18] The sunsets in Bombay that turned the bay waters iridescent are exchanged for the more menacing twilights on the Hampshire sands. The 'red bars of failing light' are remembered 'clear as ever' with a mixture of 'excitement and terror' (*SOM*, p. 7). The servants in Kipling's two worlds are similarly polarised, and where his *ayah* is remembered with profound affection, a British maid is associated with 'sorrow and darkness and a raven that "flapped its wings"' (*SOM*, p. 7). As is evident from his warm and cherished reminiscences, which are so vividly recreated to retain a freshness that speaks of the present, India was to remain a prelapsarian space in Kipling's imagination. In this 'timeless' space his sense of self was not only perfectly understood, but also reflected back to him by a loving family and a community of doting servants.

The Kipling children's expatriation proved to be a difficult and psychologically complex affair. They were not refugees escaping tyranny and oppression; they were privileged members of the Anglo-Indian community being sent 'home'. That they would face abuse and mistreatment under the care of a woman hired on the strength of a newspaper advertisement was certainly not the intention of either of their parents. Many years later, Kipling took his wife Carrie to see the place that he had spent those fateful childhood years and was still disturbed by the physical presence of the house. 'He talks of it all with horror', noted Carrie.[19] The children's experiences over the next five years were to leave them both traumatised and despairing in the face of such cruel guardianship. Like the mother of the eponymous six-year-old in 'Tods' Amendment' (in *Plain Tales*), who on hearing her son 'deliver solemn and serious aphorisms translated from the vernacular into the English', decides 'that Tods must go Home next hot weather' (*PT*, p. 152), Kipling's parents were unintentionally colluding in their children's exile, and, without realising the devastating effects of such an action, wrenching them from their Indian homeland. In the process both children had to become Anglo-Indian shape-shifters, complying with the structure, organisation and functioning of nineteenth-century English society that was filtered through the evangelical tenets of Sarah Holloway, whilst still retaining a connection to home through the letters and parcels they received from their absent parents.

The idyllic radiance of Kipling's childhood Bombay was thus measured against his more chilling experience in Southsea. For a six-year-old boy it was a fall from paradise into a Dantean hell. The only respite in this bleak existence came from the Christmases he spent with his uncle and aunt, Edward and Georgina Burne-Jones, at The Grange in Fulham. For one month of each year that he spent in Southsea, Kipling was able to recreate something akin to his life in Bombay. 'I had love and affection as much as the greediest [. . .] could desire', he writes. The smells of his father's atelier came wafting through his autobiography in the descriptions of 'uncle Ned's' studio. He roamed freely with much-loved cousins, laid claim to a special mulberry tree for 'plots and conferences', glimpsed newly created Pre-Raphaelite art and furniture and had access to aesthetic literature. His beloved 'Aunty Georgy' would read Scott's *The Pirate* or *The Arabian Nights*, with its frame-tale technique, a technique that Kipling would later make much use of in his fiction (*SOM*, p. 9). The Grange was, by the author's account, a 'jumble of delights and emotions'. It represented a 'delicious dream' that would break the grim monotony of his quotidian life at the House of Desolation (*SOM*, pp. 10–11).

There is much in the happy disorder that characterised the Burne-Jones's home that found its thematic way into *Kim*. Kipling writes in the novel: 'This was seeing the world in truth; this was life as he would have it – bustling and shouting [. . .] and new sights at every turn of the approving eye' (*Kim*, p. 121), and these sentiments from his joyous orphan freed from his colonial guardians could equally well describe its author's holidays in Fulham. At his uncle's house, Kipling would come across halls lined with sketches with only the eyes completed, making them peer out mysteriously from their frames. There were frequent visits from all manner of artists, ceramicists, writers and poets. William Morris, 'Uncle Topsy', could be found rocking back and forth reciting the Icelander sagas and a 'golden voiced' Burne-Jones was the instigator of magical games that 'thrilled' Kipling with 'delightful shivers' (*SOM*, pp 9–10). The author remembered the joy of straining over a banister to 'listen to the loveliest sound in the world – deep-voiced men laughing together over dinner' (*SOM*, p. 10). Life at The Grange flowed like the 'broad smiling river of life' on the Grand Trunk Road, where there were 'new people and new sights' for Kim to enjoy 'at every stride – castes he knew and castes that were altogether out of his experience' (*Kim*, p. 109). Similarly, 'an incessant come and go of young people and grown-ups all willing to play' with Kipling and his cousins, Margaret and Philip Burne-Jones, typified his uncle and aunt's home. The 'exoticism' that Kipling relished during his holidays, calling his cousins '"Daughter of my Uncle" or "O True Believer"' (*SOM*, p. 9), was a link to his 'lost' world in India. In Fulham, his Anglo-Indian identity was accepted and, one could argue, actively encouraged with the tales he was told or games with an Egyptian flavour that he enjoyed. In this respect,

The Grange represented a vital inclusive link between his Indian experiences and his excluded life in Southsea.

Kipling's India is solidified into an edenic space that retains the trace of a happy childhood prematurely interrupted as well as an association of an 'exotic' faraway Orient captured in books like *The Arabian Nights* that he enjoyed so much as a child. These respites were short-lived, however, and when his month was up he would return to Southsea. '[T]he delicious dream would end', he wrote, 'and one would return to the House of Desolation, and for the next two or three mornings there cry on waking up' (*SOM*, p. 11). He would be made to 'pay' for his sojourns beyond the borders of Lorne Lodge, like Kim who 'suffered the usual penalties for breaking out of bounds' at St Xavier's school (*Kim*, p. 171) or Stalky who is forced to invent elaborate ruses to enjoy time with his friends in 'strictly forbidden' dens and lairs beyond the limits of the school grounds (*S&C*, p. 29).

Deprived of his parents and, for the most part, his extended family in Fulham, Kipling ring-fenced the unpleasant aspects of his time in Southsea, and Lorne Lodge became associated with the idea of abandonment and orphanhood. His father sent him a copy of *Robinson Crusoe*, and it was the stimulus for many hours of play in which a miserable boy could escape into the self-created worlds of his imagination. Reproducing the story of this archetypal colonial tale was the means with which Kipling created a physical boundary between what is real and what was a magical 'reality', thus creating a psychic space of connectedness to his lost world of India, and the world of his beloved aunt and uncle, which had to be painfully forfeited on an annual basis:

> I set up business alone as a trader with savages [. . .] in a mildewy basement room where I stood my solitary confinements. My apparatus was a coconut shell strung with a red cord, a tin trunk, and a piece of packing-case which kept off any other world [. . .] The magic, you see, lies in the ring or fence that you take refuge in. (*SOM*, p. 8)

Robinson Crusoe is a tale, not only of colonisation and beginning again in exile, but also of being left to fend for oneself in a harsh and unforgiving environment. John McClure argues that this early game of colonisation is played out in Kipling embracing the vision of Empire,[20] a premise that is shared by Sullivan. She furthers McClure's argument with the idea that a wholehearted submission to the imperial project gave Kipling the ideological vehicle with which to heal the pain of his exile to England.[21] Yet I would argue that the connectedness that Kipling felt in trading with 'savages' (he was, in Sarah Holloway's theological eyes, not 'civilised') actually enabled the young Rudyard to reconnect to his lost homeland even while he sensed its loss. Kipling's Aunt Georgina asked him why he had kept so silent as to what went on at Lorne Lodge, and the author writes '[c]hildren tell little more than animals [and] have a clear notion of what they are likely to get if they betray the secrets of the prison-house before they are clear of it' (*SOM*, p. 11). The difficult experiences of abandonment were visited at a safe distance in his fictional account of the years he spent with Sarah Holloway, 'Baa Baa, Black Sheep'. Kristeva writes that '[w]hen others convey to you that you are of no account because your parents are of no account, that, as they are invisible, they do not exist, you are suddenly aware that you are an orphan'.[22] This painful interiority, I would argue, not only mourns the loss of an edenic childhood space, but also, in Kipling's case, mourns his 'orphaned' Anglo-Indian self that had to be necessarily sequestered from Sarah Holloway. The aggressive religious views of 'the Woman' (*SOM*, p. 6), and her cruel, dictatorial authority are reanimated in characters like the bigoted Dickensian Father Bennett in *Kim*, the unjust masters in *Stalky & Co.*, the mob of army men whose sneering jokes drive the boy in 'Thrown Away' to suicide and of course the Woman's fictional counterpart, the despotic Aunty Rosa in 'Baa Baa, Black Sheep'.

Written in 1888, Kipling's transparently autobiographical 'Baa Baa, Black Sheep', was composed a mere decade after he had left Lorne Lodge. On its publication, he strenuously maintained that it was 'not true to life'. Writing in *The Athenœum* in 1890, Kipling explained at some length that all the stories in *Wee Willie Winkie* were commendable save 'Baa Baa, Black Sheep'.[23] However, the story was reissued as non-fiction in 1935. Angus Wilson remarks that within this clearly striking story there was 'something powerful in the memory of his childhood misery that made him break through the most cherished of his tabus [sic]; the privacy of his own life'.[24] Kipling's sister Trix suggested that her brother darkened the greys of his experience to inky black for artistic purposes and in a letter to her cousin Stanley Baldwin stated that 'in some ways "Aunty" saved [Rudyard's] soul alive'.[25] However, the comments that Trix was to make later in life echo her descriptions in 'Through Judy's Eyes'. In 1947, she wrote:

> I take refuge [. . .] in our very early days together when a sturdy little boy, not quite six and a spoilt baby of three and a half – that was me – were left by their parents, who were going back to India, to face a cold world alone. And it was a very cold world, without one familiar face. And we were left with strangers who were very unkind to us. I think child psychology is better understood now. No kind and loving parents would leave their children for years without giving them any preparation or explanation.[26]

In a diary entry dated December 1888, Kipling's close friend Mrs Edmonia Hill foreshadowed Trix's comments. After briefly outlining the story of 'Baa Baa, Black Sheep', she wrote:

> It was pitiful to see Kipling living over the experience, pouring out his soul in the story, as the drab life was worse than he could possibly describe it. His eyesight was permanently impaired, and, as he had heretofore only known love and tenderness, his faith in people was sorely tried. He was a sorry guest, as he was in a towering rage at the recollection of those days. His summing up in the closing words shows the influence on his whole life.[27]

Lord Birkenhead states that the manuscript of 'Baa Baa, Black Sheep' was one of the few that were not sent to Kipling's parents.[28] He goes on to say that the Kiplings' shocked reaction when they read the story in print led to an unwillingness to recognise their own part in the affair. They appealed to Trix to say that the events were untrue, but even to placate her parents, writes Birkenhead, she was not able to contradict her brother's account.[29]

Charles Carrington writes that 'Baa Baa, Black Sheep' was a 'piece of autobiography heightened in colour, yet following the events of [Kipling's] childhood in all but a few details'. The story, along with the section dealing with Southsea in *Something of Myself* and the opening of *The Light that Failed*, is as close to a true version of events as we can imagine. Carrington argues that in Chapter One of *The Light that Failed* it is possible to 'see the unconscious workings' of the author's mind.[30] Elements of *The Light that Failed* echo certain material details but 'Baa Baa, Black Sheep' follows the events of Kipling's childhood in striking ways. In *The Light that Failed*, war artist Dick Heldar – a portrait penned with more than a little something of the writer's self – spends his childhood at the boarding house of the religiously fanatical Mrs Jennett, who exposes Dick as a liar, a sinner and subjects him to regular beatings. His companion in this dreary seaside lodging is Maisie, a character assumed to have been drawn from Kipling's early but unrequited love Florence Garrard, who lived at Lorne Lodge in the years after Kipling had left. His sister had remained there, and it was while he was visiting Trix that he first met 'Flo' and, according to Birkenhead, fell instantly in love with her.[31]

The central characters, the boy Punch and his sister Judy, are uprooted from the sunny Indian home where they are surrounded by adoring parents and servants and taken to a boarding house in the fictional town of Rocklington on the south coast of England appropriately named 'Downe Lodge'. The children have no inkling that they are to be left in this dreary place. In the 'chill dawn of a February morning'

(*WWW*, p. 265) their parents say goodbye to their sleepy children. It is a profound shock to them both when they wake up later that morning to discover that their parents have departed without trace and left them in the care of a woman whom they imagine must be their 'new white *ayah*' (*WWW*, p. 264). They have been instructed to call her 'Antirosa' but neither Punch nor his sister has any notion of 'an animal called an aunt' (*WWW*, p. 264). Alongside 'the woman in black' is her bullying son Harry and her kindly 'grey' husband who had been wounded at the Battle of Navarino and 'had expressed a wish to be called "Uncleharri"' (*WWW*, p. 265).

His new mother figure, standing flanked by her son and husband, cuts a sinister figure: 'At the doorstep stood a woman in black, and she smiled largely, with dry chapped lips' (*WWW*, p. 264). Like the kindly grandmother who undergoes a terrifying transformation to a rapacious wolf in 'Little Red Riding Hood', the threatening 'bad' mother emerges from what is, supposedly, a loving 'good' mother. Her references, which the parents agonise over in Bombay, are 'excellent' and she gives no indication of her tyrannical side, patiently going through the children's clothes with the mother (*WWW*, pp. 261, 264). Punch's privileged background has not prepared him for such a sinister paid caregiver, and his parents remain unaware of the cruelty of which Aunty Rosa is capable. The horror of the minatory 'bad' mother is reiterated in the narrator's wolfish description of her:

> At the doorstep stood a woman in black, and she smiled largely with dry chapped lips. Behind her was a man, big, bony, grey, and lame as to one leg – behind him a boy of twelve, black-haired and oily in appearance. (*WWW*, p. 264)

Her lips part to reveal a menacingly large smile that is not noticed initially by Punch, instead drawing the anxious gaze of the reader. The image is at odds with Punch's apparent lack of apprehension. He 'advance[s] without fear' and is certain that he will 'go away soon' (*WWW*, p. 264). In this split discourse we are aware that the narrator is in possession of knowledge of which the young Punch is unaware. The older 'knowing' narrator comments on the dangers that lie ahead for the younger victim, which Punch will subsequently come to understand only once he is beyond the reach of his real parents. Aunty Rosa's brutal mouth is at the centre of the tableau of the trio standing in front of the boy. Barbara Creed argues that the maternal authority of Kristeva's semiotic is represented by a powerful phallic woman and is presented in the horror genre as a terrifying negative force with the power to castrate. A 'voracious maw, the mysterious black hole that signifies female genitalia', dominates the image of the female.[32] It can be identified with the womb and thus becomes a cavernous overwhelming space. Her mouth is representative of an ambivalent fantasy of fusion with and fear of the mother's body for which this grotesque woman is a powerful substitute. Aunty Rosa's countenance is a sign of her sexual agency and implicitly her phallicism. She has plundered the masculine attributes of her incapacitated husband. He is described in the narrative as 'big, bony, grey, and lame as to one leg' (*WWW*, p. 264). Big though he may be, he has become skeletal, stripped of flesh and transparent, a desiccated testament to masculine tradition – coloured grey against Aunty Rosa's black.

Punch is dropped into a hellish environment where he must learn to fend for himself. He must learn societal rules and modes of behaviour that make little sense after his Anglo-Indian upbringing. Along with his infant sister he is, at a stroke, removed from his familiar cultural markers and must suffer the loss of a world that he has trusted as stable with no clear idea of when, if indeed at all, he will be released from this prison-like place. Harry gleefully tells the children they are 'to stay at Downe Lodge "for ever"' (*WWW*, p. 266). Punch feels discarded by his parents and is unable to fathom the reason for their enforced exile. Believing they have 'sent secret orders', he feels 'abandoned indeed' (*WWW*, p. 272). Aunty Rosa's explanation that the children are so consumed by sin they are not fit to live with their parents doesn't square with Punch's understanding of his parents' distress on the journey to England, or the obvious love his *ayah* and servants felt toward him at home in India. However, he feels acutely that he has been expelled from the sunny, welcoming paradise of his homeland. It is the narrator who explains what Punch is unable to articulate in the narrative, that he and his sister have been exiled from India:

> When a matured man discovers that he has been deserted by Providence, deprived of his God, and cast without help, comfort or sympathy upon a world which is new and strange to him, his despair [. . .] is generally supposed to be impressive. A child under exactly similar circumstances [. . .] cannot very well curse God and die. It howls till its nose is red, its eyes are sore and its head aches. Punch and Judy, through no fault of their own, had lost all their world. (*WWW*, p. 266)

There is nothing in Punch's Anglo-Indian world that corresponds to his new life in England, emblematised in the evangelical tenets of Aunty Rosa's Christian theology. Where he was loved unconditionally in India, he is despised and tormented in England. While his sister is afforded a place in Aunty Rosa's affections, 'passed, by special permit, into the kitchen and thence straight to [her] heart' (*WWW*, p. 268), he is outcast and unfairly punished. Stories that are animated by servants at the behest of an overindulged five-year-old, and devoured with relish for the thrill of the narrative (*WWW*, p. 260), become in England a trap that will lead Punch to more suffering and punishment (*WWW*, p. 271).

Punch's identity is thus shaped from the tension between England and India. His sense of self oscillates between his Anglo-Indian identity, which must be excluded in order to 'be', and a new 'Englishness' which, in its construction, must take precedence over his excluded (and increasingly repressed) Other self. Socially and theologically, in terms of class and privilege Punch is marked by his 'difference' from English culture. His new identity is formulated by western (and, by extension, imperial) edicts that define him as an 'outcast' in England. Punch's cross-cultural experiences pose a potentially dangerous threat to the white man's self-defined superiority and must be absorbed into an English system and interpreted by his image of exclusion, a 'black sheep'. Julia Kristeva argues that a nation-state functions by excluding its 'foreign' citizens. Exclusion on a state level, she argues, parallels the private exclusions that occur in the formation of identity. Such a totalising system tends to encourage exclusions. The white man's self-definition is dependent upon generating exclusions of his opposite Other. Put bluntly, one's identity, like group identity, is constructed on the exclusion of one's inner Other, which is then projected 'out' onto the image of the foreign Other.[33] Punch's experience of moving between two cultures can only be valued in terms of exclusion in the predominantly white Christian society of nineteenth-century Southsea. His 'Indian' self is condensed into a 'stranger' within, a 'black' negative of his 'white' self. The nickname 'Black Sheep', given to Punch by Aunty Rosa, becomes the marker and substitute for his affiliation to the Anglo-Indian community whose 'difference' is highlighted in its being, in Bart Moore-Gilbert's words, 'unlike metropolitan Britain'.[34]

His (undeserved) nickname is also, in Kristevan terms, an abjected image, which is a sign of pollution, of symbolic boundaries being transgressed, that in Kipling's later fiction will attest to the Englishman's worrisome anxiety as to the instability of colonial identity.[35] The white man's fear of cross-cultural contamination, ultimately realised in his horror of miscegenation, is, I would argue, a fear of existing with and not absorption of the native Other, what Kristeva describes as '[l]iving with the other, with the foreigner [that] confronts us with the possibility or not of *being an other*'.[36] Those characters of Kipling's early fiction that do manage a cross-cultural exchange do so with disastrous physical or psychological consequences. For example, McIntosh Jellaludin in 'To Be Filed for Reference' (in *Plain Tales*) abandons his life as an academic scholar, 'goes native' in India and, suffering from pneumonia brought on by alcoholism, is left in the care of his native 'wife'. Similarly, John Holden in 'Without Benefit of Clergy' (in *Life's Handicap*) is left devastated and grieving silently when Ameera, the native wife he has kept hidden from the Anglo-Indian community, succumbs to cholera after the death of their mixed-race son, Tota. In a more light-hearted but no less serious story, Kipling's intrepid policeman Strickland is forced to give up his much-loved forays into the heart of native India as a condition of his marriage to the woman he loves in 'Miss Youghal's Sais' (in *Plain Tales*).[37] And yet later writing sees an endorsement of the cohabitation that proves disastrous for his imperial workers. In his analysis of Kipling's travelogue *Letters of Marque*, Bart Moore-Gilbert argues that the 'persona of the heroic imperial actor' is continually subverted by a 'narrator [who] empathises with those of the Princely States which have rejected the nineteenth-century model of modernisation and progress which, in many eyes, legitimised imperialism'.[38] Crucially, it is when Punch is in England that his cross-cultural experience begins to muddy the waters of paternal authority by blurring the distinction between English/Indian, civilised/savage. Punch's hybridised version of the Christian creation story, bolted together with his recollection of Indian fairy tales, 'scandalize[s] Aunty Rosa' who concludes it is 'a sin, a grievous sin', although he fails 'to understand where the iniquity came in' (*WWW*, pp. 268–9). He learns that, contrary to his experience in Bombay, telling stories is a potentially dangerous activity in his new environment and brings the threat of punishment from Aunty Rosa, whose actions are sanctioned by a Christian God 'that stood in the background and counted the strokes of the cane' (*WWW*, p. 269). Kipling traced aspects of his storytelling to Harry Holloway's 'calculated torture' of entrapping him into a web of contradictory lies for which punishments would be meted out. 'Yet', he writes, 'it made me give attention to the lies I soon found it necessary to tell: and this, I presume, is the foundation of literary effort' (*SOM*, p. 6). In his Introduction to the *Wee Willie Winkie* collection, Hugh Haughton argues that '[i]n a sense, "Baa Baa, Black Sheep" is a kind of founding story of [Kipling's] own literary vocation' (*WWW*, p. 55).

Punch's identity is thus constructed under the withering (white) gaze of Aunty Rosa. It is her western ideology that captures and pinions his subjectivity; her knowledge, in effect, brings him into being and he is reconstituted in terms of his difference, his Otherness. His Anglo-Indian self is thus characterised by its marginal position in relation to the Englishness of the metropolis, the stranger within that is projected onto the 'foreigner' without in a Kristevan discourse. He becomes what he is not, in effect, not good, not truthful, not dutiful, not English, and therefore not *white*. It is his 'difference', a liminal state between Englishness and 'Indianness', which signifies and carries meaning as Punch comes to realise that his Anglo-Indian self is no longer a marker for privilege. In Aunty Rosa's house:

> There was no special place for him or his little affairs [. . .] Sprawling was lazy and wore out sofas, and little boys were not expected to talk. They were talked to, and the talking to was intended for the benefit of their morals. As the unquestioned despot of the house at Bombay, Punch could not quite understand how he came to be of no account in this new life. (*WWW*, p. 266)

The respectful attention that Punch previously assumed was his prerogative by virtue of his privileged status is no longer afforded to him. The enforced systems of (western) cultural assumptions begin to form his most interstitial perceptions of himself as a bicultural subject, his ideas of what is desirable and what is fearful. The solicitous care he received in India from his *ayah*, coupled with the unconditional love of his mother, has been the cornerstone of his internalised self-image. Aunty Rosa's cold and merciless treatment of him, which goes on in a psychically demanding and oftentimes physically brutal environment, destabilises the deep-rooted sense of 'despotic' omnipotence that characterised his relationships in Bombay. For every consoling word or gesture that his sister offers, there are beatings and humiliations from both Harry and his mother. The narrative that Punch composed with his caregivers in India is built upon a collective 'Indian' experience, a communal bond that created a sense of belonging as well as identity. In this sense his Anglo-Indian self cedes to a new English authority and his Other self, of which the diminished 'black sheep' is the defining image, subsequently identifies him.

In terms of binary oppositions, Punch has moved from the dominant side of the bar, the side that assumes the right to construct the Other within its discourse, to the side that is defined by negativity, by the English boy that he is not. Binary oppositions are always asymmetrical, and the children, uprooted from their Indian home, have to confront the difficulties of moving between cultures. In the change from one country to another, Punch loses three of the cardinal points with which his sense of selfhood has previously been mapped: his unquestioned belief in the superiority of the Anglo-Indian, his privileged place within that society and his attachments to his first and most beloved 'home'. Precociously addressing strangers in the manner he was used to in India produces only disinterest at Downe Lodge, and Aunty Rosa regards his hungry curiosity as showing off (*WWW*, p. 272). Such displays of indifference confirm Punch's loss of status as he falls from *sahib* to 'just Punch'

(*WWW*, p. 265). He struggles to understand that his status as *sahib* no longer has any meaning outside of India. A new order must be constructed, but he has little idea of what that will be.

For Punch and his sister, England is a dark and confusing *terra incognita* that is off their Anglo-Indian map, as it were. 'Their world', says Punch, 'had been Papa and Mama who knew everything, permitted everything, and loved everybody' (*WWW*, p. 265). It is a world where all desire is satisfied. Treated with deference by the native servants appointed to look after him, Punch has been affirmed by his family and servants alike as an elite member of the British Raj, giving him his unique meaning and identity whilst simultaneously reinforcing the Otherness of his native servants. In Bombay, Punch's *ayah* sang him to sleep with an 'interminable canticle' (*WWW*, p. 261). The rhythm of the canticle and not the words are what lulls the boy to sleep, and he is unaware that the relationship that offers a feeling of security and unity is about to end, just as from a Kristevan point of view the 'voiced breath' of the mother in the semiotic is symbolised by the *langue maternelle*. She argues that the indistinct echolalia of the infant anticipates the emergence of syntactical speech. This babble, jettisoned by the infant as s/he develops a recognisable language, demonstrates the oscillation between the semiotic and the symbolic:

> To rediscover the intonations, scansions, and jubilant rhythms preceding the signifier's position as language's position is to discover the voiced breath that fastens us to an undifferentiated mother, to a mother who later, at the mirror stage, is altered into a *maternal language*. It is also to grasp this maternal language as well as to be free of it thanks to the subsequently rediscovered mother.[39]

Similarly, he is able to bully the 'big *Surti* boy', Meeta,[40] into reciting a bedtime story and 'the *Hamal*' (a porter or house-boy) into animating it with tiger noises in 'twenty different keys'; but the 'obstreperous' behaviour which was accepted by 'the people of his [Indian] world' (*WWW*, p. 260) is regarded by Aunty Rosa as unacceptable.

From a Kleinian perspective, the child faced with a self that is no longer a cohesive whole adapts to this difficult situation by compartmentalising its experiences. Punch's Anglo-Indian self, representing a threat from beyond the borders of the symbolic, must be repressed if he is to survive in this new world. But before he consigns that anarchic side of himself to the abyss he must first psychically confront the mother who is responsible for his exile from his Indian homeland to an elsewhere 'beyond the seas' (*WWW*, p. 266). He does this, I would argue, through the Kleinian notion of splitting the unconscious image of his biological mother into her 'good' and 'bad' component parts. This is achieved by internalising her nurturing, life-sustaining qualities, which are associated with Punch's life in India, and projecting her frightening, life-threatening aspects – those aspects that are responsible for his exile and subsequent despairing life in England – onto Aunty Rosa. Principally a defence mechanism deployed by the ego against anxieties concerning the death-drive, Klein's concept of the splitting, introjection and projection of the part-object (and subsequently object) to maintain separation between the good object and the bad object enables the ego to be safeguarded and strengthened in difficult situations.[41] Punch's natural mother has been lost in the real world and replaced by a more threatening primary caregiver.

Punch and his sister struggle to make sense of themselves as subjects in exile from the love of their natural mother. The anger that Punch, in particular, feels is redirected toward the malevolent foster mother, Aunty Rosa. In this respect he is able to work through his feelings of abandonment without endangering the goodwill of his loving internal true mother. He is similarly 'split' in two, the Anglo-Indian Punch and the English Black Sheep, who, he wishes to believe, have little in common with one another. He thus aligns his former Anglo-Indian self, treated with respectful obedience by his *ayah* and the house-servants, to his lost Indian homeland whilst at the same time acknowledging the force of a new, paternal authority that will produce a social, ordered self to be sent back to India decontaminated, as it were, of the negative influence of his servants. In Bombay he was the centre of loving attention: 'I know I used to give orders and Mamma kissed me', he says (*WWW*, p. 279), but in England he is 'talked to, and the talking was intended for the benefit of [his] morals' (*WWW*, p. 268). Being psychically split in two forces Punch to separate from, or part company with, the Anglo-Indian part of his personality, which has now become a stranger not only to him, but also to his sister. After yet another of Aunty Rosa's chastisements Judy, who is 'awe-stricken at the catalogue of [his] crimes', says: 'You usen't to be as bad as this [. . .] Why are you so bad now?' (*WWW*, p. 274). Punished for the pleasure he finds in reading, Punch is 'left to weep himself into repentance and work out his own gospel of life' (*WWW*, p. 272).

The painful sense of loss which Punch-as-exile feels for Bombay denotes the strength of his affiliative identification with Hindustani and consequently intensifies the grief over his lost 'home'. The children's exile takes place in an environment that is culturally at odds with their Indian homeland. The difference between the two communities encourages the construction of a dual world in Punch's psychic mapping.

Psychically, the children's world is split into two parts that are divided by the past and the present. There is no one to whom the children could speak in Hindustani and it cannot explicate their 'new' English identities. Punch performs an act of hiding his Anglo-Indian self, and thus his previous Indian experiences speak of an unreachable past that can only be accessed through memory. He is told again and again to 'remember' his parents, and is instructed not to let Judy forget. The children's half-formed, clumsy English word is 'bemember' (*WWW*, p. 263), and like the Hindustani that was 'once his second-speech' (*WWW*, p. 262), Punch's ability to remember his past comes only with difficulty as he necessarily becomes immersed in a culture that is sociologically different from his original Indian surroundings.

A similar courage and determination to that shown by the 'outcast' Punch, as he struggles to manage and structure his isolating life in this forbidding environment, shows up in other stories in which children find themselves in difficult situations yet act in a manner that Kipling praises for their single-minded resolve. In 'Kaa's Hunting' (in *The Jungle Book*) Mowgli manages to resist the python Kaa's feat of mesmerism – as Kim would later do in the face of the spymaster Lurgan Sahib's attempted hypnotism – saving the lives of Bagheera and Baloo in the process. Punch's integration into the English culture of the metropolis is a sort of 'colonisation' of his Anglo-Indian self. Even though Kipling could present certain members of the Anglo-Indian community as colonial rulers in his fiction, England remained the ultimate authority. Laws, edits and codes of conduct came from the metropolis to be disseminated throughout the Indian subcontinent. Yet at times Kipling could be supremely contemptuous of MPs and government officials who, visiting during the cooler season, saw little of the harsh realities of life in India. The poem 'The Enlightenments of Pagett, M.P.', which talks of 'fools like Pagett [. . .] who duly misgovern the land', is the writer's savage take on what he saw as the error in ruling India with a metropolitan experience. Bart Moore-Gilbert argues that Britain's 'closer and more regular contact' with a post-Mutiny administration did little to dispel the feeling of incompetence and apathy that 'in Anglo-Indian eyes [. . .] were felt to characterise metropolitan conceptions of imperial rule'.[42]

In 'Baa Baa, Black Sheep', Punch is cut off from his past self, unable to revive it, and his Anglo-Indian self remains separated from the self that he is developing in England. Unable to develop in conjunction with his English experiences, the 'I' that he evolved in Bombay is arrested as he left it. India is thus transformed into an imaginary terrain that is devoid of conflict and tension. The link to his mother and his homeland is through the act of writing. Punch's father tells him to learn to write quickly so that he might establish a channel of communication (*WWW*, p. 265), but the formulaic, heavily censored letters fail to bridge the gap between his present experiences and his past life.

Punch's discourse with Aunty Rosa sees him defined according to her western values and her censorship of his Other self. Her theological ideas about the upbringing of children reshape his identity and are used to regulate his conduct, just as his mother's insistence that he 'remember' her instils a sense of duty in the boy. Therefore Punch takes on a meaningful identity only as an object under the scrutiny of a certain kind of western knowledge within Aunty Rosa's discourse in which 'the horrors were revealed to [him] with such store of imagery as [her] narrow mind possessed' (*WWW*, p. 273). Punch can only meaningfully 'exist' according to the socio-cultural ideologies of an English system, therefore he takes on the supposed attributes of a 'black sheep', an outsider. He becomes a corrupting influence, 'a liar' who resides in a permanent 'Valley of Humiliation' and is synecdochically reduced to an abjected 'dishevelled heap' (*WWW*, p. 273). Just as this discourse includes an acceptable way to conduct himself, to define his speech and actions, it also excludes, limits and restricts other ways of talking about himself. He realises that 'it would be discreet in the future to propitiate Aunty Rosa' but is confused as to what needs to be excluded in order to behave in a way that is expected of him: 'then, again, even in matters in which he was innocent, he had been accused of "showing off"' (*WWW*, p. 272). The language of the coloniser (English) overpowers and supersedes the language of the colonised (Hindustani).

Linguistically Punch-*baba* is transformed into its western-sounding equivalent of Baa Baa, Black Sheep or *black-sheep-baabaa*, if you will. The original meaning of the Hindi word *baba* is an old man, but it is a respectful appellation of father. Commanding respect according to age, it is a clear marker of a hierarchical order but at the same time can be used amongst friends to suggest a familiar closeness – rather in the way we might use 'mate' in English – as well as an affectionate term used in the nineteenth century by Anglo-Indians and native servants for children.[43] In Bombay, *baba* serves the dual function of reinforcing his *sahib* status whilst hinting at a more intimate association with a childhood state, akin to a Kristevan notion of the mother/child dyad in the semiotic chora, a psychic locale within the nurturing semiotic space. The chora retains an irreducible connection to an undifferentiated feminine space (on the cusp of the symbolic) and is, according to Elizabeth Grosz, associated with a series of sexually coded terms, such as 'mother', 'nurse' and 'imprints-bearer'.[44] Punch's recollections of his Indian homeland certainly bear the imprints of an edenic space in which a biological mother and a host of solicitous caregivers reside. Memories of his first 'home' are a stark contrast to the cold and forbidding environment of his new 'Home' in Rocklington, with its 'heath, potato fields' and endless sand dunes that stretch out before a 'great grey sea' (*WWW*, p. 267). His ventures into the town are in the company of Uncle Harry. During pauses in those walks he would sit and read epitaphs on the gravestones 'for hours' in the cemetery where 'the grey man' would rest (*WWW*, p. 275). As a result, the need for emotional support is manifested in 'Baa Baa, Black Sheep' by the repetition of the Hindustani word *baba*, which occurs seven times in the first three pages of the story, the part that deals with his experience in India. It is a word that is used exclusively by his *ayah*, who is a loving surrogate mother. This word becomes a byword for tenderness, respect and, perhaps most importantly, belonging.

Familial closeness and community affiliation were important issues for an adult Kipling. C. S. Lewis points to Kipling's need to belong to a closed circle, an 'Inner ring', bonded by filial loyalty.[45] In *Something of Myself*, the author talks about his sister's homecoming to India as completing his much cherished idea of the 'family square' (*SOM*, p. 26). Philip Mason also recognised this deeply felt need of Kipling's to be cherished in a bond of 'belonging', to guard against the threat of fragmentation that isolation brings. He writes:

> More even than most people, he wanted to be loved. More than most people, he wondered about the tenuous bond of identity. 'Who is Kim – Kim – Kim?' he wrote when he was thirty-five, and he must often as a boy have wondered: 'Who is Rudyard?' And the cracking of identity under intolerable strain was the chief preoccupation of his later years.[46]

When Kipling arrived back in India at the age of sixteen to take up a position as sub-editor of the *Civil and Military Gazette* in Lahore, he says he found himself 'moving among sights and smells that made him deliver in the vernacular sentences whose meanings [he] knew not' (*SOM*, p. 25). Though he spent less than fifteen years of his life in India, Kipling felt a lifelong affiliation to the country of his birth. The epigraph to his book of verse *The Seven Seas* is a dedication to the city of Bombay, and contains the following lines:

> Neither by service nor fee
>   Come I to mine estate –
> Mother of Cities to me,
>   For I was born in her gate,
> Between the palms and the sea,
>   Where the world-end steamers wait.[47]

The words of Hindustani in 'Baa Baa, Black Sheep', especially the term *baba*, suggest an identification that literalises his sense of exile from what they represent linguistically.

Punch's gradual acceptance of his 'exile' from the country of his birth privileges English over Hindustani with the effect that the 'vernacular' is suffused with longings for an imaginary realm of beauty, safety and unity. However, due to his traumatic upheaval, Hindustani also becomes associated with abandonment and danger. He experiences England via the personalities of Aunty Rosa and her bullying son Harry, through their gestures of anger and the meagreness of their affection. Aunty Rosa's judgement of Punch as a 'Trial and a Black Sheep' (*WWW*, p. 274) moves the boy through the processes of diminishing his Anglo-Indian self to be reconstructed as an English boy surviving in an incomprehensible universe where he is not able to cling to the life-sustaining mainstays of love, social status or affirmation that his previous life afforded. Punch's self-translation takes place through a dangerously divisive dialogue in which new perceptions of who he is in England are gauged against his earlier self-image in India. 'Black Sheep', the narrator tells us, 'had not been permitted to keep any self-respect at school: at home he was, of course, utterly discredited' (*WWW*, p. 278). Where he was 'very dear' to his Indian *ayah*'s heart, Punch feels 'grateful for any pity that the servant girls [. . .] might show' (*WWW*, pp. 261, 278).

The 'loss' of his previous edenic existence is succeeded by the recognition of the need to manufacture a new set of values in order to cope with the chaos and nullifying emptiness that characterises his life in England. Aunty Rosa's dictatorial theology offers no salvation. She tells him that 'God heard every word he had said and was very angry', but he understands that '[i]f this were true why didn't God come and say so [. . .] and dismissed the matter from his mind' (*WWW*, p. 269). Instead, he constructs an alternative moral code, striving to 'do his duty' (*WWW*, p. 263) to his mother. Battling alone in an empty, disordered universe with little to stave off the abyss save an unwavering dutiful allegiance to the 'mother' of Empire, Britannia, is a theme that is recurrent in Kipling's fiction. For his imperial heroes, maintaining a sense of self-worth is established through a dedication to duty and a readiness to work to the point of exhaustion. In stories such as 'The Bridge Builders', 'The Brushwood Boy', 'William the Conqueror' (in *The Day's Work*), 'Only a Subaltern' (in *Wee Willie Winkie*) and a handful of others with a similar theme, commitment to the ideal of Empire reveals how Kipling, according to Randall Jarrell, sought to 'justify true authority, the work and wisdom of the world, because he feels so bitterly the abyss of pain and insanity that they overlie'.[48] Shamsul Islam argues that, 'Empire [stood] for the forces of law, order and discipline [that] engaged in a constant struggle against the negative forces of chaos, confusion and disorder' that so terrifyingly characterised his childhood experiences.[49]

Punch's sense of identity, from a Kristevan point of view, his 'I' that exists as a functioning being in the world, cannot be interpreted outside of language. Reading comes with difficulty and has none of the enjoyment that the Indian tales he was told as an infant had. The 'dirty brown book filled with unintelligible dots and marks' is an extension of Aunty Rosa's 'awful' creed (*WWW*, pp. 268–9) and Punch struggles to accept that he must learn to read:

> Aunty Rosa sat him upon a table and told him that A B meant ab.
> 'Why?' said Punch. 'A is a and B is bee. *Why* does A B mean ab?'
> 'Because I tell you it does,' said Aunty Rosa, 'and you've got to say it.'
> Punch said it accordingly, and for a month, hugely against his will, stumbled through the brown book, not in the least comprehending what it meant. (*WWW*, p. 269)

It is only when he begins to read that he discovers the 'magical' properties of literature. The books, which Punch voraciously devours, ward off his fears of isolation. When he is left alone for a month, the 'package of new books' sent by his father, who 'seemed to know a young sinner's wants to the hour', block out 'the shadows of window-curtains and the flapping of doors and the creaking of shutters [. . .] and the rustling of the laurel-bushes' (*WWW*, pp. 281–2). Reading provides an alternative world and offers a few hours' respite from his grim quotidian life. Immersion in books enables him to 'pass [. . .] into a land of his own, beyond the reach of Aunty Rosa and her God, Harry and his teasements, and Judy's claims to be played with' (*WWW*, p. 271). Thus English, as the language of the coloniser, becomes equated with rescue, but is ultimately a symbol of self-control. However, the phonics of English that Punch is forced to learn come at a price. He is, in effect, made to leave behind his past in Bombay and adopt the cultural dictates of England. His bilingual status, his 'difference', is not acknowledged, let alone seen as something that should be encouraged to develop. Consequently, Punch's memories of India diminish as he establishes his new life in England. This is paralleled by the words of Hindustani that become less frequent as the narrative progresses, until they cease to appear altogether. Despite Judy's appeals to 'try and remember about Bombay', her brother reiterates that he 'can't remember' (*WWW*, p. 279). 'Under Aunty Rosa's eye', he forgets 'what manner of life he had led in the beginning of things' (*WWW*, p. 279). Even when the children are reunited with their mother, Punch remembers her only '[a] little' through the act of writing letters, '[r]emember I wrote to you every week, anyhow' (*WWW*, p. 285). 'Memories' of the visceral, pre-verbal sensations which characterise his life in Bombay have been replaced by the organising structure of the symbolic, and his feelings toward his parents are 'wholly overlaid by the unpleasant task of writing them letters' (*WWW*, p. 279).

The act of forgetting Hindustani, forgetting his Other self, is analogous not only to Punch's separation from his Indian homeland but also to his separation from India as a maternal, nurturing space populated by a collection of servants and family who would echo back both Punch and Judy's sense of self and their place in the Anglo-Indian community. The sense of gap, of the distance between his Anglo-Indian self and the coloniser's language, is the first stage in their cultural transposition. Just as Bombay is separated from the children by a sea that cannot be traversed and 'swallow[s] all [their] tiny past' (*WWW*, p. 263), so Punch's sense of identity is cleaved in two and his Anglo-Indian self can only be retrieved through memory. In this respect, English becomes the objective correlative for all the loss that Punch feels: loss of his homeland, his cultural markers, his place in society, his mother and his Anglo-Indian self. The children's exile is thus both a physical and psychogenic disconnection from their country of origin. Punch says that 'the sea must be traversed before anyone could get to Bombay' and weeps 'bitterly with Judy, into whose fair head he had driven some ideas of the meaning of separation' (*WWW*, p. 266). In Cixousian terms, the sea is a metaphor for the fluidity of the maternal feminine. In 'Manna', Cixous writes: 'suddenly the sea was pregnant and good and its belly was full of mystery and freedom and also of play'. The image of the sea, for Cixous, contains cherished childhood memories that can emerge from 'coffins like children in pyjamas' and instils within us the recognition that we can find 'the strength to vanquish monsters with a simple nod of the mother's head'.[50] But in Punch's world, the sea represents an impassable barrier to their mother, their cherished *ayah*, the servants and Anglo-Indian environment. It is an entity that 'swallowed all [Judy's] tiny past. In short, everything that has, up until the moment of separation, formed the nucleus of their self-confidence and inner security as to their self-value and sense of place in the world. In *Puck of Pook's Hill* Kipling makes much use of the image of water as a metaphor for healing psychic wounds and signifying protective childhood spaces, but in 'Baa Baa, Black Sheep' it is a 'bitter' draught that signifies Punch's fall from paradise.

Do the traces of that lost paradise where Punch's earliest frames of reference lie capture his subjectivity, thereby assigning him a place on the borders of being – or is he able to circumnavigate the 'incommensurability of translation'[51] and incorporate his lost homeland into his discourse? The mother who rescues Punch is 'a real, live, lovely Mamma, who is also a sister, comforter and friend' (*WWW*, p. 287). Punch's escape and apparent recovery from deep despair seem to conform to elements that ensure a happy ending in traditional fairy tales. J. R. R. Tolkien stresses that all complete fairy tales must have it. It is 'a sudden joyous "turn" [. . .] However fantastic or terrible the adventure, it can give to child or man that hears it, when the "turn" comes, a catch of breath, a beat and lifting of the heart, near to tears.'[52] Punch says: 'It's different now, and we are just as much Mother's as if she had never gone' (*WWW*, p. 287). But the happy ending for the young Punch comes with a caveat, as his edenic experiences in India belong to a now dead 'eternal' past. They lie on the margins of his subjectivity as a source of unnameable desire that is also infused with fear – in Kristeva terms, as a 'non-recoverable deletion'.[53] Along with 'ellipses' and 'indefinite embeddings', these are elements that, Kristeva argues, lie outside of signifying norms and as such have the ability to destabilise and undermine the symbolic order. Whilst these elements form the foundation of subversive poetic language, they are also the site of anxiety as they are an expression of primal joy and desire. Punch's mother is similarly retranslated in the young boy's psyche. She insists: 'Punch-*baba*, come back to me! I am your mother – your own mother!' (*WWW*, p. 286); but she is not the unified, whole mother of Punch's earlier life, she is a 'rediscovered mother, who is at a *stroke* [. . .] pierced, stripped, signified, uncovered, castrated, and carried away into the symbolic'.[54] Although Punch's mother may use words of Hindustani, affectionately calling Punch a '*pagal*' (an idiot/madman in Hindi)[55] (*WWW*, p. 287), they are no longer markers of the semiotic space. With Punch's fall from paradise the word takes on a more menacing inflection, as it is associated with his abjected alter ego, 'Black Sheep'. The story ends with the narrator's warning of the cost of his time at Downe Lodge, although the young boy is yet to understand it: 'when young lips have drunk deep of the bitter waters of Hate, Suspicion and Despair, all the Love in the world will not wholly take away that knowledge; though it may turn darkened eyes for a while to the light and teach Faith where no Faith was' (*WWW*, p. 287). Confronting the ramifications of maternal separation, Punch survives, but only just, and with indications of psychic damage. The introduction of a new order that will shape his future imperial life has been made at the expense of the 'Indian' side of his head.

As Kipling's fictional children move toward adolescence we see them having to leave behind their nurturing infant spaces, relinquish beauty for fear and begin the process of accepting a patriarchal law if they are to take their place among their colonial brothers (and sisters) of Empire. In the next chapter we see Kipling's colonial boys not only mastering the law of the colonising father, but finding ingenious ways to subvert it for their own ends. Throughout 'Baa Baa, Black Sheep', Punch's accumulation of knowledge via the fairy tales, adventure stories, poetry and mythology equips him with the imaginative means with which to create an alternative 'reality', and alleviates some of the distress of his wretched life. In *The Jungle Book* and *Stalky & Co.*, knowledge (found in the written word and an unwritten generative 'Law') enables Mowgli and Stalky and his friends to gain mastery not only over their geographical environment, but also over their enemies. His new 'orphaned' boys offer an alternative narrative to Punch's abandonment, and their success is dependent upon their knowledge. Yet Kipling's community of Anglo-Indian administrators, engineers, officers and foot soldiers, even though they come armed with experience and expertise, are oftentimes overpowered psychologically and physically in carrying out their arduous imperial duties in far-flung corners of the Empire.

The India of Punch's childhood has been retranslated into a place of fear and menace. Its heat-scorched cities turn sleeping men into corpses in 'The City of Dreadful Night', and its countryside hides black holes in the ground where demons snicker in 'Bubbling Well Road' (in *Life's Handicap*). This frightening, disorientating India is emblematised in Kipling's lost manuscript, a sort of anti-*Kim*, 'Mother Maturin'. No trace of the work remains. It was presumably destroyed, like so many of the author's papers. In a letter to his aunt, Edith Macdonald, he wrote that the story is 'not one bit proper but it carries a grim sort of moral with it and tries to deal with the unutterable horrors of lower class Eurasian and native life as they exist outside reports'.[56] To his much-loved cousin, Margaret Burne-Jones, he hints at cross-cultural experiences that are '[u]nderneath our excellent administrative system; under the piles of reports and statistics'. Beyond the borders of 'English life', he wrote, 'is the dark and crooked and fantastic, and wicked, and awe-inspiring life of the "native"'. His experiences of 'native' life found their way into 'Mother Maturin', 'a queer jumble of opium-dens, night houses, night strolls with natives [. . .] and one or two queer things I've come across in my own office experience'.[57] Kipling's fictional cavernous spaces, hypnotic opium dens, teeming cities where cholera outbreaks are common and fevers routine, parched landscapes that create periodic famines and unbearable heat that induces insomnia and night-stalking, are representative of a metamorphosed India after the fall that offers only the threat of dissolution. It is a terrifying space that inverts the coloniser/colonised binaries. The previously sunny, nurturing India of the author's childhood now unmans the Englishman. In his fiction set in India, Kipling hints that one of the sure-fire ways to prevent psychic collapse is to knuckle down and learn one's imperial lessons well. In the next chapter we see his colonial boys on the cusp of manhood learning that adulthood is 'the hour of pride and power,/ Talon and tush and claw' (*JB*, p. 35). To succeed in this Hobbesian environment, under the shadow of an imperial Leviathan, they must (and do) become skilled masters of his edifying 'Law'.

Notes

1. Rudyard Kipling, 'The Return of the Children', in *The Definitive Edition of Rudyard Kipling's Verse*, p. 596.
2. Rudyard Kipling, 'Baa Baa, Black Sheep', in *Wee Willie Winkie*, p. 266. Further references in this chapter are given after quotations in the text.
3. Maud Diver, *The Englishwoman in India*, quoted in Charles Allen, *Plain Tales From the Raj: Images of British India in the Twentieth Century*, p. 22.
4. Alice Fleming, 'Through Judy's Eyes', *Trix: Kipling's Forgotten Sister*, pp. 345–66.
5. Diane Simmons, *The Narcissism of Empire: Loss, Rage and Revenge in Thomas De Quincey, Robert Louis Stevenson, Arthur Conan Doyle, Rudyard Kipling and Isak Dinesen*, p. 83.
6. Lord Birkenhead, *Rudyard Kipling*, p. 45.
7. Kipling, *Definitive Verse*, p. 596.
8. None of Kipling's biographers record a breakdown after 1891.
9. Melanie Klein, 'Contribution to the Psychogenesis of Manic-depressive States', in *Love, Guilt and Reparation & Other Works, 1921–1945*, pp. 262–89.
10. Fleming, *Trix, Kipling's Forgotten Sister*, pp. 362–3.
11. Angus Wilson, *The Strange Ride of Rudyard Kipling: His Life and Works*, p. 18.
12. Zohreh Sullivan, *Narratives of Empire: The Fictions of Rudyard Kipling*, p. 110.
13. Ibid., p. 79.
14. Simmons, *The Narcissism of Empire*, p. 83.
15. Rudyard Kipling, *Land and Sea Tales for Scouts and Guides*, p. 161.
16. Kipling, *Definitive Verse*, p. 221.
17. I use the term 'Hindustani' in its historical context as it was used by Kipling to refer to both Hindu and Urdu phrases and idioms. Kipling often borrowed from different Indian languages, including Punjabi and Pashto, but as Azfar Husain has pointed out, in the main, he used Hindustani phrases and idioms to create an illusion of 'Indianness' for his Anglo-Indian and English readers. S. S. Azfar Husain, *The Indianness of Rudyard Kipling: A Study in Stylistics*, p. 61.

18. Trix, like her brother, was to retain strong memories of Henry Holloway. More than half a century later she would remember him as having 'dark eyes, set near together, and black hair, plastered with pomatum'. Alice Fleming, 'Some Childhood memories of Rudyard Kipling by his Sister', p. 169. In her later years she was still able to 'shudder with dislike' at anyone resembling him. Quoted in Birkenhead, *Rudyard Kipling*, p. 20.
19. Quoted in Birkenhead, *Rudyard Kipling*, p. 291.
20. John A. McClure, *Kipling and Conrad: The Colonial Fiction*, p. 11.
21. Sullivan, *Narratives of Empire*, pp. 27, 33.
22. Julia Kristeva, *Strangers to Ourselves*, p. 21.
23. Wilson, *The Strange Ride of Rudyard Kipling*, pp. 107, 120.
24. Ibid., p. 18.
25. Trix Fleming to Stanley Baldwin. Quoted in Andrew Lycett, *Rudyard Kipling*, p. 55.
26. Kipling Society, *Kipling Journal*, 84 (1947), 3.
27. Harold Orel (ed.), *Kipling: Interviews and Recollections*, I, p. 103.
28. Birkenhead, *Rudyard Kipling*, p. 27.
29. Ibid., p. 28.
30. Charles Carrington, *Rudyard Kipling: His Life and Work*, p. 16.
31. Birkenhead, *Rudyard Kipling*, p. 50.
32. Barbara Creed, *The Monstrous Feminine: Film, Feminism, Psychoanalysis*, p. 27.
33. Kristeva, *Strangers to Ourselves*, p. 98.
34. Bart Moore-Gilbert, *Kipling and 'Orientalism'*, p. 5.
35. Interestingly, the nineteenth-century travel writer Mary Kingsley had an altogether different experience of the moving out of the binary oppositions of the colonial space. Her descriptions of her resting place near the rapids of Ogowe, in West Africa, are uncanny in their evocation of identity being 'swallowed' by the African landscape. But her descriptions serve to erase the polarising boundaries of self/other that the white European male has put in place in order to give licence and authority to the imperial project of annexing and ruling the colonies. She writes: 'I just lose all sense of human individuality, all memory of human life, with its grief and worry and doubt, and become part of the atmosphere.' Quoted in Elleke Boehmer, *Colonial and Postcolonial Literature: Migrant Metaphors*, p. 92.
36. Kristeva, *Strangers to Ourselves*, p. 13.
37. See also 'The Gate of a Hundred Sorrows' (in *Plain Tales*) and 'The Man Who Would Be King' (in *Wee Willie Winkie*), amongst others.
38. Bart Moore-Gilbert, '*Letters of Marque*: Travel, Gender and Imperialism', pp. 22, 19.
39. Kristeva, *Desire in Language*, p. 195.
40. Kipling uses the same name as that of his childhood bearer (*SOM*, p. 3).
41. Klein developed the concept of what Ronald Fairbairn would term object relations theory in 1948. See Melanie Klein, *Contributions to Psychoanalysis* and 'The Mutual Development of Ego and Id'.
42. Moore-Gilbert, *Kipling and 'Orientalism'*, p. 70.
43. Digital Dictionaries of South Asia.
44. Elizabeth Grosz, *Space, Time and Perversion*, p. 112.
45. C. S. Lewis, *Selected Literary Essays*, pp. 249–50.

46. Philip Mason, *Kipling: The Glass, the Shadow and the Fire*, p. 299.
47. Rudyard Kipling, 'Dedication to the City of Bombay', in *The Seven Seas*, p. v.
48. Randall Jarrell, 'On Preparing to Read Kipling', p. 21.
49. Shamsul Islam, *Kipling's 'Law': A Study of his Philosophy of Life'*, p. 83.
50. Hélène Cixous, *The Cixous Reader*, p. 177.
51. Homi Bhabha, *The Location of Culture*, p. 147.
52. J. R. R. Tolkien, 'On Fairy-Stories', p. 195.
53. Julia Kristeva, *The Kristeva Reader*, p. 109.
54. Kristeva, *Desire in Language*, p. 195.
55. Digital Dictionaries of South Asia.
56. Rudyard Kipling to Edith Macdonald, 30 July 1885. Thomas Pinney (ed.), *The Letters of Rudyard Kipling* I, 83.
57. Rudyard Kipling to Margaret Burne-Jones, 28 November 1885–11 January 1886. Pinney, *Letters* I, 99.

Chapter 2

Mastering the Law-of-the-Father in *The Jungle Book* and *Stalky & Co.*

> Western wind and open surge
> Took us from our mothers;
> Flung us on a naked shore [. . .]
> 'Mid two hundred brothers
>
> And we all praise famous men –
> Ancients of the College;
> For they taught us common sense – [. . .]
> Which is more than knowledge![1]

> A Man-cub is a man-cub, and he must learn all the Law of the Jungle[2]

> An unshakable adherence to Prohibition and Law is necessary if that perverse interspace of abjection is to be hemmed in and thrust aside. Religion, Morality, Law.[3]

'I do not wish to leave the jungle,' says a heartbroken Mowgli, returning, as he must, to the man-village (*JB*, p. 52). With a profound love for his jungle 'family', the man-cub, Mowgli, as his epithet suggests, is a liminal being caught between contrasting worlds. Like the *sahib/outcaste* Punch in 'Baa Baa, Black Sheep' whose identity is founded upon his Anglo-Indian duality, Mowgli's subjectivity straddles the borders of human/animal, culture/nature, and in Kristevan topography self/Other. For critics such as Zohreh Sullivan, the marking of boundaries of self/Other necessitates an acknowledgement of the 'colonial rule of power, law and government'.[4] But as Sandra Kemp has noted, 'there is more to this duality'[5] than a self-representation that aligns the colonial subject to Empire. Whilst Kemp maintains that the duality inherent in Kipling's adolescent characters is an expression of the 'interweaving of private and public self',[6] I would argue that this duality, when viewed from a Kristevan perspective, mirrors the more profound, universal struggle of an identity that, once disentangled from the mother/child dyad, emerges into the signifying space of the symbolic. The 'double-self' that

Kipling's adolescents are subject to is magnified by the specific split in the author's own ambivalent subjectivity due to the exilic moment in his childhood. The former takes on a particular cultural inflection in his fiction as a consequence of his double socialisation in India and England. In his introduction to Kipling's early newspaper sketches, Thomas Pinney notes the author's contrasting perspectives on India. Firstly is the 'official view [that is] essentially paternalistic and administrative' and secondly, an altogether more 'personal [Kemp might say 'private'] and humane' vision that shows 'the Indian scene delighting in its variety and copiousness, and responding to the individuality of its people'.[7]

In this chapter I will explore relationships between the semiotic and the symbolic as well as their points of contradistinction in Mowgli's struggle for identity as he assimilates what Kipling calls the 'Law of the Jungle', which is a paternal law that in *Stalky & Co.* mirrors its workaday twin, the law of Empire. Mowgli never manages to come to terms with his desire for what I will argue is a semiotic spatiality, realised in narrative terms in Mowgli's love of the jungle environment and the solicitous care he receives from his loving family figures. In *Stalky & Co.*, set in an English boarding school, sleeker, more adept apprentice colonials successfully master a paternal law, preparing them to endure the rigours of colonial life, whilst simultaneously coveting 'jungle' spaces out of school bounds. Crusoe-like, the boys are free to roam and sculpt their own hideouts in the uncultivated terrain of the North Devon coastline with the tacit approval of their headmaster, 'Prooshian' Bates. Modelled on Cormell Price, Kipling's 'Uncle Crom', Headmaster Bates is neither a clergyman (unconventional for the time) nor a rigorous military man, despite the purpose of the school being generally twofold: a training ground for, firstly, entry into military academies such as Sandhurst or Woolwich and secondly, those who would go on to serve the administrative and economic interests of the Empire. A familiar character in Kipling's fiction, Bates represents the Kristevan Imaginary loving father who, unlike the stern Freudian father figure, stands in support rather than opposition over the boys in his care.

The ethics of the two collections taken together are more fully realised in *Kim*, where the eponymous hero of the novel displays, like Mowgli, an intimate knowledge and love of native India alongside a Stalky-like cunning that sees him not only gleefully subverting bumbling figures of authority, but also using his clandestine activities for the British Secret Service as a springboard for what are tantamount to adolescent pranks.

The chapter will be broken into two parts. The first section will explore the notion of Kipling's 'Law' as a representation of a Kristevan paternal authority in *The Jungle Book*, as well as uncovering a semiotic space that is continually repressed by patriarchal regulations. Kipling's disturbing portrayals of a feminised Indian landscape are emblematic of a semiotic space under threat. For example, Mother India is crushed under the might of colonial forces in 'Toomai of the Elephants', is discovered quietly disintegrating in 'Kaa's Hunting', or cleared of venomous threats by gutsy faithful servants in 'Rikki-Tikki-Tavi'. The borders of language are represented by the 'Master Words' that, when learned, enable Mowgli to communicate with every animal in the jungle (and save his life in 'Kaa's Hunting'). Submission to the Law of the Jungle must replace the nurturing, enveloping maternal space of Mother Wolf's lair if the man-cub is to move forward into adolescence. An imperial code in all but name, Kipling's Jungle Law also provides the template that allows an adult Mowgli to take his allotted place as cog in the grinding machine of Empire by working for the Forestry Commission in the last jungle story, 'In the Rukh' (in *The Second Jungle Book*). The jungle code, as taught by his mentors, Baloo, Bagheera and Kaa, not only enables Mowgli, unlike Punch, to make the experience of his orphanhood a positive one, but also empowers him to become master of both the animal and human worlds. Furthering the pedagogical and psychological development of the young boy Punch, Kipling, in this collection, will not allow his wolf-boy to be permanently damaged by the loss of the mother figure as this is, in a sense, to refuse to grow up. In *The Jungle Book*, both the law-enforced jungle community where Mowgli learns to become a dutiful citizen and the village, to which he must return, are ring-fenced from the feral heart of a feminised jungle terrain. These paternally governed domains represent a phallocentric order whereby primogenial impulses can be integrated into the words of the jungle law as well as the language of men. Mowgli must relinquish the warmth and the intimacy of Mother Wolf's cave, in addition to the howls and bays – the 'vernacular' – of his wolf brothers, if he is to be posited as a speaking subject in a colonial space.

The second section of this chapter will deal with Kipling's understanding of the role that nineteenth-century military schools play in not only perpetuating power structures, but also shaping the lives of future colonial workers. In *Stalky & Co.* the pupils' submission to an unyielding institutional authority serves to reinforce the powerful ideology of British imperialism. During their stints in the colonies, Kipling's adults will be vital players in the day-to-day running of Empire, serving the economic needs and grandiose annexing fantasies of Britain's empire builders. Cecil Rhodes was the apotheosis of nineteenth-century British imperial expansionism. He famously declared that 'all of these stars [. . .] these vast worlds that remain out of reach. If I could, I would annex other planets'.[8] Like the administrators and military guardians of Britain's economic interests in the colonies, the boys in *Stalky & Co.* begin their apprenticeship at school. The nurturing maternal space that embraces Mowgli in its familial closeness has all but disappeared in the brutalising all-male school environment in the *Stalky* collection. In its absence of protective, mothering female characters, the boys of *Stalky & Co.* must find solace in each other's company, creating familial spaces outside the boundaries of the school where aesthetic books can be read, pipes can be smoked and genuine care can be both sought after and received. The story collection sees Kipling acknowledging that school lessons are designed to mould good colonial (male) citizens, but at the same time he is not able to allow his schoolboy trio of Stalky, M'Turk and Beetle to surrender to authority so completely. Like the shrewd cat in Kipling's allegorised 'The Cat that Walked by Himself' (in *Just So Stories*), who remains undomesticated despite gaining access to and warmth and sustenance from the human cave, the boys hold in contempt the inability of the school authority to ultimately control their behaviour, lauding instead the subversive force of 'stalkying' that defines the boys' cunning, anarchic and exasperating behaviour.

The three precocious adolescent heroes of the story collection find ways to both manipulate the law of the (colonising) father and undermine it. Even though the miscreant trio are ultimately unable to overturn the crushing might of the school ethos, Kipling clearly enjoys and endorses their ingeniously disruptive pranks as much as he champions Mulvaney's rebelliousness in the *Soldiers Three* collection. Just as Kim's shape-shifting forays into the heart of native India actually work to strengthen colonial authority by neutralising threats to its northwest frontier, so Stalky's crafty individualism never challenges the monolithic edifice of Empire. Rather, it enables him to escape life-threatening situations in India, as seen in 'Slaves of the Lamp Part II'. Isabel Quigly argues that in Kipling's rendition of Stalky 'the very adjective "imperial" applies to [Stalky] because to function at all such a man needs devoted followers, childlike admirers to whom he seems godlike, unquestionably right'.[9] I would add that this attribute could just as easily apply to both Mowgli and Kim, both of whom are surrounded by loving caregivers and supportive companions. Kipling's notion of a universal Law is the skeleton on which the British imperial project is fleshed out. Britannia's colonial children will be brought up in the knowledge that they will subsequently monitor the activities of the Raj. Fulfilling their colonial destinies, the likes of Stalky, M'Turk, Beetle, Kim and the more ambivalent Mowgli will carry out the work of the British Empire, benignly 'command[ing] the natives' (*Kim*, p. 173), as Colonel Creighton reiterates in *Kim*. The notion of a ubiquitous Law, which transcends the imperialist's dictates, validates and gives licence to what Edward Said argues was Kipling's firm belief that it was India's 'best destiny' (*Kim*, p. 23) to be ruled by the British, however admiring he was of India's aesthetic attributes.[10] As this chapter is divided between *The Jungle Book* and *Stalky & Co.*, my analysis of the Mowgli stories will be taken from stories in the first collection of *The Jungle Books*. Stories such as 'Letting in the Jungle' provide an interesting riposte by 'Mother India' as to her disintegration in 'Little Toomai'. Mowgli, with the help of Haithi the elephant, wreaks revenge on the village for imprisoning and planning the execution of his adoptive parents. After destroying the village but leaving its inhabitants alive, 'Mother India' slowly reclaims the terrain for her own: 'by the end of the Rains', writes Kipling, 'there was the roaring Jungle in full blast on the spot that had been under plough not six months before' (*JB*, p. 232).

The Jungle Book opens with an epigraph that contains the lines: 'Oh hear the call! – Good hunting all/That keep the Jungle Law!' (*JB*, p. 35). Capitalised to strengthen its apparent importance, the Law is a recurrent theme that is woven through the story collection, signifying the importance that Kipling attached to his all-encompassing notion of the Law – not just *a* law, but *the* 'Law'. Adrian Poole notes that the capitalisation of commonplace words, typographically elevating their status and importance, held a fascination for Kipling throughout his writing career. He argues that the 'common feature of these capitals is that they aim for an exceptional, peremptory distinction'.[11] Primarily a moral code of conduct, which has reason at its heart but is idealised in almost mythic proportions, Kipling's 'Law' transcended all cultures, religions and castes but is something to which individuals must adhere if they were to call themselves 'civilised'. In this respect it follows what Noel Annan defines as 'the keeping of promises, loyalty to friends, bravery, generosity, respect for parents', a code to which 'all races and creeds held [. . .] good'.[12] Kipling presents the Law of the Jungle as a doctrine founded on order, which assumes that it was first implemented to counteract chaos, animals in a state of nature and nature being red in tooth and claw or, as Kipling puts it, 'the hour of pride and power,/Talon and tush and claw' (*JB*, p. 35). Indeed, Shamsul Islam notes that 'one of the main sources of primitive law [is] often generated in disorder and dispute'.[13] In Kipling topography, in a feral environment man is essentially bestial and only by acting in accordance with the edicts of a civil society does he become socialised.

In Kipling's imaginary jungle community Mowgli has to learn the Law of the Jungle if he is to function as a social creature but the jungle is, by contrast, a place that is essentially lawless. It is only the Law that has been constructed over time, 'by far the oldest law in the world' (*JB*, p. 173), that creates order out of anarchy. The Law 'arranged for almost every kind of accident that may befall the Jungle People, till now its code is as perfect as time and custom can make it' (JB, p. 173). Such an archaic law that continually evolves over generations enables surrogate parents, as custodians of the ubiquitous Law, to replace absent biological parents. Indeed, as followers of the Law, foster parents can be equally solicitous in their instruction of the cared-for child in the processes of socialisation. Mowgli's loving father figures are keepers of the paternal word (the Master Words) and are instrumental in carving out the borders of his subjectivity. From a Kristevan point of view, Kipling's notion of an atavistic moral law provides, for all its supposed unifying edits, a totalitarian discourse that denies any sort of equal relationship between the semiotic 'inside' space, which is associated not only with the Mother Wolf's warm cave, but also the 'inner' psychological danger of *dewanee* (madness or irrationality), and the 'outside' phallocentric economy where leaf, tree, animal and fish are ordered according to a patriarchal law. The Law establishes a binary opposition based on the subjugation of the maternal authority by the paternal law[14] that guarantees, in Mowgli's case, a sense of who he is and the position of master he occupies in both the animal and human hierarchies.

Mowgli's biological parents have abandoned him after the tiger Shere Khan's attack in the forest but, unlike Punch who is left devastated by his parents' absence, Mowgli is taken in by loving foster-parents who will support him, to the death if required. When Mowgli is taken to the Council Rock for his fate to be decided – accepted into the Wolf-pack or delivered to the waiting jaws of Shere Khan – Mother Wolf prepares 'for what she knew would be her last fight' (JB, p. 41) if the pack rejects the man-cub. The pack is known as Free People who are governed and bound by the Law under the leadership of Akela, the self-appointed wise wolf who leads the pack with 'strength and cunning' (JB, p. 40). However, this is not a tyrannical leadership, despite the threat of gruesome Darwinian violence that is never far away. Akela knows that his leadership will end in a fight to the death: 'the time that comes to every leader of every pack when his strength goes from him and he gets feebler and feebler, till at last he is killed by the wolves and a new leader comes up – to be killed in his turn' (JB, p. 43). Akela behaves like the benign colonial administrator – a sort of 'Chairman of the Board' in Phillip Mason's words,[15] who allows each voice to be heard, reminds the community of the overriding Law but accepts that leadership involves sacrifice, sometimes personal (he is prepared to lay down his life for Mowgli) and sometimes involving others (he persuades some of the wolves to remain loyal to the man-cub with reason as opposed to violence). The Free People are members of a community with a measure of equality among its collective but they are first and foremost subject to a higher Law that is invoked in any dispute and governs their quotidian existence. Christopher Hitchens notes Kipling's 'horror of democracy'.[16] Satires on democracy such as 'As Easy as ABC' (in *A Diversity of Creatures*), 'With the Night Mail' (in *Actions and Reactions*) and 'Kaa's Hunting', support Kipling's observation in a late Stalky story, 'Regulus', that 'democracy [is] eternally futile [. . .] in all ages and climes' (*S&C*, p. 165). Kipling most assuredly believes that without the Law, the Free People fall beyond its bounds into decadence and chaos. Disregarding both the leadership of Akela and respect for the Law, the boundaries of a communal social contract are breached. In siding with Shere Khan, Mowgli refers to his former brothers as 'jackals' (*JB*, p. 49) who are subsequently defined by chaos. Shere Khan is the embodiment of a subversive force that rocks the status quo and threatens the stability of the paternal order of the Jungle.

Resisting categorisation outside the range of the ordered animal tropology that Kipling outlines, Shere Khan is a disturbing presence in *The Jungle Books*. The animal trope can be subdivided into good colonial citizens – the wolves, the elephants, the mongoose – and troubling, disruptive colonial Others such as the monkey-people, the dholes and the jackals, who are deemed inefficient, irresponsible, unintelligible and dangerous. However, the characterisation of Shere Khan does not seem to fit quite so neatly into an imperial hierarchy of law-abiding/lawless colonial citizen. As John Thieme has pointed out, Shere Khan 'resists socialization into the order that Kipling's hero Mowgli represents'.[17] Thieme goes on to argue that the image of the tiger was treated with rancour by the British as it had more to do with the colonist's fear of being unable to wholly suppress the interiority of the Indian subject, what Sujit Mukherjee sees as the 'enduring spirit of India' that imperialism 'failed to subjugate'.[18] India was a wild, untamed force that remained both powerful and terrifying for the British imperialist. Kipling's contemporaries were at great pains to show the British Empire in a positive light, and if any moral corruption occurred, the blame was laid squarely on the shoulders of the native population. Arthur Conan Doyle's stories often revolve around returning colonialists who have been tainted by their experiences in colonial India or Africa. Kathryn Castle suggests that the implication was that a fundamentally upstanding member of the imperial mission had been 'infected with the corruption and venality endemic in the "nature" of India'.[19] Kipling affords his characters no such convenient get-out clause. Indeed, 'Thrown Away' (in *Plain Tales*) highlights the corruption and sense of futility felt by certain Anglo-Indians forced to follow the British imperial agenda. Similarly, in 'Lispeth' (in *Plain Tales*), the narrative position of the story exposes the Englishman with whom the native Lispeth has fallen in love and the English missionaries, who have been responsible for her conversion to Christianity, as racially arrogant and duplicitous. It is Lispeth who is presented as the ideal, and the English characters, far from being shining examples of Empire, are presented as conceited, hypocritical and dishonourable.

The 'unknowable' India that defies domestication by the British is, I would argue, mirrored in the characterisation of the terrifyingly feral Shere Khan. In my analysis, Shere Khan is not gendered feminine in a biological sense but rather from a Cixousian masculine/feminine delineation, that is to say, 'masculine' in terms of an allegiance to the patriarchal law and 'feminine' in terms of defying its prohibitions. I follow Cixous' use of the terms 'feminine' and 'masculine' to suggest the way in which these positions tend to subdivide under the all-encompassing law of the symbolic. Cixous argues that 'what I call "feminine" and "masculine" is the relationship to pleasure [. . .] because we are born into language, and cannot do otherwise than to find myself before words; we cannot get rid of them, they are there'.[20] In this sense Shere Khan's actions in the narrative act as a threat to the Jungle Law regardless of his gender.

If one 'reads' Kipling's rendition of Shere Khan as a manifestation of the semiotic's capacity to exist in contradistinction to the authority of the symbolic law, then the Mowgli stories are interstitial tales that lie between the schismatic power of the semiotic and the potentially brutalising totalitarianism of the symbolic. Neither situation would be compatible with Kipling's notion of a law that evolves in conjunction with the collective experiences of the jungle community. Shere Khan's vital presence in the stories therefore acts as unravelling a notional double bind that gives precedence to either one or the other. In other words, if the semiotic were allowed to run unchecked across the narrative, then chaos would ensue. It would be tantamount to the overthrow of 'civility' in the jungle. On the other hand, without Shere Khan's presence, the semiotic's potential dissidence would be repressed and the jungle Law would be commensurable with despotism. The tiger's rebelliousness not only keeps the jungle law in check, but also gives meaning and validity to its central tenets. This is why, I would argue, Kipling makes room in the narrative for a dialectic interchange between observance and non-observance of the Law. In this way Mowgli not only learns the Law of the Jungle, but also uses its lessons to ultimately slaughter Shere Khan. In a predictable identification with the Law of the Jungle, Mowgli, the hunter and ultimate Master of the transgressive power of Shere Khan, strips him of his hide. What was inside is now outside and the skinned tiger is at once abjected. His skin sits like some grotesque trophy of the colonial master on the Council Rock, seat of jungle legislature.

The Wolf Pack, together with the Council Rock, is essentially a public male domain much like the Anglo-Indian world of the Club, the Viceroy's summer Hill Station in Simla or the British parliament of the late nineteenth century. The inner circle of family life, where Mowgli is suckled with the milk of Mother Wolf, is conducted apart from the pack and remains a private sphere, symbolised in the feminine space of the wolf's cave. But as the cave is a life-giving, intimately supportive space, it is also a frightening space ruled over by Mother Wolf, who has the potential to transform into a terrifying savage beast. In awe of her ferocious capabilities, Father Wolf remarks that she 'was not called The Demon for compliment's sake' (*JB*, p. 39). The implication is that she shares a psychological similarity with Shere Khan's tendency to menacing violence. And in this respect, Mother Wolf represents the two faces of a Kristevan mother: the menacing, fecund abjected mother (although she is present, she remains silent during the proceedings at the Council Rock), and the nurturing mother who says to her man-cub on leaving the jungle, 'little naked son of mine [. . .] I have loved thee more than ever I loved my cubs' (*JB*, p. 53). Kristeva stresses the double signifying aspects of the archaic mother. Although she is a source of both life and the abyss, she is in both instances abjected from the masculine laws which govern and regulate subjectivity.[21] The processes of abjection, which Kristeva argues are necessary to subjugate the power of pre-symbolic maternal authority, are present in Kipling's narrative representation of the jungle environment. Kipling's jungle space is also subject to a similar doubling. It is a feminine space that is both warm and inviting, filled with cool pools where a tired Mowgli can dip his toes after a day of lessons, as well as a dark and threatening abyss. This ambivalent feminine space hides an eerie underground vault where an enormous blind cobra, whitened with his years in darkness, guards cursed treasure ('The King's Ankus', in *The Second Jungle Book*).

Kipling's jungle setting is a space where the conflict between desire and dread are played out. Still inseparable from the desire for the maternal body, the ghosts of solitude, of loss, of division and rejection prowl, silhouetted against the backdrop of his at once 'real' and imaginary junglescape. The setting of the jungle is 'real' in the sense that it is based upon the descriptions and photographs of the remote Seeonee Jungle that

Kipling, well known for his magpie-like tendency of turning the sparsest of information into a piece of fiction,[22] received from his Allahabad friends, Edmonia and Alex Hill.[23] Kipling writes in *Something of Myself*: 'it chanced that I had written a tale about Indian Forestry work which included a boy who had been brought up by wolves. In the stillness, and suspense, of the winter of '92 some memory of the Masonic lions of my childhood's magazine, and a phrase in Haggard's *Nada the Lily*, combined with the echo of this tale. After blocking out the main idea in my head, the pen took charge, and I watched it begin to write stories about Mowgli and animals, which later grew into the *Jungle Books*' (*SOM*, pp. 67–8).

The jungle that Kipling creates for Mowgli is a curious fusion of temporal and spatial elements, fragments of real spaces given shape and weight with a pen that was dipped directly into the ink of his unconscious. A sort of 'imaginary' internalised India that, I would argue, retrospectively encompasses what Homi Bhabha would call the 'unthought', a psychological interior space 'across which colonial man is articulated [. . .] that results in the splitting of colonial discourse so that two attitudes toward external reality persist; one takes reality into consideration while the other disavows it and replaces it by a product of desire that repeats, rearticulates "reality" as mimicry'.[24] In this sense, Kipling can not only imaginatively revisit the psychological site of his childhood abandonment, but also crucially turn Punch's trauma into Mowgli's mastery. Mowgli is recognised from the outset as 'superior'. Like Kipling's English Captains, Mowgli is able to strategically organise and lead the cattle (one is tempted to say infantry) into 'battle' to vanquish Shere Khan; like the author's colonial engineers, the man-cub can utilise technology such as the villagers' fire pot to quell a rebellion among the wolves (*JB*, p. 51). Coupled with the intellect and bravery that are crucial factors in his mastery over the jungle environment, Mowgli can shed tears 'such as men use' (*JB*, p. 52). It is perhaps this last attribute that is most touching, as it suggests a sense of empathy not only for the jungle animals over which he comes to have dominion, but also the personal debt that is owed by the orphaned boy to his adoptive wolf family and kindly teachers.

As soon as Mowgli's place in the jungle has been assured at the Council Rock, he is surrounded by a host of would-be caregivers jockeying with each other to protect, instruct and enable the boy to fulfil his destiny as a sort of jungle 'monarch'. In this neat inverse exile, Kipling sanctions Mowgli's implied inheritance of sovereignty over the jungle and all the creatures who reside there. In this respect, Kipling follows eighteenth and nineteenth-century writers who adopted the motif of 'monarch of all I survey'. This position enables the observer to assert the authority of the imperialist's position whilst simultaneously reinforcing the binary structure that his subjugation of the indigenous population makes possible. The writer is, as David Spurr argues, 'placed either above or at the centre of things, yet apart from them so that the organisation and classification of things takes place according to the writer's own system of value'.[25] Thus Kipling conveniently sidesteps the issue of the colonial 'outsider' annexing the jungle space, though the violent means with which he becomes master over his 'brothers' is uncomfortably imperialistic. Through stratagem, organisation, daring and, crucially, superior weaponry, Mowgli takes control of and ultimately tames a 'self-regulating' jungle community which the narrative implies is Darwinian in its origins.

Mark Paffard argues that the jungle is a place 'to be explored with the relish of childhood, and yet an evocation of a stereotypical "India" of dark luxuriance and hidden danger'.[26] I would go further by suggesting that the 'dark luxuriance', which Paffard argues is threatening, actually represents the covetable desire that the semiotic state holds for the socialised child in the symbolic. Intimate, solicitous spaces such as Mother Wolf's cave in Kipling's jungle world conform to the pattern that Kristeva sets up for the semiotic modality. In this sense, we can associate the jungle with the semiotic modality and its influence on the child's preoedipal relationship with the mother. Father Wolf finds Mowgli, a 'naked brown baby who could just walk' (*JB*, p. 38). He is described as a 'little atom' by Father Wolf and a 'little frog' by Mother Wolf. These images, plus the preoedipal age of Mowgli, lay out at the outset of the story not only Mowgli's amphibian duality, but also the singularity of his state of identity. In Kristevan terms, the semiotic and the symbolic are atomised into two distinct units of identity, with the symbolic not yet in ascendancy over the semiotic. Unlike Punch, the infant Mowgli settles immediately into his new family, boldly 'pushing his way between the cubs to get close to the warm hide' (*JB*, p. 38) of the loving caregiver, Mother Wolf. In contrast to the rapacious wolf-figure of Aunty Rosa in 'Baa Baa, Black Sheep', Mother Wolf is filled with a desire to take care of the abandoned child but at the same time is the undoubted strength of the semiotic space of the cave, '[she] sprang forward, her eyes, like two green moons in the darkness, facing the blazing eyes of Shere Khan [. . .] Father Wolf looked on amazed' (*JB*, p. 39). She is the protector of the cave, which is rendered as a wholly feminine space, and its (albeit unintentional) Freudian overtone is not easily missed.

Western epistemologies have highlighted the role sensory perception plays in the social and dialectic organisation of our world. There is a split between the logical human intellect and its animal corporeality. In this phallocentrically organised structure, the fecund female body is frequently aligned with a bestial, frightening corporeality and must be contained and brought under male jurisdiction.[27] Mother Wolf, terrifying though she may be, is always imaged as the keeper of the (maternal) cave and her first allegiance is to her cubs. The animal trope in *The Jungle Books* lends itself to an exploration of the split between intellect and the senses. In Kipling's jungle space, the forces of law pitted against lawlessness are metaphors for human rationality, common sense and good judgement that must tame a desirous, rebellious corporeality.[28] Shamsul Islam sees Kipling's animal trope as being two sides of Mowgli's mind: the positive qualities – represented by the tenacity of wolves, the endurance of Baloo, the bravery of Bageera and the wisdom of Hathi – and the 'Dark Powers that reside within [Mowgli's] heart',[29] of which the brutish power of Shere Khan, the lasciviousness of the *Bandar-log* and the crazed Tabaqui are manifestations. Kipling's jungle world turns on the notion that its inhabitants must rein in their bestial impulses aided by the authoritarian dictum of Jungle Law, which establishes order over chaos. Kipling's jungle space is essentially anarchic. Only by a wholehearted commitment to the higher calling of the Law and the tireless dedication needed to uphold its edicts is a workable brotherhood of animals maintained. It is a model that Kipling's imperial administrators, engineers and military personnel doggedly stick to when going about their grimly demanding workaday tasks, and they learn it from their elders and peers in the school and home environments. The experienced, 'enlightened' creatures of the jungle impart upon their young the concept of an intellectual understanding of the world built upon the foundations of sensory perception. An instance of the medieval maxim *nihil est in intectu quod non prius fuerit in sensu* (there is nothing in the intellect that was not first in sensation),[30] the notion of the intellect built upon the foundations of primary sensations has particular resonance in this collection.[31]

Father Wolf teaches the young Mowgli the 'meaning of things' (*JB*, p. 43). The conceptualisation of the jungle setting and Mowgli's understanding of his place in its hierarchy has its origin in the pre-verbal rhythmic incantations that are the substratum of the forest space:

> every rustle in the grass, every breath of the warm night air, every note of the owls above his head, every scratch of a bat's claws as it roosted for a while in a tree, and every splash of every little fish jumping in a pool, meant just as much to him as the work of his office means to a business man. (*JB*, p. 43)

Father Wolf stamps the paternal signification on all aspects of jungle life and his doing so causes the 'dark warm heart of the forest' (*JB*,

p. 44) to become deracinated from its inchoate core, which can be read as an expression of Kristeva's semiotic chora, 'a non-expressive totality formed by the drives and their stases in a motility that is as full of movement as it is regulated'.[32] Kipling, the fabulist, casts his allegorical tales in a feminised jungle setting, but it is a metonymic space in which his Law sets civility against bestiality. This organising societal structure mirrors the imperial world of his later fiction, particularly *The Day's Work*, where noble human endeavours, particularly those based upon duty in serving the common good, are valorised over egocentric carnal appetites. In other words, he champions the power of the rational mind that is able to intellectually restrain and ultimately colonise the (feminised) sensual body. This is a theme that runs through many of Kipling's Indian stories, not only *The Jungle Book*. Indeed, 'The Bridge Builders', 'William the Conqueror', 'The Drums of Fore and Aft' (in *Wee Willie Winkie*) and 'The Madness of Private Ortheris' (in *Plain Tales*) are among the stories where Kipling acknowledges and lauds the sense of duty in difficult circumstances, whereby succumbing to the blankness of fatigue, alcohol or drug-induced intoxication would not only have been understandable, but also perhaps approved of. Interwoven within the fabric of Kipling's narratives is the Cixousian notion of the coupling of masculine/feminine in 'dual hierarchical oppositions'.[33] Thus the hierarchy of Kipling's animal community is based upon the superiority of culture/male/rational over nature/female/hysteria. Angus Wilson touches on this duality in his comments on the Mowgli stories: 'where thoughts veer towards the human and movements, visions and feeling are as near to animal as a writer can hope to guess'.[34] Within the bluster of western masculine rhetoric, the status of the thinking and social subject is premised on repression of fecund (female) corporeality. In addition, a paternal discourse privileges a rational mind over the 'wild' sensual appetites that are expressed, from a Kristevan point of view, as the desire for the mother's body.[35] This curious paradox of subject and repressed Other has been spatialised in the Seeonee hills; the jungle, in effect, is constituted as a hyper-corporeal, sensual realm. Outside of lessons Mowgli enjoys the jungle setting for the sensual pleasure it gives him, '[w]hen he was not learning he sat out in the sun and slept, and ate and went to sleep again; when he felt dirty or hot he swam in the forest pools; and when he wanted honey [. . .] he climbed up for it' (*JB*, p. 43).

Kipling tacitly asserts that only his civilising, fraternal Law prevents 'socialized' creatures from reverting to an animal behaviour that is as irrational as it is wild. The animals of the jungle fear the jackal Tabaqui precisely for his tendency to lose control, to stray beyond the borders of sanity. He represents the Englishman's profound fear of 'going Fantee' made flesh:

> Tabaqui, more than anyone else in the jungle, is apt to go mad, and then he forgets that he was ever afraid of anyone, and runs through the forest biting everything in his way. Even the tiger runs and hides when little Tabaqui goes mad, for madness is the most disgraceful thing that can overtake a wild creature. We call it hydrophobia, but they call it *dewanee* – the madness – and run. (*JB*, pp. 35–6)

Tabaqui's contagious madness is a potent image of a society teetering on the brink of civilisation. Falling over the edge into the abyss of senselessness is a fate that awaits all Kipling's heroes who do not toe the imperial line and abide by its regulations. Noel Annan touches upon the fragility of society's civic structures when he poses the question of what prevents a society from destruction in Kipling's fiction and finds the answer in the notions of 'religion, law, custom, convention, morality – the forces of social control – which imposed upon individuals certain rules which they broke at their peril'.[36] In *The Jungle Book* those who refute, ignore or manipulate the Law for their own ends are subject to derision and ostracism by the wider jungle community, outcast for their lawlessness.

Daniel Karlin rightly locates this lawlessness in all aspects of the *Bandar-log* community. He argues that they are ungovernable creatures engaged in

> feckless play [. . .] inventing or appropriating a series of identities [. . .] They live from day to day, without law, without memory; they embody, if you like, that part of our nature whose floating, irresponsible and self-absorbed energy is at odds with the principle of ordered and controlled design, a threat to the ordered discourse of the jungle. (*JB*, pp. 16 and 24)

From a Kristevan perspective, the *Bandar-log* embody the 'floating' *sensible* that inscribes the semiotic modality. They represent an unfettered sensory experience that exists in contradistinction to the signifying structure of the symbolic. Mowgli recognises their lawlessness, saying the *Bandar-log* have 'no Law, no Hunting Call, and no leaders' (*JB*, p. 69). They are, in other words, asocial subjects that live outside the borders of the civilised jungle community. Mowgli is kidnapped by the *Bandar-log* who want him for their teacher and leader. Outcast and polluted, the *Bandar-log* represents everything that the Free Peoples of the jungle are not, leaderless, lawless, cruel and deranged. The *Bandar-log's* linguistic interaction is a parody of the common-sense Law of the Jungle, a sort of carnivalesque dialogic that demands our attention within the text and is reinforced by the *Bandar-log's* vociferously repeated complaint that the Jungle people never notice them. '[C]arry our words back to the Jungle-

People', they chant, 'so that they may notice us in future' (*JB*, p. 70). The actions, gestures and speech (both in patterns and context) are set in juxtaposition to the ordered logic of the Jungle Law. Baloo tells Mowgli the 'Monkey-People are [. . .] forbidden to the Jungle-People' (*JB*, p. 59). And in the light of the bear's comment, Mowgli sees that:

> What Baloo had said about the monkeys was perfectly true. They belonged to the tree-tops [. . .] But when ever they found a sick wolf, or a wounded tiger, or bear, the monkeys would torment him [. . .] Then they would howl and shriek senseless songs [. . .] They were always going to have a leader, and laws and customs of their own but they never did, because their memories would not hold over from day to day. (*JB*, pp. 59–60)

The *Bandar-log's* kidnapping of Mowgli has the unsettling effect of turning his world upside down, both literally and metaphorically. Kipling's treatment of his inverted, disorientating journey on the monkey people's 'regular roads and crossroads' that are 'all laid out from fifty to seventy or a hundred feet above ground' (*JB*, p. 61) is rendered in much lighter tones than the darker, more threatening hues of Little Toomai's journey through the forest, which will be discussed later in this chapter. But like desire for the semiotic modality that irrupts into the symbolic, Mowgli cannot help but feel a trace of exhilaration on his chaotic ride through the tree-tops: 'Sick and giddy as Mowgli was he could not help enjoying the wild rush, though the glimpses of the earth far below frightened him' (*JB*, p. 61). Common sense soon prevails, however, and rationality quickly asserts itself. Mowgli, remembering his lessons, like Kim in the face of Lurgan's mesmerism, does not surrender to this disordered state. He calls for help from Rann the kite, much to the delight of Baloo, who acknowledges: 'He has not forgotten to use his tongue [. . .] To think of one so young remembering the master Word for the birds too while he was being pulled across-trees!' (*JB*, p. 66).

Mowgli's journey ends at the Cold Lairs, a ramshackle palace that in Kristevan terms reads as a derelict feminine space, outcast by the paternal authority and made ruinous over time. It is here that the *Bandar-log* grotesquely mimic the civility of jungle society. The common sense and solemnity that characterises the Law are profaned and turned upside down by these (normally ignored) anarchic jungle creatures who incessantly babble their nonsense. In a Bakhtinian sense, they are fools given a voice, court jesters wearing the King's crown, with binary oppositions no longer demarcated but merging into one another:

> They would sit in circles on the hall of the King's council chamber, and scratch for fleas and pretend to be men [. . .] and fight and cry in scuffling crowds [. . .] and then they would all rush together in mobs and shout: 'There

> is no one in the jungle so wise and clever and strong and gentle as the *Bandar-log*.' (*JB*, p. 68)

The danger for Mowgli is that within the decaying palace there are no stable authority figures with which to restore order. Alone and abandoned to the mercy of these sinister child-like creatures in a desolate abjected landscape, Mowgli's situation attests to the fragility of the order of borders. It is the Law that stipulates difference and without its powerful and experienced keepers, Bageera, Baloo, Kaa, Father Wolf, and Akela, Mowgli has become in effect exiled from the stabilising forces of order.

Mowgli, quick and diligent learner on the cusp of taking the mantle of Master of the Jungle, recognises that the Cold Lairs, referred to by the people of the jungle as the Lost City, is the geographical heart of the *Bandar-log*'s resistance to authority but, perhaps more importantly, a site of resistance to psychological stability: 'Mowgli, who had been trained under the Law of the Jungle, did not like or understand this kind of life' (*JB*, p. 69). The speeches of the *Bandar-log* are parodies of the wise words of Akela, Baloo and Bageera. 'We are wonderful. We are the most wonderful people in all the jungle! We all say so, and so it must be true' assert the *Bandar-log*, painted by Kipling in a sinister comedic fashion; but the speeches are, according to Mowgli, 'nothing but foolish words' (*JB*, p. 69). Having no sustaining memory, they make a mockery of the ordered world of the jungle, 'they never remembered what they had seen and what they had not [. . .] they joined hands and danced about and sang their foolish songs' (*JB*, p. 69). Mowgli, recognising that the *Bandar-log* has 'no Law, no Hunting Call, and no leaders' (*JB*, p. 69), deems this type of anarchic behaviour '*dewanee*, the madness' (*JB*, p. 70). The city that the monkey-people inhabit is one of desolation and provides the setting for perhaps the most frightening part of *The Jungle Book*: that in which Mowgli is set adrift from the stabilising effect of the Jungle Law. In this sense, the abandoned 'lost' city can be read as a violated feminine space that has been left to quietly disintegrate.

Like the ambivalent megapolis of Kipling's 'The City of Dreadful Night', the Cold Lairs is a city in ruins. It is a waste ground where life no longer holds the promise of vitality and regeneration. This deserted, desolate place suggests the very borders that stand between renewal and deterioration have dissolved. The images that the name, Cold Lairs, conjures are complex and disturbing. It evokes a secret hideaway, an enclave away from society, like Stalky's dens, but takes on a sinister quality of feminine entrapment that has become a passionless, frigid site of disintegration. The feminine space is further suggested by the queen's entrance, once sumptuous with walls of 'marble tracery – beautiful milk-white fret-work, set with agates and cornelians and jasper and lapis lazuli' that cast 'shadows on the ground like black velvet embroidery' (*JB*, p. 70). The rooms have been transformed over time into 'passages and dark tunnels [. . .] and the hundreds of little dark rooms' (*JB*, p. 69). Its magnificence has decayed, and images of death permeate Kipling's descriptions. Darkness dominates the narrative, 'ruined gates', 'splinters of wood', 'worn, rusted hinges', 'trees [. . .] grown in and out of walls', 'battlements [. . .] tumbled down and decayed' (*JB*, p. 68). It has become a trap, a nest-like burrow where roofless houses are as 'empty honeycombs filled with blackness' (*JB*, p. 68). Shamsul Islam sees the images of disintegration as characterising Mowgli's psychological state of mind,[37] battling the forces of good and evil inside himself, as it were; and I would build upon this notion by adding that they represent an altogether more wretched and grief-stricken state, the melancholy of mourning that is engendered by the maternal body in the subject's drive toward socialisation.

The images of death and fragmentation in this lost city suggest a fecundity gone barren, dry and dusty in its infertility. The empty, honeycombed houses evoke the desiccation of a once yielding feminine flesh. A similar image can be found in 'The Mother Hive' (in *Actions and Reactions*). Generally regarded as one of Kipling's political allegories in which industrious effort is lauded over 'progressive' Liberal ideas. However, from a Kristevan point of view, the slow destruction of a hive and corruption of its inhabitants by the invasion of a wax moth reads eerily like the decayed feminine space of the Cold Lairs. The cavernous blackness that characterises the Cold Lairs replaces the space that once held sticky, unguent fluid, desirous and sweet, with an eerie abyss. There are images of violation and (female) fragmentation with fountains that have been 'split, and stained with red' (*JB*, p. 68), cobblestones that have been 'thrust up and apart' (*JB*, p. 68), the bloody image 'red sandstone reservoirs' is magnified, filled as they are with rain water, likewise the steps leading up to the reservoirs are red. Phillip Mason sees the appeal of *The Jungle Book* as universal because it 'comes straight from the subconscious'[38] and complies with archetypal fantasies of the inner self. I would go further by suggesting that they appeal because of a universal recognition of the trauma of exile from the maternal space that leads to the necessary abjectification of the mother's body. This empty palace foreshadows the more immediate scene of the brutalising of the maternal body in the penultimate story of *The Jungle Book*, 'Toomai of the Elephants'.

In this story, the jungle is presented as an enclosed, forbidden place that reads remarkably like the prohibited space of the semiotic. J. M. S. Tompkins argues that Kipling's jungle world is 'wild and old', a place where 'the child [is kept] in touch with its own reality'.[39] Beyond this, the passage suggests that cadenced lullabies, sung by human and animal mothers alike, are a substratum to pedagogical reasoning. The 'wild and old' can be read as a narrative encounter with pre-verbal semiotic material realised in the text. The narrative of 'Toomai of the Elephants', such as it is, follows a tired reiteration of imperial propaganda that Kipling seemed able to churn out with remarkable repetition. The self-worth to be gained in doing one's duty and persevering against seemingly insurmountable odds, the courage that was a prerequisite for intrepid colonial deeds, the honour in relinquishing one's individuality for the greater good, were part and parcel of his paradigm of Empire.

For three generations, the family of 'Little Toomai' (Kipling deems it unnecessary to furnish their surname; they are known only as Toomai of the Elephants, Black Toomai, Big Toomai and the eager apprentice Little Toomai) has been charged with attending to Kala Nag, the powerful elephant that has been in colonial service for forty-seven years. The fate of the elephant is intertwined with the Toomai family historically as well as linguistically. Kala Nag's name translates as 'Black Snake', and this is linked to Black Toomai. Both names have the connotation of excluded Other, much in the way that the 'native' is viewed by the white man elsewhere in Kipling's fiction.

> 'Yes,' said Big Toomai, [Kala Nag's] driver, the son of Black Toomai who had taken him to Abyssinia, and the grandson of Toomai of the Elephants who had seen him caught, 'there is nothing that the Black Snake fears except me. He has seen three generations of us feed him and groom him, and he will live to see four.' (*JB*, p. 135)

But this is an image whose prejudice moves in both directions, as 'Black' also summons up a young Punch having to reinvent himself according to the monocultural eyes of Aunty Rosa. The stories that paint withering portrayals of English clerics, government officials and military personnel in collections such as *Plain Tales* or in *Kim* also are telling indictments of the Englishman's bigoted gaze as much as they demonstrate his infantilisation of his native characters.

The youngest of the family, Little Toomai, is chained both by name and occupation to his native genealogy, which ensures he fills his father's role in the service of his colonial masters. He is spotted by the indomitable Peterson Sahib for his nerve and skill in averting a potentially dangerous situation involving the driving of wild elephants. The Englishman believes that Little Toomai, much to his father's dislike, has the potential to become an elephant-catcher. However, the mettle of his character is first tested, rather in the way that the schoolboys in *Stalky & Co.* or the young subalterns are elsewhere in Kipling's fiction. The precocious Little Toomai becomes the butt of both native and Peterson Sahib's jokes that his hunter status depends upon him witnessing the fabled elephant dance (all of them believe that the dance is merely a myth).

The story thus far is typically Kiplingesque, in that a young 'colt' is being put through his paces as a sort of rite of passage, but what follows is a disconcerting portrayal of the eroticised mutilation of a feminised jungle terrain. We see a threatening, pathologised[40] Indian landscape crushed by the might of colonial forces. Kala Nag takes little Toomai deep into the heart of the forest, and it is here that he sees the mythical elephant dance. From the psychological interior of this well-worn colonial tale Kipling conjures a passage that is at once sexually charged and deeply disturbing, for it offers a terrifying vision of the brutalisation of the maternal space. Where Punch was unable to neuter his wolfish surrogate mother in 'Baa Baa, Black Sheep', Little Toomai is given a ringside seat at Mother India's castration. Little Toomai is taken back to the unifying space of the semiotic modality and watches the violation and destruction of the maternal body in fascinated horror. Like Kipling's depiction of Aunty Rosa's mouth, which holds Punch in the Oedipal double bind of desirous orality and devouring jaws, the description of this encounter is an ambivalent fantasy of coveting the maternal body whilst simultaneously being repulsed by it.

As Little Toomai is taken on his journey into the heart of colonial darkness, the discontinuity of voices, which characterise the semiotic, are present in the night noises of the forest. The cacophony of 'bamboo-stem [. . .] the rustle of something alive in the undergrowth, the scratch and squawk of a half-waked bird' mingles almost imperceptibly with the landscape in 'the fall of water ever so far away' (*JB*, p. 142), and Kipling tells us that, taken together, the indistinct, nebulous noises 'make one big silence' (*JB*, p. 142). In her Lacanian reading of Kipling's fiction, Sullivan argues that colonial supervisors and servants represent 'manhood in the midst of the confusion of India's green fields'.[41] However, Little Toomai moving silently through a terrain alive with the hushed but vital sounds of the earth points to Kristeva's maternal 'music' that operates within the semiotic modality. As such it contains the unconscious impulses that are found both inside and beyond the symbolic borders of signification. In 'Revolution in Poetic Language', Kristeva argues that the semiotic rhythm within language is 'musical, anterior to judgement, but restrained by a single guarantee: syntax'.[42] The intoxicating sounds of the jungle, which lull the boy to sleep, take on a sinister aspect, for he awakes after 'some time' to a disorientated world turned upside down. There are parallels with Mowgli's experience of the *Bandar-log*, but in this story the overtone is much more ominous. Whilst Mowgli is partly thrilled by his ride along the treetops, still in some sort of command over the situation, the pre-pubescent Little Toomai rides through a surreal landscape that is bathed in 'brilliant moonlight' (*JB*, p. 142) on the back of Kala Nag. The elephants are colossal emblems of determined and durable colonial might, but have become as insubstantial as 'ghosts' (*JB*, p. 145).

The surreal images that characterise the abjected, desolate wasteland in 'The City of Dreadful Night', which will be discussed in more detail in Chapter 4 of this study, are reanimated in Kipling's descriptions of the jungle terrain. Night has been transformed into day by the transcendental magic of the moon. The faithful colonial servant Kala Nag has become the symbol of paternal authority in this fecund landscape. In an image that not only silhouettes the elephant's powerful physicality, but also his determined objective, Kipling presents Kala Nag in a mythologised tableau, 'standing up with his ears cocked' (*JB*, pp. 142–3). He is straining to catch the distant calls of his fellow elephants, united as they are in the singular purpose of crushing the fertile heart of the forest darkness. Kipling depicts an unnerving dream-like landscape whose daytime signifiers have become skewed and buckled. Little Toomai hears a noise 'so far away that it sounded no more than a pinhole of noise pricked through the stillness, the "hoot-toot" of a wild elephant' (*JB*, p. 143). The distinctly identifiable articulation of the elephants' call punctures the nebulous, hazy babble of the jungle sounds, the scrape of 'wild-pepper vines' or the 'creak' of bamboo (*JB*, p. 143), a 'hog-bear [. . .] snuffing as it digged', the 'splash' and 'rush of running water [. . .] through the bed of a river' (*JB*, p. 144). The instinctual pulse and throb of the jungle community lies underneath the elephants' signified 'voices' and is 'lost' to signified meaning. Kristeva argues that 'meaning is constituted but then is immediately exceeded by what seems outside of meaning: materiality'.[43] The materiality of these unarticulated cadences that characterise the jungle setting threatens the authority of (colonial) Law.

Kala Nag sets his sights on the 'great folds of the Garo Hills' (*JB*, p. 143), a gendered space that can be metonymically read as a fold within the maternal body. Like the feminised hills of the Himalayas that are beyond the reach of Englishmen in *Kim*, the Garo Hills represent a resistance to paternal control. Imaged in the feminine topographical features in Kipling's narrative, the semiotic oscillates dialectically with the symbolic. Rejection of the mother therefore becomes the priority of the paternal law, which is demonstrated by Kala Nag's destructive intention within the jungle space. Kipling describes the elephant as 'roll[ing] out of his pickets', moving 'as silently as a cloud rolls out of the mouth of the valley' (*JB*, p. 143), landscape and animal synthesised in one image. The journey into the forest is described in a decidedly sensuous way, an image at odds with a heat-scorched, threatening India that we find in stories from *Plain Tales* and *Life's Handicap*. In these collections India is laid bare and catalogued as if it were a cartographic exercise or a life-threatening abjected space that induces fever, madness and terror. In this story, borders become blurred in a landscape that has become both aqueous – 'a tuft of high grass washed along [the elephant's] sides as a wave washes along the side of a ship' – and vaporous: 'drifting through the thick Garo forest as though it had been smoke' (*JB*, p. 144). During the course of the journey little Toomai loses all compass points as the forest blots out bearings. He becomes both physically and metaphorically disorientated. Feeling takes over firm cartographic knowledge, suggesting through a Kristevan lens that the symbolic is giving way to the semiotic: 'He was going uphill, but though Little Toomai watched the stars in the rifts of the trees, he could not tell in what direction' (*JB*, p. 144).

The trees themselves are subject to the same disorientation, becoming animated as living things, 'all speckled and furry under the moonlight' (*JB*, p. 144). The forest, too, 'was awake below him – awake and alive and crowded', and it becomes more 'alive' the nearer Little Toomai gets to its centre. The earth becomes malleable and soft as if with a corporeal intimacy, a 'moist, warm earth' (*JB*, p. 144). The body of Kala Nag thrusts through the trees, and Kipling's description reads like a masculine penetration of the forest's yielding saplings, a remarkable description in its sexual implications given that this was reading material primarily designed for Victorian children:

> The huge limbs moved as steadily as pistons [. . .] and the wrinkled skin of the elbow-points rustled. The undergrowth on either side of him rippled with a noise like torn canvas, and the saplings that he heaved away right and left with his shoulders sprang back again, and banged him on the flank, and great trails of creepers, all matted together, hung from his tusks as he threw his head from side to side and ploughed out his pathway. (*JB*, p. 144)

This description is not only reminiscent of a Freudian primal scene that terrifies the boy witnessing this event 'all alone in the dark' (*JB*, p. 147), but also a scene of chaos where normally fixed signifiers are in disarray, to such an extent that Little Toomai wishes he 'were back in the *lines* again' (*JB*, p. 144, my emphasis) with their ordered military (masculine) structures. This passage is imbued with a rhythmic insistence on sensory impressions that give precedence to the noises of the jungle. It takes on an onomatopoeic and alliterative quality, with grass made 'squashy' by Kala Nag's powerful feet that 'sucked and squelched' (*JB*, p. 144). He is joined by other elephants, and the scene is one of 'great grunts and angry snortings' – the sexual imagery amplified markedly as the dance commences. Kipling's description of the clearing where the stamping dance will take place can be read as a vaginal opening that is skeletal, not fecund, in its inner core. It is a creeper-shrouded, desiccated abyss that engenders disintegration:

> At last Kala Nag stood still between two tree-trunks at the very top of the hill. They were part of a circle of trees [. . .] Some grew in the centre of the clearing but their bark was rubbed away, and the white wood beneath showed all shiny and polished in the patches of moonlight. (*JB*, p. 145)

And perhaps more sinister is the description of the abjected, intertwining flora with the power to bind and constrain that overhangs and wraps this frightening feminine space, giving the appearance of living things. But they are a twisted travesty of vitality, entities that overhang the borders of life: 'There were creepers hanging down from the upper branches, and the bells of the flowers of the creepers, great waxy white things like convolvuluses, hung down fast asleep' (*JB*, p. 145). They dangle like abjected markers that conceal an interiority to which life has visited, but from which it has long since departed. '[W]ithin the limits of the clearing', writes Kipling, 'there was not a single blade of green – nothing but the trampled earth' (*JB*, p. 145). The custodians of paternal authority trample the maternal space until it is stripped naked, devoid of its lushness and consigned to an empty abyss: 'The moonlight showed it all iron-gray' (*JB*, p. 145). Like a 'war-drum beaten at the mouth of a cave', the brutalisation of the forest clearing leaves a bloody 'raw earth' (*JB*, p. 147). The boy hears the grinding authority of the elephants' power as 'the crushing sound of juicy things being bruised' and trees that are 'creaking and groaning somewhere near him' (*JB*, p. 147). In response to this sadistic assault on the forest the trees seem to weep, but this elicits no compassion from the elephants, intent as they are on subjugating the landscape:

> The dew fell from the trees until there was no more left to fall, and the booming went on, and the ground rocked and shivered and Little Toomai put his hands up to his ears to shut out the sound. (*JB*, p. 147)

Mother India has indeed been brought to her knees, as when the sun rises to restore order – 'the booming stopped with the first ray, as though the light had been an order' (*JB*, p. 147) – Little Toomai sees that the elephants had 'stamped the thick grass and juicy cane to trash, the trash into slivers, the slivers into fibres, and the fibres into hard earth' (*JB*, p. 148).

The maternal realm, which has been so ruthlessly crushed in *The Jungle Book*, is exiled by the singular authority of phallocentric representations. Mowgli's experiences throughout *The Jungle Book* stem from the confusion he feels at being a 'man-cub'. Having yet to surrender to a linguistic structure that enables encounters with the inner self to be imaginatively symbolised, he remains, quite literally, the sum of two separate communities – the human and the animal, the civilised and the wild, the self and the Other – and can find no restitution in either. Unable to be posited in either realm, Mowgli's dilemma is never resolved.

In *Stalky & Co.*, however, a resolution of sorts is achieved. *The Jungle Book*, read in conjunction with *Stalky & Co.*, offers a reading of Kipling's adolescents that sees them move from the guidance of their tutors to being able to successfully master their geographical and psychic spaces armed primarily with their own cunning and ingenuity – and, crucially, by themselves. This marks a progression in the psychological development of the adolescent Mowgli. *Stalky & Co.* sees Kipling's adolescent boys performing dry runs for their future roles as colonial cogs in the machine of empire. Kipling offers yet again his idea of the Law, as set out in *The Jungle Books*. Again, the Law is a template that defines the rules of acceptable social conduct, which Annan argues were 'the keeping of promises, loyalty to friends, bravery, generosity, respect for parents' by 'which all races and creeds were held good'.[44] But the three adolescent heroes of Kipling's school stories are true masters of their school and natural environment. They subvert the rules of the school gleefully and with panache whilst simultaneously coveting the Devonian landscape, in which they find solace from the rigours of a harsh school regime, and reconnecting with Mother Earth's 'good currents', which Kim would later find so vital (*Kim*, p. 315). Mowgli's amorphous world of childhood recedes in *Stalky & Co.*, to be replaced by the trio's enlightened and transgressive subjectivity. The stability of Mowgli's subjectivity and his sense of place in the world are dependent upon the training that he receives from his elders. However, in *Stalky & Co.* the lessons that the boys learn go beyond the didactic instructions of their masters in a classroom setting. It is implicit throughout the story collection that the boys generatively teach and learn from one another. Having mastered the mechanisms of both their school terrain and countryside surroundings, and fearing neither, the boys are able to recover and reclaim for their own a feminine space by holding in contempt and thereby subverting the power of a phallocentric representation of the maternal realm.

Disparaging criticisms of the collection from those such as Robert Buchanan, who writes of 'the horrible vileness of the book [. . .] the vulgarity, the brutality, the savagery',[45] have done much to influence readers' perceptions of the stories, but Buchanan does not give Kipling credit for his masterful descriptions of the Devon countryside or the genuine comfort to be had from schoolboy camaraderie. The author's childhood memories of his time at Westward Ho! are reanimated with descriptions emerging from Kipling's retrospective gaze; it is a nostalgic viewpoint that appropriates memory and connects it to the *joie de vivre* of childhood. The undivided consciousness that characterises the semiotic is reanimated in the juvenescent sense of excitement and freedom that springs from carving covetable hideouts in the countryside:

> they flung themselves down on the short, springy turf between the drone of the sea below and the light summer wind among the inland trees. They were looking into a combe half full of old, high furze in gay bloom that ran up to a fringe of brambles and a dense wood of mixed timber and hollies. It was as though one-half of the combe were filled with golden fire to the cliff's edge [. . .] 'Fee-rocious old cove this' said Stalky. (*S&C*, pp. 31–2)

Descriptions such as these evoke what Homi Bhabha argues is 'the "deep" nation crafted in chalk and limestone; the quilted downs [. . .] the quiet cathedral towns'.[46] Rural England becomes an imagined country that offers the allure of a lost world. As a repository of archaic patterns of life and ancient familial histories, the individual is merely the sum of a conglomerate of tribes who have walked upon England's *green and pleasant land*. This 'other Eden' is a metaphorical 'fortress built by nature' where the wounds of a damaged subjectivity could be swathed by positioning oneself in the polyvalent history of England's past and, more importantly, an archaic Law whose evolution is dependent upon the collective experience of the different cultural, religious and ideological traditions of its many settler communities. Kipling's notion of the exterior sense of lineage, which is expressed in the geological layers of the English countryside, is linked to an interiority that evokes the coalescence of childhood memory. The collection does undoubtedly make an uncomfortable read when one is faced with the brutality and injustice of the school environment, but follow the boys out of bounds to their hideaways in the gorse and a complex textuality is revealed – not just, as Isabel Quigly argues, in the voices of broad Devonian, standard English, schoolboy patois, Latin and French, all of which, she argues, are skilfully employed by Kipling's trio when occasion demands, or the diverse references to classical and contemporary literature that zig-zag through the stories.[47] Kipling's elegant blurring of the distinctions between school and natural environments produces an interstitial space that topples the authority's representation of *outcast* subjectivity. His poetic rendition of the landscape as a life-affirming space reveals an author who, contrary to the harshest criticisms of this collection, resists the construction of a meagre, singular sense of (colonial) identity for his boys, and his writing in this collection expands rather than narrows the limits of their collective experiences.

In a similar way to *The Jungle Book*, the original edition of *Stalky & Co.*[48] begins with the three friends, Stalky, M'Turk and Beetle in a cave-like space, but with a crucial difference: it is a secret enclave that the boys have constructed themselves, and remains an all-male environment marked by the absence of a female nurturing presence:

> In summer all right-minded boys built huts in the furze-hill behind the College – little lairs whittled out of the heart of the prickly bushes full of stumps, odd root-ends and spikes, but since they were forbidden, palaces of delight. (*S&C*, p. 29)

Like the jungle space that has been brutalised in 'Toomai of the Elephants', Kipling again presents a castrated image of nature – 'stumps', 'prickly bushes', 'odd root-ends' and 'spikes' characterise their hideout, but the boys are not disgusted by or fearful of this stunted, uncomfortable landscape. On the contrary, they colonise it for their own, fashioning it into a coveted bolt-hole of 'forbidden' pleasure. Unlike Mowgli, the boys have not garnered this knowledge from their masters; indeed, it is a place that is 'outlawed' by the school establishment, and similarly affords no protection save that which the boys provide for one another. The knowledge of den-building and the enjoyment to be had therein is passed down from schoolboy to schoolboy. It is essentially a restorative 'female' space where the boys can forget the rigors of a bullying school situation, share confidences, smoke pipes together and read aesthetic literature without ridicule. Privates Mulvaney, Learoyd and Ortheris in *Soldiers Three* (1888) similarly find support in each other's company, but in this case the stakes are much higher. They are not just softening the blow of their brutal military existence; they must fend off madness and suicidal thoughts with their camaraderie, and, judging by *Stalky & Co.*, it is a skill learnt in boyhood.

The connection between the public school and imperial service is reinforced in the narrator's observation that 'India's full of Stalkies – Cheltenham and Haileybury and Marlborough chaps – that we don't know anything about' (*S&C*, p. 296). Ubiquitous 'stalkyism' is a continual (and much admired) means to subvert Kipling's 'Law' of Empire, albeit in the characteristically ambivalent ways that the Stalkies, Stricklands and Kims of his Indian world accomplish it. Kipling stresses that the boys have bought this 'place of retreat' (*S&C*, p. 29) at the price of their own hard work and ingenuity. They had worked 'like beavers' to create a place of 'meditation where they smoked' (*S&C*, p. 29) as their adult counterparts do in the later soldier tales. In this respect, the rigorous discipline of school life, which prepares the boys for a future as a cog in the imperial machine, is secondary to the shared experiences that extend beyond the classroom, in taboo 'palaces of delight'. These hideaways in the gorse become places where the boundaries of the subject are contested and opened up to the play of the voice of the Other. Beetle dubs their second lair the 'Pleasant Isle of Aves, for the peace and shelter of it' (*S&C*, p. 39). This is a reference to Charles Kingsley's 1857 poem 'The Last Buccaneer': Aves was a well-guarded island, an enclave of pirates living beyond the reach of the British navy, where men 'made laws so fair and free'.[49] Similarly, the boys reach their den by stealth, away from the prying eyes of their masters: 'they did not show up on the sky-line when they could move in cover' (*S&C*, p. 39). It is a shelter where 'pipes and tobacco [are] cached in a convenient ledge an arm's length down the cliff [and] their position was legally unassailable' (*S&C*, p. 39).

Stalky bullies Beetle into going forth into this untamed area of furze with the intention of claiming it for their own. Beetle pierces the furze, forcing wider the opening as he 'wormed into the gorse'. The sexual implications of the scene are made even more explicit by Stalky pressing Beetle to deeper penetration of the gorse bushes '*a tergo*'. Beetle has been transformed into something animalistic, crawling '[o]n all fours', his talk fragmented and punctuated 'between grunts of pain' (*S&C*, p. 32). The passage through the gorse is described as a tunnel at the end of which is a womb-like space. The boys feel 'inexpressible joy' at this enclosed intimate space that comprises 'a few square feet of dry turf walled and roofed with impenetrable gorse' (*S&C*, p. 32) – impenetrable, that is, only to those figures of authority back at the college. To Stalky and his compatriots it is a forbidden refuge, and despite the '[b]eastly stink of fox', they are enclosed in 'the heavy-scented acres of bloom' that are 'alive with low-nesting birds [. . .] and on the naked turf across the combe rabbits thumped and frolicked' (*S&C*, p. 33). Kipling is aware that these dens at school bring some relief from coping with a rigorous authority and bullying schoolfellows. In this respect, his trio's lives at the 'Coll.' have echoes of the author's life at Lorne Lodge, and his escape into 'ring-fenced' world of imagination was not that far removed from his fictional schoolboys' out-of-bounds hideaways. Here in their den, Stalky is monarch of this feminine space. In a decidedly callous sexual way he 'parted the tough stems before him' to make a 'window', below which is the 'deep sea sluggishly nosing the pebbles a couple of hundred feet below' (*S&C*, p. 32).

The waves from the sea, which are symphonically connected to the boys' hideout, recall the oceanic abyss of Kristeva's maternal chora. They are like the ebb and flow of pre-verbal vitality coursing below this idyllic space in the way that sound and gesture underlie discourse. Kristeva argues that the imprints of the semiotic can be transposed in literature into 'rhythms, signs [and] form [. . .] perceptible to the reader [. . .] and yet dominated, set aside, vanquished'[50] and as metaphors, the waves that break upon the shore represent a shift in the borderlines of subjectivity. In this respect they are metaphors for growth and change, movement from childhood to adulthood and between psychological territories. The connection of the waves to the boys' psychological development points to a world with which Kipling, Leonee Ormond argues, is 'particularly identified, that of the rite of passage from childhood to adulthood'.[51] The symbolism of the waves, which drenches the text with a rhythmic cadence, speaks of the porosity of boundaries between self and Other, while their distance reinforces Stalky's authoritative position in the symbolic. The image of the maternal, which occupied a place in Mowgli's imaginary realm, has in this instance been put in her place in the socio-cultural space – in the symbolic. Stalky commandingly spits on the back of an unsuspecting rabbit 'with great deliberation' (*S&C*, p. 32), reaffirming his place in the hierarchy of this world. Although Beetle, M'Turk and Stalky clearly enjoy this place and have a need to 'go native' from time to time to get away from the nullifying regulations at school, they are, 'lying on their stomachs', connected to the anthropomorphised sea that 'snored and gurgled' and the fauna around them, the birds are temporarily disturbed by 'these new animals' and the boys are wrapped in an intimate 'warm, sleepy silence' (*S&C*, p. 33). It is a space that is etymologically connected to Mowgli's world, as Kipling refers to it as 'the jungle' (*S&C*, p. 33); but it is a colonised world that is bent to the architectural will of the boys.

There is a marked difference to the wolves' cave in *The Jungle Book*, where Mowgli is under the complete protection of parental figures. Stalky's dens, as well as being devoid of females, provide secluded shelters from guardian figures *in loco parentis*, a notion that Stalky openly derides. For Stalky, *in loco parentis* is merely a weapon to enforce regulation, a morality with which to disguise the master's cruelty, in much the way it was used by the evangelical Aunty Rosa on Punch.

Beetle confides in his companions that their housemaster Prout had declared he was *in loco parentis*, to which Stalky bitterly replies: '[t] hat means he's maturin' something unusually dam' mean. Last time he told me that he gave me three hundred lines for dancin' the cachuca in Number Ten Dormitory' (*S&C*, p. 40). The boys' family configuration consists only of each other, '*Loco parentis*, by gum? But what's the odds, as long as you're 'appy? We're all right' (*S&C*, p. 40). They are, in effect, orphans but orphans without need of parents, joyously looking after one another. Stalky takes on the role of caregiver, referring to himself as 'Uncle Stalky'. The moment of writing becomes a way for the adult Kipling to rewrite 'little Ruddy's' difficult past when he had been orphaned at the House of Desolation, taking refuge in his solitary game of Robinson Crusoe (*SOM*, p. 8). Kipling can magically reinvent his parents and shrink them down into the cunning and vociferous Stalky and the regal, more literate M'Turk, and be welcomed into the loving embrace of a family circle that consists only of his peers. The surrogate parental characters of Stalky and M'Turk, distanced from the adult Kipling's feelings toward his mother and father, are made available for Kipling's engagement with the traumatic issues surrounding his childhood abandonment. In this way Kipling can not only protect his childhood vulnerability by the loving care of his compatriots, but also control and order his otherwise chaotic psychological wounding. Gaston Bachelard writes, 'The cleverer I am at miniaturizing the world, the better I possess it [. . .] Literary images that are commentaries on inversions in the perspective of size [. . .] stimulate profound values.'[52] The 'shrunken' Stalky and M'Turk replace the absent 'pater' and 'mater' in Kipling's fictionalised schoolboy world.

In *Something of Myself*, the Crusoe reference reinforces the image of a child abandoned without help or comfort. Yet it is an image that is used positively in *Stalky & Co*. The three friends revel in their outcast status, seizing any opportunity to jump the ship of paternal regulations and wash up in their haven in the gorse. Mowgli, whose age and vulnerability make him easy prey in a potentially hostile environment, learns to survive and ultimately master this world with the aid of those in authority over him. Punch's cultural vacuum leaves him vulnerable to Aunty Rosa's dictatorial regime, and he learns self-taught coping mechanisms during his time at Downe Lodge. But Stalky, Beetle and M'Turk have already mastered their lessons and distilled them into one axiom, almost Hobbesian in its brutality: that life is nasty, cruel and unjust. When Beetle makes the mistake of rising to an unfair remark made by the Classics master, King, about his inability to swim, Stalky reminds him sharply 'My Hat! You've been here six years, and you expect fairness. Well, you *are* a blithering idiot' (*S&C*, p. 75). Those expecting fair treatment are naïve and will soon find an untimely end in the rigours of colonial life, as the inexperienced, overly sensitive 'Boy' driven to a ghastly suicide in 'Thrown Away' most assuredly does.

In Stalky's world, the boys have not only learned their lessons in life well but have also, like latter-day Lords of Misrule, mastered ways in which to disrupt the status quo. Kipling presents them as anarchic pranksters, hell-bent on revenge on anyone who crosses their path. They come armed with historical knowledge. To pay King back for insinuating that their house does not wash properly, Beetle enables Stalky's plan of stuffing a dead cat into the roof of King's dormitory to come to fruition by means of the architectural knowledge he has gleaned from Viollet-le-Duc (*S&C*, p. 79). The three boys trap and torture two older boys who have been bullying a younger pupil with the help of Sir Francis Galton's *The Art of Travel* (*S&C*, p. 126). Beetle, M'Turk and most especially Stalky see little practical use in examining their unsavoury deeds, and are even less interested in contrition unless they are caught – and even then, their remorse is merely to evade punishment. They ruthlessly interpret the knowledge that they gain for their own ends. Both in and out of the classroom the lesson that they have assimilated is that life, such as it is, has no collective justice. Their individuality in this merciless school regime is dependent on and realised through their devious schemes and rebellious behaviour, to the constant irritation of their masters.

The anarchy of the trio is highlighted in their 'gloating', which Kipling likens to 'the primitive man's song of triumph' (*S&C*, p. 37). The laughter that accompanies their 'gloats' and pranks is a subversive act that has the capacity to undo the intimidating sobriety of the law of the school laughter. Cixous argues that laughter can reduce phallocentric power to a cowering confusion.[53] The very word 'gloat' highlights the moment in the text when the adolescent figures on the cusp of manhood, liminal beings neither in nor out of childhood but straddling the border between the two, laugh at the absurdity of the 'Law' that is imposed by their masters. The word 'gloat' becomes anarchy's calling card and subversive acts are reinforced by the 'words' of non-sense that syntactically surround it. For example, 'Fids! Fids! Oh, fids, I gloat! Hear me gloat!' (*S&C*, p. 37), and the oft-repeated '*Ti-ra-la-la-i-tu*! I gloat! Hear me!' (*S&C*, pp. 38, 41). It is almost a mantra to the boys, the words themselves have long since lost their meaning, but their importance lies in the joyous freedom from official regulations that 'stalkyism' brings. In these instances the law (and consequently the power of it) is made impotent before these rebellious, lawless boys. And in turn the boys find this spectacular collapse of the power of the law hilarious. The fearsome

King regards the trio as 'self-sufficient little animals' in 'need of a sharp lesson, if only to bring down their over-weening self-conceit' (*S&C*, p. 38). The adolescent is etymologically linked to an animal, and Kipling implies that the two states are comparable in his estimation. In this respect, the power of the law, manifested in both stern verbal remonstration and corporal punishment, is actually the masters' terrified defence mechanism against the imagined threat of phallic loss. It is a fear that is demonstrated in three different ways: linguistically, by the non-sense the boys talk; physically, by going outside the boundaries of the school grounds; and intellectually, by the aesthetic reading material of the boys. M'Turk has a penchant for Ruskin and De Quincey, while Beetle's eclectic reading interests are gorged by being given the run of the Head's 'brown-bound, tobacco-scented library', the Head himself 'prohibiting nothing, recommending nothing' (*S&C*, p. 259). More experienced than their peers, and like the shrewd and streetwise Kim, the trio do not betray their schemes of lawlessness as easily as their fellow pupils, who 'slink out [. . .] in haste' or 'smile nervously when questioned'. On the contrary, Kipling tells us that 'Stalky and his allies had long out-lived these manifestations of youth. They strolled forth unconcernedly, and returned, in excellent shape' (*S&C*, p. 40).

In this collection, laughter marks the crossing of a boundary between the proper and the improper, between subjectivity and the forbidden place of the Other, but more importantly, for the purposes of this study, it signifies a moment of transgression. For Stalky, M'Turk and Beetle, the pleasure obtained in defying the law is relocated in the thrill of existing momentarily in a psychological terrain outside the law. Their laughter transforms the potential terror of being outside of the paternal law into the joy of subversiveness, a state of almost Cixousian *jouissance*. Cixous' notion of 'feminine' and 'masculine' *jouissance* are linked to the ways in which both sexes experience a (sexual) pleasure that is almost impossible to articulate in language.[54] It is a pleasure that fulfils desire and contravenes the 'absurdity' of the law. Cixous argues that 'pleasure' can be had from the 'anti-pleasure' dictates of a nonsensical autocratic 'law', and for Stalky and his friends, laughter signifies a contravention of the masculine code of school.[55] Unlike Kristeva's notion of apocalyptic laughter which arises from confronting the abject borderline state from within horror – a notion that I will deal with in the latter stages of this study – the boys' laughter passes through death and abjection into life and *jouissance*. This is why the stories resound with an (albeit uncomfortable) joy that is, crucially, set in England and not India. India is an abjected, horror-filled terrain in the *Plain Tales* and *Life's Handicap* collections.

Laughter in the *Stalky & Co.* stories is far more positive and productive than the apocalyptic laughter of the kind found in stories such as 'Thrown Away', where a major and the narrator undertake in a 'grimly comic' (*PT*, p. 19) fashion the cover-up of a raw subaltern's grisly suicide. When the gruesome act is finished, Kipling's narrator laughs an apocalyptic laugh 'at the grotesqueness of the affair' and the horror of the situation is expunged in the 'laughter [that] mixed itself up with the choke' (*PT*, p. 20). Again in 'The Mark of the Beast', the narrator and the seasoned policeman Strickland engage in the sickening torture of a leper whom they believe has cursed their fellow Englishman, Fleete. Once the torture is over and Fleete has returned to his senses with no memory of the incident, Strickland has 'an amazing fit of hysterics' (*LH*, p. 207) at the horror of what they have done. The narrator too feels that they have 'disgraced ourselves as Englishmen for ever, and I laughed and gasped and gurgled just as shamefully as Strickland' (*LH*, p. 207). In the Indian stories above, the apocalyptic laughter springs from the horror of maternal abjection, dealing with the polluting affect of the bloody corpse in 'Thrown Away' and confronting a creature whose outward signs of leprosy are grotesque markers of the defilement in 'The Mark of the Beast'.

In *Stalky & Co.*, the abject is in itself a source of laughter. That is to say, the boys are recognised (and lauded by Kipling) throughout the school as outsiders, transgressors of the law and at 'home' in the Devonian countryside in a way that they never are in the harsh, masculine environment of the college. They are the anti-heroes of the school. They belong to the groups that Quigly notes are 'the intellectual or cultivated boy, the aesthete, the poet, the swot' and 'generally despised' as opposed to the 'school heroes [. . .] almost invariably athletes with the qualities that went or were thought to go with athleticism; physical strength, a masterful personality, and good looks' (*S&C*, p. xviii). Stalky, M'Turk and Beetle are characters capable of what Susan Sellers refers to as 'crossing unscathed the foul economies, in a spirited stroke, from [their] inexhaustible source of humour'.[56] Instead of being contaminated by death, alienation and abjection, the trio's laughter carves a passageway through the 'foul economies', the violent, extremely competitive, masculine school system, and turns toward a joyful and abundant affirmation of life. It is of little surprise that adult readers have viewed *Stalky & Co.* as a disturbing collection, dark and deeply seditious. However, as a pedagogical handbook for the preparation of Victorian and Edwardian youth for the rigours of colonial life, it is almost wearisomely textbook. In addition to what they learn in the classroom, the boys learn the skills of leadership, ingenuity in difficult situations, improvisation, camaraderie – these are all things that Kipling feels necessary to surviving life in far-flung colonies. The fictional college is a training ground for imperial service, where his foot soldiers and administrators can subsequently use the lessons they learned at school as survival techniques or coping mechanisms in gruelling situations.

One of the more sinister themes of the book is Kipling's notion that death is an inevitable risk of colonial life. Much is made of this idea throughout *Plain Tales* and *Life's Handicap*. In *Stalky & Co.* the casual acceptance of death is instilled into the boys from an early age. Sprinkled almost blithely among the descriptions of the pranks and jests are the references to the fate of some of the young boys who are destined to suffer bloody deaths in the service of Empire, even one 'Perowne who was shot in Equatorial Africa by his own men' (*S&C*, p. 212). The boys listen to an Old Boy tell of the death of a fellow school friend, Duncan, who had 'been shot through the lungs', but he reminds the boys that this is not an uncommon occurrence '[t]here are heaps of Duncans in the service' (*S&C*, p. 195). The young man's death is all the more poignant for the understated, almost flippant treatment with which Kipling renders it. The Old Boy has finally recognised that the injured man is an ex-pupil and they greet each other in a schoolboy fashion, the implication being that they are not long out of school, and Kipling quietly and pre-emptively connects Duncan's death to the boys sitting listening avidly to the tale on the floorboards of the dormitory. He tells the boys that:

> he said 'Hullo, Toffee!' and I said, 'Hullo, Fat-Sow! Hope you aren't hurt,' or something of the kind. But he died in a minute or two – never lifted his head off my knees . . . I say, you chaps out there will get your death of cold. Better go to bed. (*S&C*, p. 195)

The jubilation that comes through the text in Kipling's joyous rendition of the jest and pranks in the school is an act of defiance at the death that casts its shadows across the lives of these young men, in accordance with the patriarchal law of the colonial father that sends them off to far-flung corners of the Empire to witness their companions die bloodily, in madness, through illness or suicide. And in this respect the seemingly brutal laughter of the boys, far from being 'three small fiends in human likeness',[57] is an affirmation of life. Laughter affirms existence, overcomes the spectre of death and is characterised by being outside of borders and not only aligned to the maternal, but also finding solace within it. Laughter evokes a state that turns away from death and the horror of abjection, those sources of negativity which attempt to annihilate and diminish the subject.

Nevertheless, rebellious though the boys' laughter might be, it never seriously challenges the rigid masculine authority of the school. Laughter, like their dens, remains firmly off limits. The masters are custodians of the law and see the boys' wilful disobedience as well as their (feminine) hidden dens in nature as a sort of Bhabhaesque 'demonic double'[58] of the school's geographical and psychological territories. Characters that revel in an intrepid 'stalkyism', which bucks the colonial system, and have a love of a wild and ungovernable terrain are constantly in danger of being seduced by the heart of colonial darkness. Just as within Kim's psychology a constant battle rages between the 'two sides of [his] head', the Indian and the Anglo-Indian, the usurper and the upholder of colonial law, and just as Mowgli suffers from an irreconcilable allegiance to both jungle and village, so Stalky, M'Turk and Beetle face a similar dilemma. To become colonial servants these boys must, as Kim comes to do, acknowledge their outcast status and internalise the contradictions inherent in holding the dual subject position of complying with and being in opposition to the law, being in and out of bounds, as it were. One side accepts the 'stalky' tendencies that give shape to their subject positions, and the other side articulates their *difference* and the impossibility of a meaningful connection to the 'unschooled' aspects of their childhood selves within the paternal order. Escaping the rigidity of the school environment by roaming freely in the countryside is a way to postpone the inevitable acceptance of the phallocentric law.

Under the care and guidance of the Head, who is sympathetic both to their extra-curricular exploits and to the hard future that awaits them, the boys are encouraged to explore and engage with their natural surroundings; once they reach adulthood proper, the consequence of breaking the paternal law is potentially fatal. The transgressor of colonial propriety, the character (like McIntosh Jellaludin in 'To Be Filed for Reference') who in Kipling's fiction 'goes Fantee', faces madness, death and excommunication from the imperial community. By the nineteenth century, madness was precisely identified as mental illness, 'ill-being', in effect. British colonials feared that an extended working life in the punishing heat of India brought the threat of madness or going 'Fantee'. Stories such as 'The Conversion of Aurelian McGoggin' (in *Plain Tales*), 'His Brother's Keeper' (in *Abaft the Funnel*), 'With the Main Guard' (in *Soldiers Three*) and 'At the End of the Passage' deal with this notion of exhaustion and mental breakdown. Therefore their 'stalkyism' is always used according to imperial ideology once they begin their work in the colonies. In 'Slaves of the Lamp, II', Stalky is involved in a frontier war with two Afghan tribes. Heavily outnumbered, Stalky stealthily explores the wild terrain and manages to set the two warring tribes against one another just as he had done at the 'Coll.' with King and Rabbit's Eggs. Kipling's implication is clear that the template for daring (successful) colonial feats can be found in the 'stalky' instruction manual devised by the trio at school.

Despite Mowgli vanquishing Shere Khan in what is comparable to a spectacular feat of stalkyism, Bagheera reiterates that Mowgli must return to the man-village: '[t]he jungle is shut indeed to thee henceforward' (*JB*, p. 53). Similarly, the pupils of the College are fully aware of the future that awaits them. The sixth former Flint explains, '[w]e've got to get into the Army or – get out, haven't we? [. . .] All the rest's flumdiddle' (*S&C*, p. 187). With Beetle being the odd exception, the boys at this school are being trained for imperial service, ostensibly in the armed forces. But they are not the English gentlemen 'cleanly bred' and 'machinely crammed'[59] that Kipling cynically derides elsewhere in his writing. In his poem 'Arithmetic on the Frontier', Kipling, in his characteristic taciturn style, comments on the ineffectiveness of formal training when weighed against a colonial force that has scant regard for its enemies' knowledge of the local terrain:

> Two thousand pounds of education
> Drops to a ten-rupee jezail –
> The crammer's boast, the Squadron's pride,
> Shot like a rabbit in a ride![60]

Stalky, and to a lesser extent M'Turk and Beetle, are the courageous, daring, law-breaking, ingenious characters who not only 'know' their enemies' psychological terrain but can also manipulate and subvert the school rules. As with the intrepid chameleon Strickland, the precociously cross-culturally savvy Tods or the crafty dissembler Kim, Kipling lauds behaviour that goes against the colonial grain. He makes it clear that not only are the boys considered by their housemaster, Prout, as untrustworthy, but also 'there was nothing in their characters [. . .] at all commanding respect' (*S&C*, p. 29). However, Kipling makes us complicit in his admiration for the boys' miscreant behaviour. It is Stalky, and not the bumbling housemasters and school-sergeants, that we root for. Which begs the question: where is Kipling's austere and immoveable 'Law' that 'men broke at their peril'? Unlike Mowgli's teachers, most figures of authority in *Stalky & Co.* are reduced to pantomime figures that we, taking our cue from that master orchestrator Kipling, are encouraged to laugh and poke fun at. Prout's nickname, in comedic deference to his large feet and clumsy attempts to ensnare the trio, is 'Hoofer'; the substitute Maths master Brownell is presented as an arrogant, supercilious moral reformer; King, erudite though he undoubtedly is, is vilified by the boys; and a visiting MP who addresses the school with condescending rhetoric on patriotism is shunned.

Unlike the despised black sheep Punch, suffering impotently at the hands of the cruel embodiment of authority Aunty Rosa, Stalky, M'Turk and Beetle take on the masters one by one, and like the formulaic scenario of the original Punch and Judy show, set them up to vanquish them. We as an audience are supposed to laugh uproariously as each tyrannical master gets his comeuppance. However, in spite of the more odious episodes in the collection, which have aroused passionate feelings of disgust from its harshest critics, there remain the whispers of a damaged author who recognises the need for maternal protection and care. On this level, the anarchic antics of what one could rightly argue are some of Kipling's most disagreeable characters can be read as redesigned versions of the frustrated and abandoned child, now no longer cowering behind the threats and the posturing of the phallocentric power. By diminishing the power of the masters, it recognises the fragility of that monolithic edifice of power whilst simultaneously embracing the ability of a maternal space to bestow life that is, like the very nature of the symbolic, seemingly death-bound. Beyond the boundaries of school and the borders of the jungle, Kipling's colonial boys will grow into men who, in the service of Empire, will come face to face with the horror of an abjected maternal space. The lessons that they learn, both from their peers and their elders, will be the frayed and tenuous rope that will enable just a few of them to scramble up from the terrifying pit of the abyss and escape its devouring horror.

Notes

1. Rudyard Kipling, dedication to Cormell Price in *Stalky & Co*, p. 7. Further references in this chapter are given after quotations in the text.
2. Rudyard Kipling, *The Jungle Books*, p. 56. Further references in this chapter are given after quotations in the text.
3. Julia Kristeva, *Powers of Horror: An Essay on Abjection*, p. 16.
4. Zohreh Sullivan, *Narratives of Empire: The Fictions of Rudyard Kipling*, p. 180.
5. Sandra Kemp, *Kipling's Hidden Narratives*, p. 12.
6. Ibid., p. 11.
7. Thomas Pinney (ed.), *Kipling's India: Uncollected Sketches 1884–88*, pp. 18 and 22.
8. Quoted in Stephen R. Brown, *Merchant Kings: When Companies Ruled the World, 1600–1900*, p. 4.
9. Kipling, *Stalky & Co.*, Introduction, p. xxvi.
10. Yet it must be stated that throughout his writing career Kipling remained

sympathetic toward Hinduism and Islam. His stories are sprinkled with positive references to Hindu gods and goddesses. See, for example, 'The Bridge Builders' (in *The Day's Work*), 'The Miracle of Purun Bhagat' (in *The Second Jungle Book*), and *Kim*, amongst many others. For a more detailed analysis of Kipling's sympathetic attitude toward minor and major Indian religions, see S. S. Azfar Husain, 'The Religion of Rudyard Kipling'.

11. Adrian Poole, 'Kipling's Upper Case'.
12. Andrew Rutherford (ed.), *Kipling's Mind and Art*, pp. 97–125, p. 109.
13. Shamsul Islam, *Kipling's 'Law': A Study of his Philosophy of Life'*, p. 123.
14. Julia Kristeva, 'Women's Time', *Feminist Theory: A Critique of Ideology*, p. 50.
15. Philip Mason, *Kipling: The Glass, the Shadow and the Fire*, p. 167.
16. Christopher Hitchens,'A Man of Permanent Contradictions', in *Love, Poverty and War: Journeys and Essays*, p. 38.
17. John Thieme, *R. K. Narayan*, p. 152.
18. Quoted in ibid., p. 152.
19. Kathryn Castle, *Britannia's Children: Reading Colonialism Through Children's Books and Magazines*, p. 17.
20. Hélène Cixous, 'Extreme Fidelity'.
21. Kristeva, *Powers of Horror*, p. 91.
22. In the Introduction to the *Just So Stories*, Peter Levi retells the following anecdote from one of Kipling's contemporaries (who became a famous writer, Levi stresses) in a London club. During military service in India men were often called out on what was known as a 'cutting-out expedition', which involved 'chasing on horses in the dark' remembers the writer. 'Kipling never came with us,' he goes on, 'but he wrote about it with the most brilliant accuracy as I could ever have done' (Peter Levi, Introduction to *Just So Stories*, p. 9).
23. Charles Carrington, *Rudyard Kipling: His Life and Work*, p. 260, footnote.
24. Homi Bhabha, *The Location of Culture*, p. 130.
25. David Spurr, 'The Rhetoric of Empire: Colonial Discourse', p. 16. This notion typifies the Victorian anthropological and ethnographic stance, now frequently attacked by postcolonial (and other) commentators. For example, see Rebecca Weaver-Hightower's excellent analysis of imperial castaways and imperial conquests, *Empire Islands: Castaways, Cannibals, and Fantasies of Conquest*, particularly Chapter 1, 'The Monarchs of All They Survey'.
26. Mark Paffard, *Kipling's Indian Fiction*, p. 91.
27. See Jennifer Mason, 'Animal Bodies: Corporeality, Class and Subject Formation in *The Wide, Wide World*'.
28. See Rebecca Bishop, 'Writing the Body Wild: Primatological Narrative and Spaces of Animality'.
29. Islam, *Kipling's 'Law'*, p. 132.
30. See Thomas Aquinas, *Selected Philosophical Writings*.
31. Jonathan Rée, *I See a Voice: A Philosophical History of Language, Deafness and the Senses*, p. 332.
32. Julia Kristeva, *Revolution in Poetic Language*, p. 25.
33. Hélène Cixous, *The Newly Born Woman*, p. 64.
34. Angus Wilson, '*Kim* and the Stories', pp. 26–7.

35. Julia Kristeva, *Black Sun: Depression and Melancholia*, p. 15.
36. Noel Annan, 'Kipling's Place in the History of Ideas', p. 104.
37. Islam, *Kipling's 'Law'*, p. 134.
38. Mason, *The Glass, the Shadow and the Fire*, p. 167.
39. J. M. S. Tompkins, *The Art of Rudyard Kipling*, p. 69.
40. Zohreh Sullivan's term. *Narratives of Empire*, p. 25.
41. Ibid., p. 150.
42. Julia Kristeva, *The Kristeva Reader*, p. 97.
43. Ibid., p. 100.
44. Annan, 'Kipling's Place', p. 6.
45. Robert Buchanan, 'The Voice of the Hooligan', pp. 244–5.
46. Bhabha, *The Location of Culture*, p. 242.
47. Kipling, *The Complete Stalky & Co.*, p. xv.
48. 'In Ambush' opened the 1899 edition of *Stalky & Co.* Although published in *The Windsor Magazine* and *McClure's Magazine in December 1899*, 'Stalky', which now opens *The Complete Stalky & Co.*, was originally collected in *Land and Sea Tales for Scouts and Girls* (1923). At the beginning of the story in that collection, Kipling writes: 'This happens to be the first story that was written concerning the adventures and performances of three schoolboys – "Stalky", M'Turk and "Beetle". For some reason or other, it was never put into the book, called *Stalky & Co.*, that was made out of the stories' (*Land and Sea Tales*, p. 129).
49. Charles Kingsley, 'The Last Buccaneer', *The Penguin Book of Victorian Verse*, p. 349.
50. Kristeva, *Black Sun*, p. 22.
51. Leonee Ormond, Introduction to Rudyard Kipling, *Captains Courageous*, p. xxx.
52. Gaston Bachelard, *The Poetics of Space*, p. 150.
53. Hélène Cixous, 'The Laugh of the Medusa', pp. 347–62, p. 355.
54. Hélène Cixous, *Rootprints: Memory and Life Writing*, p. 53.
55. Hélène Cixous, *Coming to Writing and Other Essays*, p. 154.
56. Cixous, *The Hélène Cixous Reader*, p. 59.
57. Buchanan, 'The Voice of the Hooligan', p. 245.
58. Bhabha, *The Location of Culture*, p. 243.
59. Rudyard Kipling, 'Gentlemen Rankers', in *Barrack-Room Ballads and Other Verses*, p. 63.
60. Rudyard Kipling, *The Definitive Edition of Rudyard Kipling's Verse*, p. 45.

Chapter 3

Empire of Contradictions: Desire for the Impossible Mother India in *Kim*

> My brother kneels (so saith Kabir)
> To stone and brass in heathen-wise,
> But in my brother's voice I hear
> My own unanswered agonies.
> His God is as his Fates assign –
> His prayer is all the world's – and mine. (*Kim*, p. 300)

> [Y]ou cannot occupy two places in space simultaneously. Thatt [sic] is axiomatic. (*Kim*, p. 299)

Born to an Irish father, raised by an Indian prostitute and groomed by the British Secret Service, Kim's identity is situated between three competing discourses, Irish, Indian and Anglo-Indian. This ambivalence in ethnic classification is acknowledged by Kim in his tongue-in-cheek remark to the Pathan horse dealer Mahbub Ali, '"but *I* am a Hindu," said Kim in English' (*Kim*, p. 67). Both a colonial insider (by lineage) and a 'native' outsider (by upbringing), Kim's two-sided identity is contained within the phrase used to describe him, 'Little Friend of all the world' (*Kim*, p. 67). Unlike the mournful Mowgli, who can find no home in the Jungle or the man-village, or the Sahib/Black Sheep Punch, who is despised by everyone in England save his sister, Kim is loved and admired by English and Indian alike. The trope of parentage is in this novel established by Kim's affiliative identification with his 'replacement' guardians. An orphan with none of the attendant grief at the loss of his parents, Kim is guided through the narrative by a variety of characters vying with one another to be surrogate father figures. Thus his affiliative identification with his substitute fathers, together with the sustaining maternal space of 'Mother India', replaces Kim's 'lost' Irish father and English mother. The looming horror that characterises Kipling's treatment of India in his earlier stories is retranslated into a vibrant, welcoming India through which his picaresque hero can run with complete safety, frantically trying to exhaust his desire for Mother India. We sense Kipling's adoration for the India of his childhood, a protected environment that was filled with 'light and colour' (*SOM*, p. 3), where 'little Ruddy' was, like Kim, at the centre of these concentric circles of warmth and intimacy. The food, the landscapes and the peoples of the author's childhood were all to find their harmonious way into *Kim*, where every aspect of Kipling's colonial childhood is seemingly restored to its rightful place.

Written with the support and encouragement of his father and in an environment that was to produce the healing stories found in *Puck of Pook's Hill*, Kipling was able to imagine a multicultural India populated by a host of theologically and ideologically diverse characters and endow them with what he certainly believed to be empathetic attributes. Kipling's last major work on India, *Kim* can be read as a celebration of multiplicity. However, a novel that revolves around Kim's conflicting 'black'/white identity raises questions as to the viability of being able to sustain a plurality to which an adequate answer is not found during the course of the narrative. The contradictions of maintaining such an ambivalent subject position weigh heavily on the narrative, with Kipling unable to decide exactly where Kim's identity is situated, within the Indian or Anglo-Indian communities. Kipling would find a resolution of sorts in *Puck of Pook's Hill*, where a mythical father figure emerges from deep within the folds of the Sussex hillside and teaches the wholly undamaged, *un-orphaned* siblings, Dan and Una, that their identity and sense of place in the world is the culmination of England's heterogeneous settler history. The children are, in short, the products of plurality. In *Kim*, however, the savvy Anglo-Indian street-boy turned Buddhist disciple and British spy is ultimately unable to dodge the totalitarian colonial patriarchy, which culminates in his existential breakdown at the end of the novel.

This chapter will demonstrate the ways in which Kipling challenges the accepted traits of colonial identity. However, the writer who could expose the racial and sexual hypocrisy in the Raj[1] could not imagine an India without the 'benevolent' fist of British colonialism, which appears to be incompatible with Kim's dual Indian/Anglo-Indian identity. Kipling sidesteps the difficulties of undermining the dominant structures of British Imperialism by ensuring that the 'Indianized' side of Kim's head lies not with its indigenous peoples, but with an affinity to the land itself. 'In the *madrissah* I will be a Sahib. But when the *madrissah* is shut, then must I be free and go among my people' says Kim messianically; but when asked who his people are, he replies '[t]his great and beautiful land' (*Kim*, p. 184). Equating his psychological state of mind with a wild, 'unknowable' India, Kipling steers Kim's identity away from a cultural representation that would otherwise sublimate his 'native' side to the realm of colonial domesticity. Kipling shows us the English through the eyes of the colonised, and their portraits are not altogether flattering. However, despite Kim's protestations that the time spent in an English boarding school is 'a heavy time' and the 'strong loneliness among the white men preyed on him' (*Kim*, p. 151), there is not one native character that seriously challenges British rule. Kim's identity is nourished and developed not by militant natives disgruntled by a British presence but by a mythical Mother India that, like Stalky's dens in the Devon countryside, falls outside of the patriarchal law, and Kipling is freed from a dangerously subversive, anti-colonial stance. Kim, a name which in Hindi connotes one of high position, a ruler or king[2], is like a prelapsarian Adam running through an edenic India of implausible plenitude (poverty, disease, famine and drought are suspiciously low-key), with knowledge of and dominion over every aspect of his desire-fulfilling playground. Echoing Stalky's attitude toward the out-of-bounds spaces in the Devon countryside (albeit not quite written with the same tone), India remains an allegorical playground, a 'stupendous lark' full of possibilities (*Kim*, p. 131).

Certainly the eponymous hero of *Kim* is able to convincingly disguise himself as a lower-caste Indian, speak both Hindi and English, live at a Christian boarding school yet vanish into India's kaleidoscopic landscape. He is able to effortlessly marry a vocation of spiritual disciple with a career as a plucky British spy. Kim is the antithesis of Punch in 'Baa Baa, Black Sheep', who remains bereft of paternal protection and is cast adrift in a cold and unrelentingly harsh environment. As a white boy 'burned black' (*Kim*, p. 49), Kim remains all things to all cultures, using each as a mirror to validate every contradictory fragment of his hyphenated identity. Loved by all but reliant on no one, Kim is Kipling's most successful colonial adolescent. His archetypal colonial boy was evolving in both *The Jungle Book* and *Stalky & Co.*, but in *Kim* he reaches a sort of grandiose apex, bordering on what Diane Simmons argues is a highly developed narcissism.[3] Kim has the unlikely ability to be two sides of the same coin, both white and black. He affirms his colonial sense of self at the same time that he acknowledges his native Otherness. Kim can therefore maintain his sahib status at the very moment he disengages from the Englishman's cultural practices. Kim detests the white men who 'feed him raw beef on a platter' and is irritated that 'he must smoke by stealth' but understands implicitly that 'he was a Sahib' (*Kim*, p. 173). However, Kim is neither truly self nor wholly Other, but occupies a place on the borders of both. Like the erudite Bengali Hurree Chunder Mookerjee, Kim can embrace and see value in a white man's education but feels a deep-rooted (almost sexual) desire for the feminised Indian soil. At St Xavier's Kim had learned to write, 'magic worth anything else', but he 'yearned for the caress of soft mud squishing up between the toes' (*Kim*, p. 173). Kim's troubling blurring of identity overturns the logics of binary opposition whereby the masculine coloniser cannot acknowledge his difference whilst simultaneously sustaining a relationship to his colonised Other. Kipling's narrative becomes, in Cixousian terms, an 'ideological theatre where the proliferation of representations, images, reflections, myths, identifications, transform, deform [. . .] and invalidate in advance any conceptualisation' of self.[4] In this respect, Kim's 'difference' deceives his colonial identity as much as his 'sameness' disturbs his Other self.

Where can Kim's two-in-one identity be located within the novel? Kim struggles to find classification within the story, repeatedly affirming then questioning his heterogeneity: 'I am Kim. I am Kim. And what is Kim?' (*Kim*, p. 331). The 'unanswered agonies' (the 'what' and not who) of Kim's duality turn on the difficulties of sustaining a hybrid national identity, what Salman Rushdie argues is a conflict between the 'part bazaar-boy [and] part sahib'.[5] And throughout the novel Kipling outlines colonial 'types', the scholar, the soldier, and the priest who see the native in bas-relief to the supposed 'truths' they hold, truths that maintain the native is characterised by his deception and corruption, his 'lack' of truth. Kim is seen as a 'little imp' (*Kim*, p. 144) and 'wild animal' (*Kim*, p. 144) who has to be tied to 'the tent-pole in case he'll go through the roof' (*Kim*, p. 144) by the white men who feel that 'Injia's a wild land for a God-fearin' man' (*Kim*, p. 144). But Kipling undermines the 'truth' of these typecast labels by describing the English as 'oppressors' (*Kim*, p. 142). At the same time, Kipling undermines the colonial authority by highlighting Kim's training in the art of duplicity, a skill prized by the British Secret Service and eschewed by the Tibetan lama. Mahbub Ali tells Kim that truth can be potentially life-threatening when playing the Great Game – 'this is a world of danger to honest men' (*Kim*, pp. 192–3) – yet is astounded that the lama does not lie: 'Thou has never lied?' asks the horse-dealer. 'What need?' comes the reply. 'O Allah, hear him! "What need" in this Thy world' (*Kim*, p. 335). Similarly, Kipling's one-dimensional characterisations of the English are at odds with the complexity and richness of his Indian characters, however much the author's political allegiance lies with the British Empire's 'civilising' mission. Kipling can parrot imperial tenets in the grizzled Ressaldar suggesting the Indian 'Mutiny' was a 'madness [that] ate into all the Army' (*Kim*, p. 100), yet with savage irony lambasts an English priest for his racist bigotry.

The novel is keenly aware of the masculine/feminine, voiced/silenced, subject/object patriarchal binaries that the hegemonic colonial gaze dictates. Kim may be 'burned black as any native', speak 'the vernacular by preference' and 'consort on terms of perfect equality with the small boys of the bazaar [sic]' (*Kim*, p. 49), but he is 'white – a poor white of the very poorest', but a white nonetheless (*Kim*, p. 49). It is his white status that enables him to kick the Muslim Abdullah and the Hindu Chota Lal off the trunnions. He even manages to silence the policeman Dunnoo with 'an utterly unfounded charge sprung on the spur of the moment' (*Kim*, p. 61). Kim's colonial identity seems assured from the opening of the story, but ambivalence creeps into the narrative, for we are told his father died of opium addiction 'as poor whites die in India' (*Kim*, p. 50), and Kim, by rights, should share the same fate. He states emphatically that '[n]o man can escape his *Kismet*' (*Kim*, p. 166). His 'colonial identity' doesn't fit into a uniform category and is further complicated by his Irish genealogy.[6]

In actuality, Kim's future is the antithesis of his father's shabby life. His father's fortunes get progressively worse over the course of his life and he slips through the net of the colonial 'club', dying in obscurity. The street boy, lost to 'civilised' society is, in contrast, welcomed and exalted by the very British that allowed his father to disappear into the vast space of India. Kipling continually destabilises the accepted colonist/colonised binaries on which imperial authority depends. He compels us to question established colonial attitudes toward the native, continually moving the imperial goalposts, as it were, and asking us in the process to consciously or subconsciously collaborate in their extension. In this novel the gaze is not only an act of vision, but also an ideological stage that both articulates and validates power relationships. Encounters between characters in the novel unfold through the dynamics of a gaze, traditionally rendered in colonial fiction through the patriarchal laws of the white man. As argued in the previous chapter, almost invariably such a dynamic assigns the white man the role of viewer and the native the role of that which is viewed, establishing the binary modes of active/passive, virile masculinity/weak femininity. Kipling in *Kim*, however, destabilises an imperial ideology that offers the illusion of intellectual (and linguistic) control at the cost of diminishing the subjectivity of the native.

The ambiguous subject positioning of the major characters in the novel mirrors Kim's internal ambiguity. Difficulties of cross-cultural mutuality, deception and the problems of an identity, which occupies two disparate places in the mind simultaneously, are at the heart of *Kim*. By a neat feat of literary juggling, Kipling manages to adroitly balance two conflicting 'realities' throughout the narrative, the Indian and the English, as well as draw our attention to his shifts in perspective between each group. The imperial rhetoric orders and controls the white man and his native counterpart by a dichotomous logic of binary signifiers. But Kipling's perspectival jumps between these dual worlds create a narrative that is 'out of gear' with its colonial axioms. He performs a delicate narrative shadow dance whereby excluded Others slip from one side of the binary bar to the other with barely a syntactical stumble. Exclusion of the maternal body that guarantees a psychic identity within the symbolic can, in a colonial discourse, parallel those exclusions of the native that underwrite the white man's identity. Thus the ruling body in India forms its Anglo-Indian identity by excluding the Other, yet *Kim* transgresses the coded discourse of the imperialist and the Anglo-Indian filial loyalties. The problem of duality in *Kim* mirrors the psychological conflict within its Anglo-Indian author. The novel, like the man, is full of 'permanent contradictions',[7] to use Christopher Hitchens' perceptive phrase. As the novel progresses, Kipling presents us with a white man's vision of the black man that, like the curator's image of the lama, is blurred and out of colonial focus. Hence the binary oppositions of colonist/colonised and truth/deception are skewed and buckled. For example, Mahbub Ali's virility, loyalty and bravery are sharply contrasted with Colonel Creighton, who is presented as a curiously sexless, 'tortuous and indirect person playing a hidden game' (*Kim*, p. 165). Our chilly thrill at Kim's eerie encounters with the decidedly sinister Lurgan Sahib is matched in the frightening episode where the crone-like Huneefa performs an uncanny *jadoo* to protect Kim in the Great Game. Yet the patriarchal law of the coloniser in *Kim* would seem at the opening of the novel to be premised on the notion of a singular self-evident 'truth' that the white is, technologically at least, superior to the black, which in turn gives license to the imperial civilising which Kipling seems to be presenting as a backdrop to the novel.

The iconic image of the sahib Kim sitting astride the monstrous Zam-Zammah gun at the opening of *Kim* seems to point to this notion of the right of the white man to annex and rule over the countries that he grabs with a higher grade of weaponry. The Zam-Zammah is symbol of imperial might: 'who hold the Zam-Zammah [. . .] hold the Punjab' (*Kim*, p. 49). Kim is introduced sitting atop, assuming a position of authority as white man deftly pushing off the 'lesser breeds'. Zohreh Sullivan argues that the gun is the 'emblem of British authority'[8] and Kim is the white boy with the gun. Kipling seems to be pointing in this direction as he says, '[t]here was some justification to this [. . .] since the English held the Punjab and Kim was English' (*Kim*, p. 49). It appears that the author is implying that 'Englishness' is synonymous with a glorious image of the majestic British coloniser, annexing here and there whilst benevolently bestowing his fatherly protection on the always-ungrateful native. Kipling was to produce this kind of portrait in his stories with remarkable repetition. The near-perfect Captain Corbyn in 'A Sahibs' War' (in *Traffics and Discoveries*), the virginal George Cottar in 'The Brushwood Boy' (in *The Day's Work*) or the self-sacrificing Bobby Wicks in 'Only a Subaltern' (in *Wee Willie Winkie: Under the Deodars*) are examples of such portraits.

However, the same cannot be said for this complex and difficult novel. It is too simplistic to suggest, as Sullivan does, that Kim's deep-felt struggle is to 'attain the hierarchical position he merely mimes at the novel's opening'.[9] George Orwell argued how often Kipling was misinterpreted and to see Kim in this way captures Orwell's ironic image of 'some *pukka sahib* [. . .] kicking a coolie'.[10] Arguing that Kim is merely Kipling's colonial mouthpiece in native garb, a *pukka sahib*, is to diminish the importance of Kipling's own 'outcast' subjectivity, evident not least in how much the author identifies with his own precocious creation. Holding court in the train carriage en route to Umballa, we see Kim weaving intricate stories of his life for an audience held in rapt attention. His amphibious identity in colonial India means that Kim, like his creator, is not only able 'to think in another man's skin' (*SOM*, p. 122) but is also a master story-teller: 'as the occupants of the carriage changed, he varied [his] tale, or adorned it with all the shoots of a budding fancy' (*Kim*, p. 175). Just a little further on, we read that a supposed utopian ideal of the English character remains exactly that. The notion of 'Englishness' is undermined and the reality is rather murkier. Kim's biological father prefers opium addiction, 'drink[ing] and loafing up and down the line' (*Kim*, p. 49) to family responsibilities. Christian missionaries and 'white men of serious aspect' (*Kim*, pp. 50–1), we are told, are not to be trusted, and the soldiers of the occupying force are terrifying 'first-class devils' (*Kim*, p. 50). The parental care that Kim receives comes from a surrogate half-caste woman who, without apparent gain, takes over the responsibility of Kim's upbringing.

From an early age Kim learns to escape the colonial's rigid moral regime in order to live a 'life wild as that of the Arabian Nights' that the 'missionaries and secretaries of charitable societies could not see the beauty of' (*Kim*, p. 51). It is tempting to draw a parallel between Kim's life and the life of Kipling as a boy in Southsea. He knew by experience that the wonderful holidays he spent at the magical, unconventional home of the Burne-Joneses were not to be talked about on his return to Sarah Holloway's evangelical boarding house. From an early age Kipling was experiencing two disparate worlds, each of which would leave their mark and frame his reference points in very different ways. Peter Hopkirk notes that the Zam-Zammah at one time had a twin that was lost during a river crossing on route to Kabul. Today it lies lost, Hopkirk tells us, at the bottom of the Chenab River, forty miles from the city of Lahore.[11] The image of a twin in binary opposition is a potent one. Kim is an 'Indianised' Sahib; his 'demonic double' rests within his own psyche.

Unusually in Kipling's fiction, Kim's 'demonic double' is allowed a free rein. In this novel the imperial authority comes under scrutiny, as do its administrators, who can take a boy who does 'nothing with an immense success' (*Kim*, p. 51), encourage the murkier side of his character, that side which rejoices in small-time double-dealing and disguise, and create a duplicitous spy capable of callously betraying the lama's parental love. Viewed through the French feminist critical lens that underpins this study, I would argue that the curator (modelled on Kipling's father, Lockwood) of the Lahore Museum toes the imperial ideological line. The episode at the beginning of the novel in which Kim guides the lama to the Lahore Museum, known colloquially as the 'Wonder House' (*Kim*, p. 49), shows us a curator in possession of a cross-section of multicultural aspects of native India. Plundered, classified and timeless, statues and friezes become the metaphorical equivalent of the teeming and varied life that is relished by Kim on the Grand Trunk Road pegged out on the coloniser's dissection board. However, these abstracted illustrations of the diversity of Indian life are lying passive and codified in the museum. 'There were hundreds of pieces, friezes of figures in relief, fragments of statues and slabs crowded with figures that had encrusted the brick walls of the Buddhist *stupas* and *virharas* of the North Country and now, dug up and labelled, made the pride of the Museum' (*Kim*, p. 54). Sullivan argues that this has the effect of diminishing the 'social [. . .] complexity of India into the exquisite and timeless images displayed in a museum controlled by an English curator'.[12] Following on from this is the notion that the white man is the keeper of knowledge and that the cultural diversity of India is reduced, in the glare of the colonial gaze, to the insignificant 'forgotten workmen' (*Kim*, p. 54), excluded from their own cultural heritage. This warped colonial reasoning is premised on the notion that a white man's 'truth' and 'meaning' depend upon a series of exclusions of his *not* white native counterpart. Like the 'forgotten workmen', the colonial power renders its negative Other invisible, as a non-thing and his artistic works as well as architectural endeavours are classified by European scholars who have diminished and coded its spiritual importance according to western systems of knowledge and learning.

However, the lama's reaction to seeing the alto-relievo of the Buddha goes beyond the materiality of the carving to what it represents for him, that of a spiritual law. The lama intones the Buddhist invocation, '*To Him – the Way – the Law – Apart*' (*Kim*, p. 55). The Buddhist notion of an eternal Law recalls Kipling's notion of the archaic Law of the Jungle but with a crucial difference. In *The Jungle Books*, Kipling suggests that the jungle law evolved slowly over time to cater for all misfortunes and disputes that might occur within the jungle community. The eternal law of Buddha exists outside of time and independently of anyone who might have conceived of it. It is, as Vasant Shahane has pointed out, a law that is 'eternal and immutable and the Buddha is great because he once again made humanity aware of its existence'.[13] The curator acknowledges that the lama cannot be viewed through the colonists' gaze as a 'mere bead-telling mendicant, but [as] a scholar of parts' (*Kim*, p. 56). I would argue that the lama is in possession of a 'truth' that somehow eludes the educated western curator. He explains the tenets of Buddhism to the curator, talking at 'railway speed' (*Kim*, p. 56), heightening a portrait of the lama that can be read as a finer, more expert scholar. Elsewhere in Kipling's fiction, the image of the railway reinforces the technological superiority of the British in India. It is the curator who is seen in terms of a meaningless dead thing, frozen in time like the statues he presides over. His office is a coffin-like 'wooden cubicle partitioned off from the sculpture-lined gallery' (*Kim*, p. 55). The 'heat-split cedar door' (*Kim*, p. 55) intensifies the image, cedar being a decay-resistant wood ideally suited for coffins. The curator acknowledges the bond he shares, '[w]e be craftsmen together, thou and I', but the lama states that their friendship goes beyond artistic endeavours and touches upon philosophical reasoning, between 'priest and priest' (*Kim*, p. 60). Kipling shows the materialistic nature of the curator who longs to learn the technique 'of the conventional brush-pen Buddhist pictures' from one of 'the few in the world who still have the secret' (*Kim*, p. 60) and, ever the collector of museum acquisitions, delights in the 'open iron-work pencase [. . .] a piece of ancient design, Chinese of an iron that is not smelted these days' (*Kim*, p. 60). The author also shows us another 'secret' that the curator doesn't possess, that of a profound knowledge of the lama's spirituality. The lama, made ancient artefact by Kipling's depiction of him, brings his 'thousand-wrinkled face once more a handsbreath from the Englishman's' to *see* the curator and declares, 'I see thou dost not know. Not being of the Law, the matter is hid from thee' (*Kim*, p. 58).

The novel makes much of the difference between clear and obscured vision, which is captured in Kim's aptitude for disguise (or deceiving the eyes) that is almost artistic in its elegance. Kim is 'seen' in many guises.

He has the ability to captivate (almost) all who 'look' upon him – whilst the bigoted Reverend Bennett cannot be said to 'love' Kim, his gaze is nevertheless transfixed in fascinated horror. Whether we agree with Kipling's dubious political views or not, Kim dazzles us with his endless exuberance, irreverence and wit. Cixous writes that an 'invisible aura forms around those who are looked at well'.[14] And Kim is 'looked at well' because Kipling validates the 'Indian' side of his subjectivity that remains on the periphery of the colonist's vision and hence constantly eludes classification. Cixous argues that '[s]eeing before vision [. . .] before the eyes' narrative [. . .] is the science of the other! It is art in itself'[15] and Kipling lauds Kim's double-sided perspective, as opposed to those of the school teacher or the drummer boy, who are criticised for their myopia in regarding the native in terms of a western ideology. Sullivan argues that the 'curator's gift to the lama is sight'[16] in the form of second-hand spectacles which make the lama exclaim, 'How clearly do I see.' Certainly, the curator fills the gaps in the lama's knowledge with 'his mound of books – French and German' (*Kim*, p. 56). However, western scholars' knowledge is, like the 'photographs and reproductions' that accompany their studies (*Kim*, p. 56), merely mimicry of the real thing for, as the lama tells the curator, 'Your scholars, by these books, have followed the Blessed Feet in all their wanderings; but there are things which they have not sought out' (*Kim*, p. 57).

The 'logic' of a colonial law, which ensures the white man's relationship to his 'feminised' native counterpart, is realised in terms of binary opposition. Colonial 'Law' can only *be* because of this difference. The knowledge that western scholars do not seek out is the dangerously subversive side of this 'difference'. The lama's 'old eyes' (*Kim*, p. 57) see the knowledge gathered and bound in the books that the curator prizes as 'dried pith' (*Kim*, p. 57). The books are merely dry and dusty containers that echo with hollow ritual a 'Reformed Law' (*Kim*, p. 57) that has lost both its meaning and its vitality. It is this visceral difference that marks Kim from the beginning of the novel as a white boy 'disguised' as an Indian. He interstitially settles himself in the 'crack' (*Kim*, p. 55) in the door and as an image it works to reinforce Kim's ambivalent identity: excluded from the curator's office, he is inserted, silent but watching (being both spectator and silenced Other) into the rupture between the two worlds, that of the colonist and the colonised, east and west in the figures of the curator and the lama. Kim is emblematic of the struggle for a fixed point of reference in terms of identity. Through the curious doubling of his identity the novel continually asks the question of where the dividing line between self and Other stops. Like 'little Ruddy', who was both outcast devilish black sheep in Southsea and cherished, included

'O True believer' in the 'exotic' world of his Pre-Raphaelite relations, so Kim can assume 'two faces – and two garbs' (*Kim*, p. 81), 'Little friend of all the World' and a manifestation of the 'Powers of Darkness' to the English eye. The conflict that holding a dual-subject position engenders runs like a leitmotif throughout the novel. Kim remarks, '"I am to pray to Bibi Miriam, and I am a Sahib [. . .] No; I am Kim [. . .] Who is Kim?" he considered his own identity, a thing he had never done before' (*Kim*, p. 166). It is not until he is caught by his father's old regiment and plans are made to reinstate his 'Englishness', bleach the blackness from his real and metaphorical skin, so to speak, that Kim begins to understand what it is to be a sahib. Up until this point, his English identity is an abstract concept, nothing more than papers that hang around his neck in an amulet and some confused words that turn regimental loyalty and camaraderie into an incoherent prophecy.

Once caught, Kim learns that within the colonial system, white and black are presented as single units in a socio-cultural system and not subject to mutability. The opposition of English and Indian, imperial aggression and native passivity are contained within the English priest Bennett and the lama. Through a colonial lens, Bennett views the educated, spiritual lama with 'the triple-ringed uninterest of the creed that lumps nine-tenths of the world under the title of "heathen"' (*Kim*, p. 136). Bennett's notion of who he is as a white man and his sense of place in the colonial hierarchy is dependent on continually reinforcing the difference between the lama and himself. However, with the discovery of Kim, the concrete notions on which the imperial mission depends are shown to be constructed on foundations of sand. Bennett's colleague, Father Victor, states 'Kimball O'Hara! And his son! But then he's a native, and I saw Kimball married myself to Annie Shott' (*Kim*, p. 133). Kim's dual identity poses a problem for the priests in terms of precisely positioning the boy within the imperial system. If Bennett is not able to locate Kim within the colonial hierarchy, then how is he able to view himself in an unchallenged position of theological authority over the native population?

Like Mowgli's 'man-cub' duality, Kim's ambivalent identity is the outcome of starting life in one group but growing up in another group with conflicting languages, cultural mores and religions. Kim's sahib status, which incorporates physical markers (his whitened skin underneath his clothes) and aggressive attributes (he arrogantly displays a monarch-of-all-I-survey attitude to all native castes) are at odds with his fluid Indian side; Kim prefers the 'vernacular' to the 'clipped, uncertain sing-song of his mother-tongue' (*Kim*, p. 49), and begs to stay with the lama rather than be educated with the British. Knowing the intricacies of India's religions and adopting their customs and prayers for his own amusement or benefit, Kim's longing to remain with the lama, to be his *chela*, is genuine, we feel. Adopting an intimate pose, Kim 'squat[s] beside' the lama and, like a child holding onto 'a fold of his clothing', speaks of his love for his beloved teacher and the sorrow of an exile that is imminent (*Kim*, p. 139). The juxtaposition of the spirituality of the lama and the 'clumsy' hollow tenets of Christianity that Bennett blithely repeats leaves the two priests 'overwhelmed'. We are left in no doubt as to Kipling's admiration for his Buddhist holy man. Edward Said makes clear that 'Kipling renders [the character of the lama] with little false exoticism, that we are able to believe in the novelist's respect for this particular pilgrim'.[17] Kipling imbues the lama with an authority that equals, if not eclipses his European counterparts. Kipling writes '[d]ignified and unsuspicious [the lama] strode into the little tent, saluted the Churches as a Churchman, and sat down by the open charcoal brazier' (*Kim*, p. 136). Kipling furthers this image by describing the lama as if he is a religious statue: '[t]he yellow lining of the tent reflected in the lamp-light made his face red-gold' (*Kim*, p. 136).

In the exchange between the priests Kipling (particularly in his noticeable disgust of the Protestant priest) touches on the theme of an Anglo-Indian identity whose moral justification to rule is dependent upon an inverse image of the native. In his poem 'We and They', he questions the validity of such a viewpoint,

> All good people agree,
>   And all good people say,
> All nice people, like Us, are We
>   And every one else is They:
> But if you cross over the sea,
>   Instead of over the way,
> You may end by (think of it!) looking on We
>   As only a sort of They![18]

Certainly Kipling's portrayal of Bennett as the narrow-minded, religious dogmatist seems to bear out his observations that the native Indian has been positioned as the Other or the 'They' in relation to the Englishman's concept of a self that is colonised and governed by a patriarchal law.

The emotional and intellectual implications of Bennett's self-affirming viewpoint are that his racist bigotry is a commonplace nineteenth-century narrative. Father Victor is more sympathetic, but even he regards the Lama as an 'old beggar-man' (*Kim*, p. 160). The lama has an existential and phenomenological background that is positioned in relation to, firstly, the white man's conceptual mapping of self and Other, and secondly, the ontological limits of Christianity that negatively structure the lama's Buddhism in binary opposition. When Kim relates the lama's search for the River of Arrow to the priests, Kipling writes, '"But this is gross blasphemy,' cried the Church of England' (*Kim*, p. 137). We are left in no doubt as to where the author's sympathies lie. With a hint of wry comedy that lifts an otherwise forlorn section (Kim and the lama are about to be separated), Kipling allows us to be party to an exchange that the priests do not understand, as it is spoken in the 'vernacular'. Kim derides their lack of knowledge of Hindi, describing them as 'uncurried donkeys' and Father Victor as 'a thin fool who looks like a camel' (*Kim*, p. 136). The lama chides Kim for his comments, saying, 'it is not well to make jest of their ignorance' (*Kim*, p. 136). This exchange echoes the way in which Kipling felt that it was the Englishman's duty to understand the Indian peoples, not 'as excitable masses of barbarism [. . .] or the downtrodden millions [. . .] groaning under the heel of an alien and unsympathetic despotism',[19] but for their culture and idioms, as 'men with a language of their own which is your [the Englishman's] business to understand; and proverbs, which is your business to quote [. . .] and bywords and allusions which is your business to enter into and sympathise with'.[20]

Kipling's treatment of the Bengali intelligence operator, Hurree Chunder Mookerjee (also known as Hurree Babu or The Babu) uncovers the instability of the colonialists' belief in the absolute right of the white man to rule India, as well as his cultural, moral and intellectual superiority. Hurree Chunder's complex identification with his own sense of self, as well as how others perceive him, represents the dilemma of how his undeniable value and courageous actions are perceived by the British secret service. Our first encounter with him is at Lurgan Sahib's shop. In contrast to Kim's fluid athleticism, Kipling's description of Hurree Chunder primarily elicits our disgust: there 'entered a hulking, obese Babu whose stockinged legs shook with fat', who walked 'with the gait of a bogged cow' (*Kim*, p. 208). According to Nandi Bhatia, Kipling's mocking treatment of Hurree Chunder, particularly his speech, is a way of 'maintaining the babu's subservience by painting the picture of a silly Bengali babu who apes the Englishman with his broken English'.[21] He does indeed seem to ridicule his accent by misspelling the babu's words and highlighting his accent, 'I am of the opeenion that it [Kim's mimicry] is most extraordinary and effeecient performance' (*Kim*, p. 207). Yet Kim mirrors the babu's turn of English phrase. For example, when Kim is in possession of the foreign spies' letter, he moans 'how the deuce am I to tell Hurree Babu, and *whatt* the deuce am I to do?' (*Kim*, p. 303). Purnima Bose argues that the British created these stereotypes in response to a growing fear of the Bengali community who, having received a western-style education, were able to challenge colonial rule. The Bengalis were prominent in the Nationalist movement in India and it was precisely this open defiance of the imperial governing body that, Bose argues, led to the Bengalis being 'dismissed as comic imitations of westerners. They were virulently caricatured in the figure of the Bengali Babu: a small dark-skinned, effeminate intellectual who had an imperfect command of English'.[22] Contained within this image is the Victorian Anglo-Indian's clichéd view of an educated Bengali. *Hobson-Jobson* notes that, in Anglo-Indian circles, use of the term babu carried with it 'a slight savour of disparagement, as characterizing a superficially cultivated, but too often effeminate, Bengali'.[23] This would seem to bear out what Said suggests is Kipling's characterisation of the Babu, 'almost always funny, or gauche, or somehow caricatural not because he is incompetent or inept in his work – on the contrary he is exactly the opposite – but because he is not white'.[24]

However, this does not seem to fit with the comments Kipling inserts into the gap between his description of the Babu and his rendition of his speech. Kipling writes of Kim's annoyance that Lurgan's attention is not on Kim's antics, as it has been up until this point, but more on Hurree Chunder's reaction, 'Kim opened on him with a shower of wayside chaff. Lurgan Sahib – this annoyed Kim – watched the Babu and not the play' (*Kim*, p. 207). Lurgan goes on to explain not only his exceptional character, but also the connection that Kim has with the Bengali spy:

> From time to time, God causes men to be born – and thou art one of them – who have a lust to go abroad at the risk of their lives and discover news [. . .] These souls are very few; and of these few, not more than ten are of the best. Among these ten I count the Babu. (*Kim*, p. 209)

Neither does it fit with Kipling's observation of Hurree Chunder's fortitude, 'his day's marches [. . .] would astonish folk who mock at his race' (*Kim*, p. 317); nor, as Thomas Metcalf points out, with the way he leads the two Russian spies through the unremittingly harsh passes of the Himalayas to their downfall, despite his protestations that he is a 'fearful man' (*Kim*, p. 329).[25] We feel that Kipling's sympathy lies with Hurree Chunder's troubled sense of self in an India whose national identity has been disfigured by a British presence: '[h]e represents *in petto* India in transition', says the Russian, 'the monstrous hybridism of East and West' (*Kim*, p. 288). His companion tellingly replies '[h]e has lost his own country and has not acquired any other. But he has the most complete hatred of his conquerors' (*Kim*, p. 288). Indeed, Hurree Chunder can match Creighton for his ethnographical, botanical and cultural knowledge of India as well as his command of the western canon of literature, but is denied entrance into the Royal Society because, as Said points out, he is 'not white'. It is Kipling who makes us aware of the injustice done to Hurree Chunder because of the colour of his skin.

Kipling's 'real' and 'imagined' India in *Kim* is a complex, intricate narrative interweaving. India is 'real' in so far as it represents the various castes and a true geographical location, but the nostalgia with which Kipling renders this idyllic India of his childhood recollection heightens, in a decidedly Pre-Raphaelite way, the intensity of his array of characters' emotions, and by extension his readers' emotions. No one would argue with the emotional impact of *Kim*, however one might view its political motives; it is a novel that, as Harold Bloom argues, 'move us to tears'.[26] Capturing what has been seen elsewhere in Kipling's fiction as a frightening, chaotic India with minute details rendered with exacting clarity, expresses the emotional turmoil of most of his characters and thus intensifies the emotional response of the novel's readers. The interweaving of geographic and scientific accuracy with a style of prose that is deeply poetic brings to the novel a psychological element through which visual signifiers – such as the vibrancy of life on the Grand Trunk Road – become metaphors for Kim's struggle for identity as he journeys toward enlightenment in the novel. In *Kim* we see Kipling continually reconfiguring the colonial boundaries toward the white man and his place in colonial India. Just as Hurree Chunder represents India 'in transition', so societal contradictions in the novel (and within Kim) reveal alternative constructions of the self. The boys of St Xavier's, with their Anglo-Indian and mixed-race identities, express their thoughts in a language that is 'mixed with quaint reflections, borrowed unconsciously from native foster-mothers, and turns of speech that showed they had been translated from the vernacular' (*Kim*, p. 172). Their hybrid speech has epistemological implications; it denotes an identity that unsettles the dominant discourse of the imperialist. In this setting, Kim feels his hybridity to be acknowledged and understood. His compatriots' talk was 'not the insipid, single-word of the drummer-boys. It dealt with a life he knew and in part understood' (*Kim*, p. 172). Unlike his contemporaries – and perhaps this is why *Kim* continues to enthral modern readers – Kipling moves beyond the restrictive boundaries of the conventional representation of the native as well as the colonial administrator and the Anglo-Indian.

Kim was written in the year following the death of Kipling's beloved 'Uncle Ned', Edward Burne-Jones, a leading light of the Pre-Raphaelite Brotherhood, and its 'overlaid tints and textures' (*SOM*, p. 111)[27] owe much to their unconventional style of art. Martin Seymour-Smith argues that the appeal of the novel lies in the author 'reaping the harvest of the Pre-Raphaelitism of his youth'.[28] Kipling's writing style retains a whisper of Pre-Raphaelitism, especially in his descriptions of the Indian landscape, which are almost hallucinatory in detail and intensely emotional. *Kim* is a novel that shows the correspondence between Kipling's sharp and minute representations of the Indian landscape as well as its peoples, its cuisine, its architectural structures and mechanical objects. For example, when Kim leads the lama through the Kashmir Serai bazaar we encounter Kipling's intimate knowledge of the street-life of Allahabad and Lahore, where he would 'wander till dawn in all manner of odd places [. . .] which are not a bit mysterious [. . .] for the sheer sake of looking' (*SOM*, p. 33). As the lama and Kim pass through the bazaar Kipling's dense syntax begins to sprawl, sentences becoming longer with images that wind around one another, merging into one hazy, surreal depiction of street life:

> it was [the lama's] first experience of a large manufacturing city, and the crowded tram-car with its continually squealing brakes frightened him. Half pushed, half towed, he arrived at the high gate of the Kashmir Serai: that huge open square over against the railway station, surrounded with arched cloisters where the camel and horse-caravans put up on their return from Central Asia. Here were all manner of Northern folk, tending tethered ponies and kneeling camels; loading and unloading bales and bundles; drawing water for the evening meal at the creaking well-windlasses; piling grass before the shrieking, wild-eyed stallions; cuffing the surly caravan dogs; paying off camel-drivers; taking on new grooms; swearing, shouting, arguing, and chaffering in the packed square. The cloisters, reached by three or four masonry steps, made a haven of refuge around this turbulent sea. (*Kim*, p. 65)

Kipling's sketch of the industrial urban area, which at first frightens the more tranquil, aesthetic lama, zooms in on the microscopic life of the city. As if 'in a dream' (*Kim*, p. 65), where meaning is obscured by the play of metaphor and metonymy, the lama is '[h]alf pushed, half towed' by Kim. The water-image picks up not only the lama's search for his mythical River of Arrow, but also the fluid maternal realm. The chaotic yet coherent city life that nourishes and envelops Kim, validating and 'voicing' his Other self, is a manifestation of the semiotic realm. The fixed signifiers of the colonist who sees his native Other in antithesis (the weak, effeminate, inactive Asiatic), become, like the lama, aqueous. The teeming city, which elsewhere in Kipling's fiction is a horror-strewn wasteland, encompasses what Kristeva describes as 'the strange gamut of forgotten body relationships with [the] mother'.[29] The tones of the incoherent speech, the gestures, the colours, the sounds and smells of this vibrant city scene enable Kim to achieve a sort of corporeal fusion with an undulating maternal realm, marked by the absence of the colonial figure. During the course of the passage Kipling's fluent, rippling syntax becomes, like Cixous' *écriture féminine*, an act of *un-silencing*, *un-blinding*, *un-darkening* and *un-diluting* the Indian side of Kim's head.[30]

Although the city scene is pushed up against and enclosed within imposing symbols of colonial might, the railway station and 'arched cloisters', Kipling's description becomes a radical reinscription of the feminine as an antidote to masculine colonial alienation. The pulse and noise of the city life is written in the single lengthy, sprawling sentence that encompasses and connects 'all manner of Northern folk'. The various Indian groups have reclaimed the cloisters, even if these immobile structures are separated from the heaving square. The swirling crowd washes over the 'three or four masonry steps' that offer an island of calm and *silence* in this otherwise boisterous atmosphere, which pounds not the intellect but the senses. Kipling steps away from a description that merely 'represents' or explains native life; rather, his writing responds to and recalls what he views as that utopian life of his childhood in Bombay. The native Other is outside of the masculine coloniser's gaze at this moment in the text. The fluid, unified street life of the Kashmir Serai is as a 'fleshed' machine, where the people, like well-oiled cogs, are intricate mechanisms through which the materiality of city life can be contemplated by Kipling with a wonder that allows the native Indians to be 'spoken' of outside of the linguistic economy of the coloniser's thinking. Almost as a precursor to the stream-of-consciousness style of writing that Joyce[31] produces in the fleshy, corporeal language that characterises Molly Bloom's monologue at the end of *Ulysses*, Kipling's language is able to assume an identification with the Other, with the sounds and smells that characterise the pre-verbal realm of childhood. The frightening 'squealing brakes' give way to 'creaking well-windlasses' and the 'shrieking, wild-eyed stallions' are no longer the cause of anxiety, linked as they are to the genial polyvalent voices that fill the square with indiscernible speech. It is the life that the 'keen-eyed three-year-old baby' Kim experienced with his father, 'loafing up and down the line' (*Kim*, p. 49) instead of being sent, by western 'societies and chaplains' to a 'Masonic Orphanage in the Hills' (*Kim*, pp. 49–50).

In contrast, the routines, the people, the military manoeuvres of the colonists, jar unerringly in a novel whose native inhabitants fuse in harmony with their surroundings in the complex polychromatic life of India. The lama explains that this is emblematic of human existence according to the 'Excellent Law' (*Kim*, p. 61) of Buddhism that binds all living creatures, humans and animals alike, to an intertwining fate on the Wheel of Life. The monolithic British colonising force is at odds with the variegated Indian life that works in synthesis with both beast and nature, emblematised in the heterogeneous nature of the Grand Trunk Road. Kipling, in Chapter Five, presents the British as intruders. With barely distinguishable individual features, the Mavericks, like brutish red-coated bulls, charge through Indian fertile green fields with all the military and religious might they can muster. The British are for the most part sketched as two-dimensional stick figures, uniformly aggregated in Kipling's ironic reversal of the Victorian habit of 'lump[ing] nine-tenths of the world under the title of "heathen"' (*Kim*, p. 136). In contrast to the white-skinned group into which he was born, Kim, like Stalky out of bounds, feels much more at ease in 'the happy Asiatic disorder' into which he dives wholeheartedly (*Kim*, p. 112). Kipling speaks directly to us, stating emphatically that this life is more satisfying 'if only you allow time, [it] will bring you everything that a simple man needs' (*Kim*, p. 112). More complex characters such as Colonel Creighton, Lurgan Sahib and, to an extent, Father Victor owe much of their appeal to their cross-cultural influences. Creighton's 'fluent and picturesque Urdu' (*Kim*, p. 166) impresses Kim as much as his reputation in the bazaar (*Kim*, p. 161). The almost occult 'healer of sick pearls', Lurgan treats Kim as an 'equal on the Asiatic side' (*Kim*, p. 199). Father Victor is uncomfortable with the (partitioning) term 'Roman Catholic' to describe his religion, preferring instead the all-encompassing 'Catholic', 'you'll remember, when they ask you [Kim] your religion, that you're a Cath'lic. Better say Roman Cath'lic, tho' I'm not fond of the word' (*Kim*, p. 165). Father Victor's statement captures with striking force the Englishman's need to position the 'non-English' as Other in relation to the sense of self which has been colonised by his phallogocentric language of binary opposites.

The crucial chapter, which sees Kim returned in metaphorical chains to his white bloodline, continuing the trope of 'lost' parentage, begins with Kipling's biblical allusion to the prodigal son. However, his epigraph echoes the novel's trajectory – an opportunistic son, who by feats of cunning 'stalkyism', is able to be 'fed, forgiven and known again'. But it comes with a caveat: he must be 'claimed by bone of my bone again' (*Kim*, p. 126). The wayward son, however, does not enjoy being with his family, preferring the 'husks' to the 'fatted calf' and delights in returning to his 'styes afresh' (*Kim*, p. 126). For the cross-culturally savvy bazaar boy, the British presence – keen to bestow their cultural 'fatted calf' upon Kim – is a malignant power that forces him to be (temporally) 'orphaned' from his beloved lama and, for the first time perhaps, to feel the grief of orphanhood. Kipling's description of the appearance of British troops in the novel heightens the image of a terrifying colonising force intent on taming the landscape. His intricately woven image of the mango groves that frame the resting place of the Sahiba's entourage, where Kim is wrapped in its intimate 'family' space, is shattered by the appearance of the British troops. Kim and the lama discover 'a broad tract of grazing-ground, brown and purple in the afternoon light, with a heavy clump of mangoes in the centre' and Kim thinks it 'curious that no shrine stood in so eligible a spot; the boy was observing as any priest for these things' (*Kim*, p. 127). This unclaimed patch of land is a metaphorical, life-giving maternal space that exists independently from a paternal law, where both the lama and Kim are able to 'gaze' upon its beauty. Not codified in the name (or word) of religion or the crushing might of the British military, Kim is about to witness the colonisation of a maternal space that exists, like Kim himself, as an uncultivated subversive energy that threatens the coherence of the phallogocentric law. The white soldiers 'made small by [. . .] distance' suddenly materialise, like terrifying spectres, from 'behind the thick trunks in the cool dark of the mango-tope' (*Kim*, p. 127). The entrance to the womb-like space of the mango-tope is pierced, 'marked out' as white man's territory and spread-eagled by the soldiers.

Kipling's depiction can be read as a brutal violation that foreshadows the company officers laying claim to the tope's interior space: '[t]hey bore five-foot sticks with fluttering flags, and called to each other as they spread over the flat earth'. Pinioned, subjugated and crushed, this fertile ground is penetrated by the white man: 'At last they entered the mango-grove, walking heavily' (*Kim*, p. 127). The voices of the foot soldiers, the lowest caste in the colonial hierarchy, are rendered brutish and primitive, pig-like as they grunt their clumsy, ragged speech, 'It's here or hereabouts – officers' tents under the trees, I take it, an' the rest of us can stay outside. Have they marked out for the baggage-wagons behind?' (*Kim*, p. 127). In contrast, the lama's cadenced invocation '*Om mane pudme hum*' is in rhythmic harmony with the 'the cool [and] quiet' purified air of the plain (*Kim*, p. 127). Grateful for the 'absence of dust' (*Kim*, p. 127), and free from the desire to colonise it, the lama is able to utilise Mother India for what lies beyond the phallogocentric representation of the coloniser, the 'secret' substratum in the maternal space that, according to Cixous, nourishes thought. In her analysis of Brazilian writer Clarice Lispector, Cixous argues that Lispector understands the link between the *mater* and the *matter* as a way to relinquish the phallocentric economy in favour of a return to the 'matter' of the world, our bodies and the bodies of others that lies beneath language.[32] Similarly, on a metaphysical level the lama can be seen to embody Cixous' notion of thinking beyond established western conceptual cartography and Kipling's portrait gives him, as Said argues, a degree of verisimilitude.

Said writes, 'the lama commands attention and respect from nearly everyone. He is no charlatan, no beggarly impostor, no confidence man',[33] all the things that the British Secret Service operators encourage Kim to be. When Kim is imagining himself as a man who would be colonial king, the lama with 'the voice of authority' quietly tells him 'I will teach thee other and better desires upon the road' (*Kim*, p. 65).

Kipling's description of the *parao* at twilight, 'an hour to sundown' (*Kim*, p. 126), hauntingly evokes the transient, fragile time between light and darkness as the sun sets in a background that is lit with 'brown and purple in the afternoon light' (*Kim*, p. 127). Kipling's complex, delicate image is a threefold image that suggests the transient, the time of the child and the liminal space between childhood and adulthood. This feeds into the image of Kim caught between two worlds – the active colonial spy game, and the aesthetics of the lama's ideology. Once again, Kipling depicts a natural world that is soft and fragilely feminine. It is a warm and intimate maternal space, but he liberates it from paternal boundaries by neither defining it within a colonial discourse (it is not a frightening chaotic 'unknowable' India) nor juxtaposing it in negative terms with western masculinity. He creates a matriarchal world untouched by the law of the father. The lama's meditations within this life-affirming feminine space highlight an intelligence or 'knowingness' usually reserved for the colonial and thus associated with masculinity. In this instance it acquires an ominous, inscrutable quality in the mysterious haunting hues of the twilight. The implication is that despite attempts by the white man to categorise and label India, he will fail to 'know' the land he colonises, as classification is not sufficient to procure meaning. Kipling's word to his wise colonials is that the 'word' will always fall short of complex understanding. He seems to be suggesting that the ethnographic task undertaken with relish by the likes of Colonel Creighton can never be more than an articulation of the absurdities of the white man's law that takes no account of India's vital, living historical lineage. Creighton values Kim's duality for the gain it can bring to the British Secret Service, but has scant regard for or understanding of the depths of Kim's love for his Asiatic lama. Whilst recognising that the young 'colt' Kim has a cultural knowledge that it would be 'wrong to break' on the 'heavy cart' of St Xavier's school, and that he must be sent to Lucknow for Lurgan's tutelage, Creighton misses the longing in the boy's voice to see his beloved master, '"[s]hall I meet the Holy one there?" Kim whimpered' (*Kim*, p. 162).

The scene at the *parao* entertains the possibility of sustaining an interstitial subjectivity that does not threaten annihilation. The fecund India that offers a 'grazing ground' and a fertile 'heavy clump of mangoes' (an image that evokes the swollen uterus of pregnancy) is a feminisation of creative and not destructive energy. At this moment in the text Kim's subjective divisions are not a source of anguish, as they are to Ameera and John Tejago's mixed-race child in 'Without Benefit of Clergy' (in *Life's Handicap*), but rather a means through which the Anglo-Indian/ Indian boy can articulate his affiliative identifications and familial contradictions that exist as a consequence of having an identity that is both 'Indian' and Anglo-Indian. Thus the demarcation between the paternal and the maternal, which is sharp and distinct in other colonial texts, in Kipling's novel suggests a blurring of boundaries that unsettles the white man (as 'knowing' observer) who is the custodian and distributor of the colonial lens of 'orientalism'. The construction of the 'Orient' involved a process of hierarchisation whereby the native became the despised, uncivilised Other capable of 'infecting' the white-man. The stories of Rider Haggard, Isak Dinesen and Arthur Conan Doyle all bear hallmarks of this 'difference' between the native and the white colonial.[34] Yet Kim, who feels a lightness of being within this space, has none of the hard-pressed colonising efforts of the white. Unlike the Englishman's annexing eye, '[o]ne thing after another drew Kim's idle eye across the plain. There was no purpose in his wanderings, except the build of the huts near by seemed new, and he wished to investigate' (*Kim*, p. 127). The obvious delight with which Kipling writes of Kim's childlike desires complicates rather than simplifies both the construction of the boy's identity and his allegiance to a particular group.

In contrast to the tranquillity of Kim's experience with the lama and the Sahiba's entourage, when Kim is finally caught by his father's old regiment it is as though he is trapped like a caged animal in the Maverick's convoy. Kim is described as thoroughly downcast, 'trudging beside a baggage-cart under fire of comments from soldiers' wives' (*Kim*, p. 145). His limited dealings with white men have left him with little idea of how to escape, 'he was closely watched – Father Victor on one side, and Mr Bennett on the other' (*Kim*, p. 145). The compound is emblematic of physical boundaries of imprisonment in, and surrender to, colonial rule. To the white man, India is a 'great, gray, formless' landscape that lay 'beyond tents and padres and colonels' (*Kim*, p. 143). When travelling with the Sahiba, Kim walks 'with ten-fold pride in the train of a semi-royal procession' and enjoys 'a recognised place under the patronage of an old lady of charming manners and infinite resource' (*Kim*, p. 123). In contrast, when Kim marches with the Mavericks he moves 'through thick dust', imprisoned, beaten and called a 'little limb of Satan' (*Kim*, p. 145). The Sahiba's opposite is a 'big, shapeless white woman on a pile of bedding' (*Kim*, p. 146). The Mavericks' barracks, like their bone-like 'white tents', are sterile, calcified and lonely places. Kipling describes the men's living spaces as 'empty [and] lime-washed barracks whose floors were covered with rubbish and string and paper, and whose ceilings gave back his [Kim's] lonely footfall and where he must sleep on a 'stripped cot' (*Kim*, p. 147).

This wasteland, filled with detritus and the site of nullifying lessons, constitutes 'the very school and discipline he [Kim] had spent two-thirds of his young life in avoiding' (*Kim*, p. 147). The death-in-life that characterises the white man's existence doesn't sit well with Kim. He is recognised by the native sweeper as a 'white boy [. . .] who is not a white boy' (*Kim*, p. 148), but to the Englishman he is merely a 'wild animal' (*Kim*, p. 151) in need of domestication. The 'abominable clinging trousers' (*Kim*, p. 148) are a metaphor for a profound melancholy at the white man's law that has 'fettered [his] soul' (*Kim*, p. 148). Kim is imprisoned not only within the compound itself, but also by the coloniser's discourse, the 'white lines on a black board' reiterating the English in which 'Kim had been kicked as far as single letters' but he 'did not think well of them' (*Kim*, p. 147). Contained within this image is the Foucauldian notion of the power relationships between the settler population and the native community.[35] Discourse is controlled and catalogued by the white man and reflected back to form an image of the black man. Kim's 'story', imaged in the blackboard, is written according to the discourse (the 'white lines') of the coloniser, with scant regard for Kim's 'native' interiority. Like Joyce's Stephen Dedalus, who remarks of his English dean of studies, '[m]y soul frets in the shadow of his language'[36], Kim's Other self, his fretting soul, is retranslated by the white man's discourse into a wild animal, without benefit of the (white man's) clergy. One can draw a parallel with Punch, struggling to grasp letter-strings that make no sense to him, as well as the sense of melancholy loneliness that permeates M'Turk as he reverts to his lilting Irish accent when inebriated, an accent that Stalky and Beetle had 'carefully kicked out of him, four years previously' (*S&C*, p. 35).

Against these grey, petrified surroundings, Kipling sets his most life-affirming scenes. The image of the petrified school buildings is one of imprisonment. Kim's 'Indian' self had been free before the white man confined it within the school enclosure. This is the 'inside' from which Kim yearns to escape, a space that is entirely dominated by western ideology. However, the sense of an interned 'inside' is continually undermined by other, more positive connotations of 'inside'. The 'inside' also comes to represent Kim's Otherness, connected to the semiotic; it is a space that embodies the maternal realm, that time-before-language where identity is in an unconstructed state of constant flux and the mother/child dyad is ubiquitous. This space is associated with the ambiguous paternal/maternal figure of the lama, whose bodily and spiritual presence sustains Kim, as well as the light and open spaces of India that restore his vitality. In this novel, Kipling's Indian scenes are, for the most part, set outside in varying lights. Kipling demolishes walls, the physical boundaries of confinement, and Kim is surrounded by stunningly beautiful landscapes.

The tangled depths of Kipling's description of the Grand Trunk Road express the multiplicity of Indian life. It is only through Kim's 'bright eyes [. . .] open wide' (*Kim*, p. 109) that we can see every living thing, every fabricated caste structure, every emotion and every movement. Kim's knowledge of and desire for the native life of India is a complex, difficult concept. Here is the ethnographic classification that Colonel Creighton, like the curator, aims for, but with a crucial difference. Kim's response is a culmination of experiencing life as a living process rather than as a detached observation of 'native' culture. Each caste as 'seen' through the lens of his memory and experience, in short, his connection to his Other self. Kim's is a vision that goes beyond a scientific classification, a description that reads of joy, suffering and religiosity. Kim's portraits are filtered through his memories and experiences, which form a connection to his Other self. The 'long-haired, strong-scented Sansis' keep to 'their own side of the road [. . .] for the Sansis', Kim adds with a responsive connection, are 'deep pollution' (*Kim*, p. 109). Intimately familiar with the goings-on in the bazaar, and growing up almost exclusively within the Indian community, Kim has spent his life among many castes and has a detailed knowledge of their customs and idioms. For example, he recognises the wide, stiff-legged gait of an Indian 'newly released from jail' who still has 'the memory of his leg irons'. Kipling's description of his walking across the barred 'strong shadows', the sun mimicking the prison cell, strengthens Kim's observations (*Kim*, p. 109). The 'wild-eyed, wild haired Sikh devotee in the blue-checked clothes of his faith' is known to the 'College-trained princelings in top-boots and white cord breeches' as an expert in 'the ancient glories of the Khalsa', but Kim makes his words flesh, so to speak, by knowing that his 'temper is short and his arm quick' (*Kim*, p. 109).

The picture of Kim, like flotsam caught in the current of life that flows along the Grand Trunk, reveals his intense corporeal vibrancy as well as an imaginative realism that appeals not just to the reader's intellect but to his/her senses, and draws them into the scene. The poverty that engenders a migrant population of women workers, following the railway, carrying heavy loads of soil, is highlighted in the gang of *changars* that emerges like a column of worker ants 'through the quivering dust' (*Kim*,

p. 110). Although they belong to 'the caste whose men do not count' (*Kim*, p. 110), they too are part of the exuberance that characterises Kim's experiences on the road. Kipling portrays them as 'flat-footed, big-bosomed, strong-limbed, blue-petticoated clan of earth-carriers' who 'trot past to a chorus of quick cackling' (*Kim*, p. 110). Kipling's description of the *changars* could be read as a white man's appropriation of the customs, dress and supposed temperament of the women, much like that of the nineteenth-century European educator Gottlieb Leitner, who believed that '[n]othing can exceed the proud independence with which the Changar women move about their occupations. Their chastity is proverbial, and it is in striking contrast with the obtrusive immorality of the women of the Ghassiàra, or grass-cutting tribe that infests Lahore.'[37] However, we feel none of Gottlieb's moral indignation in Kipling's celebratory description of the women's pulsating corporeality. The women's fluidity, 'rising and falling like the back of a caterpillar in haste' (*Kim*, p. 110), is more a subversive libidinal body that disrupts western representational economies of supposed morality. The women become almost disconnected from the caste that weighs them down like the loads they must carry on their heads and, like Joyce's Molly Bloom, are retranslated into vibrant, vital entities, full of power and sensuality with 'swinging hips, and heads on high' (*Kim*, p. 110).

Kipling shifts from the monumental to the microscopic, with us barely able to perceive the textual jump, and his intricate perspectives of minutiae become integral to the text. His details of quotidian Indian life are intimately connected to the senses as he adds a touch of imagination to his 'realist' portraits. For example, the lama and Kim come to rest after travelling with the breath-taking variety of people on the Grand Trunk Road. Kim is piqued that the myriad of colours, sounds and smells that has filled his senses for the day is to the lama nothing but illusion. The lama 'sees' that the people are chained to their identities, as Kim is to his desire to be part of this overwhelming vibrancy of native life. And the description of the *changar* women gives way to a deeply libidinal description of a marriage procession. Music mingles with indistinct cries that blend into the heady sensual 'smell of marigold and jasmine stronger even than the reek of the dust' (*Kim*, p. 110). The bride's litter, a 'blur of red and tinsel' is etymologically connected to the 'haze' of the road, each subject to the lover's need for her supplication (realised in Kim's desire for the pulsating Grand Trunk Road that cuts through Mother India, and the bridegroom, waiting to take ownership of his bride). Both images are connected by the bridegroom's horse which, like Kim's asides on the various castes that pass by, turns aside 'to snatch a mouthful from a passing fodder-cart' (*Kim*, p. 110).

Kipling's sentences begin to degenerate from crystal-clear depictions, which are Pre-Raphaelite in their attention to detail, to a discourse that draws us relentlessly into a multiplicity of images and sounds. His writing pulsates and breathes with visual images as well as musical vibrations that uncover a repressed (maternal) source as the origin of his poetic vision of an India of his childhood memories. In *Souffles*, Cixous writes: 'my voice makes sound in me: my forgotten languages, my piercing sounds, my liquids, the guttural types of music with which I used to masturbate my ear drums',[38] and this passage can be read as a form of writing as song, which comes from the body and has the senses at its core. Images that are out of symbolic focus give Kim his rhythm that will, in the Himalayas, throw 'his soul after his eyes' across 'deep blue gulfs' (*Kim*, p. 282).

Animals, humans, voices and bodies fuse, and we feel consumed by a text whose signifiers no longer have any syntactical clarity. But this hardly matters, for feeling takes over logic: '[s]till more interesting and more to be shouted over it was when a strolling juggler with some half-trained monkeys, or a panting, feeble bear, or a woman who tied goats' horns to her feet, and with these danced on a slack-rope set the horses to shying and the women to shrill, long-drawn quivers of amazement' (*Kim*, p. 110). We wade through a passage filled with commingled imagery. In one sentence a juggler is linked to a bear that in turn gives way to a woman stamping the ground, her weight crushing the goat's horns (a symbol of male sexual potency) pinioned to her feet. The frantic confusion of sights culminates in a frenzy that is akin to an almost orgasmic release in her spectators. The strange sound of the text, with its overloaded confusion of sights, its heady scents and sexually charged imagery, engenders a writing that is no longer that of the Father-of-the-law to the son-in-the-symbolic, but more a writing that defies (the logic of) meaning. In a passage that focuses heavily on sensual, maternal women, the trajectory of Kipling's writing shuttles back and forth between a vibrant, rhythmic language and utilitarian descriptions of quotidian activities. The narrative boundaries between symbolic linearity and semiotic ubiquity are thus blurred. Kim comes to being, not in a Cartesian 'I think, therefore I am' abstraction, but more a Cixousian 'I *desire*, therefore I am'.

The symbol of colonial engineering is the Grand Trunk Road, but Kipling is more concerned with Kim's connective relationship to it. This superhighway pays testament to a colossal (colonial) feat of design, management and workmanship, but Kim relishes more the myriad of castes who travel along it, overjoyed to be part of the polychromatic life that traverses its path through northern India:

> Kim's bright eyes were open wide. This broad, smiling river of life, he considered, was a vast improvement on the cramped and crowded Lahore streets. There were new people, and new sights at every stride – castes he knew and castes that were altogether out of his experience. (*Kim*, p. 109)

The Grand Trunk road pushes through the Punjab like a benign 'stately corridor', with 'all India spread out to the left and the right' (*Kim*, p. 111). Cultural and religious groups, subcultures, families and companions are reduced to specks on Kipling's narrative canvas, 'little clumps of red and blue and pink and white and saffron, turning aside to go to their own villages, dispersing and growing small by twos and threes across the level plain' (*Kim*, p. 111). Kipling's macroscopic vision of the Grand Trunk Road is utopian, a space without delineated territories or subdivisions of caste. The bridge that straddles and contains 'Mother Gunga' in 'The Bridge Builders' diminishes individuals (physically as well as psychically) in the imperial workforce into one moving entity, a kind of colonial discourse that infantilises the colonised. Kipling's comments to his cousin in England on native Indians are particularly telling, 'they have to be handled like children or young horses', he tells her, and are a 'queer people indeed. Touchy as children.'[39] Sentiments such as these are echoed in stories such as 'In the House of Suddhoo', where the native Suddhoo is referred to as 'an old child' as well as 'an old dotard [. . .] completely under the influence of the [huckster] seal-cutter, by whose advice he regulates the affairs of his life' (*PT*, p. 122). But Kipling's overview of the Grand Trunk gives shape to the myriad of peoples that move along its route, cutting a rent in the smooth façade of the semiotic. Kim feels psychically connected to all that is spread out before him, 'though he could not give tongue to his feeling' (*Kim*, p. 111), evoking a pre-verbal time of coalescence.

Gorged on the visual nourishment that the Grand Trunk Road provides to his 'soul', mirrored in the actual tasting of food, Kim 'contented himself with buying peeled sugar-cane and spitting the pith generously about his path' (*Kim*, p. 111). Desperate for the lama to understand his feelings, he cries, 'This is the good land – the land of the South [. . .] The air is good; the water is good, Eh?' (*Kim*, p. 111). But the lama, whose age would, arguably, place him in one of the final two asramas, sees only illusion; the multitude of castes 'are all bound upon the Wheel [. . .] Bound from life after life' (*Kim*, p. 111). A deflated Kim suggests pausing at a *parao* (resting place). In the 'sloping' sun, an in-between time so appealing to Kipling,[40] the author presents an Indian landscape which for Kim, caught in the shadow that falls between childhood and adulthood, is truly restorative. However, we sense the adult writer's melancholy for his eponymous hero on the cusp of adulthood. It is we and not Kim, with one foot still planted in childhood, who feel the first chill of realisation that his involvement with the British imperial administrators will forever change his relationship with the country of his birth and lead him to an existential crisis of identity at the end of the novel.

The resting place, as described by Kipling, spirals out of control with sentences that lengthen and overhang their syntactical borders. What begins as a simple 'naming' process is gradually undercut by images that are redolent with the heady, sensual nostalgia of Kipling's childhood India. The passage opens with a straightforward itemisation of the *parao*. It constitutes a 'line of stalls selling very simple food and tobacco, a stack of firewood, a police-station, a well, a horse-trough, a few trees, and, under them, some trampled ground dotted with the black ashes of old fires' (*Kim*, p. 112). To a westerner's eye these are 'all that mark a *parao* on the Grand Trunk' (*Kim*, p. 112). It is a world on the 'outside', explicated by language, a world of names and knowledge that can be related to properties of the symbolic. To Kim's hybrid eye, however, the scene is a rich tapestry that weaves man, beast and plant into the undifferentiated fabric of Kim's childhood subjectivity. Kipling underwrites his dry inventory with layers that are characterised by sounds. The squawks and 'chatterings' of the birds are distinguishable from the 'men's voices' as they cry for 'oil, or grain, or sweetmeats, or tobacco' and underpinned by the 'high squeals and giggles of women' (*K*im, p. 112).

Distinct as the noises may be, however, they are symphonic, the sounds acting in rhythmic synchronisation. In this respect, the sounds, sights and smells of the *parao* articulate Kim's 'difference': his ubiquitous Other self in the maternal realm where everything is in synthesis. The kaleidoscopic nature of the *parao* reflects Kipling's idealised vision of India, a smooth, seamless spatiality that applies as much to Kim's 'Indian' identity as to a geographical space. Cixous writes that '[s]ound is a difference [. . .] like relationships between notes coming from instruments that are different but that are in harmony'.[41] The parakeets and doves, 'coming home in their hundreds', are 'chattering', the anthropomorphic 'gray-backed Seven Sisters' are 'talking over the days adventures', travellers and birds connected in the resting place of this migrant community. Kipling's words have, in Cixousian terms, 'pierced' the 'limits' and the 'difference between the human and non-human' has become blurred.[42] Each component, human and animal alike, is woven into an undifferentiated fabric where the white man's hierarchy no longer enforces any topographical gradation. The bats' rhythmic shufflings and scufflings in the branches out for the 'night-picket' are commensurate with the manoeuvres of the British military (*Kim*, p. 112).

Just as the sun lights the birds and bats, so it conjoins each living thing and every inanimate object in one spectacular panorama, 'the light [. . .] painted for an instant the faces and the cart-wheels and the bullocks' horns as red as blood' (*Kim*, p. 112). The lama proclaims that 'red' is the colour of 'desire' (*Kim*, p. 141), and in the image of the sun's fading light we sense Kipling's desire for affinity with an India which exists only in the author's sepia-tinted recollections. The author's desire, however, does not extend to a brutal colonisation of Mother India; rather, it can be read as an artistic release of the semiotic that the symbolic has schematically overwritten and diminished. The 'gossamer veil of blue' that falls 'across the face of the country' reinstates a delicate, nurturing maternal body (*Kim*, p. 112) that gives sustenance to, rather than terrorising, the itinerant population. Kipling employs a similar technique in *Captains Courageous* where, as Leonee Ormond has rightly noted, his 'feminised' ocean is intricately linked to the lives of the fishermen, their livelihood and their emotions and expectations.[43] With the fading of the light of the sun, the landscape, in that hazy, indistinct, in-between time of dusk, is transformed into a woman sensually 'changing the touch of the air' (*Kim*, p. 112). The night is subject to the same mutability, twilight 'drawing a low, even haze' across the country (*Kim*, p. 112). The humans in this landscape are not presented, like the Mavericks, as intruders. In contrast, they are in harmony with their surroundings. The travellers are seeking rest, profiting from their tranquil locale in a way that is a Cixousian 'penetration without violence'.[44] And certainly, the cool night air draws out, 'keen and distinct, the smell of wood-smoke and the cattle and the good scent of wheaten cakes cooked on ashes' (*Kim*, p. 112).

Kipling has Kim crossing the boundary of native/European, thereby aligning him with these marginal Others that operate in conjunction with the restorative aspects of the natural landscape rather than within the organising structure of the British imperial project. It is an image that will be reinforced at the moment in the novel where the lama's depiction of the Wheel of Life is torn in two by the token 'villains' of the piece. Kim learns that to be 'home' is, in a sense, to be exiled from his 'native' self. To 'live', he has to go beyond a sense of self that is configured within a grandiose imperial matrix, to one where his identity is expressed through the quotidian, '[r]oads that were meant to be walked upon, houses to be lived in, cattle to be driven, fields to be tilled, and men and women to be talked to' (*Kim*, p. 331). 'Home' for Kim is a paradisiacal India that exists within him. The 'exiled' Kim finds this edenic space not in the artefacts of the Lahore museum or even in the pictograms of the lama, but in the recovery of a lost homeland. To find his place in quotidian India is to go 'home', and the lama's Wheel of Life has more resonance with Kim's 'belonging' in the wealth of life in the midst of India than it does with Buddhist spiritual religiosity.

In this way, Kipling artistically links the lama's Wheel of Life to the image of the sun that 'was driving broad golden spokes through the lower branches of the mango-trees' (*Kim*, p. 112). The images in this passage, like the fading sun slanting between the mango trees and the lama's Wheel of Life, function like a Möbius strip that loops back upon itself in a way that Mark Paffard suggests 'wheels back to its opening scene'.[45] Whilst Paffard sees the cyclic construction of the novel as parallel to Kim's growing awareness of his place in the imperial scheme of things, Sahib and native identities occupying a more cohesive position under a benevolent British rule, I would argue that Kipling argues for a reintroduction of his notion of the 'Old Law' that has not been 'well followed' (*Kim*, p. 57). The picaresque structure of *Kim* has the protagonist, like the lama, wandering through an India that is continually on the move. Kim's identity is linked to diaspora and the coming together of two disparate communities, which ultimately initiate his wandering and mark his suffering. The loss of community leads to the finding of another key, which turns 'with an almost audible click' (*Kim*, p. 331) to a continual state of travelling. Kim is never 'home', but constantly exiled, wandering through the hills and plains of India looking for the key to a lost maternal realm. The section of the resting place closes with Kipling's image of a 'live charcoal ball in the cup of a wayside carter's hookah' (*Kim*, p. 112). The alchemic image is of a fusion of Kim's Anglo-Indian self that is ignited in the kaleidoscopic crucible of India. He connects with his Other self, and in a micro-image of mechanisation, Kipling writes of Kim's face illuminated in the red-glow of the hookah, his eye 'mechanically watch[ing] the last flicker of the sun on the brass tweezers' (*Kim*, p. 112). It is a complicated image and one that works, in a Cixousian sense, like a symphony: the charcoal ball, Kim's eye, and the sun. The symphonic quality of the image parallels the cyclic structure of the novel. Kipling underscores this with a line that refers back to an earlier description, '[t]he life of the *parao* was very like that of the Kashmir Serai on a small scale' (*Kim*, p. 112).

The fluidity of the text, the mutability of the hazy and indistinct imagery, creates a rippling textuality, which is aqueous, and is echoed in the line, 'Kim dived into the happy Asiatic disorder' (*Kim*, p. 112). It is a disorder that not only defies any white man's classification, but also mocks the colonist's inability to understand the intricacies of Indian life and see any sort of meaning in it beyond what the white man can appropriate for his own world view. Kipling's textual 'voices' cannot be interpreted through the gaze of a single perspective, but rather through two diametrically opposite viewpoints woven together in the polychromatic tapestry of the text: a symbolic discourse shot through with the cadenced pre-verbal utterances that characterise the exiled semiotic. This perspectival jump enables the corporeal drives of the semiotic to be signified in language, and is in narrative terms realised in Kipling's portrayal of the ancient mountain ranges of the Himalayas as an archaic mother figure. In this way the orphan Kim (and symbolically Kipling) can feel a sense of love and support that, unlike other parental love relationships, is not subject to the possibility of devastating separation or loss. Love experienced within and for the maternal mountain realm is beyond what Kristeva calls the 'hazards of loves',[46] and can therefore serve as a refuge against symbolic loss (of parental figures, of language and of community).

The chapter that sees the lama gradually throw off the mantle of helpless priest and begin to become a powerful father figure for Kim and a source of support on their monumental climb through the Himalayas opens with the line, '[w]ho goes to the Hills goes to his mother' (*Kim*, p. 279). In one narrative stroke, Kipling reinstates symbolic mother and father substitutes for the orphaned Kim. The descriptions of the Himalayas read as a timeless maternal realm that restores the strength of the lama whilst simultaneously filling him with desire to walk the high mountain passes. The lama, 'where he should have sunk exhausted' instead 'swung his long draperies about him [and] drew a deep double-lungful of the diamond air' (*Kim*, p. 279). The healing and restorative maternal Himalayas prefigure the two mother figures that Kim will find so therapeutic later on in the story, Lispeth, the woman of Shamlegh, and the Sahiba, as the maternal comes to take a larger role in the novel. Kim and the lama cut through the Himalayas, '[d]ay after day they struck deeper into the huddled mountains' (*Kim*, p. 279). Kipling's mountains are asexually feminised. Kim is enveloped within the topographical folds of the Himalayas, rather as a child is embraced in the soft, warm flesh of the mother. One could argue that Kipling is merely reproducing the ideological values of a colonial system in which 'masculinity' and 'culture' belong to the English. After all, the ridges of the lower Himalayas were home to several hill stations of the British Raj, including Simla and Mussoorie. Kim might be merely representative of the 'masculine' mode of Kipling's imperial vision, a vision that functions by violating and appropriating the feminine. However, the lama grows in strength the further into the heart of the Himalayas he ventures, and there is a marked absence of the white man. The returning strength of the lama is, Kipling tells us, entirely due to the nourishing effects of the mountains: 'day after day Kim watched the lama return to a man's strength [. . .] Under the great ramp to Mussoorie he drew himself together and walked as only a Hillman can' (*Kim*, p. 279).

The lama is imbued with a vigorous, healthy, sexual potency (more akin to Mahbub Ali than to the curiously asexual white men) that is appealing to a different non-colonial notion of masculinity. Kipling reinforces the image the way the lama tackles the mountain – 'with steady, driving strokes from the loins he strode upwards' (*Kim*, p. 279) – and the Himalayas seem almost complicit in the lama's masculinity that grows outside of the coloniser's gaze. The lama moves through forest out onto the 'bare hillsides' slippery sunburnt grass', then back into 'the woodlands' coolth again' (*Kim*, pp. 279–80), and the suggestion of a sensual, naked female body is not easily missed. The lama travels over this 'feminised' landscape, pausing at 'the neck of some uplifted pass' to 'stretch out his hands yearningly towards the high snows of the horizon' (*Kim*, p. 280). Kipling describes the Kedarnarth and Badrinath peaks in curiously bisexual tones; they are 'kings of that wilderness', but they lie 'like molten silver under the sun, and at evening put on their jewels again' (*Kim*, p. 280). The mountain ranges are subject to the same ambivalence as the lama, the 'effeminate' Buddhist monk has taken on attributes of formidable masculinity, and he is able to out-walk Kim at every turn. He has become, in Kristevan topography, an Imaginary father. He is transformed into the loving parent that will guide the child away from its libidinal desire of the maternal body, akin to Freud's father in individual prehistory.

There is an emotionally charged, psychological content in Kipling's depiction of the 'maternal' Himalayas and the autochthonous people who populate it. This does not suggest that Kipling's rendition of the Himalayas is powerful because they are anthropomorphic or because the landscape somehow seems corporeal – it is powerful because Kipling's presentation of the mountain range and the village-life thereon involves projecting a psychological fantasy of revisiting the maternal body in the unifying structure of the semiotic realm onto the mountain ranges. A return to the agrarian life of the hills offers a scene that demonstrates Kipling's artistic skill:

> They thawed out in the sun, and sat with their legs hanging over infinite abysses, chattering, laughing, and smoking. They judged India and its Government solely from their experience of wandering Sahibs who had employed them or their friends as *shikarris*. [. . .] The thin air refreshed [the lama], and he sat on the edge of precipices with the best of them, and when talk languished, flung pebbles into the void. [. . .] Behind the village, Shamlegh hill itself cut off all view from Southward. It was like sitting in a swallow's nest under the eaves of the roof of the world. (*Kim*, p. 306)

Like Stalky, M'Turk and Beetle in their sanctuaries in the gorse, Kim is disconnected from the unrelenting strictures of the Great Game. The text suggests that the archaic maternal realm provides a psychic blackboard on which his desire for the mother's body is chalked. Therefore, his fantasy of rejoining the maternal body underscores his portrayal of the Himalayas as feminine. Thus, in the description of the lama and Kim being spotted coming over 'the black breasts of Eua to be given cheese [and] sour milk' (*Kim*, p. 281), Kipling is not literally suggesting that breasts can be 'seen' in the mountain passes – rather, the connection with the mother and the warm closeness of her body is reinstated in the absence of the conquering (colonial) male being. India as a maternal space offers both Kim and the lama an intimate connection: 'the soft, smoky silence of evening wrapped them close' (*Kim*, p. 336).

The discourse of the lama gives Kim space enough to experience a reunion with the maternal realm in the high mountain passes, which in turn enables the mother-figure to be reborn in an Other image that is, in narrative terms, translated into the women who support Kim though his existential crisis. The mechanical 'click' with which Kim understands his identity, the matter that 'rode meaningless on the eyeball an instant before slid into proper proportion' (*Kim*, p. 331). Continuing the motif of blurred vision brought into focus, Kim 'sees' the 'roads that were meant to be walked on, houses meant to be lived in, cattle to be driven, fields to be tilled, and men and women to be talked to' (*Kim*, p. 331). Kim feels his place is in the centre of an India where the white man and his Great Game are sidelined to a speck in his peripheral vision. Kipling asserts a subject position that is underscored by the importance of the maternal realm in Kim's psyche. 'Mother Earth must do the rest', that is, restore Kim's 'Indian' identity with the help of Indian, not English caregivers (*Kim*, p. 332). Kipling argues for the importance of Kim's (and the child Kipling's) native relationships and, perhaps more crucially, his relationship to the land of his birth. 'Mother India', Kipling assures us, 'was as faithful as the Sahiba. She breathed through him to restore the poise he had lost lying so long on a cot cut off from her good currents' (*Kim*, p. 332).

As has been noted by critics such as Margaret Peller Feeley, Kim at the end of the novel 'clearly chooses the Game' over the lama's spiritual quest.[47] However, I would argue that the 'resolution' of the novel lies neither with the English nor the Indian side of Kim (and Kipling's) head. Kipling's notion of the 'Law', as laid out in *The Jungle Books*, is in *Kim* developed further into the wish-fulfilment of an impossible fantasy, the adult being reunited with the maternal body in the semiotic. Kipling, like a ventriloquist, projects through the Buddhist tenets of the lama onto a timeless and 'spaceless' imaginary screen where communal brotherhood exists beyond the boundaries of a colonial phallogocentric law. Representing life as cyclical rather than linear, this 'Most Excellent Law' does not recognise a phallic authority: 'It is not pillars but a Wheel from which I would be free', says the lama (*Kim*, p. 65). Fulfilment comes from a realignment of binary division to attain a soul in synthesis with the Great Soul, 'beyond the illusion of time and space' (*Kim*, p. 337). The Way recognises, 'neither black nor white, Hind nor Bhotiyal' (*Kim*, p. 261). This reads like a Kristevan desire for a preoedipal realm with the child existing in a fusional bliss with the 'Great Soul' of the mother's body. However, the maternal realm exists throughout the novel in the state of nature. Kim is never free of his desire for Mother India's 'good currents'. The lama's lessons on the Wheel of Life are dutifully attended to by Kim until 'they came to the Human World [. . .] for by the roadside trundled the very Wheel itself, eating, drinking, trading, marrying and quarrelling – all warmly alive' (*Kim*, p. 260). Kipling lays out, then challenges the colonial's ideological organisation of himself against the native. Kim's tangled, ambivalent Anglo-Indian identity transgresses (western) boundaries of self much as he criss-crosses India, torn between the lama's spiritual search for his mythical river and the white man's Great Game. In addition to exploring the sense of loss and dislocation that such an ambivalent subject position engenders, like Stalky, M'Turk and Beetle before him, Kim in his early stages will remain outside of the law. Kim can find restoration only in the welcoming embrace of the wild, uncolonised feminised Indian landscape, rendered by Kipling in meticulous detail and tinted with an impressionistic wash of delicate stylistic hues.

Kim invites its readers to embrace different perspectives, new ways of 'seeing'. Kipling engages his readers in unorthodox ways of considering social issues, in particular ways in which identity is constructed. And like his forerunner Dickens, Kipling also deals with the controversial issue of abandoned children. As Angus Wilson has pointed out, there is more than a nod to *Oliver Twist* in the characterisation of Kim, who Wilson argues encompasses 'the knowingness, the cunning, the humour and the appeal of the Dodger, with the gentleness and goodness of Oliver Twist'[48] or, as Harold Bloom observes, is 'both Huck Finn and Tom Sawyer'.[49] Abandoned children seemed to occupy Kipling's fiction to a greater extent than their polar opposite, the child whose protective parents remain present and full of love for the child. Characters such as the much-loved Wee Willie Winkie are lacking in dimension, and we feel an aversion to their precocity. Kipling's fascination with the physically (Little Tobra, Kim) and psychically (Punch, 'His Majesty, the King') orphaned child can be seen in terms of a fascination with the Other outcast side of himself, and in turn we feel a forbidding yet fascinating frisson of fear when reading about those that have fallen through the boundaries of civil society and transgressed the entrenched gendered and caste boundaries. Kim's relaxed and easy dealings with the prostitutes, the poor, the natives of all castes, threaten the colonial's emphasis on bodily cleanliness (racial purity becoming a sinister extension of this notion) with an erotic appeal that carries the threat of disease and miscegenation. Through representation of the cross-cultural, the illicit, and the unconventional, Kipling captures the white man's fear of the Other.

Clamped as it is, between forlorn lost boys on one side and despairing, terrified adults on the other, *Kim* remains Kipling's fantasy India beyond the boundaries of the coloniser's law. However, as we see in *Plain Tales* and *Life's Handicap*, Kipling's adults must put away such childish thoughts of an impossible reunification with an edenic India. Mother India must be abjected if the tyrannical phallogocentric order of the coloniser is to be enforced. In the next chapter India becomes a terrifying abjected site that threatens only engulfment, where his soldiers die bloodily on battlefields, suffer lonely suicidal deaths or are shot out by deserting Indian soldiers; his administrators die of disillusionment, madness, overwork or fever; his characters' cross-cultural relationships are doomed, and married couples endure gossip, boredom and adultery. For Kipling's men, surviving colonial service in India will henceforth mean having to 'buffet a path through the Pit's red wrath when God goes out to war', for his heroes wearily 'know of toil and the end of toil; they know God's Law is plain'.[50]

Notes

1. A number of the stories in *Plain Tales* revolve around the sexual intrigue that was a darker feature of Simla society. See Harry Ricketts, *The Unforgiving Minute: A Life of Rudyard Kipling*, pp. 96–7.
2. 'ha:kim', Digital Dictionaries of South Asia.
3. Diane Simmons, *The Narcissism of Empire: Loss, Rage and Revenge in Thomas De Quincey, Robert Louis Stevenson, Arthur Conan Doyle, Rudyard Kipling and Isak Dinesen*, p. 97.
4. Hélène Cixous, *The Newly Born Woman*, p. 83.
5. Salman Rushdie, *Imaginary Homelands: Essays and Criticism 1981–1991*, p. 74.
6. Kaori Nagai's study on the Indo-Irish connections in Kipling's fiction addresses this issue in more detail. Kaori Nagai, 'The Taming of the Irish Afreets', *Empire of Analogies: Kipling, India and Ireland*.
7. Christopher Hitchens, *Love, Poverty and War: Journeys and Essays*, p. 31.

8. Zohreh Sullivan, *Narratives of Empire: The Fictions of Rudyard Kipling*, p. 149.
9. Ibid., p. 150.
10. George Orwell, 'Rudyard Kipling', in Andrew Rutherford (ed.), *Kipling's Mind and Art*, p. 71.
11. Peter Hopkirk, *Quest for Kim: In Search of Kipling's Great Game*, p. 44.
12. Sullivan, *Narratives of Empire*, p. 149.
13. Vasant Shahane, '*Kim*: The Process of Becoming', in Harold Bloom (ed.), *Rudyard Kipling's Kim*, p. 19.
14. Hélène Cixous, *Coming to Writing and Other Essays*, p. 66.
15. Ibid., p. 66.
16. Sullivan, *Narratives of Empire*, p. 153.
17. Edward Said, Introduction to Rudyard Kipling, *Kim*, p. 16.
18. Rudyard Kipling, *The Definitive Edition of Rudyard Kipling's Verse*, p. 764.
19. Letter to Margaret Burne Jones, 28 November 1885–11 January 1886, Thomas Pinney (ed.), *The Letters of Rudyard Kipling* I, pp. 100–1.
20. Ibid., pp. 100–1.
21. Nandi Bhatia, 'Kipling's Burden: Representing Colonial Authority and Constructing the "Other" through Kimball O'Hara and Babu Hurree Chander [sic] in Kim'.
22. Purnima Bose, 'Survivors of the Raj, Survivors of the Empire: Narrating the Colonial and Post-colonial Encounters', p. 165.
23. Henry Yule and A. C. Burnell, *Hobson-Jobson: The Anglo-Indian Dictionary*, p. 44.
24. Said, Introduction to *Kim*, p. 33.
25. Thomas Metcalf, *Ideologies of the Raj*, p. 167.
26. Harold Bloom (ed.), *Rudyard Kipling's Kim*, p. 4.
27. Kipling is referring to the allegories and allusions with which he stuffed *Puck of Pook's Hill* and *Rewards and Fairies*.
28. Martin Seymour-Smith, *Rudyard Kipling*, p. 304.
29. Julia Kristeva, *The Kristeva Reader*, p. 180.
30. In *To Live the Orange*, Cixous writes that *écriture féminine* involves 'the work of un-forgetting, of un-silencing, of un-earthing, of un-blinding oneself, and of un-deafening oneself'. Quoted in *The Hélène Cixous Reader*, p. 83.
31. There are echoes and references in Joyce's art, particularly in *Ulysses*, but also in *Finnegan's Wake*. Eleni Loukopoulou argues that '[b]oth writers were from the periphery of the Empire and ambitious about recognition from the metropolis. They admired the quotidian, and music hall culture, and harnessed casual linguistic inventiveness in their work.' ('The Finest Stories in the World were by Kipling and Joyce', The Kent Conference, University of Sussex, 7–8 Sept. 2007; available via The Kipling Society online). In 1907 Joyce wrote: 'after all, there must be some merit in my writing [. . .] If I knew Ireland as well as R. K. seems to know India, I fancy I could write something good' (*Selected Letters of James Joyce*).
32. Of Lispector's writing, Cixous argues, 'she returns the ability not to forget matter, which we don't notice: which we live, which we are'. Hélène Cixous, *Three Steps on the Ladder of Writing*, p. 130.

33. Said, Introduction to *Kim*, p. 16.
34. For further reading see Simmons, *The Narcissism of Empire*; Catherine Hall, *Cultures of Empire: A Reader: Colonizers in Britain and the Empire in the Nineteenth and Twentieth Centuries*, and Ann Laura Stoler, *Race and the Education of Desire: Foucault's 'History of Sexuality' and the Colonial Order of Things*.
35. Michel Foucault, 'The Discourse on Language', p. 216.
36. James Joyce, *A Portrait of the Artist as a Young Man*, p. 189.
37. Gottlieb William Leitner, *A Sketch of the Changars and their Dialect*, p. 2.
38. Quoted in Verena Andermatt Conley, *Hélène Cixous*, p. 57.
39. Thomas Pinney (ed.), *The Letters of Rudyard Kipling*, p. 100.
40. Christopher Hitchens notes that Kipling captured this waning, melancholic end of days feeling in 'Recessional' (Hitchens, *Love, Poverty and War*, p. 31) – written at the height of Britannia's Empire, it sounded an eerie funereal knell long before the First World War brought the eventual acknowledgement of the sun going down on England's Imperial might.
41. Hélène Cixous, *Rootprints: Memory and Life Writing*, p. 47.
42. Cixous, *Coming to Writing*, p. 31.
43. Leonee Ormond writes: 'A series of feminine images are used to describe the skill of the fishermen or the movement of the vessels' (Introduction to *Captains Courageous*, p. xxvi).
44. Cixous, *Rootprints*, p. 47.
45. Mark Paffard, *Kipling's Indian Fiction*, p. 88.
46. Julia Kristeva, *Tales of Love*, p. 382.
47. Margaret Peller Feeley, 'The *Kim* that Nobody Reads', in Bloom, *Rudyard Kipling's Kim*, p. 73.
48. Angus Wilson, *The Strange Ride of Rudyard Kipling: His Life and Works*, p. 129.
49. Bloom, *Rudyard Kipling's Kim*, p. 4.
50. Kipling, *Definitive Verse*, p. 84.

Chapter 4

The 'Sorrowful State of Manhood': Kipling's Adults in India

> [T]here be certain times in a young man's life, when, through great sorrow or sin, all the boy in him is burnt and seared away so that he passes at one step to the more sorrowful state of manhood: as our staring Indian day changes into night with never so much as the gray of twilight to temper the two extremes.[1]

> There is a certain darkness into which the soul of the young man sometimes descends – a horror of desolation, abandonment, and realised worthlessness, which is one of the most real of the hells in which we are compelled to walk.[2]

Kim remains a character defined by the love of his various father figures and embraced by a maternal India that reflects back and nourishes the unconditional love that is afforded him. The effect of love in Kipling's most successful novel reads as 'a permanent stabilization-destabilization between the Symbolic [. . .] and the *semiotic*'.[3] In Kipling's fiction that deals with adults in India, however, the picture becomes a darker, more terrifying one. It is a 'Mother India, wan and thin', which 'takes the young civilian in' and kills him 'swiftly as [she] may',[4] that characterises his image of his birthplace in *Plain Tales* and *Life's Handicap*. How do we move from a tender and loving vision of India, typified in Kim's yearning for 'the soft caress of mud squishing up between his toes' (*Kim*, p. 173) to a frightening dystopian image of a cholera-ridden, drought-stricken Mother India who 'audit[s] her accounts with a red pencil' (*LH*, p. 149)? This chapter will attempt to deal with this complex question.

The 'bitter waters of [. . .] despair' that Punch is forced to drink during his time at Downe Lodge resurface in certain stories that feature imperial workers carrying out the work of Empire in an India that resembles a hellish abyss. The devastating loss that Punch experienced in exile from his privileged Anglo-Indian environment is replicated in those characters that equally confront the vagaries of loss – loss of self/identity, as in 'To be Filed for Reference'; of childhood, for example 'Little Tobrah'; of sanity, in stories such as 'The Mark of the Beast'; of colonial status in 'The Strange Ride of Morrowbie Jukes', and of love, as poignantly captured in 'On Greenhow Hill'. In a Kleinian sense the persecuting mother figure that has replaced the 'lost' life-giving mother, distilled in the character of Aunty Rosa, has found a new translation in the threatening, heat-scorched environment of India and the 'exotic' attraction of its native people that lures and seduces the coloniser. This chapter will deal with Kipling's Indian stories as metonymic sites of terror where colonial characters are engaged in conflict, not only with a paternal law, but also with the persecuting phallic mother that invades his vision of India. In the *Plain Tales* and *Life's Handicap* collections his adult characters are more aware than his boy heroes of the potential India has to harm them psychologically as well as physically. India has become an external site of terror that engulfs natives and colonials alike in her abjected, secret orifices, as in 'The City of Dreadful Night' and 'The Strange Ride of Morrowbie Jukes'. And the horror of India provokes an interior madness that haunts and ultimately destroys the white man, as is shown in stories that have a supernatural twist like 'At the End of the Passage'.

'The City of Dreadful Night', as well as stories such as 'The Strange Ride of Morrowbie Jukes' and 'At the End of the Passage', demonstrate the part that isolation – both physical and psychological – plays in Kipling's Indian fiction at this phase in his writing. India's particular geographic location and diverse cultural communities provide a powerful frame on which to hang an exploration of the terror of the abyss. Kristeva writes that 'the lost [maternal] object [. . .] is transposed by means of an unbelievable symbolic effort [. . .] which eroticizes the *other* [. . .] or transforms cultural constructs into "sublime" erotic objects', and Kipling's adult characters struggle to master their desire of a maternal realm, a desire that has been substituted by an eroticised Indian Other[5] that both undermines the coloniser's Christian sense of moral indignation and diminishes the potency of his perceived masculine strength. India and its peoples now pose a threat to the white adult male, where previously Kipling's Anglo-Indian children have enjoyed an (albeit hierarchical) interconnecting relationship to the indigenous population. Kristeva argues that 'the feminine as image of death is not only a screen for [a man's] fear of castration, but also an imaginary safety catch for the matricidal drive, that without such a representation would pulverize [him] into melancholia'.[6] In Kipling's fiction, the heat-scorched Indian terrain has become a place of potential death, and for the writer's imperial male to survive the rigours of Empire he must perform, in Kristevan terms, matricide on Mother India to prevent the threat of destruction. As Helen Pike Bauer has noted, implicit in the *Plain*

Tales and *Life's Handicap* collections is the idea that colonial service in India is a traumatising experience, a potentially life-threatening one that erodes a previously secure self-representation based on Empire's moral edicts and unspoken assumptions of supremacy.[7] The promise of returning 'home' or the comfort of solicitous companions is of little consolation to Kipling's imperial workforce in his nihilistic vision of India. Each homesick soldier, fevered engineer, insomniac wanderer or overworked administrator represents, in these collections, a community that is at breaking point, pushed to the edge of the abyss, weighed down by privation and deprived of an inner coalescence. Kipling's India lacks the sunny, restorative quality that would heal Kim's fragmented psyche when he sat down to write *Kim* twelve years later. At this time, Kipling's description of India is written in characteristically tongue-in-cheek tones:

> India is a place beyond all others where one must not take things too seriously – mid-day sun always excepted. Too much work and too much energy kill a man as effectively as too much assorted vice or too much drink [. . .] Good work does not matter, because a man is judged by his worst output, and another man takes all the credit of his best as a rule. Bad work does not matter, because other men do worse, and incompetents hang on longer in India that anywhere else [. . .] Nothing matters except Home-furlough and acting allowances [. . .] and the wisest thing is to escape as soon as ever you can to some place where amusement is amusement and a reputation worth the having. (*PT*, p. 15)

In *Plain Tales* and *Life's Handicap* Kipling gives voice to what Zohreh Sullivan argues are 'the colonizer's many subject positions and ambivalences'.[8] Certainly Kipling catalogues, as Pike Bauer has noted,[9] the difficult situations of ordinary soldiers as they struggle with the unremittingly hard work of the British Empire, detailing the friendships that sustain them through bouts of loneliness, homesickness and depression. He records the sense of duty that compensates for the hardships endured by imperial administrators whilst writing occasionally from an Indian perspective about lives that have been damaged by the colonising force, in stories such as, 'Lispeth', 'Little Tobrah' and 'At Twenty-Two' (in *Soldiers Three*) – the latter the author's recreation of the intolerable conditions of men working in this badly serviced coalmine, which, according to Lycett, shows that he was 'sympathetic to the plight of the Indian masses'.[10] Kipling's discourse of fragmentation can be read as an irruption of the abjected mother into the already fragile psyche of the white man that, on an unconscious level, his imperial heroes struggle against. From a Kristevan perspective, the image of a terrifying maternal Other, which disturbs the coloniser's notion of subjectivity, is the driving force behind his suffering and is present in the Indian landscape. In her manifestations, the abject maternal body in Kipling's fiction represents both death and desire. The anguish of maternal separation that Kipling's child characters experience, coupled with the subsequent loss of a ubiquitous self that characterises his adolescents, begins the process of retranslating the maternal space from a protective childhood playground of joyful and unrestricted roaming into a place of fear and death, a threatening abjected space. And the Indian stories of *Plain Tales* and *Life's Handicap*, more than any others, become the theatre where this drama of horror is played out.

'The City of Dreadful Night', curiously overlooked by a number of commentators on Kipling's art,[11] was first published in 1885 and subsequently collected in *Life's Handicap*. It is a decidedly abject text. In it we see a narrator, driven half mad with heat-fuelled insomnia and wandering a detritus-strewn landscape, trying to define and reconfigure the borders of this abjected nightmare world. In exile from the ordered daytime world of the coloniser, the narrator's identity as well as this surreal landscape is subject to mutability and as such becomes, in a Kristevan sense, 'one by whom the abject exists [. . .] a *deject*'.[12] Incapable of delineating the territory of his being, the narrator's sense of place, instead, provides him with an (albeit skewed, out of focus) meaning – his 'where' replaces his 'who'. In the metamorphosed city of Lahore, the narrator's subjectivity is comprehensively tied to this nightmarish terrain. As this space is constantly changing and morphing, the narrator as a Kristevan *deject*, is compelled eternally to reinterpret and reterritorialise his world. In the case of 'The City of Dreadful Night', Kipling stalks through his own literary past and cannibalises the images that he finds there. Kipling took the title from James Thomson's, 'The City of Dreadful Night', a poem published in 1874 and much read by Kipling as an adolescent; he discovered it while on holiday from USC.[13]

The transfigured nature of the narrator's out-of (colonial)-bounds world, which is marked by the abject, threatens to reveal the frightening brittleness of his identity. His aimless Prufrockian wanderings can be read as the psychic disorientation that occurs when the child becomes deterritorialised in its separation from the mother's body.[14] The suffering of maternal loss is mirrored in continual echoes of loss that punctuate the story: loss of sleep, loss of linear time, loss of boundaries, loss of cultural markers, loss of literary lineage. The position of the abjected mother, represented in the surreal terrain 'outside', presents a threat that is connected to the narrator's autonomous subjectivity, represented by the borders of the house, the 'inside'; but he, like Kristeva's exile, although sensing the danger of loss, 'cannot help taking the risk the very moment he sets himself apart'.[15] 'The City of Dreadful Night' mourns the loss of a nurturing maternal space, and the narrator's lonely walk, which takes him 'inside' to the heart of the walled city, reanimates that loss.

The story begins in horror: 'The dense wet heat that hung over the face of the land, like a blanket, prevented all hope of sleep in the first instance' (*LH*, p. 283) setting the scene for the narrator's need to stamp the symbolic law upon this disturbing, imprisoning 'inside'. Sliding from the parched and suffocating landscape to the narrator's insomnia almost imperceptibly, Kipling's masterful sleight of writer's hand reveals a narrative of obverse symbols. The binary oppositions of culture/nature, civility/chaos are transformed into hybrid signifiers of torment. We find the narrator embedded 'inside' in a cavernous darkness, an 'empty, echoing house', around which curls a suffocating 'dead air' (*LH*, p. 283). The metaphorical connotation of 'inside' is an important element of this story. In this instance the image of the narrator's house, as a white man's home, should represent a place of security from the dangers of 'outside', but Kipling presents it as a psychic 'prison'. The colonist's paternal authority should enclose the colonial 'inside', making it invulnerable to the threat of psychic instability but we sense the narrator's pressing need to be 'outside' of this claustrophobic interior. Beyond the walls of the house, Kipling continues to play with the notions of 'inside' and 'outside'. The narrator passes through a hellish 'outside' on his way into the walled city of Lahore, a native 'inside' that is associated with the echoic drives of the semiotic and has a connection to the past. In this respect, the image of colonial imprisonment is complicated by its connection to the 'inside' of the walled city. The colonial 'inside' that is identified with the father is an echoing, voided space. The walled city, in contrast, contains a maternal warmth in pockets of darkness that are alive with soft, comforting sounds of the night. This story challenges the normally subjugated relationship the semiotic has with the symbolic. We see a narrator wrestling with his desire for a unifying, sustaining relationship with the maternal body whilst acknowledging its 'difference' from his subjectivity.

At first the relations between the 'inside' and the 'outside' are seen as a frightening struggle between the autocratic, symbolic 'inside' and the abjected 'outside' associated with waste. Detritus is the abiding image in 'The City of Dreadful Night'. The narrator, in typical Kiplingesque style, meticulously inventories the waste of quotidian life that lies scattered about him, the 'disused Mahomedan burial-ground', the exposed fragments of bones, a 'smoke-stained lamp-shard' (*LH*, p. 283). The necropolis outside signifies immobility, a stasis magnified in the dry, discarded bones. The bones themselves are images of dusty and faded death that spares the narrator from the viscosity of the cadaver. It is a psychically manageable space, like the 'Wonder House' in *Kim* that displays centuries of 'living' history in ordered, classified groups. In this respect, the disinterred bones, which are visible under the soil, point to a ready acceptance of death as an abstract concept, a signified death. Kristeva argues that in the presence of such signification, 'a flat encephalograph, for instance – [we] would understand, react, or accept'.[16] The bleached bones appear to support a rational idea of death. But Kipling, adept at literary crafting, is rarely so one-dimensional a writer.[17] The narrator passes over the 'jawless skulls and rough butted shank-bones' (*LH*, p. 283). The July rains should hold the promise of regeneration, but instead they bring the dead from underground. And the heat from the dead air, which sets the cicalas (sic) and jackals screaming, aids the rains in enabling the bones to come rattling to the surface. Liminal spaces open up in the narrative as the moon changes places with the sun. 'It was hard not to believe that the flood of light from [the moon] above was warm' says the narrator, reinforcing the ambivalence (*LH*, p. 283). Caught between sleep and wakefulness, between the silent stasis of the house and the rustling movement outside, between life and death, the narrator enters a state of ambiguity situated on the very borders of subjectivity. It is a state that Victor Turner argues is 'neither here nor there, betwixt and between all fixed points of classification'.[18]

In a sense, 'The City of Dreadful Night' is already struggling with its literary genealogy. Kipling's piece is an uncanny rewriting of the apocalyptic poem of Thomson's that so captivated him as an adolescent at the USC. Thomson suffered from bouts of depression before his marriage to Carrie and his 'City of Dreadful Night' remains a despairing poem filled with pessimism. Set in a desolate, bleak London, it catalogues the despair of an atheist poet whose faith has evaporated, leaving nothing with which to replace it. 'Speak not of comfort where no comfort is' writes Thomson, 'Speak not at all: can words make foul things fair? / Our life's a cheat, our death a black abyss: / Hush and be mute envisaging despair.'[19] Kipling scavenges Thomson's dystopian vision to recreate what he saw as the colonial's nightmarish existence in a sun-blackened India. The vast, deserted cemetery where Thomson writes 'Perchance you find one mourner to a thousand dead'[20] finds its narrative counterpart in Kipling's image of the narrator standing in isolation before a Muslim burial ground, Thomson's 'men that were as phantoms flit and roam'[21] become 'sheeted ghosts [that] flit into the dark depths of the building' (*LH*, pp. 285–6). The trudging rhythm of the poem, with lines that seem to extend beyond their rhythmic breaks, is mirrored in Kipling's guttering sentences, as if the narrator is struggling to contain the words within their syntactical boundaries:

> More corpses; more stretches of moonlit, white road; a string of sleeping camels at rest by the wayside; a vision of scudding jackals; ekka ponies asleep – the harness still on their backs, and the brass-studded country carts, winking in the moonlight – and again more corpses. (*LH*, p. 284)

Just as Thomson is condemned to wander in a limbo of the lost, Kipling's narrator stalks through an equally ambivalent landscape where nightmare and reality have become confused and conjoined. Kipling borrowed both the title and the recurrent motif of isolation and disintegration from the poem, as well as, it seems, Thomson's pessimistic vision of urban decay. Similarly, Kipling's city is an ambivalent teeming urban space where the wreckage of humanity lies exhausted on the city's rooftops and littered by its roadside, silently disintegrating. Like the bones in the cemetery, it is a waste ground where life has lost its vitality. This ruined city suggests the very borders that stand between renewal and decay have dissolved, leaving a scattered wasteland of human debris in a grotesque pastiche of its former inhabitants that have been unearthed in the nearby Muslim cemetery.

The narrator sees a horde of 'sleeping men who lay like sheeted corpses' (*LH*, p. 283). Neither alive nor dead, these 'corpses disposed on beds in fantastic attitudes' (*LH*, p. 283) present in Kristeva's terms 'the most sickening of wastes [. . .] a border that has encroached upon everything'.[22] Kipling's description is even more horrifying, as these are not corpses but despoiled living creatures – abjection's markers made flesh, so to speak. The narrator blurs the difference between the living and the dead and so shows us the 'in-betweenness' that has begun to characterise his world. Living-dead things, he tells us, have overrun the approach to the city: 'more corpses [. . .] and again more corpses [. . .] ghosts rise up wearily from their pallets' (*LH*, pp. 284–6). Yet the story does not emphasise a fear of the corpses in themselves so much as their invasion of the perimeters of the living, and this in-between space gnaws away at the distinctions of subjectivity, like the rat that has burrowed into the turban of the Mosque's sleeping janitor and 'dashes out [. . .] at the sound of approaching footsteps' (*LH*, p. 286). The dead-in-life are everywhere:

> some face downwards, arms folded in the dust; some with clasped hands flung up above their heads; some curled up dog-wise; some thrown like limp gunny-bags over the side of grain carts; and some bowed with their brows on their knees. (*LH*, p. 284)

Corporeal decay is also connected to the terrain 'outside'. The 'grain cart atilt' and 'a few handfuls of thatch' (*LH*, p. 284) not only signal cultural decay, but also underscore bodily deterioration. This frightening space hints at a psychic 'unreality' that for the colonial has been associated with a prohibited 'beyond'. To move beyond the categories of race and gender classification is to risk losing one's colonial head. The dissemination of urban waste reflects the narrator's inner fragmentation as boundaries of subjectivity are weakened and threatened with dissolution.

The horror of 'The City of Dreadful Night' is located in its porous boundaries, its membranous inside/outside. The miasma that blows through the city implies not only bodily decay, but also the dissolution of boundaries. 'The high house-walls are still radiating heat savagely, and from the obscure side gullies fetid breezes eddy that ought to poison a buffalo' (*LH*, p. 285). In the semantic landscape of the text, the heat, the debris and the frail distinction between sleepers and corpses all imply dissolving definitions. Likewise, the proliferation of corpses signifies the 'utmost of abjection [. . .] that which has irremediably come a cropper',[23] and the story is quite literally stuffed with corpses, figuratively disinterred from below ground. The narrator's garden borders an ossuary where fragments of bones germinate and pierce the earth with the perverse life-giving qualities of night-heat and the summer rains. Kristeva argues that the 'time of abjection is double: a time of [. . .] veiled infinity and the moment when revelation bursts forth'.[24] The corporeal debris, which conversely bespeaks of the vitality of life, reveals the dereliction of a narrator whose centre has shattered in a terror of ambiguity, an 'in-between', 'composite'[25] existence where all order and structure have disintegrated. Beset by the horror of abjection, the narrator, like the colonial engineer Morrowbie Jukes, struggles to organise and catalogue the human waste that litters this most terrifying of landscapes. The 'one hundred and seventy bodies of men' that lie on either side of the road, some 'shrouded all in white', some 'naked and black as ebony' (*LH*, p. 283) are manifestations of inner disintegration as well as bodily decay. The outcast leper, 'silvery white and ashen grey' (*LH*, p. 283), attests in a decidedly Foucauldian way to a psychological disintegration.[26] The filth, which the corpse-like figures garishly display, represents what is ceaselessly cast out in order to live, whilst hinting at a defilement operating within the narrator on a wholly internal level.

The narrator too succumbs to this in-betweenness, as his narratorial position is split by a voice in the third person pronoun that enters the story from outside of its frame. This disembodied voice, like that of an uncanny doppelganger, describes the scene in clipped sentences that, ringing with clarity and authority, counterbalance the increasingly surreal description of the sleeping figures in the preceding lines. Enclosing the words in quotation marks, Kipling writes:

> 'A leper asleep; and the remainder wearied coolies, servants, small shopkeepers and drivers from the hack-stand hard by. The scene – a main approach to Lahore city, and the night a warm one in August.' (*LH*, pp. 283–4)

This calm, authoritative voice only appears once and it is, from a Kristevan point of view, the voice of reason, the voice of the symbolic. The ordered 'I' that offers a detached reportage of the scene is connected to its obverse Other voice that articulates the text's mutability. The two narratorial points of view make us aware of the borderline state to which the text has succumbed. The narrator's account of his journey starts as an editorial 'I', but quickly fragments to become the mark of migration, an 'I' that incorporates an Other. Within the narrator himself, the 'voiced breath' of the semiotic competes with the authoritative tone of the symbolic. In a surreal dual discourse, the narrator catalogues the scene and 'sees' that the 'witchery of the moonlight' (*LH*, p. 284) has morphed the landscape and the people who populate it into a frightening inversion of the daytime world. This is a world that incorporates elements of reality as well as bizarre, nightmarish visions. For example, the road to the city by day is by night transformed into a 'rigid silver statue' that is 'straight as a bar of polished steel' (*LH*, p. 283) and splits the living dead in two, while bodies fragment in a disjointed heap. Scraps of sounds like clinking bracelets and the tinkling of falling water are connected to shards of river glimpsed through gaps in the city's walls. Flashes of ragged lightning on the horizon are connected to the 'full glare of the Moon' that illuminates the entire scene like an inverted sun (*LH*, p. 284) – in Kristevan terms, a 'black sun', for she argues that the black sun metaphor sums up the 'borderline experience of the psyche struggling against dark asymbolism'.[27]

'The City of Dreadful Night' abjects Kipling's idyllic childhood vision of India. In *Kim*, *The Jungle Book* and in the English countryside in *Stalky & Co.*, Kipling's noblest hopes for humanity, love, harmony and grace imbued with splendour and might are locked into aspects of the natural world that are then valorised. For example, the details of life are beautifully 'lighted from behind like twigs on tree-tops seen against lightning' (*Kim*, p. 306), and Mowgli's lessons are punctuated with sojourns into 'the dark warm heart of the forest' (*JB*, p. 44). Endowing the external landscape with such lofty attributes enables Kipling's boy heroes to vicariously instil these attributes within themselves in the search for inner order. This visionary ideal will be reanimated in

Puck of Pook's Hill but in this story, the city, its inhabitants and the narrator are in disarray and subject to fragmentation. There is also an absence of Kipling's ideal of the transcendental, which is established by the imagination and mirrored in the natural world, and permeates the narrative of *Kim*. Such a nihilistic vision of the city is situated between an India of 'light and colour' (*SOM*, p. 3) and the sun-dappled 'sleepy stillness' (*PPH*, p. 7) of the Sussex downs. But as the skeletal remains in the cemetery are psychically connected to the sleeping corpses, so Kipling's fecund, vibrant India becomes a hybridised, borderline place of internal disintegration, like the pigeon imprisoned in niches by the 'broad diagonal bands' (*LH*, p. 285) of the moon, unable to fly, fully grown but 'squab' (*LH*, p. 285) nonetheless.

Dissolving definitions are paradoxically given shape and strength when viewed in conjunction with the artistic majesty of *Kim* and the order it brings to Kim's fragmented psyche. Kipling's edenic India that in *Kim* constitutes 'good clean dust, with no new herbage, which though living, is half-way to death already, but the hopeful dust that holds the seed of all life' (*Kim*, p. 332), in this story is inverted and polluted. The murky 'clump of tamarisk trees' (*LH*, p. 283), with their reptilian, scale-like leaves, despoil the grace bestowed by Kipling upon the natural world. The shadow that they cast, instead of leading to a path of spiritual fulfilment, dispassionately swallows life, like the startled hare that hides amongst their roots, in a whimper. Dawn, which in *Kim* offers an image of reunification with the mother figure as well as regeneration and juvenescence, is, in this story, subjected to the same mutability as everything else with a sky that is washed 'gray, and presently saffron' (*LH*, p. 288). Saffron, produced by an autumn flowering crocus, becomes a bastardised image of spring, offering no respite from the horror of this cadaverous land. The narrator is psychically inserted into the shadow that lays on the border between the symbolism of dawn as rebirth and the actuality of dawn as heralding quotidian city life – between, in effect, the idea and the reality. These are potent concepts that resonate in T. S. Eliot's *The Waste Land*.[28] In her study of Kipling Jan Montefiore argues that the subversive writing style that characterised the writers of the Modernist movement was anticipated in Kipling's prose and verse.[29]

The noises of the night, in contrast to the silence of the abjected living corpses, are warm and close, reminiscent, in Kristevan terms, of 'semiotic rhythms, which convey an intense presence of meaning in a pre-subject still incapable of signification'.[30] In the short time that the narrator rests observing this intimate scene of companionship – men sharing a pipe, seeking solace in one another's company – we as voyeurs sense his longing to be enveloped in this profoundly welcoming space.

The implication is that the narrator's goal is not to find some conclusion to his journey but that he might scrap it altogether and retrace his life to what Thomson describes as an 'antenatal night' that is 'beyond the reach of man-evolving Doom'.[31] Kipling wrote for a society that could no longer unproblematically be measured against a concept of colonial order. The so-called Mutiny of 1857 had done much to shake the confidence of the British administrators. The initial outbreaks in Dehli and Meerut inspired other mutinies in the Punjab that were, David Saul argues, 'ripe for mutiny', Lahore included.[32] David Gilmour notes that, in Kipling's time, Lahore was still haunted by the ghosts of the violent skirmishes. 'The senior men in the administration' of Lahore, he argues, 'saw themselves as descendants of the generation that had pacified the Punjab and kept it loyal during the Indian Mutiny.'[33] Kipling rarely wrote of the Mutiny, but the fear it instilled in the Anglo-Indian community is captured in 'The Undertakers' (in *The Second Jungle Book*) with Kipling's grisly description of a man-eating crocodile that gorged itself on the abundance of massacred bodies that floated down the Ganges in the wake of the Mutiny.

'The City of Dreadful Night' captures with remarkable clarity the narrator's desire to bring order to an inner chaos. Primary processes break through the text, those elements of the semiotic that are dominated by intonation and rhythmic utterances, which lead us, Kristeva argues, 'directly to the otherwise silent place of its subject'.[34] Pre-symbolic existence can be read in the indistinct strains of stringed instruments that melt into the sounds of nature itself as well as fragments of muffled conversation. Distance softens coarse music into a 'plaintive wail', the 'low grumble of far-off thunder' (*LH*, p. 288) adding to its melody. These indistinct noises, in obliterating sequential discourse, subvert the rigidity of the phallogocentric order, replacing words with sounds, as it were. In Kristevan terms, the semiotic encroaches and overpowers the authority of the symbolic, relinquishing signifiers for inchoate, rhythmic utterances.

The release of the semiotic into the narrative takes place inside the walled city amongst its indigenous population, a population that the child and adult Kipling was drawn to and entranced by. In *Something of Myself* Kipling writes of the beauty of 'far going Arab dhows on the pearly waters, and gaily dressed Parsees wading out to worship at sunset'. As an adult he describes how he would frequently 'wander till dawn in all manner of odd places [. . .] which are not a bit mysterious' (*SOM*, pp. 4, 33). Kipling's description of the city with its 'vacant main street' (*LH*, p. 285) evokes Thomson's forlorn metropolis where its inhabitants, if they meet at all, rarely speak to each other, merely 'throw[ing] in a remark from time to time' (*LH*, p. 285). But whilst Thomson presents a city with no voice, with no community in its 'soundless solitudes immense',[35] Kipling's 'voiced' silence echoes with snatches of incoherent speech that merge with fragments of music to produce the city's pulsing rhythm. Kipling writes that the sleeping city comprises 'a silence that is full of [. . .] night noises'. The binary position of cadenced sounds and meaningful syntax is therefore undermined and the text is influenced instead by the more rhythmic incantations of the semiotic. This section is defined by sounds that do not lend themselves to signification and can be read as the symbolic's authority ceding to the rippling fluidity of the signifier. For example, 'buffaloes blow [. . .] like grampuses' and men's conversation becomes a muted babble that mixes with the soft guttering of a hookah-pipe (*LH*, p. 285). The hitherto 'silenced' semiotic manifests itself in the city's echolalia, the 'voiced breath' that ripples across the text weaving its abstruse way through it. These archaic sounds, like the metamorphosed buffaloes, blow away the signifying chain of the symbolic, enabling a muted *jouissance* to emerge in the narrative. Similarly, the music of the 'stringed instrument', which is 'only just audible', is augmented by the 'rattle of the woodwork' and in turn picks up snippets of conversation over a bubbling hookah (*LH*, p. 285). Taken together in symphonic variations, these sounds indicate the rhythmic agency of the semiotic that challenges the monopoly of the symbolic.

The echoes of the semiotic, which are present in Kipling's transfigured images, rely on sensory perceptions rather than logical meanings. The sounds of the instruments and the bubbling hookah are of equal importance to the indistinct conversations of the men. As the symbolic's binary distinctions are overturned, an altogether more archaic modality brings a new energy, a new subjectivity of unity that can paradoxically hold the abject at bay. In Kristevan terms the *symbolic processes* give way to the *semiotic processes*.[36] Kipling's real-life experiences of the noises emanating from 'in and around the narrow gullies under the Mosque of the Wazir Khan' (*SOM*, p. 33) recall the mutability within its fictionalised counterpart. However, whilst the night noises summon up the warmth and security of the semiotic, their heterogeneity is broken by the 'slit of light [that] shows itself between the sliding shutters of a shop' as the symbolic works to re-establish its linguistic authority in the narrative (*LH*, p. 285). The kaleidoscopic ambiguity of Kipling's imagery, which is expressed through the rhythms, condensation and displacement of signifiers and has momentarily shaped the direction of the narrative, is subsumed by the logic of discourse. The 'noise of conversation' becomes 'more distinct' (*LH*, p. 285) as the narrator turns his attention to the work going on inside the lighted shop.

All too soon the rigid framework of the symbolic reinserts itself in the narrator's description, and the thematic and linguistic dialectic of the symbolic and semiotic are set in opposition once again as the narrator struggles for conscious mastery over semiotic echolalia. The narrator sees 'a stubble-bearded, weary-eyed trader' balancing his accounts (*LH*, p. 285). The 'three sheeted figures [that] bear him company' (*LH*, p. 285) recall the corpses that proliferate the landscape. And in this sense, the previous symphonic sounds beyond signifiers, the mutterings beyond words, recall (and are thus connected to) other meaningless but more menacing sounds, the 'yelling jackals', the cicalas, the 'high-pitched shriek' of a child (*LH*, pp. 283–4). Kipling begins to reinstate a symbolic order within the narrative. The 'more distinct' words of the trader impose an order that beats to the metronomic rhythm of day-time work, 'the work goes on steadily; entry, guttural growl, and uplifted hand-stroke succeeding each other with the precision of clock-work' (*LH*, p. 285). Yet even here, the phallogocentric order struggles to contain and control the semiotic as the 'guttural growl' of the trader is an integral part of the narrator's account. In Kipling's symbology, the policeman (Strickland, Policeman Day), the experienced soldier (Private Mulvaney), the benevolent figure of authority (Colonel Creighton, Captain Corbyn) all have the ability to restore both psychological and physical order to Kipling's stories. However, in this story the desire that threatens the very principle of symbolic order will not submit to the law-of-the-father, and its guardian, the policeman, is subject to the same mutability as the city's inhabitants. The 'bar of moonlight [that] falls across the forehead and eyes' of the turban-less policeman lying asleep on the road brings no divine vision of harmony, for 'he never stirs' (*LH*, p. 285). He remains corpse-like, lying like some grotesque signpost pointing to the mosque, where the narrator will find a proliferation of corpses.

The narrator's attempt to reach the summit of the 'Minar' is fraught with terror. Picking his way across the hordes of sleeping dead, he encounters a world that, like the 'pitch-black, polished walls of the corkscrew staircase' (*LH*, p. 273), is spiralling into chaos, where signifiers once again lose their stability and transform into ghastly nightmare images. The kites that line the staircase are subject to the same mutability as the hare, the bones, and the narrator whose shifting identity is on the brink of imminent collapse. The kites that 'snore like over-gorged humans' (*LH*, p. 288), the janitor who is a corpse that opens its eyes (*LH*, p. 288), the worshippers who are ghosts (*LH*, p. 285), are precarious signifiers. The narrator's only hope of halting this slide into obliquity seems to be to get above the horror that is, like the toxic air of the walled city, eddying all around him, threatening to engulf him at any moment and consign him to the abyss where the blankness of oblivion waits. But the panorama that awaits him is the embodiment of the nightmare realm. Unable to articulate the horror of the scene, the narrator, who momentarily loses the power of narration, calls upon his artistic precursors, Zola and Doré, to enunciate what he cannot, to paint for us an image of the thousands of bodies illuminated under a glaring moon, writhing in the torment of a sleep that eludes them. Kipling presents these corpse-like figures shuddering *en masse* as a socio-symbolic multitude in ruin:

> A small cloud passes over the face of the Moon, and the city and its inhabitants – clear drawn in black and white before – fade into masses of black and deeper black. Still the unrestful noise continues, the sigh of a great city overwhelmed with the heat, and of a people seeking in vain for rest. (*LH*, pp. 286–7)

The 'unwinking eye of the moon' presiding over this hellish scene with 'sickly warm[th]' (*LH*, p. 283) illuminates the restless inhabitants below. The narrator is looking down upon a world that has fallen through the colonial mirror. The city of the dead is briefly brought to life by the muezzin's great cry, 'Allah ho Akbar' which, resonating across the whole city, gives the narrator a fleeting sense of patriarchal order:

> What a splendid cry it is, the proclamation of a creed that brings men out of their beds by scores at mid-night [. . .] It is as though he were flinging his defiance to the summer horizon. (*LH*, p. 287)

But the respite is only temporary, for once the call is over, 'silence closes up' on the city once more (*LH*, p. 287). The last image of the story is one of death. A woman has died during the night due to the insufferable heat and her corpse pays testament to the very death-bound nature of life. The last line of the story underscores all that the narrator has witnessed on his horror-filled journey into the night with syntax that is capitalised to strengthen its potency: '[s]o the city was of Death as well as Night' (*LH*, p. 288).

The narrator of 'The City of Dreadful Night' has taken a real and symbolic journey, but what began with psychological suffering (insomnia) and physical suffering (unendurable heat) ends in a horror-filled landscape where the only hope when it comes is from the guardianship of paternal authority, yet even this solicitous space is penetrated by the abject. The '[y]ellow-skinned white-toothed pariahs' (*LH*, p. 284) threaten a child enclosed in his father's protective embrace, an image of a terrifying phallic mother with the potential to annihilate her infant. He presents this ruined city as an abyss at the bottom of which its inhabitants can find no peaceful existence and are consigned, like the recurrent motif of *Life's Handicap*, to 'beyond the pale'. Similarly, in 'The Strange Ride of Morrowbie Jukes', the protagonist falls through a gap in the steady organised world of the coloniser and falls into a horrifying abjected void that, in Kristevan terms, can be read as a terrifying vision whereby the white man is sucked back into the mother's body through her sex.

'The Strange Ride of Morrowbie Jukes' was first published in 1885 when Kipling was only still a very young man, a remarkable feat given the story's highly accomplished craftsmanship. The story charts the progress of Morrowbie Jukes, an English civil engineer working in India. This eerie tale is an examination of the coloniser's tenuous grip on the values that underpin his authority and sense of superiority, which can be read as the fragility of the paternal authority at the centre of a phallogocentric system. According to Cixous phallogocentricism is, amongst other things, 'a universal battlefield. Each time, a war is let loose. Death is always at work. Father/Son Relations of authority, privilege, force [. . .] Master/Slave Violence. Repression. We see that "victory" always comes down to the same thing: things get hierarchical.'[37] As we see in the story, Jukes is psychically at war with, not only renegade (native) sons (and daughters) of a British sovereignty but his own presupposed sense of himself as colonial master.

Pike Bauer argues that Jukes undergoes a debilitating threat to his colonial identity, not because he is isolated in some remote cantonment far from the stabilising constructs that the Anglo-Indian community provides, rather, his identity is, like Punch's, determined by just those imperial structures that give weight and meaning to his status as white man in India.[38] When he falls through the safety net of an imperial ideology that sanctions his perceived supremacy, he comes close to psychic collapse. Suffering a fevered frenzy brought about by his work in heat-scorched India, Jukes dementedly rides his horse Pornic[39] to the edge of a crater filled with sand, into which he plummets. His sanity is unhinged by a 'delirium of fever' that is mixed with 'the excitement of the rapid motion through the air' (*WWW*, p. 188). Jukes is then dementedly at 'war' with his natural surroundings, 'brandishing [his] hog-spear at the great white moon that looked down so calmly on [his] mad gallop' (*WWW*, p. 188). The 'limitless expanse of moonlit sand' (*WWW*, p. 188) illuminates the Sutlej River, which has been transformed, like the road in 'The City of Dreadful Night', into a 'shining [. . .] silver bar' (*WWW*, p. 188). It forms a psychological border between the rational world of the white man and the unmapped nightmare world that Jukes is about to enter.

The pit's bottom is a claustrophobic, abjected space and, like the mouth of Aunty Rosa, can be identified with the womb, a 'horse-shoe shaped crater of sand, opening on one side directly on the shoals of the Sutlej [. . .] with steeply-graded sand walls' (*WWW*, p. 188). Unlike the dens in the gorse bordering the sea that give Stalky and his compatriots 'inexpressible joy' (*S&C*, p. 32), this nightmare place is where Jukes is in danger of losing his colonial self, not being able to find a 'way back' to a psychic '*terra firma*' (*WWW*, p. 189). It is with horror that the engineer realises he is not alone as 'sixty-five human beings' emerge, zombie-like, from the crater's travestied uterine 'badger-holes' (*WWW*, p. 190). These crevices, like the abjected spaces of 'The City of Dreadful Night', are linked to blackness, death and decomposition. Kipling describes one of the sleeping places as a 'fetid burrow' (*WWW*, p. 201), and Jukes finds that his own sleeping place is as 'narrow as a coffin' (*WWW*, p. 199). The unfortunate victims of this hellish place are marked by pollution. 'The filth and repulsiveness of the assembly were all beyond description' says Jukes, 'and I shuddered to think what their life in the badger-holes must be' (*WWW*, p. 190).

Falling headlong into this terrifying cavity, Jukes' authority is immediately 'castrated' by his entrapment in this decidedly feminine space. He attempts to escape but at every turn he fails: 'ineffectual charges sent [him] rolling down to the bottom, half-choked with torrents of sand' (*WWW*, p. 189). Scrambling to free himself from this nightmarish space, Jukes is unable to overcome the fluidity of the sand that pulls him back toward the bottom of the pit. He finds himself trapped with a group of Indians who live in a liminal world of the half-dead. Neither part of life nor wholly excluded from it, the terrifying individuals must live out their desperate existence in this wretched pit because they revived during their cremations on the burning ghats. They are imprisoned in this hellish place and deterred from escape by snipers and quicksand. No longer included in a world of ordinary human society, these miserable creatures are family-less and casteless, outside of the 'Law', in effect. Yet these forsaken fragments of humanity still cling to life (albeit an abjected one), where they fight among themselves and must trap and eat crows in order to survive. Intriguingly, Kipling's father, Lockwood, in his study of the totemic significance of Indian animals writes: 'No decent person, of course would dine on crows [. . .] They are thieves, outcast scavengers, deceitful, and above all other creatures that hoard and hide, clever in concealing things.'[40] The crater-people, by blurring the demarcation between the living and the dead, are straddling the borders of subjectivity, are markers of abjection. They unnervingly speak in 'low equable tones, curiously in contrast to the strident babble with which natives are accustomed to make hideous' (*WWW*, p. 198), regarding Jukes 'with the most chilling indifference' (*WWW*, p. 194). He is no longer at the centre of the colonial system, having been cast to its margins by his fall into the abyss. Jukes is the embodiment of colonial authority, but here he is outside of borders, and his stern edicts carry little weight in this environment. Used to commanding the natives, he is surprised that the 'people [of the pit] showed not the faintest sign of curiosity – that curiosity which is so rampant, as a rule, in an Indian village' (*WWW*, p. 194).

To compensate for the horror of his situation, Jukes uses the rational thinking of the colonial engineer. He estimates the size of the crater ('a level piece of ground about fifty yards long by thirty at its broadest'), the slope of the hill ('about thirty-five feet high'), and the ghastly burrows the inhabitants occupy: 'a series of eighty-three semicircular, ovoid, square, and multilateral holes, all about three feet at the mouth' (*WWW*, p. 189). Jukes attempts to reinstate the borders of the symbolic with logic, to create order out of chaos. However, Jukes' panicky efforts only reinforce the helplessness of his situation: he says that the 'sensation of nameless terror which I had in vain attempted to survive overmastered me completely' (*WWW*, p. 193). Social and physical deprivation causes the normally stout-hearted, rational colonist to temporarily succumb to blind terror, which provokes a bestial insanity: 'I verily believe that, for a few minutes, I acted as one mad. I hurled myself against the sand-slope. I ran round the base of the crater, blaspheming and praying by turns [. . .] I dared not face the death of a mad dog among that hideous crowd – and so fell, spent and raving, at the curb of the well' (*WWW*, p. 193).

Hope seems to be revived when Jukes meets Gunga Dass, a junior government worker whom he remembers as a 'jovial, full-stomached, portly Government servant with a marvellous capacity for making bad puns in English' (*WWW*, p. 191). But his transformation into an abjected inhabitant of this nightmare environment repulses the Englishman. Jukes is drawn into a struggle to control his terror of Dass by trying to 'see' him in terms of who he was in the colonial world, but Dass's shabby, emaciated appearance makes this impossible: 'the man was changed beyond all recognition. Caste-mark, stomach [. . .] and unctuous speech were all gone' (*WWW*, p. 191). Dass represents death-in-life: 'I looked at the withered skeleton, turbanless and almost naked, with long matted hair and deep-set cod-fish eyes' (*WWW*, p. 191). He now lies outside the codified world of Empire and as such defies just those lessons in the master/slave dialectics that British men (like Jukes) have learned in their military academies back home. Seen through a Kristevan lens, Dass will not 'agree to the [. . .] rules of the game'.[41]

This abjected wreckage of humanity informs Jukes that he is now one of the desolate inhabitants in this pit of despair. And he is 'astonished' to learn that Dass feels himself 'superior or at least [. . .] an equal' (*WWW*, p. 193). Like Punch, it is not the situation itself that Jukes finds most bewildering, but his own collapse of authority. As an Anglo-Indian he expects to be treated with grateful obedience, but in this 'reeking village' of the damned, a hierarchy based upon superior strength and cunning outweighs the white man's sense of mastery (*WWW*, p. 192). His initial reaction to the manner in which he is treated is irritation, but this is quickly followed by the shock of realisation that the border between Sahib and native, previously held in place by a British military force and their technological skill, has irrevocably broken down:

> even in these days, when local self-government has destroyed the greater part of a native's respect for a Sahib, I have been accustomed to a certain amount of civility from my inferiors, and so on approaching the crowd naturally expected that there would be some recognition of my presence. As a matter of fact there was, but it was by no means what I had looked for. The ragged crew actually laughed at me – such laughter I hope I may never hear again. (*WWW*, p. 190)

As Mark Paffard argues, the 'ragged crew' no longer recognises his assumed superiority as imperial representative.[42] On the contrary, Jukes is now counted as a 'companion' among the '[r]epublic of wild beasts penned at the bottom of [the] pit' (*WWW*, pp. 194, 201).

Unable to tolerate the degeneration of humanity that is laid out before him, Jukes finds himself in a terrified abyss but must join the others in the same brutal fight for existence if he is to survive. In this surreal world, Jukes literally eats crows and incorporates their abjected status into his sense of selfhood. He is reduced by hunger, exhaustion and fear to a panicky wreck. In the 'agony of nervous dread' he collapses on the ground, 'spent and raving' (*WWW*, p. 193). Just as Punch loses his status of 'sahib', so Jukes is 'stripped' of his colonial authority by the natives' indifference to it. 'Two or three men trod on my panting body', he says, 'but they were evidently used to this sort of thing' (*WWW*, p. 193). The only law seems to be a Darwinian one. Those who prove stronger in the fight for food, shelter and self-preservation are better equipped to last in this environment:

> I had left the world, it seemed, for centuries. I was as certain then as I am now of my own existence, that in the accursed settlement there was no law save that of the strongest, that the living dead men had thrown behind them every canon of the world which had cast them out; and that I had to depend for my own life on my strength and vigilance alone. (*WWW*, p. 199)

In a continent that has been overpowered by the iron fist of military and technological might and is ruled by a race of white men who wholeheartedly believe that it is India's best destiny to be governed by the British, the 'canons', which Jukes laments being cast away, are in fact the coloniser's notion of 'fair play' and 'civilised' behaviour as well as bowing to the will of superiors – everything, in short, that a governing body expects of its subjugated peoples in order to rule. As invaders of the Indian subcontinent, the British relied upon their military strength, gruesomely displayed in the swift and bloody reprisals to the Mutiny. The historian David Saul writes: 'The mutiny at Benares and the subsequent unrest in the outlying districts unleashed a terrible European backlash. Rows of gallows were erected the day after the rising and were soon filled with scores of suspected rebels [. . .] At the same time volunteer hanging parties were roaming the Benares area with one gentleman executioner boasting of the "artistic manner" in which he had strung up his victims "in the form of a figure of eight".'[43] The difference seems to be that in this anarchic space Jukes has no military might to reinstate his authority save the brute strength he can muster. The playing field has been levelled and Jukes comes to realise that his existence is, like Darwin's notion of the state of nature, precarious, hunger-filled, brutish and by no means assured. It is a world where he can survive only on his cunning and fitness.

In the Darwinian anarchy that characterises the behaviour of the pit's inhabitants, Jukes can only rely upon inner strength to stop himself from being overpowered both physically and psychically: 'I had to control myself here with both hands, lest the blind terror should lay hold of me a second time and drive me raving round the crater' (*WWW*, p. 195). But all societal markers of morality, culture and hierarchy are continually undermined by the horror of abjection. The sahib Jukes, 'a representative of the dominant race', is as 'helpless as a child and completely at the mercy of his native neighbours' (*WWW*, p. 196). Beset by abjection, he feels variously 'sick and faint with horror', 'numbed and helpless', and is overcome by the 'sensation of a nameless terror' (*WWW*, pp. 203, 201, 193). Each stage of his escalating insanity is characterised by laughter. The 'absurd' contrast of his colonial life makes the government engineer who is not possessed with an 'imaginative temperament' (*WWW*, p. 200) 'laugh heartily' (*WWW*, p. 192). Laughter, Kristeva argues, is the 'trans-syntactic inscription of emotion [. . .] the most subtle manifestation of [. . .] abjection'[44] and Dass, who can be read as the representative of abjection, bursts through Jukes' assumed colonial authority with a terrifying apocalyptic laugh. His laughter not only undermines the Englishman's ineffectual threats and supposed morality, but questions the very foundations of colonial and paternal authority, 'he [Dass] was laughing all the while in the same mirthless wheezy key that greeted my first attempt to force the shoals' (*WWW*, p. 194). 'Morality', Jukes comes to realise, 'is blunted by consorting with the Dead who are alive' (*WWW*, p. 206). Dass, through his 'malevolent', 'wheezy chuckles' (*WWW*, pp. 200, 195), announces the horror of the abject. By 'naming' the abject with such apocalyptic laughter, Dass symbolically reaches into the unconscious to uncover a repressed fear of not only annihilation by engulfment in abjected feminine flesh, but also of reverting to what the white man unequivocally believes is 'bestiality' of the native. Jukes comes to recognise his own 'bestial' nature in a pit 'so full of terror' (*WWW*, p. 200). Associating himself with the native community in a perverted companionship, he says, '[o]ne does not protest against the doings of a den of wild beasts; and my companions were lower than beasts' (*WWW*, p. 194).

The story ends with the appearance of Dunnoo, a faithful servant who has followed the tracks of Jukes' horse and finally (if a little unbelievably) rescues him from the crater; but only after he has, as Pike Bauer and Angus Wilson rightly note, gazed into the abyss and seen there the spectacular disintegration of the code by which he has lived in India as an imperial servant.[45] And with its collapse, his Anglo-Indian identity buckles and shatters: 'you are dead, my dear friend' Gunga Dass tells Jukes gleefully, '[i]t is not your fault, of course, but none the less you are dead *and* buried' (*WWW*, p. 195). Jukes is removed from the society that has perpetuated those values which the white man appropriates for his own: a racial and social superiority, the self-appointed role of moral protector to the infantilised native and the belief in an ideological system that can echo back and amplify his colonial status. And, as J. M. S. Tompkins has pointed out, the tale is all the more terrifying for the detached way in which Jukes lays bare the precarious nature of British authority.[46]

The life-affirming native friendships, coupled with the sustaining environment of India that gave shape to and nurtured Kim's ambivalent identity, have yet to be imaginatively realised by the author in this hellish space. India is subject to the same mutability as the inhabitants of her cave grave. Jukes tries to escape across the seemingly benign shallow pools that flank the crater, but they turn out to be quicksand: 'I felt an indescribable drawing, sucking motion of the sand below. Another moment and my leg was swallowed nearly to the knee' (*WWW*, p. 200). Kipling anthropomorphises India into a terrifying she-devil, gleefully revelling in the colonial's impotence: 'the whole surface of the sand seemed to be shaken with devilish delight at my disappointment'

(*WWW*, p. 200). Although Jukes almost succumbs to madness, he manages to escape with his sanity intact. This eerie tale uncovers what David Gilmour argues is the 'vulnerability of the Englishman when he [has] strayed beyond the protection of Anglo-India'.[47] In this story, the terror that his fever precipitated remains an external malignant force. In 'At the End of the Passage', the terror is presented on a wholly internal level as the protagonist is infected with an uncanny inner horror.

'At the End of the Passage' is an example of Kipling's horror of the abyss, which can be viewed as the threat to the paternal authority from irruptions in the narrative of a maternal space. The story concerns four Anglo-Indians whose occupations are emblematic of the bedrock of Empire – a physician, a civil servant, a surveyor, and an engineer. Even though tensions are apparent in their precarious friendships, they each depend upon one another for a companionship that acts as a meagre antidote to the monotony of their daily routines. The engineer, Hummil, out of a sense of duty (unnecessarily, as it turns out), endures not only painful isolation, but also a psychic disturbance in his effort to continue his work for the Empire. Like 'The City of Dreadful Night', this disturbance is represented climatically in the parched landscape, but Kipling adds a twist, a spectral vision of a frightening doppelganger. So catastrophic are these potential threats to Hummil's psychic stability that a spiralling narrative of madness finds its harrowing conclusion in his death. Kipling implies that the men's sense of duty to the monolithic edifice of Empire hides a growing awareness of the meaninglessness that lurks behind their quotidian work.

The men's allegiance to the imperial mission is founded on the repression of this realisation, which, if acknowledged, can lead to depression and suicide. Hummil guesses that his subordinate's death may have been just such a suicide, and the 'brown purple haze of heat' that obscures 'sky, sun [and] horizon' is a contributing factor (*LH*, p. 156). 'I judge no man this weather' (*LH*, p. 161), he bluntly states, but the physician Spurstow's taciturn response is, 'suicide is shirking your work' (*LH*, p. 161). The doctor's flippant retort hints at an internal battle between the daytime work of Empire (that will be dealt with in more detail in the following chapter) and the night-time world of insomnia and night terrors. The ghastly conclusion to this internal conflict is self-destruction, and the narrative is fixed in an ever-present fantasy of suicide, a fantasy that has been portended in an earlier tale of suicide in 'Thrown Away'. Hummil allows his subordinate's death to be filed as an accidental death, saying: 'A man hasn't many privileges in this country, but he might at least be allowed to mishandle his own rifle. Besides, some day I may need a man to smother up an accident to myself' (*LH*, p. 161). The story records the spectacular failure of the law-of-the-father to prevent Hummil's psychic fragmentation, a failure that sees binary oppositions overturned.

In this story, the European's world is covered over by the climactic conditions that seem to blow from the mouth of hell. Charles Allen argues that Kipling's 'Hot Weather' imagery is irrevocably tied to the mental breakdowns of his imperial characters.[48] The forgotten outposts where Hummil and his compatriots eke out their daily lives are in conflict with the perceived ordered world of the coloniser, which is regulated by binary oppositions between sahib and native. When the boundaries disappear through overwork, boredom and exhaustion there follows a descent into hell, where the border between reality and dream, order and chaos becomes hazy and indistinct. The epigraph that opens the story sets the tone for the narrative that follows.

> The sky is lead and our faces red,
> And the Gates of Hell are opened and riven,
> And the winds of Hell are loosened and driven,
> And the dust flies up in the face of Heaven [. . .]
> And the soul of a man is turned from his meat,
> Turned from the trifles for which he has striven
> Sick in his body, and heavy hearted,
> And his soul flies up like dust in the sheet. (*LH*, p. 156)

Hell is a metaphor for the chaotic, malignant Indian weather coupled with a detritus-strewn wasteland and overwhelms the narrative, thereby inverting the supposed power of an imperial system designed to prevent its subjects from going 'worst mucker' (*DW*, p. 291). Sullivan maintains that 'Kipling's worst fear [was] going "worst mucker" amid the multiple tyrannies and invisible structures of everyday colonial life.'[49] However, a tension is created between desire for the maternal body and the strictures of a masculine paternal law; this is what drives Kipling's colonial characters to madness and suicide. Characters like the Brushwood Boy shield themselves against the onslaught of desire with an exemplary dedication to duty. Armed with a code of practice that favours war and camaraderie over emotional and sexual desire, Kipling's 'successful' colonial adults are able to keep their desire for the maternal body in (albeit repressed) check.

Kipling's ironic narratorial voice implies that the stress, sleeplessness and loneliness of carrying out governmental work in almost unendurable climatic conditions actually induces a panicky madness and suicidal impulses. The men's living conditions are tied to a landscape that petrifies and 'condemns' any vitality:

> From time to time clouds of tawny dust rose from the ground without wind or warning, flung themselves tablecloth-wise among the tops of parched trees, and came down again. Then a whirling dust-devil would scutter across the plain for a couple of miles, break, and fall outward, though there was nothing to check its flight save a long low line of piled railway-sleepers white with the dust, a cluster of huts made of mud, condemned rails, and canvas, and one squat four-roomed bungalow that belonged to the assistant engineer. (*LH*, pp. 156–7)

Kipling seems to suggest that a dangerous force, which takes the shape of blood-like 'tawny' dust devils, undermines the stability and calcifies the power of the colonial world. The leitmotif of the railway that will energetically run across the narrative of *Kim* is, in this story, inert and lifeless due to the destructive effect of the dust whipped up by the malignant wind.

Kipling's vision of an abjected landscape is at the ruinous heart of an imperial darkness that threatens the colonial's masculinity. In Kristevan terms, the power of the phallic mother, narratively endowed with 'savage' climatic adornments of an all-encompassing heat-scorched landscape, creates an environment where the male subject can come to grief. In this overwhelming Dantean hell the men's attempts to create order, through work or friendship, are ineffectual. The fear of aloneness which this space induces, cannot be countered by such diversions as work, card games or dinners. The civil servant Lowndes 'wearily' exclaims 'Oh, heavens! What is there to do?' (*LH*, p. 162), but in this environment his entreaty is spoken not with passion but exhaustion. Spurstow suggests beginning poker again, this time with outrageously high stakes, but the surveyor, Mottram (Kipling's logical 'surveyor' of the scene), says that there 'isn't enough excitement in it, and it's foolish' (*LH*, p. 162). Having exhausted their usual 'manly' options, Mottram spies a 'worn and battered little camp-piano', which is the 'wreckage of a married household that had once held the bungalow' (*LH*, p. 162). The image of a married couple, however dusty and wrecked that may be, punctures the sorrowful bachelor existence of these men who have traded potential marital happiness for their allegiance to Britannia. The consequences of imperial duty, which amplify the men's frustrated existence, are communicated through the metaphor of the broken-down piano. Ghosts of memory, of a vibrant, life-affirming England (and 'Home') are set against this nullifying landscape. Mottram manages to 'bring the rebellious notes into a sort of agreement, and there rose from the ragged keyboard something that might have once been the ghost of a popular music-hall song' (*LH*, p. 162).

The piano becomes an important image not only for the process of remembering, but also as a metaphor for the connection between the reality 'outside' and a psychic 'inside'. Kipling hints that the 'rebellious notes' of the dilapidated piano, which are reminiscent of the Cixousian scansions that characterise a female space, can stave off the madness that their futile colonial existence induces. Mottram sings an old 'song of the streets' (*LH*, p. 162). The English streets are imaginatively connected to but mockingly contrasted with the dust-strewn wasteland of India. Kipling uses the Indian landscape as a link to England in stories such as 'The Madness of Private Ortheris' (in *Plain Tales*), but in this tale the connection has a much darker outcome. Mottram's companions grow silent and nostalgic for a world they have been separated from and cannot hope to retrieve except, like Punch, through their memories of the past. The melancholic sound of the piano becomes an elegiac lament for a youth beyond hope of recovery. Made even more pitiable by its faulty notes, it is nevertheless warm and close, reminiscent of the 'semiotic rhythms' that the narrator of 'The City of Dreadful Night' finds so appealing. Kipling poignantly says, '[v]ery simple indeed were the tunes to which Mottram's art and the limitations of the piano could give effect, but the men listened with pleasure, and in the pauses talked all together of what they had seen or heard when they were last home' (*LH*, p. 163). The nostalgic effect of the hymns and popular songs keep the men's fear of the debilitating Indian environment at bay. The 'dense dust-storm' that has 'sprung up outside, and swept roaring over the house, enveloping it in a choking darkness of midnight' goes unheeded by Mottram as he continues to play one badly picked out tune after another. Moreover, Mottram's defiant playing continues once the storm has abated. In this sense the disturbing abjected mother figure has been vanquished and the more nurturing mother of the semiotic, realised in Mottram's 'more directly personal songs' (*LH*, p. 163) takes her place momentarily in the narrative.

The men exist in an isolated outpost, a troubling microcosm of the imperial world that has, for them, long since lost any meaningful political motive or even a unifying sense of order. A pre-verbal realm is recalled in the 'crazy tinkle' of the piano (*LH*, p. 163) that melts into and fuses with the men's memories of home and tempers the threat of annihilation. The 'Evening Hymn' that Mottram sings is taken up by Hummil, who 'chants' its words, words that are like a talisman to the exhausted men:

> Glory to thee, my God, this night
> For all the blessings of the light.

That shows we really feel our blessings. How does it go on? –

> If in the night I sleepless lie,
> My soul with scared thoughts supply;
> May no ill dreams disturb my rest –
>
> Quicker, Mottram! –
>
> Or powers of darkness me molest!

The Hymn is associated with memories of home in both Lowndes' and Mottram's minds, 'Summer evenings in the country, – stained-glass window, – light going out, and you and she jamming your heads together over one hymnbook' (*LH*, p. 164). Mottram never says who the 'she' is: a mother, sister or sweetheart, perhaps? But in a sense her precise identity hardly matters, for 'she' represents female companionship, security, unity and above all, intimacy. The hymn releases a torrent of memories of England. The 'smell of hay' recalls a 'moon as big as a bandbox', and the syntax collapses into a checklist of memory 'bats – roses – milk and midges' (*LH*, p. 164). Its alliterative conclusion is that of 'mothers', prompting Spurstow to recollect his 'mother singing me to sleep [. . .] when I was a little chap' (*LH*, p. 164). This interjection in the story demonstrates that 'memory' of the semiotic can be a subversive threat to the phallogocentric order. The sound of music, however limited in its execution, not only stays the anthropomorphised dust-storm, successfully silencing the raging wind that shakes the 'tattered ceiling cloth' (*LH*, p. 163), but also creates an intimate space of shared memories that shore up the men's anxieties. The masculine camaraderie, of which their poker game is emblematic, is unable to achieve the same heightened sense of companionship.

Reminiscent of the symphonic quality of the trader's house in 'The City of Dreadful Night', in this story ordered discourse, which is associated with the symbolic, has been replaced by the music that is 'associated [. . .] with the most sacred recollections' of the welcoming space of 'home' (*LH*, p. 163). Kipling's descriptions of the memories, which Mottram's tunes evoke, conjure the close intimacy of the maternal realm. Language, shot through with pulsing musical inflections, emerges from the tattered cloth of remembrance. Yet, for Hummil, the act of remembering reiterates the hopelessness of the men's situation and once cherished memories are extinguished in the 'darkness [that] had fallen on the room', leaving him 'squirming in his chair' (*LH*, p. 164). Hummil breaks the silence: 'you sing it when you are seven fathom deep in Hell! It's an insult to the intelligence of the Deity to pretend that we're anything but tortured rebels' (*LH*, p. 164). Pike Bauer argues that the small place of refuge the men are trying to create through 'ritual and memory'[50] is consumed by the desolation of their isolating quotidian lives. The power of memory to strengthen the spirit is just an illusion, a temporarily healing illusion but an illusion nonetheless, whose only power lies in its ability to nostalgically look back rather than provide the men with an alternative to their wretched existence. The songs that were sung to them by a mother in a world that they cannot reach only emphasises their isolation. However profound a connection was made by the men's shared memories of home, Hummil still takes his own life, and Kipling's implication is that it could just have easily been any of the four. The unifying maternal realm, which enables the men to feel some kind of comfort, is continually undermined and overpowered by their nullifying existence in a dismal colonial world.

This story is, to a large extent, Kipling's examination of the devastating consequences of the men's ability to cope with what is, I would argue, a devouring female space reified in the febrile environment of India. Hummil hallucinates an uncanny doppelganger, which moves through his house. This eerie spectre can be read as a Kristevan 'alien *double*'[51] that represents a projection of the semiotic impulses which have been stirred in Hummil's unconscious. Unable to bear what is identified as dangerous to the psyche, Hummil psychically splits himself in two 'as a defence put up by a distraught self'.[52] The welcoming embrace of sleep eludes him and he suffers a painful insomnia. And yet sleep, when it does come, produces no restful state. Like the dream world of 'The Brushwood Boy', Hummil's night-time world holds childhood horrors: 'He had slept back into terrified childhood' (*LH*, p. 169). Echoing Punch's terrified daytime world, where, left alone, the child gradually loses his sight and imagines 'nameless terrors' and ghosts that flap around him (*WWW*, p. 282), Hummil's nameless terror is 'a blind face that cries and can't wipe its eyes [and] chases him down corridors' (*LH*, p. 170). If, as Kristeva argues, 'the theme of suffering-horror is the ultimate evidence of such states of abjection within a narrative representation',[53] then the engineer's wretched nightmare vision bears witness to the violent split in adult masculine exteriority and a repressed interior Other. Isolated, without the weekly ritualised companionship of the other men, Hummil is subsumed by this demonic abjected Other. In Kristevan terms, he has been unable to ward off his fear of 'his very own identity sinking irretrievably into the mother',[54] thereby suffering a loss of a sense of the totality of his subjectivity, a loss that ends in his self-destruction.

Hummil's companions are fearful for their friend's mental state of health, but are duty-bound to their imperial tasks and unable to stay with him. They return a week later to find that he is dead. On a closer inspection of his body, they are confronted with the terrifying image of a demon that is fixed in the glassy, dead eyes of the engineer. Spurstow takes a photograph and the unnameable image can still be seen, something that defies rational scientific explanation: ''Tisn't in medical science [. . .] Things in a dead man's eyes' (*LH*, p. 174). Mary Hamer argues that 'there is no need for magical explanations, for "the Dark Places" or for the unspeakable image in the eye. These very phrases take us straight back to the unconscious and the child before command of language.'[55] It becomes emblematic of an abyss and its horror – 'leave that horror alone', says Lowndes (*LH*, p. 175). The body of Hummil, with its life-in-death stare, carries with it the full force of the abject.[56] This decidedly Gothic story uncovers the precarious stability of the paternal authority that is continually threatened by the powerful but abjected Other of Kipling's early fiction.

Desire and horror, attraction and repulsion lie at the heart of Kipling's early fiction. The geographical site of rebellion that Kipling found in the night-time world of Lahore and Allahabad finds its metaphoric counterpart in his early stories of India. The internal struggle between the desire for the unknowable night-time India captured in *Life's Handicap* and the reassurance of daytime work of the Empire, brought into sharp relief in *The Day's Work*, underlines the dichotomy of Kipling's narrators as distanced and dispassionate spectators and ambivalent voyeurs, clearly enjoying what he saw as the intimate and ethereal India. However, the need for boundary control over the self is metaphorically played out in the British imperial civilising mission over the teeming, seemingly ungovernable population of the Indian subcontinent. Kipling's colonial characters, on their way into the heart of a dreaded Indian darkness, send out an impassioned entreaty that calls across the text. Those that wrench themselves free from the corpse of abjection are in themselves survivors. In answer to the grieving, frightened men in a limbo of the lost, Kipling's survivors recite a melancholic elegy that proclaims the white man's lost youth. India as an artistic expression of the semiotic already under the sway of the autocratic symbolic brings Kipling's dejected imperial adults to the very brink of existence and forces them to stand petrified at the edge of the abyss, alone, save for the unnameable, unspeakable anguish buried deep in the desire for a perpetually unreachable Other.

In the epigraph to this chapter, I included part of an address that Kipling made to students at McGill University. His personal recollections of the 'great depression, despondencies, doubts [and] waverings' (*BOW*, p. 20) of his youth can be countered, he tells the students, by an attempt to 'lose yourself, in some issue not personal to yourself – in another man's trouble, or preferably, another man's joy' (*BOW*, p. 20). Submission to the ideology of Empire as well as hero-worshipping its orchestrators will be a 'good enough' issue in Kipling's subsequent fictions of India. But, Kipling adds, 'if the dark hour does not vanish [. . .] if the black cloud does not lift [. . .] let me tell you again [. . .] the despair and horror mean nothing [. . .] you are not yet sufficiently important to be taken seriously by the Powers above or beneath us' (*BOW*, p. 20). Thus Kipling relinquishes the needs of the individual for the good of the whole: the individual empire builder can crumble, but his collapse does not cause even a ripple in 'Britannia''s iron robes. In the next chapter we see Kipling embracing a new ideal of Empire and consolidating the polarising tenets of the likes of Cecil Rhodes and Sir Alfred Milner, retranslating himself as imperial apostle along the way. Repressing the desire for reunification with an edenic India, Kipling will subsequently '[t]ake up the White Man's burden' to 'veil the threat of terror' from 'sullen peoples, [h]alf devil and half wild'.[57] However, as I hope to demonstrate in this chapter, Kipling's vision of Empire with its insistence upon a dedication to duty, predominantly from the stories in the aptly titled *The Day's Work*, is a flimsy protection against the mourning of a lost maternal realm, a repressed semiotic space that will be reanimated in the dreams and opium-induced hallucinations of Britannia's imperial custodians.

Notes

1. Rudyard Kipling, 'The Dream of Duncan Parrenness', in *Life's Handicap*, pp. 294–5.
2. Rudyard Kipling, address to students of McGill University, Montreal, 1907, 'Values in Life', in *A Book of Words*, p. 20.
3. Julia Kristeva, *Tales of Love*, p. 16.
4. Rudyard Kipling, 'A Vision of India', in *The Works of Rudyard Kipling, XVII: Early Verse*, p. 63.
5. Julia Kristeva, *Black Sun: Depression and Melancholia*, p. 28.
6. Ibid., p. 28.
7. Helen Pike Bauer, *Rudyard Kipling: A Study of the Short Fiction*, p. 11.
8. Zohreh Sullivan, *Narratives of Empire: The Fictions of Rudyard Kipling*, p. 11.
9. Pike Bauer, *Rudyard Kipling*, p. 3.
10. Andrew Lycett, *Rudyard Kipling*, p. 209.
11. Francis Green calls this 'excellent first class journalism' (quoted in *Kipling: The Critical Heritage*, p. 157). Angus Wilson says that it is 'only the most crudely brilliant of the stories that resulted from [Kipling's] misery of insomnia' (*The Strange Ride of Rudyard Kipling*, p. 37). A contemporary commentary comes close to describing the eeriness of the tale. Mrs Oliphant, reviewing *Life's Handicap* in *Blackwood's Magazine*, Nov. 1891, says, '[n]ever was there a more astounding picture than that, all done

in black and white, which is called 'The City of Dreadful Night'. We pant in the air which is no air, we sicken for the evanescent breath of dawn' (quoted in *Kipling: The Critical Heritage*, p. 141). Paffard and Kemp miss it out altogether and Sullivan gives the tale a perfunctory mention but sees its narrative function as a means for the narrator to 'distance himself from immersion in the destructive element' (*Narratives of Empire*, p. 23).

12. Julia Kristeva, *Powers of Horror: An Essay on Abjection*, p. 8.
13. Martin Fido, *Rudyard Kipling*, p. 30.
14. See Caren Kaplan, 'Deterritorializations: The Rewriting of Home and Exile in Western Discourse'.
15. Kristeva, *Powers of Horror*, p. 8.
16. Ibid., p. 3.
17. In his autobiography, Kipling comments on the editing process: 'read your final draft and consider every paragraph, sentence and word, blacking out where requisite. Let it lie by to drain as long as possible. At the end of that time, re-read it aloud alone and at leisure' (*SOM*, p. 121).
18. Victor Turner, *Drama, Fields and Metaphors: Symbolic Action in Human Society*, p. 232.
19. James Thomson, 'The City of Dreadful Night', in *The City of Dreadful Night and Other Poems*, XVI, pp. 39–42.
20. Ibid., I. 51.
21. Ibid., VII. 16.
22. Kristeva, *Powers of Horror*, p. 3.
23. Ibid., pp. 3–4.
24. Ibid., p. 9.
25. Ibid., p. 4.
26. Michel Foucault's argument of the connection between leprosy in the Middle Ages and the animality of madness in the Classical Age can be found in *Madness and Civilization: A History of Insanity in the Age of Reason*. Whereas in the Renaissance, madness was seen as almost ubiquitous (the Reason of God was beyond humanity), by the eighteenth century it was synonymous with existing in an 'unreality', and 'melancholics' and 'maniacs' suffered exclusion and confinement. By the nineteenth century madness was precisely identified as mental illness, 'ill-being', in effect. British colonials feared that an extended working life in the punishing heat of India brought the threat of madness, or going 'Fantee'. Stories such as 'The Conversion of Aurelian McGoggin' (in *Plain Tales*), 'His Brother's Keeper' (in *Abaft the Funnel*), 'With the Main Guard' (in *Soldiers Three*) and 'At the End of the Passage' deal with this notion of exhaustion and mental breakdown.
27. Kristeva, *Black Sun*, p. 151.
28. When addressing members of the Kipling Society at their Annual Luncheon, Eliot stated that 'Kipling had accompanied me ever since boyhood [and] traces of [his art] appear in my own mature verse where no diligent scholarly sleuth has yet observed them' ('The Unfading Genius of Rudyard Kipling', p. 9). Robert Crawford has subsequently tracked down some of those traces of Kipling in Eliot's poetry. For his excellent analysis of Kipling's influence on Eliot's work see Crawford, 'Rudyard Kipling in *The Waste Land*'.

29. See Jan Montefiore, *Rudyard Kipling*.
30. Julia Kristeva, *In the Beginning Was Love: Psychoanalysis and Faith*, p. 62.
31. Thomson, *The City of Dreadful Night*, XVIII, pp. 948, 950.
32. David Saul, *The Indian Mutiny*, p. 397.
33. David Gilmour, *The Long Recessional: The Imperial Life of Rudyard Kipling*, p. 20.
34. Julia Kristeva, *Desire in Language: A Semiotic Approach to Literature and Art*, p. 167.
35. Thomson, 'The City of Dreadful Night', I. 44.
36. Kristeva, *Black Sun*, p. 65.
37. Hélène Cixous, *The Newly Born Woman*, p. 64.
38. Pike Bauer, *Rudyard Kipling*, p. 6.
39. It is interesting to note here that Jukes' horse shares the name of the setting for Robert Browning's 'Gold Hair: The Story of Pornic'. The verses detail the grisly corpse of a girl whose skull when disinterred is found supported by a mound of golden coins. Alice and Lockwood Kipling had a mutual admiration for Browning's art; indeed his poetry provided the catalyst that brought them together. Their son came to similarly appreciate the poet. Harry Ricketts argues that Browning's poetry was 'to prove a major influence on Kipling's own development as a writer' (*The Unforgiving Minute*, p. 21).
40. Lockwood Kipling goes on to say that, '"The swan (noble type) has flown away, the tiger (the king) has made the crow (the knave) his minister," is a much-quoted verse from a popular tale' (John Lockwood Kipling, *Beast and Man in India: A Popular Sketch of Indian Animals in their Relations with People*, pp. 30–1).
41. Kristeva, *Powers of Horror*, p. 2.
42. Mark Paffard, *Kipling's Indian Fiction*, p. 33.
43. Saul, *The Indian Mutiny*, p. 233.
44. Kristeva, *Powers of Horror*, p. 204.
45. Pike Bauer, *Rudyard Kipling*, p. 8; Wilson, *The Strange Ride of Rudyard Kipling*, p. 72.
46. J. M. S. Tompkins, *The Art of Rudyard Kipling*, p. 199.
47. Gilmour, *The Long Recessional*, p. 31.
48. Charles Allen, *Kipling Sahib: India and The Making of Rudyard Kipling*, p. 133.
49. Sullivan, *Narratives of Empire*, p. 78.
50. Pike Bauer, *Rudyard Kipling*, p. 4.
51. Julia Kristeva, *Strangers to Ourselves*, p. 183.
52. Ibid., p. 183.
53. Kristeva, *Powers of Horror*, p. 141.
54. Ibid., p. 64.
55. Mary Hamer, 'Kipling and Dreams'.
56. Kristeva, *Powers of Horror*, p. 207.
57. Rudyard Kipling, *The Definitive Edition of Rudyard Kipling's Verse*, p. 323.

Chapter 5

The Ascent from the Abyss: Dedication to Duty in *The Day's Work*

A stone's throw out on either hand
From that well-ordered road we tread,
 And all the world is wild and strange:
Churel and ghoul and *Djinn* and sprite
Shall bear us company to-night,
For we have reached the Oldest Land
 Wherein the Powers of Darkness range.[1]

Not for Voices, Harps or Wings or rapt illumination,
But the grosser Self that springs of use or occupation,
Unto which the Spirit clings as her last salvation.
Heart may fail, and strength outwear, and Purpose turn to Loathing
But the everyday affair of business, meals and clothing,
Builds a bulkhead 'twixt Despair and the Edge of Nothing.[2]

Kipling, the artist, perceived with great clarity the physical and mental strains that were part and parcel of the lives of administrators carrying out the quotidian work of the Empire. In his fiction, he went some way toward addressing their difficulties by imaginatively cataloguing their apprehensions, frustrations, illnesses and fatigues. The stories in *Plain Tales* and the best of the tales in *Life's Handicap*, written whilst Kipling was in India and newly arrived in London, detail empire builders who are psychologically battered, worn down and wretched. The overall quality of the *Life's Handicap* collection is uneven; David Sergeant argues that Kipling's success pressured the writer into bulking out the collection with previously uncollected material to 'release [the London stories] in volume form as soon as possible'.[3] His characters confront an imperial landscape that is bereft of the moral values of the metropolis. In these collections Kipling is frequently damning in his appraisal of the Indian Civil Service (ICS) as an administrative body, and of the effect its oftentimes unnecessary bureaucracy had on the lives of its foot soldiers.[4] Men sent out by the military or the Indian Office in London were reduced to anonymous disposable quotas, summed up by Private Ortheris: 'I'm a Tommy – a bloomin', eight-anna, dog-stealin' Tommy, with a number instead of a decent name' (*PT*, p. 215). Faced with an administration that prioritises ubiquitous colonial authority at the expense of individual suffering, Kipling's fictional heroes, if they are to survive imperial service, must pull themselves back from the edge of a psychic abyss and reorientate themselves in an India that Kipling describes through the eyes of his journalist narrator in 'The Man Who Would Be King' (in *Wee Willie Winkie*):

> the telephone becomes a tinkling terror, because it tells you of the sudden deaths of men and women that you knew intimately, and the prickly-heat covers you with a garment, and you sit down and write: 'A slight increase of sickness is reported from the Khuda Janta Khan District. The outbreak is purely sporadic in its nature, and, thanks to the energetic efforts of the District authorities, is now almost at an end. It is, however with deep regret that we record the death, etc.' (*WWW*, pp. 214–15)

The Day's Work is a collection of twelve stories that were, for the most part, written between 1893 and 1896 while Kipling was living in Brattleboro, Vermont. The collection was published while Kipling and his family were wintering in South Africa as guests of Cecil Rhodes. The overriding theme of the collection is the multifaceted nature of duty. From imperial duty in 'The Bridge Builders' and 'The Brushwood Boy', familial duty, in 'In the Tomb of his Ancestors', professional duty of the kind displayed by the engineer, Mr Wardrop, who doggedly fixes his ship's shelled engine in 'The Devil and the Deep Blue Sea', collective duty, in 'The Maltese Cat', to duty to work to one's limits in 'The Walking Delegate', this collection sees a subtle shift in his writing. In it, he moves from detailing the microcosm of individuals' lives to the broader vision of their contribution to the imperial cause. In this collection Kipling's newly minted imperial administrators, Scott in 'William the Conqueror', Findlayson in 'The Bridge Builders' and George Cottar in 'The Brushwood Boy', lift their eyes to the colonial horizon and perceive the autocratic, regimented wheels of Empire of which they are merely the atomised cogs. These characters, unlike the disorientated Morrowbie Jukes and the deeply disturbed Hummil, emerge from the horror that India represented to the colonial white man and begin the tireless search for individual meaning in their workaday colonial lives. Kipling's Englishman could find a sense of worth in a moral purpose executed through an unstinting dedication to duty. By working within the paternal authority rather than railing against it, the power of maternal India, so threatening in previous stories, is not only diminished, but also brought under the jurisdiction of the white man.

In the stories that I have chosen to focus upon from *The Day's Work*, we see Kipling's characters turning away from the cynical acceptance of imperial ideology that marked the stories in *Life's Handicap* and *Plain Tales*. Kipling's imperial heroes, in this collection, tackle their unsettling anxieties by reconfiguring their world in a metaphysical as well as a material sense. In this respect, Kipling's imperial men can give shape and meaning to their otherwise fragmented psyches through the cult of Britannia, which denies the possibility of a desirous identification. His colonials may exist, as Bonamy Dobrée argues, 'alone in a blank universe, without any support beyond their own constructions and efforts', but he goes on to argue that they 'do not succumb, and they do more than avert their eyes; they construct their lives as a rebuke'.[5] Scott, Findlayson and Cottar avoid the pitfalls of their predecessors and reconstruct a colonial world around their dedication to Britannia's calling, whether through constructing immense bridges to open trade and communication lines, feeding starving children in a catastrophic famine, or fending off threats to the Raj by their heroic endeavours in fierce border wars. Devotion to duty thus becomes a means to assuage the psychological damage of imperial life in the Indian subcontinent, as well as a safeguard against future crises. Throughout *The Day's Work*, Kipling's ideal of his heroes is to shoulder the immense burden of responsibility by refusing to give up when enormous physical and mental strains conspire against them. Indeed, the narratives of 'William the Conqueror', 'The Bridge Builders' and 'The Brushwood Boy' suggest that the white man's organisational skills, feats of engineering and bravery in wars are all the more commendable because of his obstinate refusal to give up in the face of seemingly insurmountable odds.

Kipling's notion of duty incorporates the responsibility of one man for the well-being of another. The camaraderie that exists amongst Mulvaney, Learoyd and Ortheris in the *Soldiers Three* stories is one among many such examples. However, friendships that bear the weight of another's depression, anxiety and loneliness, as important as they are as support structures, fall short of a dedication to his grandiose vision to take up the calling of Empire for Empire's sake. A thematic strand that runs through *The Day's Work* is that one can survive imperial service, if one clings to the tenets of the nineteenth-century imperial fantasy. In many respects Kipling is parroting the arguments put forward in John Stuart Mill's 1859 pamphlet, 'A Few Words on Non-Intervention', which could be read as an apologia of imperial power. In a letter to Margaret Burne-Jones in 1885, Kipling shows that he appears to accept the principles of imperial ideology. He writes: 'We spend our best men on the country like water and if ever a foreign country was made better through the "blood of the martyrs" India is that country [. . .] Yes the English in India do do a little for the benefit of the natives and small thanks they get.'[6] In exalting the ideal of Empire rather than its greedy, economic reality, he sought to bring a paternal order to his broken characters and in doing so afford them an ennobling reason for their presence as occupiers in the Indian subcontinent.

However, Kipling's endorsement of the 'civilising' mission of the British Empire compromises his previously sympathetic portrayals of individual suffering. Gilmour argues that whilst his imperial characters in *The Day's Work* are 'well-drawn and fairly accurate portraits' of colonial administrators, 'the very similarity of the [them], their work and their sense of duty, tends to diminish the quality of the fiction'.[7] Martyrdom for a higher calling of Empire is now the goal of his exhausted heroes. Kipling's colonials, in psychic bits and pieces, become greater than the sum of their damaged parts. Their rallying point is centred upon what the author saw as the imperial community's (inherently paternal) values: an emphasis on cleanliness of mind and body, and the value of hard work, good leadership and courageous deeds. Through these values the despairing (colonial) male can not only find the means with which to heal himself, but also avert his desirous gaze from an exoticised maternal realm and find his place in an unbroken masculine history.

In the early Indian stories Kipling's characters do not, indeed cannot, realise an imaginary union with a life-affirming maternal India, however much they cling to the hope of it. With the exception of Kim, his colonials can never hope to enjoy cross-cultural relationships with their colonised counterparts. Kipling is very clear on this point; many of his cross-cultural relationships are doomed, and those who continue to seek connections with the native risk being cast out of the imperial community, as shown in stories such as 'Beyond the Pale', 'Miss Youghal's Sais' and 'To Be Filed for Reference' (in *Plain Tales*). His heroes cannot have their colonial cake and eat it, too. The white man's relationship to his native counterpart must be aligned according to the hierarchical structures of Victoria's colonial rule. Characters who do not respect this master/servant dialectic are cast beyond the boundaries of the imperial community. They exist in a curious half-world between the two communities. McIntosh Jellaludin in 'To Be Filed for Reference' is an example of Kipling's fear of penetrating the Other side of India too closely, the price of which, Mark Paffard has rightly noted, is 'degradation and death'.[8] Lewis Wurgaft observes that 'Kipling was known for his unusual knowledge of native life, and for his intimacy with "wild" or "filthy" Indians from frontier regions [and] was familiar with natives and their customs and was constantly holding chats with "filthy" tribesmen who regarded him as a "Sahib apart".'[9] Yet at this point in his writing there is a sense in which the author is reining in his desire for an impenetrable India in favour of inclusion in the colonial community. The desiccated yet all-powerful matriarch, Queen Victoria (the 'Widder of Windsor', as Kipling refers to her), becomes a maternal agency that covers up the abject Mother India. And standing behind the 'Widder' in London is Kipling's grandiose vision of the helmeted, trident-carrying Britannia as his imperial goddess of action. Dobrée argues:

> She ['Britannia'] is a goddess not only by the fact of her being, but in her very nature, for she exacts much toil from her votaries, much of the silent endurance, abnegation, and loyalty that he [Kipling] loves. The Empire then is to be cherished, not so much because it is in itself an achievement, but because, like old Rome, it is the most superb instrument to cause man to outface the universe, assert himself against vacancy.[10]

Kipling's ideal of Empire, personified in the mythic Britannia, reads like the worship of the Virgin Mary. According to Kristeva, the image of the Virgin Mary represents a maternal semiotic that has been 'castrated' from its fecund driving force. She is the paternal symbolic mother who is impregnated by the Word. The primal sexual scene is missing from the Virgin's history and thus the carnal semiotic mother is missing in her discourse. Like the Virgin Mary, Britannia is brought into existence and sustained by the Word, the name of the Father.[11] The worship of this phallic matron in Kipling's new, purposeful adult colonial world is a way of both ensuring the power of a paternal order, and fighting off the remnants of an abject Mother India. As I hope to demonstrate in this chapter, Kipling's allegiance to a colonial authority includes an attempt to incorporate a frightening Mother India with her outlawed *jouissance* through a cult of an imperial goddess. Britannia's 'presence' in *The Day's Work* is Kipling's immaculate conception; she is a figure sculpted without *jouissance*, and hence no abject status. Her body is tattooed with the Word of the Law and is not frightening to the father's imperial sons. Similarly, Kipling's new colonial figures must worship her with an asexual dedication to duty, repressing the desires that characterised their relationship to the maternal realm of India in his earlier stories.

In *The Day's Work*, India – as both a mentally mapped geographical and colonial space, much as in *Plain Tales* and *Life's Handicap* – is still ungovernable, its people still infantilised. The heat still rages and the famines are still prevalent, but Kipling's colonial characters have become like benevolent father figures, selflessly carrying out the work of the British Empire. In this new vision of Empire, Kipling's administrators are responsible for the lives and well-being of thousands of native Indians. They wield a benign authority that sees them, like kindly fathers, admonishing wayward native children with rebellious intentions or rewarding those that prove loyal to the imperial enterprise. The daytime work of the Empire takes precedence over, and is seen to be more valuable than, night-time encounters with 'exotic' natives in India's underground 'forbidden' world of the bazaars. However, Kipling's colonial male, I would argue, merely suppresses his desire for the night-time India, and it resurfaces in dreams or delirium. This repression is implicit in the very title of the collection itself; *The Day's Work* incorporates not only the unspoken topic of the *night's* intrigue, but also the night's oblivion. On the mantelpiece in Kipling's Naulakha home, Lockwood carved 'Do the task of the day, for the night cometh when no man can work.' A precarious route exists for the colonist to find a way back to the maternal realm, but in this collection the path of the night-stalker is characterised by opium-induced hallucinations or surreal dreamscapes, what Kemp argues is 'the idiom of dream and paranoid fantasy'.[12] Kipling himself was attracted to this 'night-time' world of the Other India.

In *Something of Myself* Kipling, upon returning from a night of wandering the streets of Lahore, driven out by the heat, describes taxis perfumed with 'hookah-fumes, jasmine-flowers, and sandalwood' (*SOM*, p. 33). It is in such taxis that he uncovers what he imagines is the 'real' India, if his native driver is in a talkative mood. Memories of India are evoked by smells and sights recreated in 'Mandalay' as 'them spicy garlic smells, /An' the sunshine an' the palm-trees an' the tinkly temple-bells', and Kipling's observation that '[m]uch of Indian life goes on in the hot weather nights' (*SOM*, p. 33) puts India and its peoples in antithesis to the European coloniser whose empire-building is carried out by those dedicated engineers, soldiers and administrators as well as their wives, sisters and mothers, as demonstrated in 'The Drums of Fore and Aft' (in *Wee Willie Winkie*), 'William the Conqueror' and 'The Daughter of the Regiment' (in *Plain Tales*). This newly circumscribed India is akin to a sort of impregnable 'family square', forming a magic circle of protection that keeps nightmares and unclean desires at bay. During a fearful night spent in Lurgan's shop, Kim discovers that the lures of magic, superstitions, and benign and vengeful gods are reduced to fanciful curios by day for a resourceful colonial worker who knows his multiplication tables by heart, is dedicated to imperial values and can thus manage to map an 'unmappable' India.

In 'The Bridge Builders', the opposing orders of Kipling's India, waking world and dream world, routines and chaos move, as Zohreh

Sullivan argues, from the quotidian to the mythic.[13] The narrative is split into two parts. The first part concerns the efforts of chief engineer Findlayson as he oversees the construction of a great railway bridge that will cross the Ganges. As the bridge is nearing completion, a storm causes immense flooding that threatens the destruction of the bridge. Findlayson is swept downstream with his Lascar, Peroo, during the night in a little boat. Driven to a small island, he is given opium by Peroo to stave off hunger and exhaustion. The second part of the story concerns the two men witnessing, through their drug-induced hallucinations, India's gods arguing over the fate of the coloniser's bridge and whether they can allow the bridge to withstand a real and symbolic deluge. In this sense, the bridge is a metonym for Empire.

The governing body of the British Empire is also given elevated status and it is locked into a dispute, which now transcends Findlayson's personal perspective (he has no part in the gods' discussion), over the fate of colonial India as well as the validity of British rule. Kipling ennobles India with mythic status, and the setting is elevated from the wreckage of quotidian life that we see in 'The City of Dreadful Night'. Her voice rings clear in the narrative through her gods arguing over the allegorical building of an iron bridge that will straddle 'Mother Gunga'. Sullivan sees the story as reinforcing Kipling's credentials as imperial propagandist.[14] However, Findlayson's devotion to Empire in the form of his stoic endurance to see if his bridge (and reputation) will be engulfed by the floodwaters is interspliced with a psychological study of the engineer's difficulties in finding individual fulfillment or personal meaning in an imperial world. He hopes his efforts will earn him government recognition – 'The least that Findlayson, of the Public Works department, expected was a C.I.E; he dreamed of a C.S.I.' (*DW*, p. 31) – but he also realises the fragility of a reputation that will stand or fall on the precariousness of nature:

> For himself [Findlayson] the crash meant everything – everything that made a hard life worth the living. They would say, the men of his own profession – he remembered the half-pitying things that he himself had said when Lockhart's big waterworks burst and broke down in big heaps and sludge and Lockhart's spirit broke in him and he died. (*DW*, p. 44)

The story is ambivalent in its attempt to reinforce colonial might whilst simultaneously undermining the mastery of the white man. Findlayson is not only the chief engineer of such a colossal construction, he is also the designer of pivotal devices that bear his name in recognition of their originality, such as the 'Findlayson truss' (*DW*, p. 32) or the 'Findlayson bolted shoe' (*DW*, p. 44). Yet this remarkable engineer is reduced to an impotent eavesdropper on the celestial council that decides the fate of his beloved bridge.

Findlayson's bridge is a complex image within the narrative. It is both an emblem of imperial might and a device that will contain and transform the nature and purpose of India's mythical river, reducing its status, in effect, to a facilitator of Britannia's commercial and military interests. The following dizzying passage opens up a panoramic view of the sheer scale of the colonial enterprise at the same time as it magnifies the minutiae of imperial expansion. Kipling captures the macroscopic and the microscopic nature of the all-encompassing colonial enterprise. However, the abiding image in this passage is the 'corporeal' damage that is inflicted on 'Mother Gunga'. There is an overriding sense of grief and loss for a Mother India that will soon be subjugated by 'Britannia's' iron fist:

> Findlayson, C.E., sat in his trolley on a construction-line that ran along one of the main revetments – the huge stone-faced banks that flared away north and south for three miles on either side of the river – and permitted himself to think of the end [. . .] At either end rose towers of red brick, loopholed for musketry and pierced for big guns, and the ramp of the road was being pushed forward to their haunches. The raw earth-ends were crawling and alive with hundreds upon hundreds of tiny asses climbing out of the yawning borrow-pit with sackfuls of stuff [. . .] The river was very low, and on the dazzling white sand between the three centre piers stood squat cribs of railway-sleepers, filled within and daubed without with mud, to support the last of the girders as those were riveted up. In the little deep water left by the drought, an overhead-crane traveled to and fro along its spile-pier, jerking sections of iron into place, snorting and backing and grunting as an elephant grunts in the timber yard [. . .] East and west and north and south the construction-trains rattled and shrieked up and down the embankments, the piled trucks of brown and white stone banging behind them till the side-boards were unpinned, and with a roar and a grumble a few thousand tons more material were thrown out to hold the river in place. (*DW*, pp. 31–2)

The construction site is immense, and as manager of this colossal project, Findlayson is aggrandised in Kipling's imperial landscape as commander-in-chief of Mother India's brutal violation. As well as enhancing his engineer's political status as European bridge-builder and commander of a vast native workforce, the author also 'defaces' Mother India's native sons. The workforce is refracted through a European lens that defines and shapes the existence of its members in terms of their usefulness to the construction of the bridge. Their individual identities are lost amongst the thousands of 'tons of material'. Connected with dirt, this image reinforces the barbaric or degenerate nature of the 'native'. Kipling's East is peopled by a slave force to be used as 'asses', as well as helpless childlike peoples in need of guidance from their European rulers. What Said argues is the construction of 'Kipling's White Man as an idea, a persona and style of being' begins to emerge from the shadows of his fiction.[15] Similarly, the white man will 'clean' the land with 'iron underfoot'.[16] Underneath the image of benevolent white colonial is the threatening dictator prepared to subdue the native peoples of its colonies with brutality and force.

Said argues that this treatment of Kipling's colonial characters was much in evidence in *Kim*.[17] Certainly, the perspective in the example above is catalogued and itemised in much the way that Asiatic artefacts in the 'Wonder House' were in *Kim*. Yet Kipling's breathtaking descriptions, whilst they bestow majesty upon the feat of colonial engineering, are not static, timeless relics decaying in a dusty museum, and are all the more threatening for it. The fluidity and disorder that Kipling's sprawling sentences produce evoke a living, breathing but crucially colonised Indian workforce charged with inflicting 'corporeal' damage on the banks of the river. The 'raw earth-ends' that are left suggest a Mother India in torment at the tortuous hands of the willing agents of the Raj, but she, unlike her workers, will not submit to colonisation so easily. Peroo asks Findlayson, 'What do you think Mother Gunga will say when the rail runs over?', to which the engineer replies, 'She has said little so far' (*DW*, p. 36). However, Peroo chides the Englishman for his confidence for the 'allowance' in his calculations, saying, 'There is always time for her [. . .] Mother Gunga eats great allowances' (*DW*, p. 36).

As if to reiterate Peroo's warnings, Kipling's image of the 'revetments' give the impression that both the mighty bridge and its ant-like workers are in need of protection against the force of the body of water that has until now been diminished to a trickle by the drought. The huge 'stone-faced flanks' suggest an indestructible edifice that is seemingly set rigid and impassive against an onslaught by a climatically unstable India. However, the solidity of the impressive 'seven and twenty' brick piers that support his bridge, a staggering 'one mile and three-quarters in length', are built upon the fluid sands of the riverbed (*DW*, p. 31). The symbol of colonial engineering and technological superiority is the railway line, and it is presented balanced precariously atop this shifting terrain: 'Above [the piers] ran the railway-line fifteen feet broad' (*DW*, p. 31). The passage above not only presents a deep contradiction between solid architectural design and the precariousness of the geographical terrain, but it foreshadows the near-destruction of Findlayson's bridge and his colonial reputation.

If the project is successful, the bridge will span the thus far untraversable river and will further the white men's economic and military gain in India. Like the soldiers who brutally penetrate the feminised landscape in *Kim*, the masculine power of the British imperial mission is frighteningly displayed in the anthropomorphised towers, the 'ramp of the road being pushed up to their haunches'. Where Kipling admonishes the occupying soldiers in *Kim*, here he suggests that we approve of the actions of his empire builders. '[U]nder the bellies of the girders, clustered around the throats of the piers', an 'invisible staging' supports the truss that will force the banks of the river apart and pinion Mother Gunga ready for 'lattice side-work and the iron roof' to be forced between her embankments (*DW*, p. 32). The earth around the river bed is similarly anthropomorphised. The 'raw earth-ends' suggest a brutal assault where the earth is left bleeding, and the asses that crawl and swarm around are like maggots feeding on a decaying wound. A painful, nightmarish image, Mother India is left cut and bloody as the colonial workers endlessly gouge 'sackfuls of stuff' from her interior.

The opening cut into the river is a 'borrow-pit' that is 'yawning', recalling the crater into which Morrowbie Jukes tumbles headlong. Mother India has not only been bound but her mouth cannot form words of protest as her throat is relentlessly emptied by asses driven by the 'rattle of driver's sticks'. The 'dazzling white sands', like bones that are exposed because the river has lost its protective layer of water, read as a woman with her translucent, vibrant flesh exposed to the brutalising effects of the masculine cranes that 'grunt and snort' as she suffers a horrifying assault carried out with 'jerking' ram-rods of iron. The sexual image is distorted even more by the image of 'cribs' of railway sleepers. The crib not only cruelly emphasises the result of colonial penetration into the unwilling flesh of Mother India, but also suggests a newly conquered India that is 'birthed' by the European encounter with her and is subsequently pinioned under the 'thousands of tons' of black and white stone.

India's mouth, although gagged in a metaphorical sense, is not voiceless. The native Peroo 'counted himself' as one of the three bridge builders even though Findlayson and his 'cub' assistant Hitchcock see the construction of the bridge as 'two [white] men's work' (*DW*, p. 34). This is as close as Kipling can come to a conjoined native and white perspective in this collection. He is a sort of corporeal bridge who warns of the danger in underestimating the power of nature. He has travelled all over the world, is an experienced seaman; in his 'knowledge of tackle and the handling of heavy weights, Peroo was worth almost any price he might have chosen to put upon his services' (*DW*, p. 34). Certainly Kipling emphasises and gives validity to his importance in the story.

Jan Montefiore argues that Peroo is 'the most intelligent person in the story'.[18] He has a contempt for the guru who caters to the spiritual needs of the native workers, but sees his necessity in order to shape and give meaning to the workers' lives: 'he is a very holy man', says Peroo, '[h]e never cares what you eat as long as you do not eat beef, and that is good, because on land we worship Shive [. . .] but at sea on the Kumpani's boats we attend strictly to the orders of the Burra Malum (the first mate)' (*DW*, p. 36). Peroo is Kipling's 'bridge' between the competing Indian and British voices. He represents an alternative to the imperial bridge and this notion is distilled in his antithetic understanding of the imperial consequences of the bridge's construction. He can say that 'My honour is the honour of this bridge' (*DW*, p. 35) whilst simultaneously seeing the cost to Mother India that the bridge will entail: 'We have bitted and bridled her. She is not like the sea, that can beat against a soft beach. She is Mother Gunga – in irons' (*DW*, p. 37).

Like Gunga Dass in 'The Strange Ride of Morrowbie Jukes', Peroo takes charge of the Englishman's welfare when the situation threatens to overwhelm Findlayson. 'The Bridge is mine', says Findlayson, 'I cannot leave it' (*DW*, p. 45). But in this story the native Peroo, like Umr Singh, the Sikh Ressaldar, who doggedly remains loyal to his dead English Captain in 'A Sahib's War', willingly bears the weight of his white master's dreams of imperial success as well as assuming responsibility for Findlayson's physical and mental well-being, giving him opium to stave off hunger and madness:

> 'Wilt thou hold it [the bridge] up with thy hands, then?' said Peroo, laughing. 'I was troubled for my boats *before* the flood came. Now we are in the hands of the Gods. The Sahib will not eat and lie down? Take these, then. They are meat and good toddy together, and they kill all weariness, besides the fever that follows the rain. I have eaten nothing else to-day at all.' (*DW*, p. 45)

The Lascar as an interstitial figure, who speaks across cultures, assumes authority over the white man telling him '[t]hou hast dealt long with the Gods when they were contented and well-wishing. Now they are angry. Speak to them!' (*DW*, p. 45). He can act as a broker between the two cultures as well as an interpreter of the different aspects of the mother figure. From a Kristevan perspective, the excluded mother figure has come back to disturb the symbolic's ordered sphere, and she does so as a terrifying phallic mother who not only threatens engulfment in her flooding feminine flesh but demands that the bridge that chains her falls: 'Heavenly Ones, take this yoke away! Give me clear water between bank and bank! It is I, Mother Gunga that speak. The Justice of the Gods! Deal me the Justice of the Gods!' (*DW*, p. 50).

The river Ganges is rendered as feminine throughout this story, but her strength gains as the story progresses and she becomes a more frightening entity. 'The bridge challenges Mother Gunga,' states Peroo almost blithely. 'But when *she* talks I know whose voice will be the loudest' (*DW*, p. 41). The tumult has been gathering since Findlayson received the coolly economical warning, '*Floods on the Ramgunga. Look out*' (*DW*, p. 38). The colossal undertaking of the workers is then seen in reverse as they work through the night to shore up the bridge. The power of the daytime British Empire is transformed into an image of its workers scrabbling blindly in the gathering dusk:

> Engine after engine toiling home along the spurs after her day's work whistled in answer till the whistles were answered from the far bank. Then the big gong thundered thrice for a sign that it was flood and not fire; conch, drum, and whistle echoed the call, and the village quivered to the sound of bare feet running upon soft earth. The order in all these cases was to stand by the day's work and wait instructions. The gangs poured in by the dusk; men stopping to knot a loin-cloth or fasten a sandal; gang-foremen shouting to their subordinates as they ran or paused by the tool-issue sheds for bars and mattocks; locomotives creeping down their tracks wheel-deep in the crowd, till the brown torrent disappeared into the dusk of the river-bed, raced over the pilework, swarmed along the lattices, clustered by the cranes, and stood still, each man in his place. (*DW*, pp. 39–40)

Kipling's new imperial figure of the lone hero is spotlighted amongst this chaotic scene that, in turn, feeds into the glorified late -Victorian image of the strong man in command of the natives.[19] Findlayson clings to hard work, camaraderie with Hitchcock, the junior 'cub' he treats as an equal and reliance upon Peroo's experience to fortify his inner strength when the stress of completing an imperial project, together with the coming flood and total exhaustion, conspires against him. Findlayson stands between an uncontrollable abjected Mother India – which threatens to devour not only his engineering ambitions, but also his corporeal self at the same time – and an autocratic imperial system that will accept 'no excuses in his service' (*DW*, p. 44). If the bridge falls, 'Mother Gunga would carry his honour to the sea with the other raffle', but Findlayson knows that the 'Government might listen, perhaps, but his own kind would judge him by his bridge, as that stood or fell' (*DW*, p. 44). The only recourse left to him is to frantically work through the mathematical calculations of his bridge design, '[h]e went over it in his head, plate by plate, span by span, brick by brick, pier by pier, remembering, comparing, estimating, and recalculating, lest there be any mistake' (*DW*, p. 44). For Morrowbie Jukes, calculating the topographical nature of the unearthly crater helps to ward off the threat of breakdown. Similarly,

Punch measures the interior of the house in handspans to ward off the crippling isolation he feels when left alone. But the coloniser's empirical calculations prove to be little defence against the looming threat of a devouring female space, 'through the long hours and through the flights of formulae that danced and wheeled before him [Findlayson] a cold fear would come to pinch his heart. His side of the sum was beyond question; but what man knew Mother Gunga's arithmetic?' (*DW*, p. 44).

The conflict between the rational daytime work of the empire builder and the night-time dream realm of the Indian gods is imaged in the black (Peroo) and white (Findlayson) men's joint hallucination. The unease of the gods is pitted against colonial labours. Hanuman, considered one of the most intelligent and powerful of Hindu divinities, states: 'They [the British] toil as my armies toiled in Lanka, and they believe that their toil endures' (*DW*, p. 52). Ancient India and British India fight for supremacy in the narrative but, contrary to Sullivan's reading, I would argue that Kipling does not let either side win out. Instead, Ganesh, chiding Mother Gunga for her impatience, says the work of the British is 'but the shifting of a little dirt. Let the dirt dig in the dirt if it pleases the dirt' (*DW*, p. 52). Krishna, who lives in the human world, says of the gods' fate: 'The end shall be as it was in the beginning [. . .] The flame shall die upon the altars and the prayer upon the tongue till ye become little Gods again' (*DW*, p. 58).

Findlayson's bridge in the present, which is emblematic of the British occupiers' absolute belief in their ability to endure, is connected to the immense passage of time through which the gods have reigned in India. Kipling implies, as he does elsewhere in his fiction, that the halcyon days of the British occupation of India are coming to an end and meaning must be found, not with collective might, but with individual courage and toil. Their rule, like the gods' existence, is, as Krishna says, merely the dreams of the sleeping Brahm. Sullivan states that Brahm's dreams come to nothing in the cold light of the daytime work of the British Empire, 'the irony is clear', she argues, 'the gods exist as long as Findlayson remains in his opium dream. And the colonists exist as long as the natives remain asleep. Rationality, consciousness, enlightenment will gradually awaken the sleepers, and then the gods will die.'[20] But Sullivan's interpretation does not address Indra's difficult question: 'The deep sea was where she [Mother Gunga] runs yesterday, and to-morrow the sea shall cover her again as the Gods count that which men call time. Can any say that this their bridge endures till tomorrow?' (*DW*, p. 51). Kipling's ironic voice is clear when he suggests that men like Findlayson work, not for the glory of the ICS, but to stave off the horror of their meaningless existence. Empires and altars will be painstakingly constructed and worshipped at, but will inevitably diminish, only to be reconstructed in another guise. Says Indra: Brahm's 'dreams come and go, and the nature of the dreams changes [sic], but still Brahm dreams' (*DW*, p. 59). The workaday lives of Britannias army of soldiers and administrators, and not political or ideological agendas, which are of little compensation, will divert men's horror of the abyss. Krishna states that '[t]he matter is with the people. *They* move, and not the Gods of the bridge-builders' (*DW*, p. 58).

Kipling's reverence for quotidian work in the service of the British Empire, a theme that dominates 'The Bridge Builders', is elevated to almost mythic heights in 'William the Conqueror', but with an added dimension: that of stubborn persistence in seeing the job through to its completion. Where Findlayson crumbles in doubt, Scott, Kipling's hero in 'William the Conqueror', works himself almost to death to avert further disaster in a famine-stricken southern India. He does it, not with ostentatious self-promotion, but with a quiet altruism that Kipling summarises in the epigraph that opens the story:

> I have done one braver thing
> Than all the worthies did;
> And yet a braver thence doth spring,
> Which is to keep that hid. (*DW*, p. 157)

Scott's selfless acts demonstrate, as Randall Jarrell argues, Kipling's aching need to 'celebrate and justify true authority, the work and wisdom of the world, because he feels so bitterly the abyss of pain and insanity that they overlie'.[21] Kipling's notion of service – the need to cling to a belief-structure and dedicate one's weary existence to furthering an ideal – reaches an apex in 'William the Conqueror'. The story sees Kipling obsessed with building a rampart of unwavering adherence to service to shore up the struggling, lonely colonial whose political *raison d'être* has been spirited away in an abject pit of the undead, nullified in lonely outposts or almost washed away in violent flood-waters. 'William the Conqueror' details the efforts of British relief workers as they attempt to turn the tide of famine in Southern India. From all departments of the Government of India, officers and administrators are being drafted in to organise the distribution of grain to the famine-stricken south. From the Punjab comes the engineer, Scott; his friend, the policeman Martyn; and Martyn's sister, Wilhelmina (although she is known by her nickname as 'William'), who has, against the wishes of her brother, obtained permission to join the relief team. For months Scott and Martyn organise the grain supplies, travelling through the worst hit areas to get the supplies through and collecting a convoy of starving people along the way. William, with the wife of Jim Hawkins, commander in chief of famine operations, stays behind at the central relief camp but works tirelessly, looking after a growing band of abandoned children. During their arduous tasks William and Scott begin to fall quietly in love with one another, but neither will make their feelings explicit until the job in hand is completed.

Charles Carrington writes that Kipling 'painted in the backcloth [of southern India] with a Pre-Raphaelite brilliance of colour and accuracy of detail'.[22] However, the tedious monotony of the Anglo-Indian Club as well as a desiccated India serves as backdrop to Scott's quotidian life. Describing Scott and Martyn's station, Kipling writes:

> It was a hot, dark, breathless evening, heavy with the smell of the newly-watered Mall. The flowers in the Club gardens were dead and black on their stalks, the little lotus pond was a circle of caked mud, and the tamarisk-trees were white with the dust of days. (*DW*, p. 157)

This desolate image is one of imprisonment. 'Inside' the club, like the narrator's house in 'The City of Dreadful Night', represents an enclosure. The political dogma of an imperial agenda, a Kristevan law of the father, in effect, has foreclosed any possibility of giving meaning to the lives of Kipling's overstretched workers of Empire. Scott had been sent here 'much against his will, for he hated office work [. . .] to serve during the hot weather on the accounts and supply side of the Department' (*DW*, p. 160). This is the 'inside' from which Scott needs to escape. It is a space entirely dominated by a paternal authority that defines his worth in purely monetary terms. Kipling writes that his nullifying office work is defined by a system 'where each man's pay, age, and position are printed in a book, that all may read [and] it is hardly worth while to play at pretences in word or deed' (*DW*, p. 160). The imperial space presents itself as self-sufficient, lacking nothing. There is a bandstand where 'the native Police band [are] hammering stale waltzes', a 'polo-ground', a 'high-walled fives-court, hotter than a Dutch oven', 'white-washed barracks' where men would 'listlessly loaf', 'meeting the same faces night after night at dinner, and drawing out their office-work till the latest possible hour, that they might escape that doleful company' (*DW*, p. 158).

The enclosed 'inside' of the club, mapped as such by Scott's mind, is analogous to a drought-stricken southern India, 'a dry, hot dawn, in a land of death' (*DW*, p. 168), populated by 'a regiment of little brown men' and 'wailing, walking skeletons' (*DW*, p. 168). This army of undead creates an association of the 'inside' as a corporeal dimension of the self. From Scott's point of view, his white 'body' offers no security of colonial identity as the native is etymologically fastened to the 'regiments' of the British military. The nullifying heat-scorched Indian landscape threatens physical destruction to black and white alike. Scott escapes the imprisoning 'inside' of both the dusty club and the parched landscape through the joyful positivism associated with action. William confides to one of her admirers that she likes 'men who do things' (*DW*, p. 161), a sentiment echoed by the head of the famine relief who says of Scott, '[t]hat's a good man [. . .] If all goes well I shall work him – hard.' Kipling emphatically states that 'this was Jim Hawkins' notion of the highest compliment one human being could pay another' (*DW*, p. 169). Scott's selfless deeds spring not from blind imperial loyalty, but from a stubborn refusal to be beaten down when the situation seems hopeless. Exhausted and ill, his 'steadfastness bore his body to the telegraph-office at the railway station, and dictated a telegram to Hawkins saying that the Khanda district was, in his judgement, now safe and he "waited further orders"' (*DW*, p. 183). His challenging, life-affirming engagement with an abjected Indian space, a colonial heart of darkness, sees him taking on duties that have previously been associated with women. He drives the bullock carts, work traditionally given to 'coolies', he milks goats, bottle-feeds starving Indian children, which makes him the butt of Martyn's jokes, 'What a lark! I'd have given a month's pay to have seen him nursing famine babies' (*DW*, p. 179). However, Kipling encourages an admiration of Scott's selfless deeds when they are performed for the good of the whole. In this respect, he exchanges his masculine male 'inside' for an 'outside' that subverts his 'I am white, I am male, I am ruler' role. To be 'inside' India's furnace-like melting pot blurs matters of historical and cultural affiliative identifications as well as sexual identity.

Kipling's characterisation of William demonstrates, according to Carrington, 'a new sort of woman' whose more fully developed gender role the author had not been able to depict until this story.[23] Elsewhere in Kipling's fiction, white women are by turns hysterics, seductresses, matronly mother figures or ghostly one-dimensional characters. Kipling negates William's physical beauty in his opening description, thereby introducing an unconventional heroine at the outset. Her face is marred with the 'big silvery scar' that marks a 'Delhi sore' (*DW*, p. 161). She is equal to (and on occasions outmatches) a man at every turn. She 'never set foot on the ground if a horse were within hail', 'had altogether fallen out of the habit of writing to her aunts in England, or cutting the pages of the English newspaper' (*DW*, p. 161), is fluent in Urdu and has fragments of Punjabi, has had her head shaved due to a life-threatening bout of typhoid fever. Rather than see her as a shadow of a man, she encapsulates a Cixousian 'newly born woman' in that her character describes a particular subjectivity that destabilises the foundation of sexual difference. In this respect, William embodies the desexualised characteristics of Britannia and her work for the imperial project takes precedence over her culturally imposed 'femininity'.

William, like Scott, is defined by her deeds. At one point in the story, Scott's work brings him close to the camp. In an attempt to buoy William's spirits, 'Mrs Jim' assures her that Scott will take time out to visit her in the camp. But William knows better, '"It'll take him off his work [. . .] He won't see fit," [she] replied without sorrow or emotion. "It wouldn't be him if it did"' (*DW*, p. 182); and Kipling's implication is that she would think the less of him if he did shirk his duties, even for the woman he loves. When Scott prepares a report on the possibility of repairing a broken-down reservoir to augment the water supply when the rains come, William sits late into the night, 'reading page after page of the square handwriting' (*DW*, p. 181). She, like Scott, learns to milk goats to feed the starving children. Working herself almost to exhaustion, she is described as 'pulled down a bit' but otherwise 'in great form' (*DW*, pp. 184–5). In terms of her feminine agency, William has overturned the autocratic authority of the phallogocentric ideal that women are defined by lack and are passive Others. Connected to Scott in both (masculine) name and deed, William's characterisation refutes the idea that fear and inactivity bind one to a horror of the abyss and the systems that support the binaries of difference. In this story, Kipling tacitly acknowledges that his characters are capable of changing the way subjectivity is constructed. Both Scott and William can rewrite the oppressive narrative of colonial identity that 'sees' its opposite (women and native) from the other side of the bar. And the ideal of Empire becomes the vehicle through which his heroes (male and occasionally female) can accomplish great deeds.

Throughout the story, commitment to following a course of action can avert the anxiety that the crippling famine induces, and Kipling lauds those men and women who take an active role in psychologically paralysing situations:

> No one was better than the big Canal officer [Jack Hawkins] who never lost his temper, never gave an unnecessary order, and never questioned an order given. (*DW*, p. 180)

> Hawkins reported at the end that they all did well – but Scott was the most excellent, for he kept good coined-rupees by him, and paid for his own cart repairs on the spot, and ran to meet all sorts of unconsidered extras, trusting to be recouped later [. . .] but Government vouchers cash themselves slowly, and intelligent and efficient clerks write at great length, contesting unauthorised expenditures of eight annas. (*DW*, p. 180)

In order to truly become a conqueror of the abyss, Kipling's heroes must put aside the Latin 'impots', Greek tragedies, Shakespearian sonnets and dusty histories of ancient rulers that were sleepily attended to in the stuffy classrooms of their youths, in favour of working shoulder to shoulder with their colonial compatriots in the field. His imperial man of action who rematerialises at Bateman's in the form of a hedger described as a 'poacher by heredity and instinct' who was 'more "one with Nature" than a whole parlour full of poets' (*SOM*, p. 106), can by his deeds for the community at large achieve personal glory. Thus in 'William the Conqueror' Kipling detaches the British Empire from its annexing, commercial reality that gives license to those eager to pillage India's lands and emasculate its peoples. In one narrative stroke, he transforms the individual's inner nullification into the gratifying world of humanitarian duty. Men are made mythic by dint of their humble unsung deeds:

> He [Scott] had no desire to make any dramatic entry, but an accident of sunset ordered it that, when he had taken off his helmet to get the evening breeze, the low light should fall across his forehead, and he could not see what was before him; while one waiting at the door beheld, with new eyes, a young man, beautiful as Paris, a god in a halo of golden dust, walking slowly at the head of his flocks, while at his knee ran small naked Cupids. (*DW*, p. 174)

Widening the image of god-like colonial hero to include a geographical space, Kipling's mythologised Empire becomes, in 'The Brushwood Boy', a prelapsarian playground that offers the man of action a hallowed refuge from the now distant abyss. A terrifying India and its dead-in-life population have become, as Sullivan argues, 'marginalized into non-existence'.[24] In this story, while Kipling's goddess of Empire, Britannia, guides the trajectory of her new-cast imperial son, she is not able to entirely silence the ghost of a coveted Mother India who is reanimated in the outcast space of his hero's dream world.

Like 'The Bridge Builders', 'The Brushwood Boy' operates on two levels. Firstly, there is the outer world where Kipling charts the flawless progress of the subaltern groomed for imperial life, and secondly there is George Cottar's chaotic and surreal inner dream world, set in sharp relief to his colonial success. As argued in the previous chapter, Kipling's rendition of a frighteningly chaotic India that disrupts the ordered psychological state of the colonial's mind heralds a closing-off of the avenues of discovery that Kipling so enjoyed when the 'night got into [his] head' and he strolled the streets of Lahore (*SOM*, p. 33). As we have seen in 'William the Conqueror', he establishes limits of propriety on the white man's interaction with his native counterpart and imposes jurisdiction on desirable communication with the native India of bazaars and opium dens. Hence the dream world as a site for libidinous impulses, in this story, creeps furtively toward centre stage. Like the dream-imagery that exposes desire in the condensation and displacement of quotidian events, the tropes in Cottar's surreal dream landscape act as a signpost to exactly those points of fracture that, for Kristeva, constantly threaten the symbolic order. Cottar's dream world is the place of the secret and the 'incommunicable' (*DW*, p. 293). Kipling's treatment of the dream world is not a simple set of binary oppositions between self and Other. Rather, it incorporates an interstitial space that includes the writtenness of the subject's identity, whilst simultaneously extending the limits of acceptable conduct within the imperial community. In this sense it is a metaphor for 'an entire structure of investigation, not merely "writing in the narrow sense", graphic notation on a tangible material'.[25] The myths and behaviours governed by inherited traditions and conventions of the kind that Stalky and his friends learn in their school in England are the foundations of political and philosophical attitudes of colonial service overseas. But just as Stalky and his compatriots, with their dens in the gorse, escape the rigid masculine order of school life in the more feminine realm of the natural world, so Cottar sneaks away from his colonial responsibilities by means of furtive sojourns into his unconscious.

'The Brushwood Boy' is a curious tale of feminine and masculine duality. Cottar's ventures into his dream world are at odds with the sexually potent, masculine world of Empire, yet he is lauded as one of its shining lights. Driven by insatiate desires and a longing for reunification with what I will argue is a maternal realm, he is crushed by the weight of Kipling's notion of colonial duty and is, in his waking world, at least, consigned to a future life that conforms to imperial strictures. The line of demarcation that separates the dream world from reality sees Cottar surreptitiously crossing its border. The day is where the work of the Empire is accomplished and its laws enforced, but the murky waters of Cottar's unconscious seep into and disrupt the paternal imperial hegemony. As in 'The Bridge Builders,' the protagonist is involved in a descent into the unconscious, this time into the surreal world of dreams. However, Findlayson's visions are opium-induced. Having no control over them, he is merely allotted the role of passive spectator to events that unfold before him. Although in 'The Bridge Builders' the chasm between the Indian psyche and western rationality is metaphorically bridged, albeit fleetingly, Cottar's barely manageable night-time world remains exiled from his 'Englishness'. He is able to exercise a certain control over his dreams yet is fully aware that they must on no account interfere with the realisation of a successful school and military career.

After proving himself on the school playing fields and via military service in India, Cottar's stint abroad entitles him to return 'Home' to the promise of marriage to one of the 'Herefordshire Lacys' (*DW*, p. 305). 'The Brushwood Boy' is a crucial story in my study as it links several phases in the progression of infant to adulthood within one tale. Cottar's earlier pre-Indian experience contains elements common to 'Baa Baa, Black Sheep'. Like Stalky and Kim, he moves through adolescence learning (but curiously *not* exploiting) the 'law' (of the father) before applying his training on the military fields of India, winning the respect of his company and his superiors in the process. However, like Kim, he remains strangely innocent of sexual advances from the older women he encounters. Sexually, at least, Cottar's libidinous development remains arrested at a pre-adolescent stage.

The story opens with an infant Cottar's cry of fright as he wakes from a nightmare, '[a] child of three sat up in his crib and screamed at the top of his voice, his fists clinched and his eyes full of terror' (*DW*, p. 283). Kipling implies that the terrors of the dream have their source in real life, thereby establishing at the outset Cottar's daytime connection to his night-time world. The policeman Tisdall, whom Georgie had met earlier in the day on the Down, is transformed into the ghoulish authoritarian 'Policeman Day' of his nightmare. The confusion of Georgie's account adds a hazy blurring between reality and dream, 'It was a policeman! He was on the Down – I saw him! He came in. Jane *said* he would' (*DW*, p. 283). What is clear, however, is the crossing of boundaries between the dream world and the waking world. As Sullivan points out, whilst the contents of the nightmare itself do not seem particularly threatening,[26] the original manuscript holds a much more plausible explanation for the boy's terror. He exclaims, 'It was – it was a policeman. He came in froo the window an' ate the rug! I saw him do it!' Harper, the housekeeper, tries to reassure the frightened boy by saying, '"Nonsense Master George. Policemen never come through windows. They live in the Garden just like Ponto. Go to sleep."'[27] The implication is that the boy's waking life has been penetrated by his dream. Sullivan argues that Georgie's ultimate fear is to be eaten by the policeman,[28] but I would argue that the policeman consuming the rug can be read as an infant's fear of being engulfed or overwhelmed not by a person, but by the autocratic authority of the paternal word.

As his childhood progresses Georgie begins to gain a certain mastery over his night-time world. Continuing a bedtime story left unfinished by his mother, Georgie is 'delighted to find that the tale came out of his own head [. . .] as though he were listening to it "all new from the beginning"' (*DW*, p. 284). The feelings toward his mother in the real world are reanimated in the joyous elements of his unconscious discourse. Thereby, he has found a 'forbidden' route to the mother in the semiotic realm. However, he realises that his newly gained 'power' must remain 'secret'. Kipling felt that storytelling could be a potentially dangerous act. Addressing the Royal Academy in May 1906, Kipling tells the story of a 'masterless man' with the ability to describe 'a most notable deed' of a member of the tribe. The storyteller's words 'became alive and walked up and in the hearts of all his hearers'. Misunderstanding that the 'magic' was in the words and not the man, the members of the tribe promptly killed the unfortunate storyteller (*BOW*, pp. 3–5). Cottar's ability to 'magically' change stories remains hidden 'for fear of being laughed at' (*DW*, p. 284), in much the way that Punch realises his mistake when he scandalises Aunty Rosa by reshaping her Christian creation story with fragments of Indian mythology. Like Punch, whose ventures into the liberated world of the imagination must be disguised in play, Georgie's 'tales faded gradually into dreamland, where adventures were so many that he could not recall the half of them' (*DW*, p. 284).

The dream world, where he can realise prohibited desires, remains 'out of bounds' and Cottar, like Stalky, comes to internalise this notion once he is at school: 'English public school[s] do not encourage dreaming' (*DW*, p. 287). In this respect, Cottar's unconscious dreams increasingly come to resemble Kristeva's abject and must be cast out for his colonial 'I' to exist. The abject is what 'disturbs identity, systems, order', respecting neither 'borders [nor] rules.'[29] Policeman Day of the dream world, Cottar's real-life schoolmasters and army officers are the paternal law's enforcers, who outlaw his desire for a lost maternal realm and demonstrate a contingent aggression toward a maternal realm. The boy's unconscious fantasy of maternal prohibition is chastised in the image of Policeman Day devouring the rug, consuming, in effect, the lost maternal figure, what in Kristevan terms is a 'Melancholy Cannibalism', 'the intolerable other that I crave to destroy so as better to possess it alive. Better fragmented, torn up, swallowed, digested [. . .] than lost.'[30] Thus the cannibalistic act manifests the anguish of losing the mother figure to become a socialised subject. These feelings of penetrating a forbidden space and the fear of being consumed by the desire to cross these boundaries will, during the course of the boy's school, military and colonial training, be repressed and transferred onto the wild, jungle-like terrain and the frightening figures of his dreams. Cottar's dreamscape represents a feminised space where the paternal law is continually under threat of annihilation. Elsewhere in Kipling's Indian fiction, this threat meant losing one's colonial head and 'going Fantee'. In Cottar's nightmare realm, the danger of loss of control necessitates an augmentation of rationality and strength of character in the daytime world. The abject dream world, as it exists at the borders of his colonial self, recalls Kipling's earlier treatment of Hummil's crippling fear of isolation in 'At the End of the Passage' that must be decoded and disciplined into a more manageable state.

The beginnings of his newly created dream world transform his infant experience of being left alone to cry in his cot into an edenic space of childhood, populated exclusively by 'little boys and girls' that Georgie can run races with. The landscape is similarly paradisiacal, 'ships ran high up the dry land and opened into cardboard boxes; or gilt-and-green iron railings that surrounded beautiful gardens turned all soft, and could be walked through and overthrown so long as he remembered it was only a dream' (*DW*, p. 284). But the real world remains on the periphery of this utopian existence. Recognition of his dream-state creates a sort of 'conscious' dream where the laws of the physical world apply and he once again becomes an 'orphaned' boy (with shades of Kim): 'instead of pushing down houses full of grown-up people (a just revenge), he sat miserably upon gigantic door-steps trying to sing the multiplication-table up to four times six' (*DW*, p. 284). However, these moments of realisation are few. For the most part, the boy can navigate his way through this surreal kaleidoscopic landscape with a Kim or Stalky-like poise and self-assurance, commentating on its temporal space whilst magically transforming its narrative structure with, like his bedtime stories, fragments drawn from memories of the waking world.

Georgie creates a favourite playmate in the shape of the 'brushwood girl', whom he names 'Annie*an*Louise'. At one point in his dream, he begins to sink in his dream-sea, thinking he must surely drown. However, his newly-created companion saves him with a nonsensical but magical incantation, 'Ha! Ha! said the duck laughing' (*DW*, p. 284) and, 'since laughing is a way of [. . .] displacing abjection,'[31] at once the floor of the seabed lifts and Georgie emerges with a 'twelve-inch flower-pot on each foot' (*DW*, p. 285). The image of water evokes the Cixousian notion of a fluidity of the pre-verbal maternal realm.[32] Unlike the welcoming waves that break upon the foot of the cliffs where Stalky has built his 'out of bounds' den, the sea is a frightening entity. The malevolent image of a maternal sea here will be reanimated in the terrifying elements of the boy's dreams later on in the story. Georgie's desire for the 'out of sight', lost mother is articulated through language. Kristeva says that '[l]anguage learning takes place as an attempt to appropriate an oral "object" that slips away and whose hallucination, necessarily deformed, threatens us from the outside'.[33] The mother figure that Georgie inarticulately cries alone for in the real world is recreated in the 'dream-sea', which is prompted by a real-life experience of being taken to bathe in the sea by his nurse. Colonising the maternal realm with words temporarily assuages the threat of engulfment that his desire for the pre-verbal mother figure provokes, imaged in the terror of drowning.

Georgie is most afraid of being overwhelmed by forces he is unable to control. His dream world is a 'reality' where meaning disintegrates and, if acknowledged, has the power to annihilate his self-constructed world: 'he could never hold that knowledge more than a few seconds ere things became real' (*DW*, p. 284). Similarly, his first tentative ventures outside, where social structures should be managed and controlled, are accompanied by a corresponding threat of potential destruction. The first time we see the boy outside his nursery is on a visit to Oxford. Here Georgie is exposed to the frightening world of predominantly adult males, where an 'enormously fat man' stops his mouth with bread and cheese and tries to give him an intoxicating draught of 'auditale' (*DW*, p. 285). He is led away to watch a performance of a puppet show called 'Pepper's Ghost'. The instigator of these chaotic events is Mr Pepper, who is 'beyond question a man of the worst' (*DW*, p. 285). The puppeteer can be read as the 'grown-up' who propels George to the border of the symbolic and the semiotic and blurs the distinction between his conscious and unconscious worlds. The show, like the pit into which Morrowbie Jukes falls or the wonderland at the end of the rabbit hole, has a hallucinatory air, where 'people's heads came off and flew all over the stage' (*DW*, p. 285). In 'Pepper's Ghost', decapitation, a metonymic image of castration, along with the skeletons 'that danced bone by bone' (*DW*, p. 285), recalls Jukes' sense of disorientation at finding his imperial authority 'castrated'.

However, Georgie is oddly disconnected from the fear that this performance should provoke to a boy of his age. He is told there is 'no need to be frightened', no doubt by a concerned 'grown up', as this illusory, nonsensical world is created and amplified with mirrors (*DW*, p. 285). In the narrative, mirrors are etymologically connected to his mother: 'a mirror was the looking-glass with the ivory handle on his mother's dressing table' (*DW*, p. 285). And in a Lacanian sense, the mirror is connected to the moment that a child recognises its own image, an image that is disconnected from the mother/child dyad. The 'mirror stage' is the moment where the child's ego begins to be formulated via (mis)identification with its own mirror image. It is at this moment that the boy sees 'a little girl dressed all in black, her hair combed off her forehead exactly, like the girl in the book "Alice in Wonderland"' (DW, p. 285). Interestingly, the psychoanalytic implications of *Alice in Wonderland* have much in common with Cottar's unconscious dream world. He, like

Alice, slides into an erratic, chaotic dreamland where the laws of the daytime world no longer apply. Both the mother and the girl have their counterparts in the dream world. The mother will become transfigured into the terrifying 'Sick Thing' and the girl is a would-be saviour. In 'Baa Baa, Black Sheep', Punch exchanges his 'real, live, lovely Mamma' (*WWW*, p. 287) for the wolfish Aunty Rosa, which mirrors the two faces of the mother figure, the 'good' and the 'bad'. Similarly, Georgie substitutes his mother in the real world for the terrifying 'Sick Thing', akin to the transformation of the life-giving mother into the abject, phallic mother.

The boy's dream world at this moment in his childhood points to a liminal state between childhood and adulthood where maternal elements are yet to be fully abjected. When Georgie meets the girl who will subsequently replace 'AnnieanLouise' as the 'brushwood girl' in his dreams, he becomes oddly reticent. He explains the cut on his thumb, caused by a 'savage triangular hack' (*DW*, p. 286), and receives the girl's lisping sympathies. The raw wound covered over by the 'di-ack-lum' plaster is an example of corporeal waste and as such should provoke a sense of horror and disgust, but both Georgie and the girl are drawn to it with fascination. It is the nurse sitting next to Georgie who voices the cultural and individual disgust for the rent in the boy's skin through which the inside has seeped and sits like an abject trophy. The scab sticks to the surface of the skin, no longer part of the interior map of the body but not yet wholly separated from it. Georgie deems the wound received from 'his first real knife', his 'most valuable possession' (*DW*, p. 286). The children's fascinated horror of Georgie's scab acts as a point of connection between them. Similarly, in the dream world, he feels a deep bond to his brushwood girl.

In his dream world Georgie becomes a 'devisor of territories, languages, works'.[34] His infantile ego, when threatened with the conflicting impulses of love and hate, reacts by splitting his mother into her 'good' and 'bad' components. The Kleinian notion of the two internalised maternal figures – on the one hand the nurturing, life-giving mother whose breast accords complete gratification and on the other the discordant, terrifying phallic mother – are literalised in Cottar's dream images of the 'Sick Thing' and the brushwood girl. His companion shows him a way to pass 'across unexplored territories and unknown seas'. He is described by Kipling as being 'unspeakably happy' in a place that fills him with 'incommunicable delight' (pp. 353, 352). Cottar has travelled to the borders of self, the 'world's end', to meet his brushwood companion, and this makes 'everything [. . .] entirely well with him' in this place that is 'beyond the most remote imaginings of man' (*DW*,

p. 294). However, the underlying threat to this manufactured world is the 'Sick Thing', the aggressive, annihilating mother, who instils in Cottar his greatest fear and over whom he can exercise no control.

The anxiety experienced by the boy in such a threatening situation results in a splitting that affects both the menacing object and his sense of a coherent self, which literally breaks into pieces. This fragmentation of self is, according to Klein, an expression of the death drive and with it the disintegration of self from within.[35] The aggressive, phallic mother who threatens obliteration resides in a world that materialises with the 'rustle of unrolling maps' (*DW*, p. 294). Like a creeping pollutant, this uncharted protean landscape unfurls and multiplies to form 'a sixth quarter of the globe' (*DW*, p. 294). The infant's fear of being devoured and engulfed by this monstrous feminine entity becomes a terrifying possibility in an anthropomorphised landscape whose 'straits [. . .] yawned and widened'. The road becomes a rotting cadaver and the sea rabid with maniacal intent, 'lash[ing] back at him [with] black, foamless tongues of smooth and glossy rollers' (*DW*, p. 294). Like a man crazed with fever or madness, Cottar's psychic terrain has gone 'Fantee' – the colonialists' greatest fear. It is a place that constantly shifts, with little to stabilise it: 'the islands slipped and slid under his feet [. . .] till he found himself utterly lost in the world's fourth dimension, with no hope of return' (*DW*, p. 294). The gardens that were previously 'beautiful' have now become 'moist and dripping [. . .] where a mob of stony white people, all unfriendly, sat at breakfast tables covered with roses' (*DW*, p. 296). India is obliquely alluded to in this menacing place, as the brushwood boy and his companion meet 'in the middle of an endless hot tropic night' to enter the 'huge house' where he will meet the object of his greatest fear, the 'Sick Thing', who lies in a bed shrouded in 'mosquito-netting' (*DW*, pp. 296–7). The 'Sick Thing' can be read as a corpse-like phallic mother who exists at the very borders of subjectivity. She represents 'death infecting life'.[36]

Until this point in the narrative, the Sick Thing had remained on the periphery of Cottar's dream realm. Its portents are the shadowy 'They' and 'Them' who reside on an 'inland', which is strenuously avoided as he becomes more proficient in mapping his psychic space. However, the 'Sick Thing's' appearance in the penultimate dream of the story represents shifts from the border into the heart of Cottar's dream world itself. In the 'middle of an endless hot tropic night', together with his companion, he finds 'a huge house [. . .] somewhere north of the railway station' (*DW*, p. 296). The house is surrounded by a garden, 'all moist and dripping', that recalls the maternal jungle space that is so ruthlessly crushed by the elephants in 'Toomai of the Elephants'. The children pass through this space with mounting trepidation, moving through the complex warren of corridors in the house until they reach the room where the Sick Thing lies on a bed. It is a vision of pure terror, 'the least noise, Georgie knew, would unchain some waiting horror' (*DW*, p. 296). It poses a danger to his ego in so far as its precarious instability questions his ability to control the situation. The brushwood girl, companion and protector to the boy, turns out to be no match for the terrifying power the phallic mother wields in this world. When the two enter the room, 'Georgie was disgusted to see that she was a child [. . .] she could do nothing whatever if Its head came off' (*DW*, p. 297).

It is the 'Sick Thing', however, that breaks the silence with a cough that shatters the stillness, causing its guardians, 'They' and 'Them', to come rushing 'from all quarters' to overwhelm the boy (*DW*, p. 297). The cough erupting in an expulsion of acoustic rhythms that articulates the Sick Thing's archaic authority is magnified, swelling and thickening until powerful enough to shatter the ceiling in a cascade of plaster. In *Kim*, the inchoate sounds of the *parao* are signifiers of the welcoming maternal space of the semiotic; here, the incoherent menacing noises are harbingers of terror. Coming face to face with the 'Sick Thing', whose head, like 'Pepper's Ghosts', threatens continually to topple, forces the boy to confront the horror of abjection. It is her bodily and vocal emissions that summon the stony white figures to rush into the room, presenting a threat of annihilation. In this womb-like room, reached through a labyrinthine network of 'whitewashed passages', the boy meets the object of his desire and his horror. Cottar sees the shifting axis of meaning and sensory perceptions blur the demarcation line between desire/fear, mother as Other, revealing the perilous instability of the symbolic as it struggles to stamp its provisional authority on the pulsations of the semiotic. The boy and girl escape 'through the stifling garden', accompanied by 'voices chanting behind them', until they reach the 'safety' of the lamppost and brushwood pile (*DW*, p. 297). However, the Sick Thing remains undefeated. The last dream that Cottar experiences inexplicably sees all the terrifying elements of his dream diminished at the same time that his companion has grown into a woman: '"They" for some dreamland reason, were friendly or had gone away that night.' The house of the Sick Thing has become 'a pin-point in the distance to the left'. Just as he had been able to colonise and control the natural aspects of his dream world, so he has similarly moved the Sick Thing to the margins of his unconscious. The melancholic subterranean sounds can still be heard, but now 'there was no panic' (*DW*, p. 301).

The maternal figure of the 'Sick Thing', however, is not vanquished but reclaimed in the mother figures in the outside world, although its power, as in the dream world, is significantly decreased. Cottar is surprisingly unaware of the attentions of the ladies of the camp and it is left to the more experienced men of the camp to comment: 'If only Cottar knew it, half the women in the station would give their eyes – confound 'em! – to have the young 'un in tow' (*DW*, p. 290). Mrs Zulieka, who George meets on his way home to England, tries to seduce him, and again he is oblivious to her entreaties: 'turning from parental affection', she 'spoke of love in the abstract [. . .] and in discreet twilights after dinner demanded confidences [. . .] She learned all that was necessary to conviction and, being very much a woman, resumed (Georgie never knew that she had abandoned) the motherly attitude' (*DW*, p. 300). Similarly, the Oedipal drama is re-enacted upon his return to England, where Cottar's lips are territorialised by his mother as she 'kisse[s] him on the mouth', which Kipling recognises 'is not always a mother's property' (*DW*, p. 304). But yet again the eroticism of this moment is lost on her son, as is her delight at finding him still a virgin, and its power is weakened by the 'profane and incredulous laughs' of his father (*DW*, p. 304).

The masculine world of the empire builders, who have learned their trade on the playing fields of England, enables Cottar to transpose and translate the loss of the maternal figure onto a third party – the father whose word constitutes the form and symbol of paternal authority. Unlike Stalky, school, for Cottar, is the reassuring 'real world, where things of vital importance happened' (*DW*, p. 288). School in this story is not a brutalising, dispassionate environment; rather, it is a place where a boy wins 'his growth and chest measurement' (*DW*, p. 287) by a rigorous regime of physical exercise to which regular doses of corporal punishment are added. Youths like George Cottar will go on to find service as colonial administrators of the British Empire, and we sense Kipling's growing approval of the benefits that 'work' produces in this repressive regime, despite the ambivalences that the dream world throws up. With the prospect of marriage to the decidedly straight-laced Miriam Lacy at the end of 'The Brushwood Boy', Kipling's lost motherland and desire for the bounteous semiotic mother figure is increasingly diminished. The fecund, archaic maternal figure that has in earlier stories been written with a retrospective nostalgia for the loss of coalescence, the transcript of which was India and its peoples, is finally succumbing to the will of the symbolic.

From this point on in Kipling's fiction, the 'phantasmatic mother who also constitutes, in the specific history of each person, the abyss that must be established as an autonomous *place* and distinct *object*'[37] becomes transfigured into the figure of Britannia. Like the nameless, bruised and defiled woman of Eliot's 'The Fire Sermon', whose 'feet are at Moorgate' and 'heart/Under [her] feet',[38] Mother India attests to the constant threat of fragmentation. The monstrous, bloody finger that laid bare abjection in previous Indian stories has been sheathed and now, cold and sterile, points to India as the site of the Other. As the character of George Cottar demonstrates, the borders of self have been established and bleeding boundaries cauterised with surgical precision. By combining the now dead eternal past, to which his childhood self belonged, with the authoritative Law of the present, Kipling is able to give a sense of meaning to the wretched lives of his colonial heroes. A wholehearted submission to the imperial project will begin to emerge in the wake of the nostalgic yearning for the lost 'Thing' that has marked his story collections up until this point.

Kipling's golden ideal of Empire in *The Day's Work*, whereby his art is bolted to a completed ideology of imperialism, has replaced the unarticulated cacophony of voices shrieking from the abyss. The means to repair the damaged mother image is accomplished through a narrative reworking of a lost England. The territory of Cottar's English country home (eerily similar to the gardens and house in his dream world) enables him to take his place in the paternal hierarchy. Father and son 'went out to smoke among the roses, and the shadow of the old house lay across the wonderful English foliage, which is the only living green in the world' (*DW*, p. 302). Characters like the black sheep Punch, the downcast Mowgli or the terrified Hummil, unable to preserve their identity in the face of the devouring, engulfing maternal figure, find reparation in the reworking of England as a site of mythical healing in *Puck of Pook's Hill*. Kipling's reformed maternal figure is Britannia, and at her majestic feet lie all the polyvalent tribes that make up generations of Britain's settler population. *Puck of Pook's Hill* continues the reorganisation of self that Kipling started in *The Day's Work*. India as a site of difficult, life-threatening desire has been finally exorcised. The feminised terrain of the heat-scorched Indian plains is replaced by an unproblematic pastoral of England. Kipling's reimagined historical tales, with Britannia at their heart, offer an alternative life-affirming identity to his colonial wretches who have been spiritually ruined by their desire for Mother India. The rewards for Kipling's 'exiles' are many, for he promises them that '[t]here's no place like England – when you've done your work' (*DW*, p. 303).

Notes

1. Rudyard Kipling, epigraph to 'In the House of Suddhoo', *Plain Tales from the Hills*, p. 115.
2. Rudyard Kipling, 'The Support', epigraph to 'On the Gate', *The Definitive Edition of Rudyard Kipling's Verse*, p. 767.
3. David Sergeant, *The Art of Kipling's Fiction*, p. 89.
4. Kipling had little regard for the policies of the Viceroy Lord Ripon or members of the Viceroy's council. David Gilmour writes: 'During the Simla season of 1885 Kipling had suggested in the *Gazette* that Lord Dufferin's Councillors [. . .] transmigrated after death into "the bodies of the great grey Langurs."' Gilmour, *The Long Recessional: The Imperial Life of Rudyard Kipling*, p. 76.
5. Bonamy Dobrée, *Rudyard Kipling: Realist and Fabulist*, pp. 66–7.
6. Thomas Pinney (ed.), *The Letters of Rudyard Kipling* I, p. 98.
7. Gilmour, *The Long Recessional*, p. 79.
8. Mark Paffard, *Kipling's Indian Fiction*, p. 54.
9. Lewis Wurgaft, *The Imperial Imagination: Magic and Myth in Kipling's India*, p. 108.
10. Dobrée, *Rudyard Kipling*, pp. 44–5.
11. For a further discussion of the myth of the Virgin Mary see Julia Kristeva, 'Stabat Mater' in *The Kristeva Reader*, pp. 160–86.
12. Sandra Kemp, *Kipling's Hidden Narratives*, p. 51.
13. Zohreh Sullivan, *Narratives of Empire: The Fictions of Rudyard Kipling*, p. 120.
14. Ibid., pp. 126–7.
15. Edward Said, *Orientalism*, p. 226.
16. Kipling, 'A Song of the White Men', *Definitive Verse*, p. 282.
17. Said, *Orientalism*, p. 226.
18. Jan Montefiore, *Rudyard Kipling*, p. 44.
19. Toward the end of the nineteenth century the British Empire was seen as a civilising force carried out by men that possessed what Sir James Stephen (one-time member of the Viceroy's Council) called 'the masterful will, the stout heart, the active brain, the calm nerves, the strong body' (quoted in Gilmour, *The Long Recessional*, p. 79).
20. Sullivan, *Narratives of Empire*, p. 126.
21. Randall Jarrell, 'On Preparing to Read Kipling', p. 21.
22. Charles Carrington, *Rudyard Kipling: His Life and Work*, p. 276.
23. Ibid., p. 276.
24. Sullivan, *Narratives of Empire*, p. 134.
25. Gayatri Chakravorty Spivak, translator's note and preface in Jacques Derrida, *Of Grammatology*, p. lxix.
26. Sullivan, *Narratives of Empire*, p. 131.
27. Collection of Manuscripts of Rudyard Kipling, in Pierpont Morgan Library, Department of Literary and Historical Manuscripts, New York (call number MA0979). Quoted in Sullivan, *Narratives of Empire*, p. 131.
28. Sullivan, *Narratives of Empire*, p. 131.
29. Julia Kristeva, *Powers of Horror: An Essay on Abjection*, p. 4.

30. Julia Kristeva, *Black Sun: Depression and Melancholia*, p. 12.
31. Kristeva, *Powers of Horror*, p. 8.
32. See Introduction to Rudyard Kipling, *The Day's Work*, n. 16.
33. Kristeva, *Powers of Horror*, p. 41.
34. Ibid., p. 8.
35. Melanie Klein, *Developments in Psychoanalysis*, p. 296.
36. Kristeva, *Powers of Horror*, p. 4.
37. Ibid., p. 100.
38. T. S. Eliot, 'The Waste Land', p. 62.

Conclusion: This Other Eden – *Puck of Pook's Hill, Rewards and Fairies*

> Take of English earth as much
> As either hand may rightly clutch [. . .]
>   Lay that earth upon thy heart,
>   And thy sickness shall depart!
>
> It shall sweeten and make whole
> Fevered breath and festered soul.[1]
>
> We shall go back by the boltless doors,
> To the life unaltered our childhood knew –
> To the naked feet on the cool, dark floors,
> And the high-ceiled rooms that the Trade blows through:[2]
>
> And what should they know of England who only England know?[3]

The cultural dichotomy that Kipling faced as a consequence of spending his earliest years in India – brought up predominantly by his native servants – and his formative years in England at Downe Lodge and USC meant that his sense of self was inextricably linked to the Anglo-Indian community, where English was the dominant language and its culture the assumed superior, and native India, where Kipling's early linguistic and social frames of reference lay. For the bicultural children of his Indian fiction, the search for subjectivity stems not from the geographical location that they are born into, but rather from making sense of and understanding the collective experiences of themselves as willing or unwilling travellers between two disparate worlds. Characters such as the appropriately named Adam, son of Kipling's Kim-like master of disguise, Strickland, in 'The Son of His Father' (in *Land and Sea Tales*) attest to Kipling's knowledge of the language and everyday life of native India that becomes fused in Adam's sense of identity operating within what was considered appropriate in the Anglo-Indian community. This blurring of the division between the Indian and the Anglo-Indian frames of reference both frighten and upset Adam's mother, but not, it seems,

Kipling's narrator, who sees the enriching experience a cross-cultural upbringing can be:

> Mrs. Strickland tried to teach him a few facts, but he revolted at the story of Genesis as untrue. A turtle, he said, upheld the world [. . .] 'it's awful,' said Mrs. Strickland, half-crying, 'to think of his growing up like a little heathen.' Mrs. Strickland had been born and brought up in England, and did not quite understand eastern things. (*LST*, pp. 224–5)

Punch's bitter despair is a direct consequence of the nineteenth-century practice of expatriating Anglo-Indian children to England. Similarly, in Kipling's case, his exile separated him from his 'best-beloved' India. Mowgli is never at ease either in his adoptive jungle home or the man-village. Whilst Kim deftly moves between both the Anglo-Indian and Indian communities he is also left in a limbo state between the two at the end of the novel. For his Anglo-Indian characters, identity is mapped out on the terrain in which they live and Kipling's art reflects the difficulties of giving precedence to either Anglo-Indian or Indian intellectual and cultural discourses. Edward Said, in his memoir *Out of Place*, describes the effect of his own cross-cultural upbringing on the formation of his identity. Having had a Protestant Palestinian father who was also an American citizen, a mother born in Nazareth, a youth 'between worlds' in Cairo and Jerusalem, Said felt as though he was never 'of' anything.[4] Kipling's own upbringing mirrors elements of Said's, and that ambivalent sense of identity created the contrary viewpoints that can be found in his fiction. Through his art, Kipling continually modifies his own fractured sense of self with a cast of characters in a variety of settings that create the illusion of being 'of' something. On the composition of his autobiography, Said finds some elements that he argues are common to the writing process, namely that '[a]ll families invent their parents and children, give each of them a story, character, fate and even a language'.[5] In Kipling's case, the abandoned boy left to fend for himself finds or invents playmates and playgrounds, adult companions and restorative places, nowhere more so than in the 'far green spaces' of the Sussex downs.

As we have seen in Kipling's Indian stories, particularly those which use his frame-tale technique, a (usually) white, male narrator together with a host of voices explore and articulate disparate subject positions that cross class, race and (tentatively) gender boundaries. Nevertheless, the narrator is nearly always tied to the English political perspective within his tales, however sympathetic he is toward the fate of his heroes and the peoples that they govern. The 'inside' of his Indian stories, however, will always remain a matter of an ambivalent cultural identity.

His stories can be located within a western cultural discourse, which is 'enclosed' but punctuated occasionally by forays into fanciful escapism. Both Strickland's and Kim's exuberant escapades into 'forbidden' Indian spaces are psychically policed by the likes of the loafers Peachy and Dravot and the mixed-race opium addict Gabral Misquitta, who represent the sordid underside of venturing 'outside' of imperial edicts.

Kipling wrestled with ways that he could imaginatively represent the 'two sides of his head'. However, it was to prove a difficult undertaking in his Indian stories. Even in his last word on India, *Kim*, the author could not find a resolution to his troubling sense of Anglo-Indian identity. Like the Reverend Casaubon's unfinished manuscript, 'The Key to all Mythologies', which his wife Dorothea is expected to make sense of in George Eliot's *Middlemarch*, the ex-scholar McIntosh Jellaludin's magnum opus on India turns out be nothing more than a 'big bundle, wrapped in the tail of a petticoat, of old sheets of miscellaneous note-paper, all numbered and covered with fine cramped writing [and] McIntosh ploughed his hand through the rubbish and stirred it up lovingly' (*PT*, p. 248). 'Mother Maturin', Jellaludin's 'rubbish', was Kipling's (colonial) fantasy of capturing, containing and making coherent his imperial experience, perhaps even his Anglo-Indian identity. This was a seemingly impossible undertaking in India, but in Edwardian England Kipling found the means with which to realise his utopian conception of Empire as a unifying structure that would bring together all of England's past settler communities. His 'new' England was no longer a grey land full of cold and condemnation, but a fabled 'far green space' whose history could be expanded to include rather than exclude the 'foreigner'. It was a country that the displaced Kipling could finally call 'home'.

Upon settling in Sussex, situated in what he considered to be 'the most marvellous of all foreign countries [he] had ever been in',[6] Kipling composed the captivating children's stories *Puck of Pook's Hill* and its sequel *Rewards and Fairies*. The purpose of the books, Kipling wrote, was 'to give children *not* a notion of history but a notion of the time sense which is at the bottom of all knowledge of history and history understanded [sic] rightly means love of one's fellow men and the lands they live in'.[7] Harry Ricketts argues that the *Puck* collections represent time as a continuously moving entity where the present is merely the 'moving edge of the past'.[8] Leaving behind the parched plains of India where his eager subalterns earn their imperial stripes, Kipling recreates his notion of service and duty in the long-gone Empires of England's history.

Written before his vision darkened to murky cynicism in his journalistic pieces of the First World War in *Sea Warfare*, the two collections remain Kipling's lasting testament to his ideal of Empire. In these collections, Kipling is still didactic (his spokesperson, however, is mercifully not the smug, all-knowing narrator of his Indian tales but the magical, playful Puck), but as Gilmour points out, he was taking a 'pastoral sabbatical from haranguing his fellow countrymen about their responsibilities'.[9] These collections examine the ways in which a fragmented and disorientated identity can be healed and mapped properly through a lost 'time' of childhood, which is brought to life in the protected Sussex home of the fictional siblings Dan and Una, harking back to an age of unity, continuity and wholeness. In these collections the maternal space, which has been abjected, diminished and brought under colonial jurisdiction in his Indian fiction, takes centre stage in the Sussex landscape. A problematic Mother India has been transformed into Kipling's goddess of Empire, Britannia. 'Land and the People, persisting through Time and all its revolutions,' writes Carrington, 'are the theme of the two "Puck" books.'[10] And pastoral Sussex, with its dappled glades and bubbling streams, is where the healing space of the maternal realm is mapped out.

The importance of Kipling's house at Bateman's is underscored in the epigraph that heads the chapter in *Something of Myself*, 'The Very-Own House', which deals with him finally settling down in England. The fragment of verse, whose quietly insistent iambic rhythm and simple but deceptively sturdy end rhymes endow the house with almost totemic significance, reads:

> How can I turn from any fire
>   On any man's hearth-stone?
> I know the wonder and desire
>   That went to build my own. (*SOM*, p. 103)

Charles Carrington writes of what securing the purchase of Bateman's meant to Kipling and his wife, after deliberating on it two years previously and missing out: 'There was no doubt in their minds: this was the dream-house [. . .] of their private baby-talk, and they snatched it out of the market.'[11] Kipling's image of his home in Sussex, like his vision of England, captures the ancient resilience of its foundations, where its various owners have little long-lasting affect. Their presence adds to rather than diminishes the past history of the house. There is a sense of boyish excitement that characterises his first view of it. 'We had seen an advertisement of her', he says, 'and we reached her down an enlarged rabbit-hole of a lane' (*SOM*, p. 104). This is an interesting metaphor with regards to psychic ambivalence in two ways. In 'The Brushwood Boy', *Alice* was referred to in association with the dark underside of the unconscious self, sliding signifiers and a world in chaos with the potential for malevolence. At the end of the 'rabbit-hole', one could lose one's head on the whim of an unstable matriarch. But Kipling's use of it in the context of 'coming home' to Bateman's recalls the troubling search for identity that governs *Kim*. The bazaar boy's repeatedly unanswered self-questioning, 'Who is Kim and what is Kim?', could equally apply to an author 'coming home' to that 'most marvellous of foreign countries'. The question of identity is also a strong thematic strand in *Alice*; even the caterpillar's scornful 'Who are *You*?' satirises her ambivalent identity in Wonderland. Similarly, the didacticism, such as it is in the *Puck* stories, is focused on Dan and Una's sense of themselves by opening for them a magical rent in the linear structure of time to create a fluid, commingled history of England's past, coupled with the potentiality of a future that is reliant on an understanding of the connection one has to the past. Kipling's history is 'alive'. It defies rules, sequencing and order. It is at once disorientating and thrilling, much like the serpentine world that Alice finds herself tumbling into. At the end of Lewis Carroll's novel, the little girl embarks upon the transition to adulthood armed with a sense of place in her disordered world. Similarly, Dan and Una become the vital pieces of Kipling's spatial psychic landscape of England, which intimately connects foreign invaders from the past to the minutiae of the children's quotidian playground in their tiny corner of the Sussex downs.

Puck of Pook's Hill and *Rewards and Fairies* primarily detail Dan and Una's encounters with Puck, one of the last remaining People of the Hills. Puck possesses magical powers, knows intimately the healing power of various herbs and plants and is on friendly terms with Kipling's quiet keeper of England's natural landscape, the hedger Hobden. Through this mythical sprite the children hear stories of England's colonised past conveyed with the aid of historical figures, which Puck brings from the past. Kipling snakes through time and history, at one moment detailing fallen deities in ancient Weland before heralding the emergence of a Norman conquest, then on to a melancholic account of a splintered and warring Roman Empire in its death throes. These collections can be read as Kipling's emotional catharsis, for in them he finds reparation for new incarnations of his twin exiles, Punch and Judy, in a world where their dual Anglo-Indian/Indian identities 'belong'. The mixed cultural heritage of the children's Anglo-Indian world comprises mythic, religious, linguistic and social praxes that compete for the children's loyalties and affiliations. Their sense of place in the world is, like Mowgli's, fragile and on the borders of two separate communities. In this respect their movement from one community to another, from one country to another, represents an exile that is never quite understood by either Punch or Judy. In the same way, Kipling and his sister experienced an unfathomable expatriation where the positivism of their bicultural background was, for the most part, ignored. Kipling's sister Trix (Judy's corporeal twin) said of their abandonment '[l]ooking back I think the real tragedy of our childhood days [. . .] sprang from our inability to understand why our parents had deserted us'.[12] But Puck teaches Dan and Una that England has the capacity to weave each immigrant community's cultural conventions into its pluralist historical tapestry, which in turn enriches the children's sense of their own national identity.

Similarly, Kipling's mixed cultural background, which led to his expatriation to England, made him sensitive to the dynamics of exclusion. Throughout the early Indian stories the notion of exile, and of the border between what were considered appropriate and inappropriate patterns of behaviour, looms large in the narratives. The stories also critique the Anglo-Indian tendency to psychically 'name' the 'native' as its excluded Other. Kipling's adult yearnings for the soft underbelly of an India, which to European sensibilities was 'beyond the pale', were underscored by the menace that such a deep-rooted connection to the Other engenders. This threatening subject position is transposed onto an adult Kipling's recollections of his childhood in Bombay that rely heavily on sensory perceptions for their affect: 'I have always felt', he writes, 'the menacing darkness of the tropical eventides, as I have loved the voices of the night-winds through palm or banana leaves, and the song of the tree-frogs' (*SOM*, p. 3). In adulthood, his recollections take on a shrewder perspective, as he is more aware of the divisions between the Anglo-Indian and Indian communities: 'I would wander until dawn in all manner of odd places – liquor shops, gambling and opium-dens, which are not a bit mysterious', the implication being that they are not mysterious to Kipling's intimate cross-cultural affiliations (*SOM*, pp. 3, 33). His perceptions were perhaps based on experiences that were more intimate than those of his European readership. In *Puck of Pook's Hill* Kipling manages to give a voice to the Anglo-Indian boy, the 'Indian' side of whose head has been gagged by a sovereign western discourse. In the *Puck* tales, Kipling *controls* time, history and, perhaps most crucially of all, viewpoint. He restructures temporal linearity while simultaneously establishing an unrestricted narrative space where the author's bicultural identity and his solicitous (native) caregivers can be imaginatively reinstated. In Kipling's reimagined history of England, the Roman occupation comes after the Norman Conquest. However, Parnesius's understanding of the structures of power that shape (and ultimately corrode) the Roman Empire, and the cross-cultural bonds of friendship that give meaning to his life, are given value when seen in conjunction with the friendship of Sir Richard and Sir Hugh and the dedication they have to shape a 'new' England.

By restructuring England's pluralist past and giving it a Norman and Roman lacquer, Kipling constructed a schematic from the skeletal remains of history that vivified his childhood bicultural experience. Immersing the children in a 'living' history that encompasses the Roman occupation and Viking plundering, local pirates and smugglers, evangelical religious groups that drove away the magical hill people and stone-age paganism, Puck indirectly instructs the children on the importance of England's cultural diversity, and of those men and women who have worked the land to keep it fertile in a physical as well as a metaphysical sense. Like Kipling's exhausted soldiers of the northern provinces, the administrators living out their lonely lives in a 'far-away, desolate, by-white-men-forgotten district',[13] the men and women who are brought forward in time to tell Dan and Una of their past embody a vision of Empire that has service and duty to humanitarian ideals at its centre. Kipling bolts together scraps of history, ancient mythology, Celtic magic and Tudor royalty, and in Donald Mackensie's words, 'sets flickering patterns of meaning [and] cross-connections' that are 'not generated by historical sequence'.[14] In his autobiography, Kipling explains the writing process in which he:

> Worked the materials in three or four overlaid tints and textures, which might or might not reveal themselves according to the shifting light of sex, youth, and experience. It was like working lacquer and mother o' pearl, a natural combination into the same scheme as niello and grisaille, and trying not to let the joins show. So I loaded the book up with allegories and illusions and verified references until my old Chief would have been pleased. (*SOM*, p. 111)

In recharacterising his fragmented sense of Anglo-Indian selfhood by reinterpreting it in a Sussex setting, Kipling creates not only a sense of 'belonging' for his tribe of fictional orphans, but also validates the dedicated service of his army of imperial administrators, foot soldiers, subalterns and engineers. By imaginatively excavating Britain's ancient civilisations, buried deep in the geological strata of the Sussex soil, he unearths what Gilmour calls the 'connecting layers of a continuous past', where the exile's fragmented identity and his/her sense of not belonging anywhere could be finally connected and brought 'home' by becoming part of the intertwining histories of England's peoples.[15]

Kipling's 'new' England is a babbling, protean world that is reanimated and given authority by the quintessential time-traveller, myth-modifier and shape-shifter Puck, who stands with one shoeless foot in childhood and the other in adulthood – his magical self 'cleaved middlin' close to people', says Kipling's Everyman Hobden (*PPH*, p. 152). Carrington argues that Kipling is humbled by the 'historical figure of Hobden the Hedger, who is relevant to the life of the [valley] in all its phases'.[16] But I would tend to view Hobden as Martin Seymour-Smith views him: the hedger, he argues, is 'seen through falsely aristocratic and patronising eyes'.[17] As a Kiplingesque hero, however, he remains a man of the soil who spends his days and years tirelessly working the valley and thus, Kipling implies (as with his colonial soldier administrators), his wizened hedger is able to discern more of the 'real England' than the aristocratic landowner whose fields he tends. This, in turn, enables him to perceive cultural traditions at first hand.

Puck of Pook's Hill opens with the children Dan and Una practising a pared-down version of *A Midsummer Night's Dream*. It has been shaped and précised by their father, who rarely appears again in the stories despite being the implied instigator of events thereafter. Like one of the thematic strands woven through *A Midsummer Night's Dream*, *Puck of Pook's Hill* questions the configuration of identity. In a forest space beyond the reach of Athenian law, the lovers of *A Midsummer Night's Dream* relinquish their individual identities (through magical means) to recover the wholeness being one half of a couple affords. Similarly, Dan and Una's conscious awareness of their island's history, as well as their imaginative conceptualisations of who (and where) they are, is modified within a pastoral space where the 'house-rules' no longer apply. The difficulties of 'aloneness' that are encountered by Stalky and his compatriots as well as by Kim, Mowgli and Punch are erased in the children's Sussex environment. They are not in any sense alone or 'orphaned', but umbilically linked to the encircling, imaginative embrace of their unseen writer-father. He, like the Headmaster at the 'Coll' in the *Stalky* stories, or Uncle Ned during Kipling's stays at The Grange, is both complicit in and openly approving of their unparented roaming through the countryside.

The magical and the quotidian are given a shared 'reality' in this collection through the character of Hobden. He calmly accepts the appearance of folkloric Puck within the borders of the land he works hard to maintain and, through a genealogy that stretches back through the centuries, he forms a present-day link to his valley's long-standing traditions. In Kipling topography, Hobden is the common man (similar in status to the Mechanicals in *A Midsummer Night's Dream*) who dispenses gobbets of moral fortitude in the guise of pithy, agrarian wisdom.[18] As in the Shakespearean play, a sense of 'belonging' within a community is the foundation of identity. Puck, as Oberon's mischievous servant and as Dan and Una's magical guide, is the instigator of both the losing and finding of identities, as well as the traveller who moves freely between the human and magical worlds.

Similarly, Puck shows Una and Dan that the friendships that develop among individuals, whose common purpose is to serve the greater good, are directly responsible for the subtle shifts in a sense of national identity. For example, the pairing of the Norman Sir Richard Dalyngridge and the Saxon Hugh in 'Young Men at the Manor', 'The Knights of Joyous Venture' and 'Old Men at Pevensey' and the friendship based upon mutual respect between the Roman Legionary Parnesius and the Pict warrior Allo in 'On the Great Wall' have consequences that change the way that characters perceive their allegiance to a particular ethnic group. Victor Kiernan argues that within Shakespeare's play, identity is not so much lost but consumed in a hazy integrated state where individual selfhood is almost impossible to separate out. 'In the strange and magical world of the forest', he argues, 'characters form relationships as a coping mechanism against an unsettling environment' without the steadying security of a regulated city-space.[19] Kipling's empire builders and administrators who find themselves struggling to survive in a forbidding and often frightening colonial space in his Indian tales are, in *Puck of Pook's Hill*, shown to form sustaining friendships with native islanders; and in the case of Sir Richard, to develop a lasting affiliative identification to one of England's Saxons in the process. A sort of allegory of the British Empire in reverse, Kipling's utopian England is a place where the coloniser's psychic map is redrawn to incorporate an affiliative identification with its subjugated peoples. England is presented as a life-affirming space where supernatural elements coexist with the quotidian. This feminised space has previously been attributed to Kiping's ideal of India, which consists of the 'soft air' and 'good clean dust' (*Kim*, p. 332) that we find almost solely in *Kim*.

Andrew Rutherford, amongst others, makes the pertinent point that *Puck of Pook's Hill* was written with the Boer War still fresh in Kipling's artistic imagination, and the heavily allegorical 'Roman Empire (prototype and symbolic equivalent of the British) is in decline'.[20] Parnesius's (ultimately nullifying) defence of the Wall enables Kipling to explore his well-worn aphorism of the self-redemptive value of hard work completing the job at hand. Benita Parry also argues that '[e]mbedded in his Indian fiction are [Kipling's] ideas and feelings which are neither casual interpositions nor contingent representations of a moral vision merely symbolized by Empire, but are an essential part of colonialism conceived as the triumphant expression of the white world's destiny'.[21] Parry's comments are relevant to my analysis of *Puck of Pook's Hill* in that Kipling's difficult 'ideas and feelings' toward his birth-place find a harmonious way to be integrated into his notion of a retranslated English national identity.

The children make their way to an enchanted fairy-ring to rehearse their version of the play after dinner, 'when the shadows were growing' (*PPH*, p. 7). The early evening brings a textual anticipation of the 'inbetween' time of twilight. Unlike the frightening night-time realm of 'The City of Dreadful Night', with its dead-in-life population moving through a bastardised moonlit scene, the mutability in the children's world constitutes a solicitous space from which all frightening elements, including corporeal decay, have been banished (the historical figures that are brought here have no notion that they have been 'dead' for centuries). Passing from one state of being to another is intensified by the very name of the meadow, 'Long Slip', where their 'theatre' stands, for it is the site where the magical world 'slips' into the children's reality. In Kipling's descriptions of the Sussex landscape, a dreamlike maternal space endures more readily than the author's allegorical didacticism. Seymour-Smith argues that had Kipling 'concentrated upon the poetic expression of [the dreamlike quality of his descriptions], instead of linking it all with the children's talk of Latin and tea [. . .] he could have achieved much more than he did: two timeless books'.[22] The meadow is the symbolic equivalent of an Indian feminine space, encircled by a 'little mill-stream, carrying water to a mill two or three fields away' (*PPH*, p. 7). The banks of the mill-stream are 'overgrown with willow, hazel and guelder-rose' (*PPH*, p. 7). There is a Pre-Raphaelite attention to minutiae in Kipling's rendition of the meaning-charged flora. The drooping willows[23] and tangle of hazel and guelder-rose[24] are a vital, if rather soporific, component of this feminised setting.

The interconnection between the mill-stream banks and vegetation has occurred over a passage of time and the uninterrupted union of plant life to stream is part of the continuum of nature's seasonal cycles. Kipling's vivid descriptions create a meadow that is not only vivified, but also characterised by a proliferation of sounds. Like instrumental components in a symphony, the wildlife is integral to an evocation of this edenic space, '[t]hree Cows [that] had been milked [. . .] were grazing steadily with a tearing noise that one could hear all down the meadow; and the noise of the mill at work sounded like bare feet running on hard ground. A cuckoo sat on a gatepost singing his broken June tune, "cuckoo-cuk"' (*PPH*, p. 7). This delicate description, which relies for its effect on rhythmic pulsations created by syntax, recalls Kipling's rendition of the *parao* in *Kim*. The kaleidoscopic nature of the *parao* represents Kim's ubiquitous 'Indian' self, where everything is in synthesis and he is in complete harmony with his natural surroundings. The *parao*, however, is a stopping-off point, a sort of narrative oxbow lake, outside not only of Kim's obligations as a British spy and the demarcated borders of life that the Grand Trunk Road represents, but also of the narrative's trajectory. But in the topography of Kipling's Sussex, the symphonic quality of the landscape is present wherever one's eye roams or ear strains. Thus the maternal realm, previously associated with the Indian landscape, is rediscovered in this 'Other Eden' of the Sussex countryside.

Just as the banks of the mill-stream are obscured by overhanging foliage, so there is no neat dividing line between the children's encounters with the magical world and their ordered world of home. Both operate within the confines of the valley and both migrate into each other. In 'Gloriana' (*Rewards and Fairies*) the children have seen the pair of green shoes that once belonged to Queen Elizabeth in a glass case at Brickwall House. When Puck brings Elizabeth through time to meet the children she explains that these very shoes, which they stare at through the dusty glass case of a museum, burst when she made the decision to send her two courtiers to their doom to halt a serious threat from Spain. Like the artefacts in the 'Wonder House' in *Kim*, the shoes are connected to the pulsing corporeality of a woman's life. The blood that flows through her body finds its symbolic counterpart in the suggestion of the courtiers' blood having turned her green shoes red: she 'stamped her red foot' (*RF*, p. 215), we are told. The children learn the emotional cost of imperial leadership, in this case individual sacrifice for the good of the community. It is a lesson that Kipling's imperial heroes learn on the hoof, as it were, during their time in the colonies. It is also an implied lesson in 'Baa Baa, Black Sheep', and one that Punch never quite comes to understand during his time at Downe Lodge. He remains scarred by the actions of parents who sacrificed their children's happiness to bestow upon them a sense of English nationhood. In 'Gloriana', Dan not only understands Queen Elizabeth's sense of responsibility and culpability, but also is able to give her benediction by expressing his awareness of her dilemma without reproach: 'I don't see what else she could have done,' he states. He is also aware of the loyalty of the courtiers who sacrificed their lives for their queen: 'I don't see what else they could have done' (*RF*, 217). In this respect, Dan is able to give voice and licence to Kipling's notion of service, duty and the hardships that his colonial adults and children endure without leaving his secluded 'Willow Shaw Kingdom'.

The nature of the children's Edwardian utopia, whilst it inverts the configurations of reality and imagination, conversely imbues the dead past with a contemporary realism. The dreamlike quality of the children's summer afternoons in the meadow is sharply contrasted with the melancholy 'realism' of the stone-age, Roman, medieval and Elizabethan tales that detail violent, bloody struggles of conquering nations, empire-building and warring factions. Like elements of the Brushwood Boy's dreamscape that can be pushed over and walked through, the hazy 'real' world of grown-ups, houses, responsibilities and rules is pushed to the margins of Kipling's other 'reality' of vanished Empires and plague stricken-communities where courageous deeds, unifying friendships and acts of self-sacrifice are all played out. And perhaps clearest of all, Kipling's ideal of dedication to duty resounds through the two collections, as exemplified in the image of the slave-ring in 'Cold Iron'. Puck takes the orphaned boy of the story to live among the fairies. To wear such a ring is to accept that he must:

> Go among folk in housen hence-forward, doing what they want done, or what he knows they need, all Old England over. Never will he be his own master, nor yet ever any man's. He will get half he gives, and give twice what he gets, till his life's last breath; and if he lays aside his load before he draws that last breath, all his work will go for naught. (*RF*, p. 198)

But Kipling reiterates that the weight of duty can be shouldered if loving foster parents and caring teachers have overseen one's childhood experience. Puck says that Lady Esclairmonde and Sir Huon 'were comforted to think that they had given the Boy a good store of learning to act and influence on folk in housen' (*RF*, p. 199).

In *Puck of Pook's Hill*, the natural landscape together with its restorative capacity is an important element of Kipling's textural weaving of literature, myth, landscape and history into the complex tapestry of individual subjectivity. The children will learn that the characters Puck brings forth have walked through their lands, seen the construction of their landmarks, fought battles in their hills; thus the natural world becomes an eternal bridge between past and present, between memory and experience. The 'thick, sleepy stillness of meadow-sweet and dry grass' (*PPH*, p. 63) echoes not only the endless continuum of time, but also the fecund feminine hills that have not been woken 'for a thousand years' (*PPH*, p. 9) and subsequently give birth to a host of England's long-dead sons and daughters. Earlier in Kipling's fiction, from *Life's Handicap* to *Stalky & Co.* and to a lesser extent *Kim*, the maternal space has remained 'excluded', out of (paternal) bounds, as it were, but in these collections a feminised landscape provides the stage for Kipling's exploration of England's ancestral past, furthering the borderline 'status' of the paternal realm and hence the paternal authority. In Kristevan topography the semiotic, with its notion of non-linear time, is brought from the margins of the phallogocentric order and displaces its autocratic totalitarianism with its gentle, life-affirming natural surroundings – presided over by the equally gentle and mischievous but omniscient Puck, who can be seen as adjunct to characters like the savvy 'friend of all the world', Kim.

The mill-stream, which meanders through and around the fields, connecting the mundane with the mythic, is an important image in the *Puck* stories. As with the den that Stalky and his companions fashion close to the sea, or the lama's spiritual River of Arrow, the relationship between time, memory and subjectivity is communicated through the metaphor of water. However, whilst Stalky remains a masculine coloniser of his feminised hideaway, reinforced by the separation of the sea from his den on the cliffs, in this story the water is not only an integral part of the setting – the stream's course traces a path and is connected to the adult world by providing essential power to run the mill. The mill is the utilitarian endpoint of the stream that passes through the meadow, and in this respect the stream is symbolic of the children's journey from childhood to the functional world of adults. The stream is also inextricably linked to memory, as it encircles the spot where the past will irrupt into the present. History, in this collection, is connected to memory and the fluidity of 'becoming'. Ripples of moments across time are reinforced by the narrator's comment that 'a grown-up who had seen it said that Shakespeare himself could not have imagined a more suitable setting for his play' (*PPH*, p. 7). Water is thus not only the link between the adult and child worlds, the magical and quotidian, but is also a metaphor for the process of becoming, for the flow between an exterior temporality and an interior desire for the 'timeless' maternal realm. In *Limonade*, Cixous writes: 'the secret of water was forgotten, but when one wishes for it with all of one's being, one loves it anew as it was loved in the beginning'.[25] In this respect, the water that trickles through the stories invokes the Cixousian notion of an awareness of alterity and of a profound connection with the Other, and is intimately linked to memory.

Water is the image that opens 'The Knights of Joyous Venture'. The children are sailing their little boat over the pond until 'they reached the overgrown banks beyond the garden', where 'they pulled themselves up stream by the low branches' (*PPH*, p. 45). Lying 'beneath a roof of close green, watching the water trickle over the flood-gates down the mossy brick chute from the mill-stream to the brook' (*PPH*, p. 45), the children's resting place marks the point of entry into Sir Richard's memories. He sits 'in the comfortable crotch of an old ash-root on the bank' (*PPH*, p. 46) to recount his tale. Ash leaves, along with oak and thorn, are used to make the children forget their encounters. Kipling's ironical voice breaks through the narrative to imply that Sir Richard's memories are stored in the substratum of the children's consciousness. In a Kristevan sense, entry into the symbolic order demands a 'forgetting' of the semiotic realm; it is impossible to articulate what is pre-verbal. Nevertheless, traces or echoes of the semiotic remain and impact upon the regulated order of the paternal law. The feminised geographic space of the meadow and its link to the paternal order attests to the porosity of subjectivity in *Puck of Pook's Hill*, which earlier in Kipling's fiction was marked by borders of demarcation. The wild and desirable maternal realm in *The Jungle Book* was put in its socio-symbolic place in *Stalky & Co.*, loathed and feared in *Life's Handicap*, subject to a troubling ambivalence in *Kim* and finally brought under phallogocentric jurisdiction in *The Day's Work*. In this collection, the meadows and downs, alive with the sounds of wildlife and the blur of summer colours, are vital elements that psychically link the children's interior and exterior sense of temporality. The maternal realm, as it figuratively bubbles and streams and winds its way through the children's edenic playground, is no longer in exile from the paternal order but instead enables the 'time' of the child to be an important part of Dan and Una's perception of 'who' and 'what' they are; perceptions that continually troubled Kim during the course of his journey.

In 'Cold Iron', the children are wearing boots for the first summer of their childhood. Wearing boots is a sign of growing up, and the children 'hated them so'. Taking them off to feel, like Kim, their toes digging into the earth and paddling 'joyfully over the dripping turf' takes them symbolically back in time 'where the shadows lay the *wrong* way, like evening in the East' (*PPH*, p. 185, my emphasis). Their childhood is characterised by an awakening consciousness that leads to a notion of where one's subjectivity can be located in the process of creating identity. As they are introduced to a growing number of people from the past, Dan and Una gradually become aware that their own 'histories' are given meaning by an immersion in the collective memories of Britannia's long-dead peoples. But this is done subliminally, as Puck ensures the children have no recollection of events by touching their eyes (and thus controlling their gaze) with leaves of oak, ash and thorn. At the end of 'Cold Iron' the children agree to wear their boots, and can even see the advantages in growing older as they are able to (playfully) challenge the magical authority of the mischievous sprite. He cannot bear the 'cold iron' of the nails in their boot soles, so they try to trick him into not coming close enough to throw the 'forgetting' leaves in their eyes. The story ends with Dan and Una's joyful, unrestrained laughter ringing clear through the meadows as they stand with one booted and one bare foot apiece. It is a poignant image of unconditionally loved children coming to the end of a wholly undamaged childhood.

The desolate Punch, imprisoned in his Rocklington nursery, which is a basement room that is 'half underground', learns in his solitude that 'all Fairyland' could 'be won by the mere opening of a book' (*WWW*, p. 272). But both Dan and Una, with the aid of their writer-father, bring fairyland tumbling into their world. Reciting their play three times in succession on Midsummer's Eve in a fairy ring near Pook's Hill, the children bring Puck, the Robin Goodfellow of art and mythology, from his hideaway in the hills. Literature, in this instance, is not confined to the page, to the written word. With the help of Puck, stories break through the borders of syntax to become living, dynamic entities. The power of the creative force of literature encourages the children to expand the limits of their perception of both time and memory and subvert the paternal word that dominates subjectivity and thus identity. In this sense the non-scribal nature of the maternal realm displaces the notion of subjectivity being circumscribed by the phallogocentric order. For example, the People of the Hills break through the fictionalised limits of oral and written folk-tales to become tangible 'living' ancestors. The '[g]iants, trolls, kelpies, brownies, goblins, imps; wood, tree, mound and water-spirits; heath-people, hill-watchers, treasure-guards, good people, little people, pishogues, leprechauns, night-riders, pixies, gnomes, and the rest' (*PPH*, pp. 10–11) are commensurate with figures from the human world, and pay testament to the diversity of ethnicity that Kipling believes makes up the rich cultural tapestry of ancient Britain.

In *Kim*, there are aspects of the lama's cultural heritage that have been confined to a dusty, static museum and restrained by the white man's ethnological evaluation. The archaeological fragments which planted the germ of the collections in Kipling's fertile imagination are taken from the soil and resuscitated in his fiction. In this sense, cold and broken remnants of the past are scrutinised, catalogued and given meaning; they are remnants that are made flesh, so to speak. Dan and Una go beyond the perimeter of the world of their (writer) father to reinstate a maternal realm imaged in the splitting of the hills: 'You've done something', says Puck to the children, 'that Kings and Knights and Scholars in the old days would have given their crowns and spurs and books to find out. If Merlin himself had helped you, you couldn't have managed better! You've broken the Hills – you've broken the Hills!' (*PPH*, p. 9). The opening up of the hills, in addition to being a distinctly vaginal image, represents an unfolding of perception that questions the way in which history is written by the aggressor who regards its colonised population as its mirror image, pouring all its 'lack' into its Other shadowy, looking-glass twin. The 'small, brown' shoeless Puck, wearing a 'dark blue cap, like a big columbine flower' (*PPH*, p. 8), is the native Englander and is associated with a space before colonisation, a time of magic that is in itself tied to England's soil and the maternal realm. He is the 'oldest Old Thing in England' (*PPH*, p. 9) – which evokes the frightening 'Sick Thing' in the brushwood boy's dreamscape, although here the 'Thing' is loving rather than menacing. Stuart Hall argues that cultural identity concerns 'becoming' as well as 'being'. In other words, identity cannot be found simply by turning back time to a pre-colonial era, to a past 'which is waiting to be found, and which when found will secure our sense of ourselves into eternity'.[26] Puck's presence, together with the dead historical figures which Kipling reanimates in a contemporary Sussex landscape, show the Other as a positive force that is in the process of 'becoming' rather than having 'been'. Their personal stories are not appropriated by the dispassionate texts of scholars, but are entirely their own, brought to life with their own 'voiced breath'. In this respect Puck teaches Dan and Una that their sense of identity is dependent upon building bridges between the polyvalent British past and their Edwardian present.

Dan and Una have learned their Edwardian lessons well. Una can recite lines from the vigorously heroic 'Horatius', but has no notion of the daily drudgery of the soldier's life. Her view of the valiant Roman defending the bridge across the Tiber is imbued with a poetic vigour that belies the realities of a foot soldier of the ancient Roman Empire like the one she will subsequently meet. Puck succinctly makes this point to the children when he scorns their use of the word 'fairies' to describe the People of the Hills, a description that infantilises them whilst simultaneously diminishing their power:

> Besides, what you call *them* are made-up things the People of the Hills have never heard of – little buzzflies with butterfly and gauze petticoats, and shiny stars in their hair, and a wand like a school-teacher's cane for punishing bad boys and rewarding good ones. (*PPH*, p. 13)

Similarly, Dan's knowledge of Latin is reduced to dusty 'impots', a 'beastly Latin' (*PPH*, p. 95) that keeps him from joining his sister in the fields. Latin as a living, breathing language that is present in the children's contemporary English, like the lama's cultural identity, is ironically counterpointed by a notion of history belonging to an unreachable past. The 'foreignness' of the past and the 'alien' Others who recount their tales are perceived as an important part of the children's process of 'becoming'. Their strangeness, their difference is to be celebrated as an inseparable part of the present rather than consigned to bookshelves and museum exhibits to be picked over by scholars and weary schoolchildren. In *Something of Myself*, Kipling remarks,

> My main interest [at USC] as I grew older was C – [W. C. Crofts], my English and Classics Master [. . .] Under him I came to feel that words could be used as weapons, for he did me the honour to talk at me plentifully; and our year-in year-out form-room bickerings gave us both something to play with. (*SOM*, p. 21)

Parallels can be seen in 'The Propagation of Knowledge', a late *Stalky* story, where Beetle learns that past literatures can be bent into any critical shape and their meanings refracted in the lens of contemporary analyses. Beetle's awareness of the malleability of words and ideas recalls Punch's shock of realisation that in England, Christian theology holds the moral high ground over Indian mythology. Aunty Rosa is the evangelical keeper of a western cultural tradition that 'blacks' out Punch's Anglo-Indian interiority. Her colonisation of Punch's Anglo-Indian identity establishes a power that takes its assumed authority from a dominant 'English' history. Homi Bhabha argues that the 'discourse of post-Enlightenment English colonialism often speaks in a tongue that is forked, not false. If colonialism takes power in the name of history, it repeatedly exercises its authority through the figures of farce.'[27] Punch's 'difference', his Anglo-Indian identity, is repeatedly ridiculed and viewed as 'black' against Aunty Rosa's 'Englishness' – but as the *Puck* stories suggest, Aunty Rosa's sense of Englishness is derived from a Christian discourse which has scavenged scraps from earlier mythologies to claim for its own, that has merely superseded earlier pagan beliefs, and takes no account of her island's migrant history. Punch is thus culturally imaged as the degenerate, amoral twin of her Christian son, Harry.

In the *Puck* stories Kipling inverts the power structure of England as an outwardly colonising nation, presenting it as a nation articulated by its settler communities. Such a position ensures that the voice of authority comes not from a contemporary priest, scholar, industrialist or military commander, but from the indigenous Puck, who stands outside of the white man's 'law'. In this order, the disavowed Anglo-Indian voice of Punch (and indeed Kipling himself) can be reinstated and his bicultural experience is commensurate with the competing discourses of England's pluralist past. With the précised words of Shakespeare, which have, it seems, a magical potency, children have inadvertently awoken the sleeping hills, instilled a sense of the magical to the quotidian and brought the perished past into the living present. Words are, in this instant, not to be used as weapons by those in authority, but rather they break through pages of history books to reveal a kaleidoscopic ethnicity. Puck will introduce the children, through the voices of the past, to the cultural diversity that lies beneath the soil under their feet, and teach them that they are merely a transitory part of the continuum of England's green spaces.

Puck emphasises the link between time, land and history by cutting a clod of turf from the middle of the fairy ring and giving it to the children. He calls this ritualistic act 'taking seizin' (*PPH*, p. 12), an old commercial custom that involved giving a piece of soil to a new buyer, the implication being that until one had clasped the earth in one's hands the land was not truly owned. Puck emphatically states that 'you weren't lawfully seized of your land – it didn't really belong to you – till the other fellow had actually given you a piece of it' (*PPH*, p. 12). This archaic 'legal' custom takes on a deeply symbolic meaning for, as Helen Pike Bauer rightly notes, the children spend the greater part of the stories taking possession of their own history,[28] its myths and its actualities, the supernatural and the natural, the desires and the deeds of its peoples, as a preparation to shape its future. Just as land is commercially passed from one person to the next, so Dan and Una come to understand that they are symbolic custodians of their island's ancient heritage, a heritage that is bound to the land and not the ideology of its governing body. Kipling also implies that an unexpected benefit of taking hold of the soil and tangibly feeling the responsibility of guardianship is that the earth is imbued with healing properties. As Kipling's poem 'The Charm' (used in the epigraph to this chapter) shows, the soil can calm the 'fevered breath' and 'festered soul' of his battle-worn foot soldier, overworked administrator and under-appreciated engineer.

The gods in the 'The Bridge Builders' fleetingly discuss this notion but Findlayson, ever the empire builder, misses the point entirely, which is why his work is nothing more significant than 'the shifting of a little dirt' (*DW*, p. 52). Findlayson's sense of himself is always tied to his place in the imperial landscape and not to the actual land on which he toils. His bridge, which is built to push forward the economic and military interests of the British Empire, 'chains' the river and is emblematic of the colonisers' misguided belief that their Empire will endure the passage of time. Findlayson represents Kipling's recognition of the fragmented nature of his empire builders, torn between the warring considerations of dedication to service and the self-defeating acceptance of the ultimate transience of their hard-won deeds. Findlayson, like Hummil, Morrowbie Jukes, Colonel Creighton, Scott and countless other imperial administrators who have little regard for India's immense time frame, and little more for the soil they claim in the name of Empire, sees his intellectual and architectural efforts ultimately swallowed by the monumental passage of time. This is the elliptical moral of Parnesius's story in the *Puck* stories. The centurion's father warns his son of the precarious nature of empires in the monumental span of time: 'It began before your time or mine [. . .] He went back to the time of Diocletian; and to listen to him you would have thought Eternal Rome itself was on the edge of destruction, just because a few people had become a little large-minded' (*PPH*, pp. 89–90). Yet Kipling's irony makes a Roman father's comments all the more poignant, for we *know* that the 'Eternal' Roman Empire will indeed fall, as Kipling knew the British Empire would fall. The remnants of once-monumental empires will be reclaimed by the soil and their ragged monuments recycled by future empire builders.

The first tale in the collection, 'Weland's Sword', foreshadows the transitory nature of the coloniser's enforced cultural practices as well as the impermanence of empires. The story concerns the fortunes of the blacksmith Wayland-Smith, formerly the disempowered Norse god Weland and the wayward Saxon novice monk, Hugh. As a conquering force the Norsemen brought their gods, the 'Old Things' (*PPH*, p. 14). The mighty gods required terrifying blood sacrifices in veneration of their omnipotence. Over the course of time, the people grew increasingly resentful at having to sacrifice members of their community along with their precious livestock. Gradually they abandoned the gods, and their altars fell into disrepair. As Kipling emphatically states in 'The Bridge Builders', the power of the gods is dependent upon the strength of its adherents' belief: 'The end shall be as it was in the beginning', states Krishna in the tale, '[t]he flame shall die upon the altars and the prayer upon the tongue till ye become little Gods again' (*DW*, p. 58). In 'Weland's Sword' we see Kipling describing the fulfillment of Krishna's prophecy. Norse paganism splinters as Christianity, a religion that required no sacrificial bloodletting, begins to take hold. With their power diminished, the gods scattered; some were found living half-lives as ghosts to scare lonely travellers, many left England's shores, but one Weland, swordsmith to the gods, remains in Sussex, eking out a living as a lowly blacksmith.

Unable to return to Valhalla until he is thanked for his work, he spends his days and years in drudgery, shoeing horses for ungrateful farmers whose place in the dominant Christian hierarchy empowers them to both abuse and underpay the 'heathen' blacksmith. The novice Hugh, who Kipling portrays more for his vitality of life than his scholarly training, appears, 'his gown swishing through the shiny dew and his fishing-rod across his shoulders spear-wise' (*PPH*, p. 19), and finally releases Weland from the bonds of his earthbound toil. A typical

Kiplingesque hero, Hugh recognises the value of unappreciated work that cuts across religious and race boundaries: '"Heathen or no heathen" said the novice, "you took his help and where you get help you must give thanks"' (*PPH*, p. 18). To show his appreciation, Weland fashions a sword for the young Saxon. The sword is a magical object over which he whispers runic chants and on which he carves 'Runes of Prophesy' (*PPH*, pp. 19–20). The charm that he breathes over and etches into the sword enables it to 'sing' of the joys and sufferings of its wielder, as well as sound a warning of an imminent attack. Magically associated with the 'Old Things', the sword also has a profound connection to the land, as the 'evening dew' cooled the blade after it was forged. The sword, Weland says, is a 'gift that shall do him [Hugh] good the wide world over and Old England after him' (*PPH*, p. 19). The sword also protects future defenders of 'Old England', both in far-flung corners of the globe and from subsequent colonising attacks at home. 'It is not given for goods or gear' say the Runes on the blade in the poem that ends the Norman triptych, 'But for the Thing' (*PPH*, p. 80). The runic rituals, which are associated with a fluid musicality as well as water, empower the sword to 'sing' and allude to a time before Christian 'law' and all of these spiritual elements are expressions of the unnameable (maternal) *Thing*, which translates into Kipling's warrior goddess, Britannia.

Weland places the sword in Hugh's sleeping hand, and Puck tells the children that 'the young fellow gripped it in his sleep' (*PPH*, p. 20). Hugh, even in his unconscious state, recognises the value of action over learning, Kipling seems to whisper into the narrative. A defiant Weland strides 'as far as he dared' (*PPH*, p. 20) into the monastery and flings his blacksmith's tools upon the altar. Hugh tells the Abbot about his encounter with Wayland-Smith, to which the Abbot replies, 'Son Hugh, it needed no sign from a heathen God to show me that you will never be a monk. Take your sword, and keep your sword, and go with your sword, and be as gentle as you are strong and courteous' (PPH, p. 20). The sword is ostensibly to be used in battle against a Norman invasion. However, Hugh balks at the slaughter of a Norman knight, and instead uses it as the starting point of a friendship that develops between himself and the knight whose life he spares, Sir Richard Dalyngridge. In the following three tales, 'Young Men at the Manor', 'The Knights of Joyous Venture' and 'Old Men at Pevensey', the sword becomes an emblem of both camaraderie and reparation.

During the course of the next three tales we see the strong bond of friendship forming across Norman and Saxon cultural divides. Like Kipling's last major work on India, *Kim*, which relies on its eponymous boy hero being able to traverse cultural barriers with ease, the relationship that Sir Richard and Hugh form is an implied cornerstone of their subsequent 'shared' national identity. However, in Kim's case his conflicting 'black'/white identity raises important questions as to whether a sense of plurality can be sustained, to which an adequate answer is not found during the course of the novel. But in the Knights' tales Kipling imagines a fantasy of wholeness that is dependent on a conglomerate Norman/Saxon blending, out of which emerges a richer and more solicitous 'new' English identity. Kipling's imaginative journey with Kim ends before the boy has reached adulthood proper, but the Norman triptych demonstrates a more constructive path through life, as the Knights' relationship is not subject to a political affiliation. Indeed, the very nature of their cross-cultural friendship undermines any claim to an affiliate Norman or Saxon identity. This blending of affiliative identifications into harmonious familial relationship remains solely in the subjunctive tense in *Kim*.

Kipling takes us through the entire lifespan of his two heroes, from the vigours of youth and battles in England, through to treasure-hunting adventures overseas in Africa – adventures which leave Hugh crippled – then on to a middle age, where Norman and Saxon successfully guard England against a second Norman invasion. As Pike Bauer has pointed out, what starts as a Norman invasion of Saxon England (the conqueror and the conquered)[29] gives way to Kipling's actual purpose of creating a shared national identity, of putting down roots in a foreign country and participating in the subsequent shaping of its pastoral idealisation of English life. The Norman knight De Aquila declares, 'I am not Norman, Sir Richard, nor Saxon, Sir Hugh, English am I', exclaiming, 'In fifty years there will be neither Norman or Saxon, but all English' (*PPH*, pp. 71, 68). Kipling's notion of 'Englishness' is thus not tied to the conquering group that 'outlaws' its defeated native population and absorbs their cultural genealogy into its own, but to cohabitation with the 'native' population – of being able to recognise the Other in oneself. 'By recognising *our* uncanny strangeness', Kristeva argues, 'we shall neither suffer from it nor enjoy it from the outside.'[30] Kipling's vision of a unifying national identity, in this sense, breaks down barriers of 'foreignness' that can be seen to embody Kristeva's notion that the 'foreigner is within me, hence we are all foreigners. If I am a foreigner, there are no foreigners.'[31] In short, Kipling's England represents a commingled, multi-levelled continuous community that is rooted in England's soil and not its warring ideologies.

In *The Day's Work* Kipling glorifies the ideal of the British Empire because it brought meaning to his world-weary colonials, desperate for release from their nullifying imperial tasks carried out in the heat-scorched atmosphere of the Punjab. His imperial heroes speak little of religion to shore up their arduous lives as their portraits come from a writer who, as Bonamy Dobrée argues, 'has small opinion of Christianity because it has not eliminated the fear of the end'[32] and holds no traditional Hindu, Muslim or Christian gods dear for, as 'The Bridge Builders' shows, they are proven to be transitory. Kipling's heroes in *The Day's Work* believe in the ideology of the British Raj simply because their deeds could be blessed and their lives given meaning on the altar of his goddess of Empire. For his imperial administrators, engineers and soldiers, Empire represents what Shamsul Islam sees as 'the forces of law, order and discipline which engaged in a constant struggle against the negative forces of chaos, confusion and disorder that so terrifyingly characterised the modern age'.[33] Service, duty and devotion to Britannia's cause come through the often unrecognised toil of building a sturdy edifice of Empire on the shifting political terrain of India.

However, in the *Puck* stories the efforts of England's metaphorical bridge-builders are valorised, precisely because they divert meaninglessness. In 'Young Men at the Manor', Sir Richard is given Hugh's estate by Richard's Lord De Aquila as part of the spoils of a conquering faction, with the proviso that if he can hold it, it is his. Sir Richard manages to do so only by securing the friendship of Hugh. Together they manage to evolve an alliance between Saxon and Normans that ensures a successful defence against possible threats from 'robbers and nightwalkers' (*PPH*, p. 33). Like Scott and William, Findlayson and George Cottar, they work tirelessly in safeguarding their valley with an unwavering perseverance to seeing their governing duties through to completion. The work that is put into the land, keeping 'the roof on the hall, the thatch on the barn and the plough on the furrow' (*PPH*, p. 31), is rewarded in the reaping of a metaphorical seed of splendidly healthy male companionship, emphasised by De Aquila's allegorical exclamation, 'I have never seen such bright straw,' (a straw that has been cultivated by hybridised Norman/Saxon Englishmen). 'Send me three bags of the same seed yearly' (*PPH*, p. 35) he proclaims. For Kipling's conquering imperials, such as Morrowbie Jukes and the coolly self-certain Colonel Creighton, the veneer of Empire and Anglo-Indian relations stood as both infallible and invincible. However, Sir Richard and Hugh's combined efforts lay bare Kipling's criticism of Empire as a complex network of government departments that buries the deeds of its workers under a mountain of bureaucratic paperwork. For every dedicated Findlayson and Cottar in Kipling's Indian fiction, there is a hard-working Otis Yeere whose ambitions and morale are crushed:

> Fortune had ruled that Otis Yeere should be [. . .] one of the rank and file who are ground upon the wheels of the Administration; losing heart and soul, and mind and strength, in the process. Until steam replaces manual power in the workings of the Empire, there must always be this percentage – must always be the men who are used up, expended, in the mere mechanical routine.[34]

The manual labour over which Sir Richard presides characterises life at the Manor and is seen as an integral part of both overseeing an occupied land and developing a connection to the soil. In this respect, Sir Richard, the Norman invader, together with Hugh, truly forms an apolitical bond with the Saxon peoples through their dedication to hard work for the good of the community. Guarding England's green spaces with his great friend Hugh, he comes to feel a deep connection to the land, acknowledged in his declaration, 'I set out to conquer England three days after I was made a knight. I did not then know that England would conquer me' (*PPH*, p. 28). Kipling's proposition is that the invader can form a bond with the land that he has taken by force. Sir Richard becomes so captivated by the 'soft valley soil' (*PPH*, p. 25) that he is prepared to safeguard England against the threat of a second Norman invasion. Dan and Una thus become aware of their island's long ancestry and their place within it. For centuries, these settlers have, like Dan and Una, fished in the same 'bed of a brook' and moved through its valleys with 'trees closing overhead' making 'long tunnels through which the sun worked in blobs or patches' (*PPH*, p. 25). Others have seen the beauty of the land, the 'bars of sand and gravel, old roots and trunks [that] were covered with moss or painted red by the irony water' (*PPH*, p. 25). Like his rendition of the Himalayas or Stalky's den on the cliffs, Kipling's Sussex landscape is similarly anthropomorphised. His image of water as a corporeal body connects the maternal realm to the time of the child. The pools where the children fish, their 'most secret hunting-grounds' (*PPH*, p. 25) are connected by 'sheets of thin broken water that poured themselves chuckling round the darkness of the next bend' (*PPH*, p. 25). The Pre-Raphaelite minuteness of detail, '[d]own in the tunnels', of this maternal space is painted by an artist who knows the intricacies of his Sussex valley to such an extent that he can almost palpably sense the pulse of the land. Similarly, Sir Richard is given, by dint of his being part of the colonising force, an English estate, but it is only by understanding the nature of the earth on which his men toil that he becomes 'part' of land himself. He finally becomes at 'home' in a foreign land not through subjugating the people whose ancestors have lived there for centuries by force, but by governing with understanding of and compassion for those who work the land to ensure the land's continued fertility and thereby the success of the estate.

In the Roman stories that form the triptych that follows, Puck introduces the children to another member of a conquering army; but this time the Roman Legionary Parnesius is British-born, which could be seen as an analogue to Kipling's own identity as a second-generation expatriate. The theme of becoming psychically bound to England's soil in the previous stories is developed further. During the course of the tales 'A Centurion of the Thirtieth', 'On the Great Wall' and 'The Winged Hats', we see the life span of Parnesius from his childhood and adolescence through to his military career as a centurion. The strong friendship he forms with fellow centurion Pertinax, their defence of Hadrian's Wall from local Pict marauders and foreign Viking invaders, forms the greater part of the tales, which finish with his middle age and retirement. In this respect, the tales parallel the trajectory of George Cottar in 'The Brushwood Boy'. Parnesius's life story has much to do with what Rutherford argues is Kipling's approval of empire-building, 'not for the sake of empire so much as for the qualities which it develops in the empire-builders'.[35] I would further this line of thinking by suggesting that the qualities of duty, service and fidelity to comrades, which Rutherford sees as developing during imperial service, can be traced back to the familial relationships that characterise Parnesius's childhood years.

The young Roman, like Punch and Kim, has never set foot in the land of his father's birth. He is brought up by a Numidian, a 'dear, fat, brown thing with a tongue like a cow-bell' (*PPH*, p. 87), who recalls Punch's *ayah* – who 'sat in the moonlight at the doorway' to his nursery and lulled him to sleep with a [. . .] canticle' – (*WWW*, p. 261) as well as the shadowy native brothel-owner who takes care of a very young Kim. Parnesius's mother is likened to the goddess Demeter and evokes the figure of the 'adored' mother who rescues Punch from his miserable life in Rocklington, making her a type of 'mythic' mother figure. As the mythic is linked with the mother, so Kipling sees a loving family as a universal substratum of psychic stability. Parnesius says that 'all good families are alike' (*PPH*, p. 87) and Una recognises the similarities in her own familial circle (*PPH*, p. 87). Parnesius's childhood mirrors the children's. It is an edenic space of protected exploration, where he is playfully 'hunted' through 'the gorse bushes' by his clever, athletic governess Aglaia (*PPH*, p. 86). Like Kipling himself, Parnesius has a witty mother and a father who loves and understands his children. Rather touchingly, and very much like the kindly but ineffectual 'Uncle Harry', his father is forced to discipline the boy at the behest of his mother. Parnesius, however, suffers no ill effects, and Kipling stresses the loving relationship between the mother and her son. He spends summers visiting 'many friends', riding 'as many ponies as we wished' (*PPH*, p. 87).

At the borders or limits of this mythical playground is the constant threat of wolves, but Parnesius implies that the love of the family and servants provide a sort of magical protection and the children are ring-fenced in this magical world. Parnesius says that this magical world ended when he 'was about sixteen or seventeen' (*PPH*, p. 87). Compare this with Kipling's own experience of childhood in Southsea, where the wolf-like Sarah Holloway was responsible for his upbringing. The escapism he found in recreating magic worlds depended upon building an enclosed imaginative space away from the pressures of such a brutalising existence. In *Something of Myself*, he writes, '[t]hus fenced about, everything inside the fence was quite real, but mixed with the smell of damp cupboards. If the bit of board fell, I had to begin the magic all over again [. . .] The magic, you see, lies in the ring or fence that you take refuge in' (*SOM*, p. 8). In contrast with the terrors of abandonment that the young Kipling suffered, Parnesius's youth is spent in an idyllic pastoral setting. There are echoes of a young Kim, but Kipling manages to 'un-orphan' his little Roman so his childhood space becomes not only a joyful playground, but is populated by a life-affirming troupe of adults who nurture rather than admonish his investigative explorations.

This marks a narrative evolution from Kipling's previous assertions in *Stalky & Co.* that life in a boarding school, away from the protection and unconditional love that characterises family life, is a valuable training ground for colonial life. Kipling emphatically states that the sheltered upbringing of 'the Boy' in 'Thrown Away' is precisely what causes him to come to grief once he is on his own in India. The cynical narrator of this story tells us in a voice that drips with irony:

> To rear a boy under what parents call the 'sheltered life system' is, if the boy must go into the world and fend for himself, not wise. Unless he be one in a thousand he has certainly to pass through many unnecessary troubles; and may, possibly, come to extreme grief simply from ignorance of the proper proportion of things. (*PT*, p. 14)

The 'Boy' does indeed come to 'extreme grief'. Unable to cope with military life in India, the jokes of his fellow soldiers at his expense or the cutting remarks of his colonel, he rides to a dâk-bungalow thirty miles outside the cantonment to commit a grisly suicide. In 'A Centurion of the Thirtieth', Kipling stresses the importance of family life and remaining within the family circle. He sees it as crucial to Parnesius's social and psychological development. The centurion explains to the children in 'On the Great Wall', 'your fate will turn on the first true friend you make', and Puck explains, 'if you try to make yourself a decent chap when you're young, you'll make rather decent friends when you grow up' (*PPH*, p. 102). Rutherford argues that Parnesius's vision of a happy childhood 'give[s] warm reality to the elusive concept of civilisation, and make[s] the defence of the Wall meaningful in human terms'.[36] To further this I would argue that it also imaginatively recreates an alternative existence to the miseries that Kipling's other fictionalised abandoned children suffer. Implicit in Kipling's decision to keep his Roman soldier in the life-affirming closeness of the family circle throughout his formative years is the notion that a cherished childhood strengthens the man. When the adolescent children finally leave home, they are able to find their metiers because of the loving support they received as children. Their governess rather proudly remarks that '[c]hildren [at sixteen] you went away. Men and a woman you return' (*PPH*, p. 88). Such an observation can be poignantly counterpointed against the words that Meeta says to a six-year-old Punch through his tears: '"[c]ome back [. . .] and be a *Burra Sahib*" (a big man)' (*WWW*, p. 262). Meeta's remark is made all the more sorrowful as we are aware of the devastating consequences of Punch's exile from the family home.

Once again the image of water is connected to borders between childhood and adulthood. Whilst taking the waters at the Roman spa-town Bath, Parnesius's siblings decide upon their life paths. His sister gets married, his younger brother studies medicine, his elder brother shuns the army for philosophy and Parnesius is delighted at finding himself able to take on the mantle of 'man of action' by joining the Roman army. The realities of soldiering, however, are not so easy. As Kipling presents the pomposity of London MPs who deem to understand the workings of colonial life better than the soldiers in the field,[37] Parnesius tells his father that the 'Roman-born officers and magistrates looked down on us British-born as though we were barbarians', to which his father replies ' I know they do [. . .] but remember, after all, we are the people of the Old Stock, and our duty is to the Empire' (*PPH*, p. 89). Kipling highlights his ubiquitous 'Law' on which his ideal of Empire is founded. Transgressing the 'Law' for personal or economic gain threatens the stability of imperial government, undermines its right to rule and leads to an inevitable endemic corruption. In *The Jungle Book*, Kipling admonishes the renegade wolves that defy the wolf pack 'Law' by ousting Akela. Similarly, Parnesius's father repeats the author's warning:

> It began before my time or yours [. . .] The great war with the Painted People broke out in the very year the temples of our Gods were destroyed. We beat the Painted People in the very year our temples were rebuilt. Go back further still [. . .] There is no hope for Rome [. . .] She has forsaken her Gods, but if the Gods forgive *us* here, we may save Britain. (*PPH*, pp. 89–90)

Kipling sees the inevitable decline of the Roman Empire, but there is work to be done in one of its outcrops, and therein lies his imperial hero's self-worth. Parnesius is sent to defend Hadrian's Wall against the threat of invasion, but unlike Sir Richard's successful neutralisation of threats to England's borders, his mission is doomed to failure. The tide of invasion from the North cannot be held at bay. However, Kipling lauds Parnesius's resolve to defend the Wall at any cost, and his dogged determination to stay at his post even though the odds of survival are minimal. Once again we are reminded of the Findlaysons and Hummils of the author's fictionalised world of Empire in *The Day's Work*, whose deeds can come to naught, whose spirits can be broken and they can do little but rage against the dying of their imperial lights. Defence of the Wall constitutes a noble act in and of itself, despite being, as Parnesius quickly learns, the career terminus for all the outcasts of the Roman Empire. Most are sent because of criminal misdemeanours or, like the friend he will meet, fighting for justice and fairness in an Empire bereft of Kipling's 'Law'. He stands alone, like so many of the author's colonial heroes, shouldering the heavy burden of imperial duty. The welfare of the wild, 'uncivilised' Picts is as much his responsibility as his military defence of the Wall. In this respect, Parnesius perfectly embodies Kipling's humanised imperial archetype.

Dan and Una prepare to listen to the beginning of the end of the 'eternal' Roman Empire, as they are poignantly coming to the end of their own childhood, in a more funereal part of the wood:

> they climbed up Long Ditch into the lower end of Far Wood. This is sadder and darker than the Volaterrae end because of an old marlpit full of black water, where weepy, hairy moss hangs round the stumps of the willows and alders. But the birds come to perch on the dead branches, and Hobden says that the bitter willow-water is a sort of medicine for sick animals. (*PPH*, p. 113)

The maternal 'far green spaces' that have been crushed by the might of the paternal order can conversely be used as a *parao* that restores the broken spirit of Kipling's lost and lonely men of action in spite of its 'stumps' and 'dead branches'. The *jouissance* of the maternal realm, although moribund and diminished in the image of the blackened 'Far Wood', has a place in the phallogocentric order that the children must comply with. In this sense, the 'bitter waters of despair' that Punch is forced to drink are an antidote to the suffering of loss and are an integral part of his psychic mapping. It is necessary to know the death-like nature of loss if one is to truly know the redemption that reunification brings. Kipling quietly acknowledges this as the sun began to set over his own days:

> In the long run these things [at Southsea], and many more of the like drained me of any capacity for real, personal hate for the rest of my days. So close must any life-fulfilling passion lie to its opposite. 'Who having known the Diamond will concern himself with glass?' (*SOM*, p. 12)

The maternal realm in Kipling's fiction remains a 'lost territory'[38] that idealises the relationship the child has with the mother in the semiotic. Its appearance in the feminised landscapes of India and Sussex points to a continuous crossing of boundaries between the semiotic and the symbolic. This crossing forms the dialectic between the fragmentary and reconstructed identities of his adolescent and adult characters. The many images of the mother figure are vital entities in the formation of identity. In 'The Knife and the Naked Chalk', a mother tells her wearied son, 'whether you live or die, or are made different. I am your Mother [. . .] There is only one Mother for the one son' (*RF*, p. 275). In this one sentence, Kipling acknowledges the ubiquitous nature of the mother figure that underscores his mythology of Empire. In her many guises of nurturing, life-affirming caregiver, abjected, terrifying phallic Other, and desexualised goddess, the mother figure is crucial at all stages of the mapping of identity.

Appended to the all-embracing love of a biological mother is the worship of the mythic mother, Britannia, and the hope that she continues to offer her wretched and despairing sons of Empire long after they have left the warm embrace of their own mothers. Although Kipling's fictional adults can never be reunited with their mothers in an undifferentiated semiotic realm, they can find 'wholeness' in the service of Empire. The empathetic voice of childhood that issues a *cri de cœur* in 'Baa Baa, Black Sheep' and *The Light that Failed* is hushed after the death of his best-beloved daughter Josephine in 1899, and (almost) silenced after the loss of his only son John at the battle of the Loos in 1915; but in between, although marked by separation and loss, Kipling's childhood self echoes across the years and Kipling the author, in answer, composes a survivor's lamentation. His rendition of the semiotic modality and the nurturing mother who resides therein, transposed in the past onto India and its peoples, has found a new translation in the Sussex landscape and the men and women who occupy this rustic Arcadian space.

Until these collections, India has been the site of the maternal realm in Kipling's fiction, but it is always a troubling place and as a pastoral it continually fails. The author thus moves India to Sussex and, in one textual transfiguration, eliminates from his psychic paradise all the ambivalences that cause anxiety. India is displaced onto Sussex in a Freudian sense but this does not take account of the wholly convincing transformation of one problematic edenic space into another unproblematic one. India, in its reformed state, passes from death and fragmentation into a coherent, life-affirming whole, what in Kristevan terms is 'the passage from one sign system to another [. . .] the destruction of the old position and the formation of a new one'.[39] Kristeva acknowledges the Freudian processes of 'displacement' and 'condensation' in poetic texts, but she adds a third, that of 'transposition', which enables the speaker to occupy a position that both accepts and transgresses the word of the father. The law subsequently evolves over time to accommodate these delicate infringements to ameliorate the socio-cultural structure. How like Kipling's Jungle Law this seems – and how like the *Puck* stories, where the maternal realm can finally coexist with a paternal authority.

The *Puck* stories tie together the sorrowful threads of separation, loneliness and loss that are left hanging in Kipling's Indian fiction and express his impossible but ever-hopeful dream of re-entering, through doors that his artistic vision has unbolted, a utopian space of coalescence where the author's excluded Anglo-Indian self can be finally included in this welcoming pluralist psychic pastoral.

Notes

1. Rudyard Kipling, 'A Charm', Introduction to *Rewards and Fairies*, p. 181.
2. Rudyard Kipling, 'Song of the Wise Children', *The Definitive Edition of Rudyard Kipling's Verse*, p. 90.
3. 'The English Flag', in Kipling, *Definitive Verse*, p. 221.
4. Edward Said, *Out of Place: A Memoir*, p. 14.
5. Edward Said, 'On Writing a Memoir', p. 8.
6. Rudyard Kipling, letter to Charles Norton, 30 November – 8 December 1902, in Thomas Pinney (ed.), *The Letters of Rudyard Kipling* III, p. 113.
7. Rudyard Kipling, letter to Edward Bok, July 1905, in Pinney, *Letters* III, p. 189.
8. Ibid., III, p. 189.
9. David Gilmour, *The Long Recessional: The Imperial Life of Rudyard Kipling*, p. 171.
10. Charles Carrington, *Rudyard Kipling*, p. 444.
11. Ibid., p. 432.
12. Alice Fleming, 'Some Childhood memories of Rudyard Kipling by his Sister', p. 171.
13. Rudyard Kipling, '"The Biggest Liar in Asia" (by One Who Knows Him)', in Thomas Pinney (ed.), *Kipling's India: Uncollected Sketches 1884–88*, p. 81.
14. Donald Mackenzie, Introduction to Rudyard Kipling, *Puck of Pook's Hill* and *Rewards and Fairies*, p. xxii.
15. Gilmour, *The Long Recessional*, p. 172.

16. Carrington, *Rudyard Kipling*, p. 444.
17. Martin Seymour-Smith, *Rudyard Kipling*, p. 338.
18. See 'The Land', Kipling's epigraph to 'Friendly Brook' (in *Diversity of Creatures*). Generations of Hobdens are described in just this manner to their various imperial overseers and landowners alike. A sample of the lines that follow outlines the rich seam of rustic sagacity that runs through the poem:

    When Julius Fabricius, Sub-Prefect of the Weald,
    In the days of Diocletian owned our Lower River-field,
    He called to him Hobdenius – a Briton of the Clay,
    Saying: 'What about that River-piece for layin' in to hay?'
    And the aged Hobden answered: 'I remember as a lad

    My father told your father that she wanted dreenin' bad.
    An' the more that you neglect her the less you'll get her clean.
    Have it jest *as* you've a mind to, but, if I was you, I'd dreen'
    (Kipling, *Definitive Verse*, p. 601)

19. Victor Kiernan, *Shakespeare: Poet and Citizen*, p. 212.
20. Andrew Rutherford, 'Officers and Gentlemen', p. 186.
21. Benita Parry, *Delusions and Discoveries: India in the British Imagination, 1880–1930*, p. 221.
22. Seymour-Smith, *Rudyard Kipling*, p. 338.
23. An image associated with loss and abandonment, recalling Scott's 'A wreath of willow to show my forsaken plight' (*The Fair Maid of Perth*). In *Hamlet*, Gertrude announces that Ophelia climbed into a willow tree overhanging the water where she would subsequently drown. In the painting of Ophelia, now hanging in the Tate Britain in London, by Pre-Raphaelite John Everett Millais, a rather spiky willow dominates the upper left corner, but its association with sadness has the added Victorian symbolism of forsaken love.
24. Both hazel and guelder-rose are important in Celtic mythology, the former being associated with creativity and the latter associated with female suffering and menstrual cycles.
25. Quoted in Claudine Fisher, 'Cixous' Concept of "Brushing" as a Gift', in Lee A. Jacobus and Regina Barreca (eds), *Hélène Cixous: Critical Impressions*, p. 114.
26. Stuart Hall, 'Cultural Identity and Diaspora', p. 394.
27. Homi Bhabha, *The Location of Culture*, p. 122.
28. Pike Bauer, *Rudyard Kipling*, p. 64.
29. Ibid., p. 64.
30. Julia Kristeva, *Strangers to Ourselves*, p. 192.
31. Ibid., p. 192.
32. Bonamy Dobrée, *Rudyard Kipling: Realist and Fabulist*, p. 44.
33. Shamsul Islam, *Kipling's 'Law': A Study of his Philosophy of Life*, p. 83.
34. Rudyard Kipling, 'The Education of Otis Yeere', in *Wee Willie Winkie*, p. 19.
35. Rutherford, 'Officers and Gentlemen', p. 185.
36. Ibid., p. 189.

37. See Rudyard Kipling, 'The Enlightenments of Pagett, M.P.'
38. Julia Kristeva, 'Stabat Mater', in *Tales of Love*, p. 234.
39. Julia Kristeva, 'Revolution in Poetic Language', in *The Kristeva Reader*, p. 111.

Bibliography

Primary Bibliography

Eliot, T. S. (ed.), *A Choice of Kipling's Verse* (London: Faber and Faber, 1973).

Gilbert, Elliot L. (ed.), *O Beloved Kids: Rudyard Kipling's Letters to his Children* (London: Weidenfeld and Nicolson, 1983).

Kipling, Rudyard, 'The Enlightenments of Pagett, M.P.' [1890], in *The Sussex Edition of the Complete Works in Prose and Verse of Rudyard Kipling*, vol. 32 (London: Macmillan, 1937–9), p. 49.

Kipling, Rudyard, *Plain Tales from the Hills* [1890], ed. Andrew Rutherford (Oxford: Oxford University Press, 2001).

Kipling, Rudyard, *Life's Handicap* [1891], ed. A. O. J. Cockshut (Oxford: Oxford University Press, 1987).

Kipling, Rudyard, *Life's Handicap* [1891], ed. P. N. Furbank (London: Penguin, 1987).

Kipling, Rudyard, *Departmental Ditties and Other Verses* (Calcutta: Thacker, Spink, 1892).

Kipling, Rudyard, 'The Potted Princess' [1893], in Jack Zipes (ed.), *Victorian Fairy Tales: The Revolt of the Fairies and Elves* (London: Routledge, 1989).

Kipling, Rudyard, *The Jungle Books* [1894/5], ed. Daniel Karlin (London: Penguin, 1987).

Kipling, Rudyard, 'Baa Baa, Black Sheep' [1895], in Hugh Haughton (ed.), *Wee Willie Winkie* (London: Penguin, 1988).

Kipling, Rudyard, *Wee Willie Winkie* [1895], ed. Hugh Haughton (London: Penguin, 1988).

Kipling, Rudyard, *The Seven Seas* (London: Methuen, 1896).

Kipling, Rudyard, *Captains Courageous* [1897], ed. Leonee Ormond (Oxford: Oxford University Press, 2008).

Kipling, Rudyard, *The Day's Work* [1898] (London: Penguin, 1988).

Kipling, Rudyard, *Stalky and Co.* [1899], ed. Isabel Quigly (Oxford: Oxford University Press, 1999).

Kipling, Rudyard, 'A Sahibs' War' [1901], in Craig Raine (ed.), *A Choice of Kipling's Prose* (London: Faber and Faber, 1987).

Kipling, Rudyard, *Kim* [1901], ed. Edward Said (London: Penguin Books, 1989).

Kipling, Rudyard, *Just So Stories* [1902], ed. Peter Levi (London: Penguin, 2000).

Kipling, Rudyard, *The Five Nations* (London: Methuen, 1903).

Kipling, Rudyard, *Puck of Pook's Hill and Rewards and Fairies* [1906/1910], ed. Donald Mackenzie (Oxford: Oxford University Press, 1993).
Kipling, Rudyard, *Actions and Reactions* (London: Macmillan, 1909).
Kipling, Rudyard, *Soldiers Three and Other Stories* (London: Macmillan, 1914).
Kipling, Rudyard, *Barrack Room Ballads and Other Verses* (London: Methuen, 1915).
Kipling, Rudyard, *A Diversity of Creatures* [1917], ed. Paul Driver (London: Penguin, 1987).
Kipling, Rudyard, *The Works of Rudyard Kipling XVII: Early Verse* (New York: Charles Scribner's Sons, 1917).
Kipling, Rudyard, *Land and Sea Tales for Scouts and Guides* (London: Macmillan, 1923).
Kipling, Rudyard, *Debits and Credits* (London: Macmillan, 1926).
Kipling, Rudyard, *A Book of Words* (London: Macmillan, 1928).
Kipling, Rudyard, *The Naulahka* (London: Macmillan, 1928).
Kipling, Rudyard, *The Light that Failed* (London: Macmillan, 1929).
Kipling, Rudyard, *Something of Myself and Other Autobiographical Writings* [1930], ed. Thomas Pinney (Cambridge: Cambridge University Press, 1991).
Kipling, Rudyard, *The Definitive Edition of Rudyard Kipling's Verse* (London: Hodder and Stoughton, 1986).
Kipling, Rudyard, *Letters of Marque* (Amsterdam: Fredonia Books, 2001).
Orel, Harold (ed.), *Kipling: Interviews and Recollections*, 2 vols (London: Macmillan, 1983).
Pinney, Thomas (ed.), *Kipling's India: Uncollected Sketches 1884–88* (London: Macmillan, 1986).
Pinney, Thomas (ed.), *The Letters of Rudyard Kipling*, 6 vols (Iowa City: University of Iowa Press, 1990–2005), I: 1872–89 (1990), II: 1890–99 (1990), III: 1900–10 (1996).

Secondary Bibliography

Achebe, Chinua, *Morning Yet on Creation Day* (New York: Anchor Press/ Doubleday, 1975).
Adams, Jad, *Kipling* (London: Haus, 2005).
Adams, Jad, 'Decadent of Hearty? Kipling's Dilemma', in *Kipling Journal* 82 (2008), 9–27.
Allen, Charles, *Kipling Sahib: India and the Making of Rudyard Kipling* (London: Little Brown, 2007).
Allen, Charles, 'Ruddy and the Gods: the Young Kipling and Religion', The Kent Conference (University of Kent, 7–8 Sept. 2007).
Allen, Charles (ed.), *Plain Tales from the Raj: Images of British India in the Twentieth Century* (London: Deutsch, British Broadcasting Corporation, 1975).
Allen, Jeffner, and Iris Marion Young, *The Thinking Muse: Feminism and Modern French Philosophy* (Bloomington and Indianapolis: Indiana University Press, 1989).
Allen, Richard, and Harish Trivedi (eds), *Literature and Nation: Britain and India 1800–1990* (London: Routledge, 2000).

Althusser, Louis, 'Ideology and Ideological State Apparatuses', in *Lenin and Philosophy* (New York: Monthly Review Press, 2001).

Amis, Kingsley, *Rudyard Kipling and His World* (London: Thames and Hudson, 1975).

Anderson, Benedict, *Imagined Communities: Reflections on the Origin and Spread of Nationalism* (New York: Verso, 1991).

Annan, Noel, 'Kipling's Place in the History of Ideas', in Andrew Rutherford (ed.), *Kipling's Mind and Art* (Stanford: Stanford University Press, 1964), pp. 97–125.

Appadurai, Arjun, 'Understanding Gandhi', in Peter Homans (ed.), *Childhood and Selfhood: Essays on Tradition, Religion and Modernity in the Psychology of Erik H. Erikson* (London: Associated University Presses, 1978), pp. 113–43.

Aquinas, Thomas, *Selected Philosophical Writings*, trans. Timothy McDermott (Oxford: Oxford University Press, 1998).

Arnold, Matthew, 'A Summer Night', in Timothy Peltason (ed.), *Selected Poems* (London: Penguin, 1994).

Ashcroft, Bill, Gareth Griffiths, and Helen Tiffin, *The Empire Writes Back: Theory and Practice in Post-Colonial Literature* (London and New York: Routledge, 1989).

Auden, W. H., *Selected Poems*, ed. John Fuller (London: Faber and Faber, 2005).

Bachelard, Gaston, *The Poetics of Space*, trans. Maris Jolas (Boston, MA: Beacon Press, 1969).

Bakhtin, M. M., *The Dialogue Imagination* (Austin: University of Texas Press, 1981).

Balint, Michael, 'Early Developmental States of the Ego: Primary Object Love', in *Primary Love and Psycho-Analytic Technique* (London: Tavistock, 1965).

Baneth, Emilienne, '"Ship Me Somewhere East of Suez": Rudyard Kipling's Strange Exile from Himself', <http://english.chass.ncsu.edu/jouvert/v6i1-2/baneth.htm> (last accessed 17 Sept. 2014).

Barthes, Roland, *The Pleasure of the Text*, trans. Richard Miller (London: Jonathan Cape, 1976).

Beck, Aaron T., Gary Emery and Ruth Greenberg, *Anxiety Disorders and Phobias: A Cognitive Perspective* (Cambridge, MA: Basic Books, 2005).

Benveniste, Emile, *Problems in General Linguistics*, trans. Mary E. Meek (Coral Gables, FL: University of Miami Press, 1971).

Berkeley, Michael, *Baa Baa Black Sheep: An Opera in Three Acts* (Oxford: Oxford University Press, 1995).

Beyer, Stephen, *The Cult of the Tara: Magic and Ritual in Tibet* (Berkeley: University of California Press, 1973).

Bhabha, Homi, 'Difference, Discrimination and the Discourse of Colonialism', in *The Politics of Theory* (Colchester: University of Essex, 1983).

Bhabha, Homi, 'Remembering Fanon: Self, Psyche and the Colonial Condition', in P. Williams and L. Chrisman (eds), *Colonial Discourse and Postcolonial Theory* (New York: Columbia University Press, 1994), pp. 112–23.

Bhabha, Homi, 'Boundaries, Differences, Passages', keynote address, Volkswagen Foundation, Dresden Conference (Dresden, 14–16 June 2006).

Bhabha, Homi, *The Location of Culture* (London and New York: Routledge, 2006).

Bhatia, Nandi, 'Kipling's Burden: Representing Colonial Authority and

Constructing the "Other" through Kimball O'Hara and Babu Hurree Chander in *Kim*', *South Asia Graduate Research Journal* 1.1 (1994): 1–13.

Birjepatil, J., 'Hybridity and History in Rudyard Kipling', http://akbar.marlboro.edu/~birje/home.html (last accessed 17 Sept. 2014).

Birkenhead, Lord, *Rudyard Kipling* (London: Weidenfeld & Nicolson, 1978).

Bishop, Rebecca, 'Writing the Body Wild: Primatological Narrative and Spaces of Animality', *Culture, Theory and Critique* 49, 2 (2008).

Bloom, Harold (ed.), *Rudyard Kipling's Kim* (New York, New Haven, Philadelphia: Chelsea House Publishers, 1987).

Blyth, Ian, and Susan Sellers (eds), *Hélène Cixous: Live Theory* (London and New York: Continuum, 2004).

Boehmer, Elleke, *Colonial and Postcolonial Literature: Migrant Metaphors* (Oxford: Oxford University Press, 1995).

Bose, Purnima, 'Survivors of the Raj, Survivors of the Empire: Narrating the Colonial and Post-colonial Encounters', unpublished doctoral thesis (University of Texas, 1993).

Bowlby, John, *Attachment and Loss*, 2 vols (London: Pimlico, 1997–8), I: Attachment (1997), II: Separation, Anxiety and Anger (1998).

Bray, Abigail, *Hélène Cixous: Writing and Sexual Difference* (New York: Palgrave Macmillan, 2004).

Brennan, Timothy, 'The National Longing for Form', in Homi Bhabha (ed.), *Nation and Narration* (London: Routledge, 1995), pp. 44–70.

Breuer, Joseph, and Sigmund Freud, 'Studies on Hysteria (1893–5)', in *The Standard Edition of The Complete Psychological Works of Sigmund Freud*, vol. 2, trans. James Strachey (London: Hogarth, 1953–74).

Brogan, Hugh, *Mowgli's Sons: Kipling and Baden-Powell's Scouts* (London: Jonathan Cape, 1897).

Brown, Stephen R., *Merchant Kings: When Companies Ruled the World, 1600–1900* (Vancouver: Douglas & McIntyre, 2009).

Bruss, Elizabeth W., *Autobiographical Acts: The Changing Situation of a Literary Genre* (Baltimore: Johns Hopkins University Press, 1976).

Buchanan, Robert, 'The Voice of the Hooligan', in *Kipling: The Critical Heritage* (London: Routledge and Kegan Paul, 1971).

Carrington, Charles, *Rudyard Kipling: His Life and Work* (London: Macmillan, 1955).

Castle, Kathryn, *Britannia's Children: Reading Colonialism through Children's Books and Magazines* (Manchester: Manchester University Press, 1996).

Cixous, Hélène, *Souffles* (Paris: Des femmes, 1975).

Cixous, Hélène, 'Sorties: Where is She . . .', in Elaine Marks and Isabelle de Courtrivon (eds), *New French Feminisms*, trans. Anne Liddle (Amherst, MA: University of Massachusetts, 1981), pp. 90–8.

Cixous, Hélène, *The Poetics of Gender*, ed. Nancy K. Miller (New York: Columbia University Press, 1986).

Cixous, Hélène, 'Extreme Fidelity', in Susan Sellers (ed.), *Writing Differences: Readings from the Seminar of Hélène Cixous*, trans. Ann Liddle and Susan Sellers (Milton Keynes: Open University Press, 1988).

Cixous, Hélène, *Coming to Writing and Other Essays*, trans. Sarah Cornell, Deborah Jenson, Anne Liddle and Sellers, ed. Deborah Jenson (Cambridge, MA: Harvard University Press, 1992).

Cixous, Hélène, *The Cixous Reader*, ed. Susan Sellers (London: Routledge, 1994).

Cixous, Hélène, *Three Steps on the Ladder of Writing*, trans. Sarah Cornell and Susan Sellers (New York: Columbia University Press, 1994).
Cixous, Hélène, 'The Laugh of the Medusa', trans. Keith Cohen and Paula Cohen, in Robyn R. Warhol and Diane Price Herndl (eds), *Feminisms: An Anthology of Literary Theory and Criticism* (Basingstoke: Macmillan, 1997), pp. 347–62.
Cixous, Hélène, and Mireille Calle-Gruber, *Rootprints: Memory and Life Writing*, trans. Eric Prenowitz (London and New York: Routledge, 1997).
Cixous, Hélène, and Catherine Clément, *The Newly Born Woman*, trans. Betsy Wing (Minneapolis: University of Minnesota Press, 1986).
Cody, David, 'Kipling's Imperialism', <http://www.victorianweb.org/authors/kipling/rkimperialism.html> (last accessed 17 Sept. 2014).
Cohen, Morton (ed.), *Rudyard Kipling to Rider Haggard: The Record of a Friendship* (London: Hutchinson, 1965).
Collingwood, R. G., *The Principles of Art* (Oxford: Oxford University Press, 1938).
Collits, Terry, 'Theorizing Racism', in C. Tiffin and A. Lawson (eds), *Describing Empire, Postcolonialism and Textuality* (London and New York: Routledge, 1990), pp. 61–9.
Conley, Verena Andermatt, *Hélène Cixous* (Hemel Hempstead: Harvester Wheatsheaf, 1992).
Cornell, Louis L., *Kipling in India* (New York: St Martin's Press, 1966).
Crawford, Robert, 'Rudyard Kipling in *The Waste Land*', *Essays in Criticism* vol. 36:1 (1986).
Creed, Barbara, *The Monstrous Feminine: Film, Feminism, Psychoanalysis* (London and New York: Routledge, 2007).
Crook, Nora, *Kipling's Myths of Love and Death* (London: Macmillan, 1989).
Cross, T. N., 'Rudyard Kipling's Sense of Identity', *The Michigan* Review 4 (1965), 245–52.
David, Saul, *The Indian Mutiny* (London: Penguin Books, 2003).
De Mann, Paul, 'Autobiography as De-facement', *Modern Language Notes* 94: 5 (1979).
Derrida, Jacques, *Of Grammatology*, trans. Gayatri Chakravorty Spivak (Baltimore: Johns Hopkins University Press, 1974).
Derrida, Jacques, *Writing and Difference*, trans. Alan Bass (London: Routledge, 2005).
Deutsch, Karl W., and Norbert Wiener, 'The Lonely Nationalism of Rudyard Kipling', *Yale Review* 52:4 (1963), 499–517.
Digital Dictionaries of South Asia, <http://dsal.uchicago.edu/dictionaries/> (last accessed 17 Sept. 2014).
Diver, Maud, *The Englishwoman in India* (London: Blackwood, 1909).
Dobrée, Bonamy, *Rudyard Kipling: Realist and Fabulist* (London: Oxford University Press, 1967).
Douglas, Mary, *Purity and Danger* (London: Routledge and Kegan Paul, 1966).
Edel, Leon (ed.), *The Letters of Henry James Letters, Vol IV, 1895–1916* (Cambridge, MA: The Belknap Press of Harvard University Press, 1984).
Eliot, T. S., *Selected Essays* (London: Faber and Faber, 1932).
Eliot, T. S., 'Rudyard Kipling', in *On Poetry and Poets* (London: Faber and Faber, 1957).
Eliot, T. S., 'The Unfading Genius of Rudyard Kipling', *The Kipling Journal* 26: 129 (1959).

Eliot, T. S., 'The Waste Land', in *Selected Poems* (London: Faber and Faber, 1976).
Ellman, Richard (ed.), *Selected Letters of James Joyce* (London: Faber and Faber, 1975).
Fanon, Frantz, *Black Skin, White Masks*, trans. C. L. Markmann (New York: Grove Press, 1967).
Fanon, Frantz, *The Wretched of the Earth*, trans. C. Farrington (London: Penguin Modern Classics, 2001).
Fido, Martin, *Rudyard Kipling* (London: Hamlyn, 1974).
Fink, Bruce, *The Lacanian Subject: Between Language and Jouissance* (Princeton: Princeton University Press, 1995).
Fink, Bruce, *Lacan to the Letter: Reading Écrits Closely* (Minneapolis: University of Minnesota Press, 2004).
Flanders, Judith, *A Circle of Sisters: Alice Kipling, Georgiana Burne-Jones, Agnes Poynter and Louisa Baldwin* (London: Penguin, 2001).
Fleming, Alice, 'Some Childhood Memories of Rudyard Kipling by his Sister', *Chambers Journal* (1939), pp. 168–78.
Fleming, Alice, *Trix, Kipling's Forgotten Sister: Unpublished Writings of Trix Kipling*, ed. Lorna Lee (Otford, Kent: Pond View, 2003).
Fletcher, John, and Andrew Benjamin (eds), *Abjection, Melancholia and Love: The Work of Julia Kristeva* (London and New York: Routledge, 1991).
Forster, E. M., *A Passage to India* (Harmondsworth: Penguin Books, 1979).
Foucault, Michel, *Madness and Civilization*, trans. Richard Howard (New York: Pantheon, 1965).
Foucault, Michel, 'The Discourse on Language', in *The Archaeology of Knowledge*, trans. A. M. Sheridan Smith (New York: Pantheon, 1972).
Foucault, Michel, 'Interview with Michel Foucault' in Paul Rabinow (ed.), *The Foucault Reader* (New York: Pantheon, 1984).
Gallop, Jane, *Reading Lacan* (Ithaca and London: Cornell University Press, 1988).
Gilbert, Elliot L., 'The Aesthetics of Violence', *English Literature in Transition, 1880–1920* 7:4 (1964), 207–17.
Gilbert, Elliot L., *The Good Kipling* (Manchester: Manchester University Press, 1972).
Gilbert, Elliot L. (ed.), *Kipling and the Critics* (London: Owen, 1966).
Gilmour, David, *The Long Recessional: The Imperial Life of Rudyard Kipling* (London: John Murray, 2002).
Goonetilleke, D. C. R. A., *Images of the Raj* (London: Macmillan, 1988).
Green, Martin, *The English Novel in the Twentieth Century: The Doom of Empire* (London: Routledge & Kegan Paul, 1984).
Grosskurth, Phyllis, *Melanie Klein: Her Word and Her Work* (London: Hodder & Stoughton, 1985).
Grosz, Elizabeth, *Space, Time and Perversion* (London and New York: Routledge, 1995).
Hagiioannu, Andrew, *The Man Who Would Be Kipling* (New York: Palgrave, 2003).
Hall, Catherine, *Cultures of Empire: A Reader: Colonizers in Britain and the Empire in the Nineteenth and Twentieth Centuries* (Manchester: Manchester University Press, 2000).
Hall, Stuart, 'Cultural Identity and Diaspora', in P. Williams and L. Chrisman

(eds), *Colonial Discourse and Postcolonial Theory* (New York: Columbia University Press, 1994), pp. 392–403.

Hamer, Mary, 'Kipling and Dreams', in Readers' Guide, The Kipling Society online, <http://www.kipling.org.uk/rg_dreams.htm#endpassage> (last accessed 17 Sept. 2014).

Hanks, Robert, 'A sheep that bites: the revival of Rudyard Kipling's fortunes has now spawned an opera', *The Independent*, 3 July 1993, <http://www.independent.co.uk/arts-entertainment/classical-music--a-sheep-that-bites-the-revival-of-rudyard-kiplings-fortunes-has-now-spawned-an-opera-robert-hanks-explores-tonights-cheltenham-premiere-1482501.html> (last accessed 17 Sept. 2014).

Havholm, Peter, *Politics and Awe in Rudyard Kipling's Fiction* (Aldershot: Ashgate, 2008).

Haynal, André, *The Technique at Issue: Controversies in Psychoanalysis from Freud and Ferenczi to Michael Balint* (London: Karnac Books, 1988).

Hitchens, Christopher, *Love, Poverty and War: Journeys and Essays* (London: Atlantic Books, 2005).

Hopkirk, Peter, *Quest for Kim: In Search of Kipling's Great Game* (Ann Arbor: University of Michigan Press, 1999).

Hotchkiss, Jane, 'The Jungle of Eden: Kipling, Wolf Boys, and the Colonial Imagination', *Victorian Literature and Culture* 29:02 (2001), 435–49.

Husain, S. S. Azfar, *The Indianness of Rudyard Kipling: A Study in Stylistics* (London: Cosmic Press, 1983).

Husain, S. S. Azfar, 'The Religion of Rudyard Kipling', *Journal of King Saud University*, vol. 3, Arts 2 (1991), 141–64.

Hyam, Ronald, *Britain's Imperial Century 1815–1914: A Study of Empire and Expansion,* 3rd edn (New York: Palgrave Macmillan, 2002).

Inden, Ronald, *Imagining India* (Oxford: Blackwell, 1990).

Islam, Shamsul, *Kipling's 'Law': A Study of his Philosophy of Life* (New York: Macmillan, 1975).

Islam, Shamsul, *Chronicles of the Raj* (London: Macmillan, 1979).

Ives, Kelly, *Cixous Irigaray Kristeva: The Jouissance of French Feminism* (Worcestershire: Crescent Moon, 1996).

Jacobus, Lee A., and Regina Barreca (eds), *Hélène Cixous: Critical Impressions* (Amsterdam: Gordon and Breach, 1999).

James, Lawrence, *The Rise and Fall of the British Empire* (London: Abacus, 1996).

JanMohamed, Abdul R., 'The Economy of Manichean Allegory: The Function of Racial Difference in Colonialist Literature', in Henry Louis Gates, Jr. (ed.), *Race, Writing and Difference* (Chicago: University of Illinois Press, 1986).

Jarrell, Randall, 'On Preparing to Read Kipling', in Harold Bloom (ed.), *Rudyard Kipling* (New York: Chelsea House, 1987), pp. 9–22.

Joyce, James, *Finnegan's Wake* (London: Bradford & Dickens, 1960).

Joyce, James, *A Portrait of the Artist As a Young Man* (New York: Viking Press, 1964).

Jung, Carl, *The Archetypes and the Collective Unconscious*, 2nd edn, trans. R. F. C. Hull (Princeton: Princeton University Press, 1992).

Kaplan, Caren, 'Deterritorializations: The Rewriting of Home and Exile in Western Discourse', *Cultural Critique* 6 (1987), 187–98.

Kemp, Sandra, *Kipling's Hidden Narratives* (Oxford: Blackwell, 1988).

Kiernan, Victor, *Shakespeare: Poet and Citizen* (London: Verso, 1993).

Kingsley, Charles, 'The Last Buccaneer', in Daniel Karlin (ed.), *The Penguin Book of Victorian Verse* (London: Penguin, 1998).
Kinkead-Weekes, Mark, 'Vision in Kipling's Novels' in Andrew Rutherford (ed.), *Kipling's Mind and Art* (Stanford: Stanford University Press, 1964), pp. 197–234.
Kipling, John Lockwood, *Beast and Man in India: A Popular Sketch of Indian Animals in Their Relations with People* (London: Macmillan, 1904).
The Kipling Society, *The Kipling Journal*, 1929–2007.
The Kipling Society Online, *The New Reader's Guide to the Works of Rudyard Kipling*, <http://www.kipling.org.uk/bookmart_fra.htm> (last accessed 17 Sept. 2014).
Klein, Melanie, *Developments in Psychoanalysis* (London: Hogarth, 1952).
Klein, Melanie, 'The Mutual Development of Ego and Id', *Psychoanalytic Study of the Child* 7 (1952).
Klein, Melanie, *Contributions to Psychoanalysis* (London: Hogarth, 1967).
Klein, Melanie, 'Early Stages of the Oedipus Conflict', *International Journal of Psycho-Analysis* 9, 167–80. Reprinted in *The Writings of Melanie Klein*, vol. 1 (London: Hogarth Press, 1975).
Klein, Melanie, *Envy and Gratitude and Other Works, 1946–1963* (New York: Simon & Schuster, 1975).
Klein, Melanie, *Love, Guilt and Reparation & Other Works, 1921–1945* (New York: Delta, 1975).
Knoepflmacher, Ulrich, 'Female Power and Male Self-Assertion: Kipling and the Maternal', *Children's Literature* 20 (1992), 15–35.
Knoepflmacher, Ulrich, 'The Hansel and Gretel Syndrome: Survivorship Fantasies and Parental Desertion', *Children's Literature* 33 (2005), 171–84.
Kristeva, Julia, *Powers of Horror: An Essay on Abjection*, trans. Leon Roudiez (New York: Columbia University Press, 1982).
Kristeva, Julia, 'Women's Time', in N. Keohane, M. Z. Rosaldo, and B. C. Gelpi (eds), *Feminist Theory: A Critique of Ideology*, trans. Alice Jardine and H. Blake (Brighton: Harvester, 1982).
Kristeva, Julia, *Revolution in Poetic Language*, trans. Margaret Waller (New York: Columbia University Press, 1984).
Kristeva, Julia, *In the Beginning Was Love: Psychoanalysis and Faith*, trans. Arthur Goldhammer (New York: Columbia University Press, 1987).
Kristeva, Julia, *Kristeva Reader [The]*, ed. Toril Moi (Oxford: Blackwell, 1987).
Kristeva, Julia, *Tales of Love*, trans. Leon Roudiez (New York: Columbia University Press, 1987).
Kristeva, Julia, 'Interview with Julia Kristeva', in Elaine Baruch and Lucienne Serrano (eds), *Women Analyze Women* (New York: New York University Press, 1988).
Kristeva, Julia, *Black Sun: Depression and Melancholia*, trans. Leon S. Roudiez (New York: Columbia University Press, 1989).
Kristeva, Julia, *Strangers to Ourselves*, trans. Leon Roudiez (New York: Columbia University Press, 1991).
Kristeva, Julia, *Desire in Language: A Semiotic Approach to Literature and Art*, trans. Thomas Gora, Alice Jardin, and Leon S. Roudiez, ed. Leon S. Roudiez (Oxford: Blackwell, 1993).
Kristeva, Julia, 'Foreign Body: A Conversation with Julia Kristeva and Scott L. Malcomson', *Transition* 59 (1993), 172–83.

Kristeva, Julia, *New Maladies of the Soul*, trans. Ross Guberman (New York: Columbia University Press, 1997).

Kristeva, Julia, *Melanie Klein*, trans. Ross Guberman (New York: Columbia University Press, 2000).

Kucich, John, 'Sadomasochism and the Magical Group: Kipling's Middle Class Imperialism', *Victorian Studies* 46: 1 (2003), 33–68.

Lacan, Jacques, *Écrits: A Selection*, trans. Bruce Fink (New York: Norton, 2004).

Lane, Christopher, *The Ruling Passion: British Colonial Allegory and the Paradox of Homosexual Desire* (Durham, NC: Duke University Press, 1995).

Leach, Robert, *The Punch and Judy Show: History, Tradition and Meaning* (London: Batsford Academic and Educational, 1985).

Lechte, John, *Julia Kristeva* (London: Routledge, 1990).

Leitner, Gottlieb William, *A Sketch of the Changars and their Dialect* (Charleston, SC: Bibliobazaar, 2009).

Levy, Steven T., and Andrew C. Furman, *Influential Papers from the 1950s* (London: Karnac Books, 2003).

Lewis, C. S., *Selected Literary Essays*, ed. Walter Hooper (Cambridge: Cambridge University Press, 1969).

Likierman, Meira, *Melanie Klein: Her Work in Context* (London and New York: Continuum, 2001).

Lohman, W. J. Jr., *The Culture Shocks of Rudyard Kipling* (New York: Peter Lang, 1990).

Longford, Elizabeth, *Victoria R.I.* (London: Weidenfeld and Nicholson, 1964).

Loukopoulou, Eleni, 'The Finest Stories in the World were by Kipling and Joyce', The Kent Conference (University of Kent, 7–8 Sept. 2007).

Lycett, Andrew, *Rudyard Kipling* (London: Phoenix, 2000).

Lyons, John, *Semantics*, 2 vols (Cambridge: Cambridge University Press, 1977), I.

Macaulay, Thomas Babington, 'Minute of 2 February 1835 on Indian Education', in *Macaulay, Prose and Poetry*, selected by G. M. Young (Cambridge, MA: Harvard University Press, 1957).

McBratney, John, *Imperial Subjects, Imperial Space: Rudyard Kipling's Fiction of the Native-Born* (Columbus: Ohio State University Press, 2004).

McClure, John A., *Kipling and Conrad: The Colonial Fiction* (Cambridge, MA: Harvard University Press, 1981).

Mason, Jennifer, 'Animal Bodies: Corporeality, Class and Subject Formation in *The Wide, Wide World*', Nineteenth-Century Literature, 54:4 (2000).

Mason, Philip, *Kipling: The Glass, the Shadow and the Fire* (London: Jonathan Cape, 1975).

Mason, Philip, *A Matter of Honour* (London: Peregrine, 1976).

Mauss, Marcel, *The Gift*, trans. W. D. Halls (London: Norton, 2000).

Marshall, David, 'Exchanging Visions: Reading *A Midsummer Night's Dream*', *ELH* 49 (1982).

Metcalf, Thomas, *Ideologies of the Raj*, The New Cambridge History of India, vol. 3, part 4 (Cambridge and New York: Cambridge University Press, 1994).

Miller, Alice, 'Depression and Grandiosity as Related Forms of Narcissistic Disturbance', in Andrew P. Morrison (ed.), *Essential Papers on Narcissism* (New York: New York University Press, 1986), pp. 323–47.

Montefiore, Jan, *Rudyard Kipling* (London: Northcote, 2007).

Montefiore, Jan (ed.), *In Time's Eye* (Manchester: Manchester University Press, 2013).
Moore-Gilbert, B. J., *Kipling and 'Orientalism'* (London and Sidney: Croom Heim, 1986).
Moore-Gilbert, B. J., '*Letters of Marque*: Travel, Gender and Imperialism', *Kipling Journal* 281 (1997).
Morey, Peter, *Fictions of India: Narrative and Power* (Edinburgh: Edinburgh University Press, 2000).
Nagai, Kaori, *Empire of Analogies: Kipling, India and Ireland* (Cork: Cork University Press, 2006).
Najder, Zdzislaw, *Joseph Conrad* (Cambridge: Cambridge University Press, 1983).
Nicolson, Adam, *The Hated Wife: Carrie Kipling, 1862–1939* (London: Faber and Faber, 2001).
O'Flaherty, Wendy Doniger, *Dreams, Illusions and Other Realities* (London and Chicago: University of Chicago Press, 1984).
Oates, Joyce Carol (ed.), *Telling Stories: An Anthology for Writers* (New York: Norton, 1998).
Obraztsor, Sergie, *My Profession*, trans. Ralph Parker and Valentino Scott (Moscow: Foreign Languages Publishing House, 1950).
Obraztsor, Sergie, *My Profession*, 2nd edn, trans. Doris Bradbury (Moscow: Raduga Publishers, 1985).
Oliver, Kelly, *Reading Kristeva: Unraveling the Double Bind* (Bloomington and Indianapolis: Indiana University Press, 1993).
Oliver, Kelly, *French Feminism Reader* (Lanham, MD: Rowman & Littlefield, 2000).
Oliver, Kelly, *The Portable Kristeva* (New York: Columbia University Press, 2002).
Oliver, Kelly, and Lisa Walsh, *Contemporary French Feminism* (Oxford: Oxford University Press, 2004).
Oliver, Kelly, and S. K. Keltner (eds), *Psychoanalysis, Aesthetics, and Politics in the Work of Julia Kristeva* (New York: State University of New York Press, 2009).
Olney, James, *Metaphors of Self: The Meaning of Autobiography* (Princeton: Princeton University Press, 1972).
Orel, Harold (ed.), *A Kipling Chronology* (Boston, MA: G. K. Hall, 1990).
Orwell, George, 'Rudyard Kipling', in *Dickens, Dali and Others: Studies in Popular Culture* (New York: Reynal and Hitchcock, 1946), pp. 140–60.
Orwell, George, 'Rudyard Kipling', in Andrew Rutherford (ed.), *Kipling's Mind and Art* (Stanford: Stanford University Press, 1964), pp. 70–84.
Osborne, John, *Look Back in Anger* (London: Penguin, 1982).
Paffard, Mark, *Kipling's Indian Fiction* (New York: St. Martin's Press, 1989).
Page, Norman, *A Kipling Companion* (New York: Macmillan, 1984).
Parry, Benita, *Delusions and Discoveries: India in the British Imagination, 1880–1930* (London: Verso, 1998).
Phillips, John, and Lyndsey Stonebridge (eds), *Reading Melanie Klein* (London and New York: Routledge, 1998).
Pike Bauer, Helen, *Rudyard Kipling: A Study of the Short Fiction* (New York: Twayne, 1994).
Plotz, Judith, 'The Empire of Youth: Crossing and Double-Crossing Cultural Barriers in Kipling's *Kim*', *Children's Literature* 20 (1992), 111–31.

Poole, Adrian, 'Kipling's Upper Case', in Philip Mallet (ed.), *Kipling Condensed* (London: Macmillan, 1989), p. 137.

Rabaté, Jean-Michel (ed.), *The Cambridge Companion to Lacan* (Cambridge: Cambridge University Press, 2003).

Ragland-Sullivan and Mark Bracher (eds), *Lacan and the Subject of Language* (New York: Routledge, 1991).

Randall, Don, *Kipling's Imperial Boy: Adolescence and Cultural Hybridity* (Basingstoke: Palgrave, 2000).

Ricketts, Harry, *The Unforgiving Minute: A Life of Rudyard Kipling* (London: Chatto & Windus, 1999).

Rée, Jonathan, *I See a Voice: A Philosophical History of Language, Deafness and the Senses* (London: Flamingo, 1999).

Reynolds, David, *Britannia Overruled: British Policy and World Power in the Twentieth Century* (New York: Longman, 2000).

Rosenthal, Michael, *The Character Factory: Baden-Powell's Boy Scouts and the Imperatives of Empire* (New York: Pantheon, 1984).

Rushdie, Salman, *Imaginary Homelands: Essays and Criticism 1981–1991* (London: Granta/Viking, 1991).

Rushdie, Salman, *Shalimar the Clown* (London: Vintage, 2006).

Rutherford, Andrew, 'Officers and Gentlemen', in Andrew Rutherford (ed.), *Kipling's Mind and Art* (Stanford: Stanford University Press, 1964), pp. 171–98.

Rutherford, Andrew (ed.), *Kipling's Mind and Art* (Stanford: Stanford University Press, 1964).

Said, Edward, *The World, the Text and the Critic* (Cambridge, MA: Harvard University Press, 1983).

Said, Edward, *Cultural Imperialism* (New York: Alfred A. Knopf, 1993).

Said, Edward, *Orientalism*, rev. edn (New York: Vintage, 1994).

Said, Edward, 'On Writing a Memoir', *London Review of Books* 21:9 (1999).

Said, Edward, *Out of Place: A Memoir* (London: Granta, 1999).

Sandison, Alan, 'Kipling: the Artist and the Empire' in Andrew Rutherford (ed.), *Kipling's Mind and Art* (Stanford: Stanford University Press, 1964), pp. 146–67.

Saul, David, *The Indian Mutiny* (London: Penguin Books, 2003).

Schwartz, Henry, *Writing Cultural History in Colonial India* (Philadelphia: University of Pennsylvania Press, 1977).

Segal, Hanna, *Introduction to the Work of Melanie Klein* (Bath: Heinemann, 1964).

Sellers, Susan, *The Hélène Cixous Reader* (London: Routledge, 1994).

Sergeant, David, *Kipling's Fiction* (Oxford: Oxford University Press, 2013).

Seymour-Smith, Martin, *Rudyard Kipling* (London: Macdonald, Queen Anne Press, 1989).

Shahane, Vasant A., *Rudyard Kipling: Activist and Artist* (Carbondale, IL: Southern Illinois University Press, 1975).

Shengold, Leonard, 'An Attempt at Soul Murder: Rudyard Kipling's Early Life and Work', *The Psychoanalytic Study of the Child* 30 (Yale University Press, 1977), 683–724.

Shershow, Scott Cutler, *Puppets and 'Popular' Culture* (Ithaca, NY: Cornell University Press, 1995).

Shusterman, David, *The Quest for Certitude in E. M. Forster's Fiction* (Bloomington and Indianapolis: Indiana University Press, 1965).

Simmons, Diane, *The Narcissism of Empire: Loss, Rage and Revenge in Thomas De Quincey, Robert Louis Stevenson, Arthur Conan Doyle, Rudyard Kipling and Isak Dinesen* (Brighton and Portland: Sussex Academic Press, 2007).
Smith, Anne-Marie, *Julia Kristeva: Speaking the Unspeakable* (London: Pluto Press, 1998).
Smith, Anna, *Julia Kristeva: Readings of Exile and Estrangement* (New York: St. Martin's Press, 1996).
Speaight, George, *The History of the English Puppet Theatre* (London: George G. Harrap, 1955).
Spengemann, William, *The Forms of Autobiography: Episodes in the History of a Literary Genre* (New Haven and London: Yale University Press, 1980).
Spurr, David, 'The Rhetoric of Empire: Colonial Discourse', in *Journalism, Travel Writing and Imperial Administration* (Durham, NC: Duke University Press, 1993).
Stewart, J. I. M., *Eight Modern Writers* (Oxford: Oxford University Press, 1963).
Stewart, J. I. M., *Rudyard Kipling* (London: Victor Gollancz, 1966).
Stokes, Eric, *The English Utilitarians and India* (Oxford: Clarendon Press, 1959).
Stoler, Ann Laura, *Race and the Education of Desire: Foucault's "History of Sexuality" and the Colonial Order of Things* (Durham and London: Duke University Press, 1995).
Stone, Wilfred Healey, *The Cave and the Mountain: A Study of E. M. Forster* (Stanford: Stanford University Press, 1966).
Suleri, Sara, *The Rhetoric of English India* (Chicago: University of Chicago Press, 1992).
Sullivan, Zohreh T., *Narratives of Empire: The Fictions of Rudyard Kipling* (Cambridge: Cambridge University Press, 1993).
Sutherland, John, 'The Ideas Interview: Julia Kristeva', *Guardian Online*, 13 March 2006 <http://www.guardian.co.uk/education/2006/mar/14/highereducation.research1> (last accessed 17 Sept. 2014).
Thiong'o, Ngugi wa, *Decolonising the Mind: The Politics of Language in African Literature* (Portsmouth, NH: Heinemann, 1981).
Thieme, John, *R. K. Narayan* (Manchester and New York: Manchester University Press, 2007).
Tolkien, J. R. R., 'On Fairy-Stories', in *The Tolkien Reader* (New York: Del Rey, 1986).
Thomson, James, 'The City of Dreadful Night', in *The City of Dreadful Night and Other Poems* (London: Reeves & Turner, 1888).
Tompkins, J. M. S., *The Art of Rudyard Kipling* (London: Methuen, 1965).
Trilling, Lionel, 'Kipling', in Andrew Rutherford (ed.), *Kipling's Mind and Art* (Stanford: Stanford University Press, 1964), pp. 85–94.
Turner, Victor, *Drama, Fields and Metaphors: Symbolic Action in Human Society* (Ithaca, NY: Cornell University Press, 1974).
Ussher, Jane, *Managing the Monstrous Feminine: Managing the Reproductive Body* (London and New York: Routledge, 2006).
Weaver-Hightower, Rebecca, *Empire Islands: Castaways, Cannibals, and Fantasies of Conquest* (Minneapolis: University of Minnesota, 2007).
Waddell, L. Austine, *Lhasa and Its Mysteries* (New York: Dover, 1988).
Wilson, A. N., *The Victorians* (London: Arrow Books, 2003).

Wilson, Angus, *The Strange Ride of Rudyard Kipling: His Life and Works* (London: Secker & Warburg, 1977).
Wilson, Angus, '*Kim* and the Stories', in Harold Bloom (ed.), *Rudyard Kipling* (New York: Chelsea House Publishers, 1987).
Wilson, Edmund, 'The Kipling that Nobody Read', in Andrew Rutherford (ed.), *Kipling's Mind and Art* (Stanford: Stanford University Press, 1964), pp. 17–69.
Wordsworth, William, *The Prelude: The Four Texts (1798, 1799, 1805, 1850)* (London: Penguin Books, 1995).
Wurgaft, Lewis D., *The Imperial Imagination: Magic and Myth in Kipling's India* (Middleton, CT: Wesleyan University Press, 1983).
Young, Robert, *Colonial Desire: Hybridity in Theory, Culture and Race* (London: Routledge, 1995).
Young, W. Arthur, and John H. McGivering, *A Kipling Dictionary* (New York: Macmillan, 1967).
Yule, Henry, and A. C. Burnell, *Hobson-Jobson: The Anglo-Indian Dictionary* (Ware: Wordsworth Reference, 1996).
Zipes, Jack, *Victorian Fairy Tales: The Revolt of the Fairies and Elves* (London: Routledge, 1989).

Index